CONTENTS

CHRISTOPHER MARLOWE

This major work brings together, for the first time in a single volume, all the recognized sources of Marlowe's dramatic works. Many of the forty-two texts presented here are of outstanding interest in their own right. Together they illuminate the cultural milieu which fostered Marlowe's talent, and deepen our appreciation of his dramatic methods.

Each of the texts is presented in a form accessible to modern readers; works in Latin or foreign vernaculars have been translated, and modern spelling and punctuation have been used throughout. The sources for each play are examined individually, and each text is annotated.

Few libraries can provide the range of sources contained in this one volume. The editors have included virtually complete texts of works such as the *English Faust-book* from which Marlowe borrowed heavily, and provide substantial extracts from other books with which he was no doubt familiar. This book is an invaluable resource for all those interested in Marlowe and the development of Elizabethan theatre.

William Tydeman is currently Professor of English at the University of Wales, Bangor. **Vivien Thomas** is a former lecturer in English at the University of Wales, Bangor. They co-authored *The State of the Art: Christopher Marlowe* (1989).

CHRISTOPHER MARLOWE

The plays and their sources

Edited by

Vivien Thomas and William Tydeman

Routledge
Taylor & Francis Group

LONDON AND NEW YORK

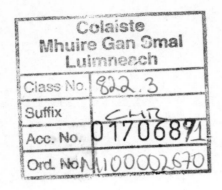
First published 1994
by Routledge
11 New Fetter Lane, London EC4P 4EE

Reprinted 1999

Simultaneously published in the USA and Canada
by Routledge
29 West 35th Street, New York, NY 10001

Transferred to Digital Printing 2003

Routledge is an imprint of the Taylor & Francis Group

© 1994 Vivien Thomas and William Tydeman

Typeset in Baskerville by
Ponting–Green Publishing Services, Chesham, Bucks
Printed and bound in Great Britain by
T.J.I. Digital, Padstow, Cornwall

British Library Cataloguing in Publication Data
A catalogue record for this book is available from
the British Library

Library of Congress Cataloging in Publication Data
Christopher Marlowe: The plays and their sources /
edited by Vivien Thomas and William Tydeman.
p.   cm.
Includes bibliographical references (p.) and index.
1. Christopher Marlowe, 1564–1593–Sources.
2. English drama–Early modern and Elizabethan,
1500–1600–Sources.
I. Thomas, Vivien.   II. Tydeman, William.
PR2676.C48   1994
822'.3–dc20   93–34070

ISBN 0–415–04052–3

CONTENTS

Doctor Faustus

The Massacre at Paris

CONTENTS

The Jew of Malta

Edward II

viii

PREFACE

Christopher Marlowe: The plays and their sources brings together for the first time in a single volume all the recognized sources of Marlowe's works for the theatre. Few libraries, outside the major academic centres, can supply enquiring readers with the appropriate materials for extending and deepening a critical appreciation and understanding of Marlowe's dramatic methods: our chief purpose in compiling this work has been to facilitate what we believe to be a fruitful aspect of Marlovian studies. The aim has been to include virtually complete texts of such works as the *English Faust-book* or Perondinus's *Life of Tamburlaine* of which it is reasonable to assume that the dramatist made use, along with selections from such other books as it is likely that he knew.

We have presented our material in a form accessible to today's readers by making those works originally written in Elizabethan English conform to current practice as far as possible. In selecting our texts for reproduction, we have gone to the earliest original versions, or to editions which it is at least feasible that Marlowe himself consulted. Where a Latin or a European source survives in a translation accessible in Marlowe's own day, we have used it, but in a number of instances, we have arranged for modern versions of non-English texts to appear, several of them especially prepared for this edition.

In reproducing our material we have been guided by the following editorial principles: sources and extracts from them have been printed verbatim, but with the original spelling, punctuation, capitalization, paragraphing or typographical features made to conform to present-day usage (except in cases where no contemporary equivalent for a sixteenth-century form exists). Proper names have presented difficulties, particularly in the case of place-names, since we feel that the wholesale adoption of current forms ('Istanbul' for 'Byzantium' or 'Constantinople', say) would be unhelpful or misleading; therefore in many instances (and on occasions where identification is at best equivocal), we have retained the name adopted in the original and provided a gloss.

ix

Within the texts all necessary glosses (within square brackets) have been kept to a minimum, but these occasionally take the form of more extended explanations, with longer and more complex explications reserved for the notes. At certain points we have been reluctantly compelled to cut material out for reasons of space or relevance: summary comments are employed to indicate where a considerable amount of material has been omitted, with ellipses to indicate more minor omissions. Editorial emendations have been confined to points where they have been felt essential in order to clarify the sense: these adjustments are also contained within square brackets.

We believe that, while conforming to good academic practice, our methods will allow the material to be read on its own terms with the minimum of editorial intervention. However, considerations of space have ruled out what many will regard as the ideal method of presentation which provides relevant parallel passages from the plays themselves in the form of footnotes to each page (as in T.J.B. Spencer's *Shakespeare's Plutarch*, Penguin Books, 1964). We have had to assume that the majority of those hoping to derive full benefit from this collection will wisely choose to work with a reliable edition of Marlowe's plays within easy reach. We have also had to resist including much material related to Marlowe's incidental borrowings and passing allusions, in order to concentrate attention on works of truly central significance. Our defence must be that such areas receive their proper consideration in major annotated editions of Marlowe's dramas, to which we would direct the interested reader on points of both substance and detail.

This enterprise has obviously involved calling on the good offices of numerous colleagues, scholars, librarians and friends; they include staff at the Bodleian and the British Libraries, the New York Public Library, and the libraries of Bristol University and of the University of Wales, Bangor. At the latter institution particular thanks go to Dr Ann Illsley, Inter-Library Loans Librarian, Dr I.G. Jones of the Computing Laboratory, and Dr Valerie Rumbold of the School of English. Professor John Russell Brown advised and encouraged us from the outset, and shaped our final proposal; Dr John Henry Jones generously shared with us his researches into the nature of the *English Faust-book*. Bruce Griffiths, John Ellis Jones, the Revd W. Alexander Jones, Caterina Maddelena, and Anthony Pearson guided our faltering steps in French, Latin, Italian, and German, by supplying us with much-needed translations of selected passages, and answering queries; John Jennison provided a full English version of Pedro Mexía's original account of Tamburlaine for purposes of comparison; Peter Llewellyn undertook the most formidable task of all by rendering Perondinus's florid Latin into highly readable English. Gareth Wyn Jones devoted many painstaking hours to drawing a map which incorporates the majority of the place-names relevant to the plays. Gail Kincaid and Michelle Harrison dealt patiently and cheerfully with our requests amid other pressing secretarial duties. At Routledge Julia Hall was only the last in a long sequence of understanding and helpful editors who brought our work to ultimate fruition.

To all those who have willingly supplemented our efforts we tender sincerest thanks; for the faults which still remain we alone must bear responsibility.

Vivien Thomas
William Tydeman
Bangor, North Wales

TEXTS AND SOURCES

Throughout the volume all references to Marlowe's plays are based on the texts to be found in *Complete Plays and Poems* edited by E.D. Pendry, Everyman's Library, Dent, 1976. The physical location of each source-item reprinted in the main body of the book is given at the start of each entry, while fuller bibliographical information has been arranged in sequence under the heading 'Primary Texts' in the Select Bibliography placed towards the end of the work.

INTRODUCTION

An urge to establish the origins or trace the genesis of works of literature may smack too much of Darwinian imperatives or Teutonic tenacity to find much favour today. Even readers wary of the current critical new broom which seeks to sweep away the author as the controlling, or even a determining agent in the creation of literary constructs might agree that to over-emphasize the significance of a writer's borrowings has its dangers. In the past perceived similarities between texts all too frequently generated incautious claims that one must plainly have borrowed from the other, where more stringent examination might have led to the conclusion that such resemblances were merely casual or fortuitous, or that they demonstrated little more than the fact that several works could be indebted to a common or even a commonplace original. Moreover, wherever doubt as to chronological precedence arose, as in the case of many early texts, efforts to establish the relative roles of debtor and creditor were customarily inclined to usurp a place on the critical balance-sheet more profitably reserved for calculating the intrinsic quality of what actually confronted the appraiser.

Yet at a period when many distinguished academics have become convinced that the concept and function of the author require to be reassessed, and indeed reasserted, in the face of a refusal in some quarters to deny the overt creator not simply primary importance in the processes of creativity but any kind of independent status at all, the validity of reviewing a writer's probable and possible debts to others has gained renewed momentum, whatever the errors and shortcomings of the past. No form of art, least of all literature, begets itself spontaneously. Far from being the unconscious beneficiary of a self-engendering phenomenon, the literary artist might more accurately be considered as one who creates linguistic artefacts through a process of receiving, rejecting, shaping, assembling, sharpening, or synthesizing a virtually limitless range of competing sense-impressions acquired in a wide variety of ways. If the modes of acquisition undoubtedly include

1

the accumulation of data arising from one's own personal experience of life, they emphatically do not *exclude* the vicarious assimilation of others' responses transmitted by way of conversation or correspondence, or through books. Hence, for those who take such a view the more thorough our familiarity with even a selection of the multiple stimuli to which a writer becomes subjected, the more sensitively the achieved artistic product can be evaluated and understood. Thus, since the nature of an author's sources and their handling constitutes a vital element in the critical appraisal of the act of writing, the identification and exploration of those materials from which a writer has clearly derived stimulus and motivation should make a claim on the attention of every informed student.

It is claimed increasingly that all literary texts are of necessity inextricably inter-related. But to investigate the part played by pre-existing written materials in shaping an author's output not only bears strongly on critical disputes centring on questions of the absolute autonomy of any aesthetic product, but on the exploration of literature from a socio-historical standpoint. In the particular context of the Elizabethan theatre, where our focus is on a body of work produced at high speed in order to satisfy an expanding clientele, in a mode for which there were few contemporary models available, to consider pertinent sources and their treatment can help readers define and understand more precisely the cultural milieu which fostered that astonishing upsurge of talent which revolutionized the national drama in little more than a single decade.

The Elizabethan dramatic corpus came into being at a time when plagiarism was not viewed as an infringement of copyright or an assault on designated intellectual property. Few authors had inhibitions as to the propriety of appropriating promising subject-matter from the wealth of locations made recently accessible as a result of a revolution in communications transmitted through the agency of the printing industry. As a newly popular urban amusement the public stage required a steady supply of novel and intriguing fare with which to meet an eager demand, and since pure invention was not in itself sufficient to cope with this contingency, books of every type assumed an essential place in stimulating and facilitating dramatic composition. Through first-hand study of those raw materials on which playwrights tended to rely, by comparing such bald and seemingly unpromising arguments and narratives with the finished artefacts almost miraculously derived from them, a profounder insight may be gained into the particular aims, conventions and demands of the genre during Elizabeth's reign.

Moreover, it can be argued that it is ultimately through contemplating the multiplicity of materials available to the late Tudor dramatist that we as readers and perhaps playgoers can grasp most successfully what these craftsmen regarded consciously or otherwise as the true nature, the correct structure, and the precise purpose of their chosen genre. To study the unmodified, unrefined prior manifestations of matter now familiar in the form of narrative, dialogue, situations, and *dramatis personae*, is to become aware of the principles and conventions, expectations and restrictions, which both overtly and tacitly governed the building of works for stage presentation even in an era as apparently aesthetically unfettered as the late sixteenth century. To reflect on the motivation behind particular acts of addition, suppression, alteration or development by which a source-text was transformed into finished composition, is to become possessed of a privileged insight into a writer's mental laboratory. For a moment we ourselves share the excited realization that from the dense tracts of print before us a figure, a phrase, an incident is slowly emerging to become (often with a minimum of authorial adjustment) something charged with that potent authority which inheres in all great art.

Such experiences have long been possible in the case of Shakespeare, most notably since the publication of Geoffrey Bullough's monumental *Narrative and Dramatic Sources of Shakespeare* between 1957 and 1975, a definitive tool whose very existence legitimizes the exploration and analysis of source-materials as offering an illuminating approach to literary study. Bullough's eight volumes have proved invaluable through supplying generous extracts (and occasionally complete texts) drawn from works difficult of access or impossible to locate and scan outside major research libraries. Such helpfully assembled evidence offers scholars the opportunity to assess for themselves whether or not a particular authenticated source, a possible original advanced for consideration, or an interesting analogue previously disregarded, has relevance. This may apply not only to broadening an understanding of the evolving genesis of an individual play or poem, or to acquiring a fuller insight into the writer's working methods at different stages in his career, but also for cultivating the ability to form an overview of Shakespeare's artistry as it developed and matured. Bullough's canvas is fortunately sufficiently wide to enable him to provide a portrait of an author growing increasingly sophisticated in his response to often copious source-materials, while the editor's own critical commentaries (themselves becoming more authoritative and central as the project develops) represent a major contribution to Shakespearean scholarship in their own right.

While our compilation is necessarily more limited in scope, both in terms of what we have found space to include and what we have contributed on our own account, our principal aim has been to offer the same kind of assistance as Bullough does Shakespeareans to those who wish to gain fresh access to the dramatic writings of Christopher

Marlowe. But some essential differences will be obvious. Bullough's work, which grew from a projected five volumes to eight, covers the whole of Shakespeare's output, non-dramatic as well as dramatic. We have endeavoured to set as much material before the reader as can be included in one volume, but we have not attempted to emulate the comprehensiveness of Bullough. We have concentrated for the most part on major sources, 'major' in the sense that they supplied Marlowe with the bulk of his material and also in the sense that they are substantial works of importance in themselves. Several Marlowe plays depend very closely on a source of this kind, whether an established classic, as with Virgil's *Aeneid* from which *Dido Queen of Carthage* springs, or a newly published topical work like the *English Faust-book* which underpins *Doctor Faustus*. Possible sources and analogues feature less prominently in the case of *The Jew of Malta* and to a lesser extent *The Massacre at Paris*. Only the first half of the latter piece can be shown to make extensive use of a single source, and *The Jew* seems almost an exercise in doing without sources. In such cases it is not possible to do more than advance tentative suggestions.

We have been unable to find space for Marlowe's poems, perhaps a harsh decision in the case of *Hero and Leander*, a major work though presumably unfinished. The poem derives from a poem of the same name by the fifth-century Greek poet Musaeus. This work, which Marlowe almost certainly read in the original Greek as well as in Latin translation, was highly valued in the sixteenth century, and gave rise to a number of versions in various European languages. Gordon Braden (1978) gives a stimulating account of this phenomenon. It would have proved impossible to deal adequately with this linguistically complex subject within the confines of the present volume: there is no known English translation contemporary with Marlowe, and that by George Chapman, published in 1616, is too idiosyncratic to cast much light on Marlowe's version.

Of that astounding generation of young dramatists who effected the transformation of English playwriting during the 1580s and 1590s Marlowe has a claim to be regarded as the best educated, at least in the formal sense of the term. Almost alone among the 'University Wits' he supplemented the twelve terms of residence at Cambridge required to obtain his BA degree with three further years of study which culminated during the late summer of 1587 in the conferment of his Master's award. Whatever the somewhat irregular circumstances in which that qualification appears to have been pursued and eventually granted, there can be little doubt as to Marlowe's general intellectual calibre. At all events his chosen vocational path certainly provided him with far more favourable opportunities for wide and penetrating reading

4

than were vouchsafed to the majority of his contemporaries, not least William Shakespeare.

Such privileged circumstances must have obtained at least from the time when he entered King's School, Canterbury under the terms of a capitular scholarship around Christmas 1578. Thanks to the painstaking researches of the late William Urry (1988) we can now scan the detailed inventory of the extensive collection of books owned by John Gresshop, Marlowe's headmaster, who died in February 1580. If, like many teachers, Gresshop made the contents of his personal library available to his more promising pupils, Marlowe could have obtained early access to a fine representative range of texts in both the vernacular and the classical tongues, and found his knowledge increased and his imagination stimulated by as ample a private collection as that possessed by any university tutor of the day. Among upwards of 350 volumes Gresshop, a former Student of Christ Church, Oxford, owned works by most of the principal ancient and modern authors, including the philosophers Plato and Cicero, the poets Homer, Virgil and Juvenal, the historians Thucydides and Julius Caesar, and the dramatists Aristophanes, Sophocles, Plautus and Terence; the latter pair no doubt appear thanks in part to their high profile in the contemporary school curriculum. Curiously, the tragedies of Seneca which had so signal an influence on the development of European vernacular tragedy do not feature. However, it would be fanciful to propose that this absence accounts for Marlowe's relative freedom from Senecan traits in his dramas.

Among poets Ovid features several times, and Marlowe (who was to translate the *Amores* at some point during his brief career) may have first encountered the Roman through the pages of Thomas Churchyard's version of the *De Tristibus* or Arthur Golding's rendering of the *Metamorphoses*, both of which were on Gresshop's shelves. Late medieval writers such as Petrarch and Boccaccio were there, along with the continental humanists Marsilio Ficino, Lorenzo Valla and Juan Luis Vives, to whose ranks the Englishman Thomas More must be added, his *Utopia* being among the Canterbury volumes. Contemporary religious controversy was well represented with works by Luther, Beza, Bucer, John Knox and Bishop John Fisher. Works in the English vernacular included Chaucer's poems, one of the versions of Robert Fabyan's *Chronicles*, Ascham's *The Schoolmaster* of 1570, and Tottel's celebrated miscellany, *Songs and Sonnets* of 1557. Jerome's Vulgate Bible complemented a copy of the Geneva Bible and two copies of the Greek New Testament, while the principal reference work, to which Marlowe was to have recourse in either its original Latin or later French version, was Sebastian Münster's *Cosmographia*. Marlowe may have employed further items later in his career: he almost certainly read Geoffrey Fenton's

Discourse of the Civil Wars in France as part of his preparations for writing *The Massacre at Paris*, while Philippus Lonicerus's history or chronicle of the Turks supplied a small but telling detail which appears in the second part of *Tamburlaine the Great* (See *Tamburlaine* Text 10, pp. 151–2). He may also have consulted the *Flores historiarum* by Matthew Paris while working on *Edward II*, even if he borrowed nothing from it.

Such may have been Marlowe's introduction to 'serious' reading. The more prescriptive features of his schooling need concern us less in that he undoubtedly followed the relatively standard syllabus laid down for most mid-sixteenth-century educational establishments, which would certainly have involved him in reading the principal Latin authors, and learning to compose prose and verse in that language. However, what may prove to be of greater significance in assessing the creative use to which he put his reading when he turned to the craft of playmaker is to determine what factors affected his concept of drama as a genre, and the extent to which the experiences of his formative years influenced that conditioning. For example, what plays had he read or seen before taking up his pen, what critical discussions of the theory and practice of drama came to his notice, what were his *expectations* of drama? Above all, how far did his conception of the form lead him to refashion what he quarried from his sources? Does the episodic structure of *Tamburlaine*, for instance, derive from the epic pattern of the typical religious cycle sequence? Is *Doctor Faustus* deliberately modelled on the basic structure of the moral interludes in vogue during the later Middle Ages and early Tudor period? What led Marlowe to cast his plays in the moulds that he did?

It has long been recognized that the reading and performing of plays, especially the comedies of Terence and Plautus, achieved some prominence in the classrooms of Tudor Britain, and that therefore it is entirely possible that up to the time he proceeded to Cambridge late in 1580 Marlowe had not only read the works of the principal Roman dramatists, but may well have himself participated in performances of their works while at school in Canterbury. The fact that all those admitted to Parker scholarships at Corpus Christi College had to be possessed of singing abilities above the average suggests that the future playwright's musical skill may also have made him a more than eligible performer in those 'Tragedies, Comedyes and interludes' which we know were presented at the school until at least the 1560s. In 1562–3, for example, the Canterbury Cathedral Chapter granted Anthony Russhe, Gresshop's predecessor as headmaster, the sum of £14. 6*s*. 8*d*. for 'settinge out of his plays in Christmas'. It seems unlikely that the tradition would have lapsed before Marlowe became a pupil at King's School in 1578, but unfortunately records of performances for the relevant years have not survived to confirm or refute the belief that Marlowe must have appeared in plays while at school, and been influenced by them.

We know even less about the types of drama that Marlowe might have witnessed outside the confines of King's School. The Canterbury records carefully presented by Giles Dawson in the Malone Society's seventh volume of *Collections* (1965) make it clear that, while presentations by local civic groups are sparsely documented, the cathedral city played host on numerous occasions throughout the century to touring companies of both professional and amateur players. Such visitors during Marlowe's youth included the Queen's Men, Leicester's Men, Pembroke's Men, Lord Strange's Men, Sussex's Men, and Worcester's Men, and he could obviously have watched some of their presentations. But as yet the repertoire set before the citizens of Canterbury remains unknown, and, until it emerges, attempts to assess ways in which specific live performances may have coloured Marlowe's notions of drama must prove abortive.

Nor does a sharper picture result if we examine the extant records of dramatic activity in Cambridge during Marlowe's six and a half years of at least nominal residence. The splendid contribution made by Alan H. Nelson to the indispensable *Records of Early English Drama* series (1989) greatly facilitates the search for Marlowe's experience of Cambridge dramatics between 1580 and 1587, but despite the fine mesh of Nelson's net, very few hard facts concerning plays Marlowe might have witnessed, or taken part in, have been brought to the surface. Corpus Christi College was certainly the scene of a 'show' in 1575–6, of comedies (doubtless Latinate) presented in 1576–7, 1577–8, 1578–9 and 1581–2, and of unspecified 'plays' in 1582–3, but whether this tradition lapsed remains uncertain. The theatrical highlight of Marlowe's time at Cambridge would appear to have been the staging of a satire on the unfortunate Gabriel Harvey, then a Fellow of Pembroke Hall, presented at Trinity College in February 1581, and entitled *Pedantius*. Marlowe can scarcely have failed to know of it and may even have watched it in performance, but there is no evidence to support the conjecture.

In short, there is sadly little documentation to substantiate Urry's entirely reasonable claim that drama 'performed in Cambridge would have provided another dimension of his education' (Urry 1988: 55), although the statement would seem to be justified in the light of the importance both dons and students attached to college presentations. Furthermore, the university's virtually total ban on public performances by troupes of visiting professional players, exercised with increasing severity within a widening area from 1570 onwards, meant that Marlowe's possible opportunities for watching the work of London-based companies were confined to venues which could only be lawfully visited during periods of absence from his *alma mater*. Curiously, the city of Cambridge itself never seems to have boasted a thriving communal religious drama of the type so relatively accessible at other East Anglian centres.

However, such records as do survive permit a handful of conclusions to be drawn from the context in which Marlowe may have encountered practical theatre, not the least of which is that the majority of those college presentations which have been identified were either classical Latin comedies and tragedies (with the former very much in the ascendant), or imitations of classical dramas composed in Latin by European and frequently British authors. Presentations in English were far more rare, the best known being William Stevenson's *Gammer Gurton's Needle* staged around 1550–1 at Christ's College. However, it is significant that as late as December 1593 the Vice-Chancellor John Still should be informing Lord Burghley that an invitation issued to the Cambridge students to present 'A Comedie in Englishe' before the Queen at Christmas could not be honoured by reason of the players 'havinge no practize in this Englishe Vaine', claiming that 'Englishe Comedies, for that wee never used any, wee presentlie have none', and asking 'liberty to play in latyn' (Nelson 1989: 346–7). Hence we must assume that if Marlowe's dramaturgy owes anything to performances to which Cambridge gave him access, the chances are that any such influence was exercised through the agency of an ancient tongue.

In the absence of concrete evidence of Marlowe's experience of drama in performance, we are forced to assess in a more abstract fashion those forces which affected his selection and treatment of his source-materials. In addition to the practical examples afforded him by presentations of Plautus, Terence and Seneca, he was fairly certainly acquainted with such early works of literary theory as Aristotle's *Poetics*, Horace's *Ars Poetica*, the commentaries of scholars such as Donatus, and their Renaissance manifestation in the writings of Castelvetro, Minturno, Scaliger and others, though their most popular English formulation in Sir Philip Sidney's *Apology for Poetry* was to appear in print only after Marlowe's death.

At the same time we should bear in mind that 'Elizabethan playwrights bowed to the authority of the ancients in dramatic principles, but in dramatic conventions they followed the dictates of public taste. . . . Only principles, the fundamental truths which govern dramatic form, can be given as rules for all time. . . . Conventions, though they are invaluable contemporary hints, apply only to the theatre of the writer's time' (Hyde 1949: 3–4). Hence an awareness of contemporary stage practices must accompany any study of such rudiments of dramatic theory as Marlowe may have acquired by dint of formal application. Although a handful of playwrights clung staunchly to the precepts of the ancients, the majority of writers for the English stage embraced the independently conceived native traditions and conventions which, by drawing on both Gothic and classical aesthetics, ensured that the prescriptive stranglehold prevailing in Italy in the sixteenth century and France in the seventeenth did not prevent the masterworks of the Elizabethans and Jacobeans from emerging into the light.

To discuss in detail the salient features of Elizabethan dramaturgy as they affected Marlowe's work would once again require more space than can be found in the present context, but there can be little doubt that the contemporary understanding of what constituted the essential components, purpose and import of a successful play helped to determine Marlowe's selection and treatment of his principal sources. Even with such a limited perspective it becomes quite central to an evaluation of his authorial skills to be mindful of the pressures exerted on him by contemporary perceptions of theatrical form and structure, theme and content, plot and character, ethical imperatives and style.

As Doran (1954) argues, one of the principal problems with which any Elizabethan dramatist, not relying exclusively on pure invention, had to grapple was how to shape from often disparate and almost always diffuse raw materials a single completed dramatic action, which, although other subordinate actions might be interwoven to create complementary juxtapositions, had to exclude extraneous elements that might detract from the central focus. Given the Elizabethan audience's apparent thirst for variety and abundant action, the dangers of narrowing the dramatic spotlight to an excessively slender beam can readily be perceived. The intricate questions of what to incorporate and what to omit from the wealth of matter accessible to the playwright, of how to transform shapeless, repetitive or otiose resources into a cogent and integrated new entity, were governed largely by the overriding need to produce that intensity of effect arising from a sense of informing purpose and the achievement of a tight organic structure, while satisfying the medium's predilection for diversity (even prodigality), contrast and ingenuity.

If we adopt the general assumption that Marlowe's professional stage career was launched with *Dido Queen of Carthage* (with or without the collaboration of Nashe), then this adaptation of Books I, II and IV of the *Aeneid* presents for inspection a novice dramatist tailoring his chosen material to the requirements of both contemporary audiences and current stage practice. By opening *in medias res* with the brawling of the gods, Marlowe effected his exposition without having recourse to the devices of prologue, chorus, dumb-show or soliloquy to which several of his predecessors had been attached. The presence of the gods helps to frame the actions of the mortals, and the coolly comic dimension thus occasionally introduced serves as contrast to the frenzied human emotions portrayed through following (in the main) Virgil's narrative. However, Marlowe appears to have been dissatisfied with his original, going outside the Latin poet for some of his borrowings and incorporating a parallel but entirely invented love-relationship between Iarbas and Anna, which creates the type of multiple plot much favoured at this period. By concluding the play with a flurry of deaths Marlowe again conformed to the Elizabethan ideal of treating plot as a unit of action completed with the culmination of the dramatic proceedings.

In terms of adapting a possibly recalcitrant sequence of materials for the stage, *Tamburlaine the Great* presented the dramatist with problems far more acute than those encountered with *Dido*. While there was no shortage of competing accounts to select from, all the extant *vitae* of the conquering Tartar (apart from those too succinct to supply enough matter to fashion the piece to the required dimensions) demanded skilful condensation in order to sharpen that intensity of effect that theatre requires. Although inherent formlessness was an established feature of the evolving chronicle play, and the fundamentally episodic structure of both parts of *Tamburlaine* does not always avoid the charge, Marlowe was at pains to choose from his sources such elements as would allow his protagonist's exploits to be seen as one structured sequence, even if the individual episodes are rarely differentiated in terms of any form of psychological progression. The events portrayed seem only inter-related in so far as they represent steps in a chronological sequence; it is one of the play's weaknesses that one perceives no necessary connection between Tamburlaine's meteoric rise, his bloody triumphs and his ultimate demise, although many attempts have been made to discover one. Only the titanic figure of the eponymous hero himself confers on the *mélange* of incidents any measure of coherence, and even here it is less the case that his career creates a pattern – from obscure bandit to world conqueror, from aspiring usurper to cataclysmic sadist – but that he acts as a kind of common denominator in a welter of narrative phases.

It was not only in order to achieve the desired degree of coherence that Marlowe discarded many of the features with which Tamburlaine's several chroniclers endowed him. His aim was in part to exclude elements which might detract from his protagonist's sublime superiority. Thus Tamburlaine's crippled condition is suppressed, while the splendour of his physique is intensified. In the climactic rivalry with Bajazeth too the Tartar is again privileged: while boastfulness and vaingloriousness are made the Ottoman's primary characteristics rather than the worthiness and martial valour brought out in several accounts, Tamburlaine's own sadistic treatment of the Turkish emperor thus takes on a measure of just retribution: *hubris* meets its classic deserts in tragical textbook fashion.

Typical of Marlowe's care for coordination in *Tamburlaine* is his use of the *Theatrum Orbis Terrarum*, the famous contemporary atlas produced by Abraham Ortelius (1527–98), when plotting his protagonist's conquering progress. Ethel Seaton was able to demonstrate convincingly that 'Marlowe's Map' provides firm evidence that here is a playwright far from casually indifferent in matters of geography, one who 'used this source at least with the accuracy of a scholar and the commonsense of a merchant-venturer, as well as with the imagination of a poet' (Seaton 1924: 34).

If Marlowe confronted a surfeit of competing narratives in creating a synthesized portrait of Tamburlaine, with *Doctor Faustus* he could draw almost exclusively from a single original in the shape of P.F.'s version of the German *Faustbuch*. Yet even here the 'editorial' aspects of his task were real enough, since the Faust material was prolix and diffuse, requiring the dramatist to observe ruthless principles of selection in order to allow the linear progression of Faustus's descent into despair to emerge from the somewhat inconsequential plethora of anecdotal detail with which the legend had become encrusted. Marlowe's dramatic talents are nowhere more apparent than in the eclecticism with which he wove together the variegated threads that went to compose *The History of the Damnable Life and Deserved Death of Doctor John Faustus*, following to some extent the broad design of the native morality play.

Marlowe's major device for concentrating the audience's attention must be deemed to be the creation of the symbiotic relationship between Faustus and his fiendish mentor Mephostophiles. The playwright transmuted the casual contact of the Faust books into a complex fluctuating relationship which supplied a dimension of continuity to what could otherwise have been a series of unrelated adventures. Unlike Tamburlaine, Faustus is no mere common denominator; with Mephostophiles perpetually at his dupe's elbow (a blistering irony makes the ostensible master the slave), throughout the action Faustus is accompanied by a visual reminder of that inescapable doom which will ultimately overwhelm him, and it is our awareness of this that bestows a thematic unity on the most heterogeneous of escapades. Given the fondness for 'the mixed perfected brew' Elizabethan audiences evidently displayed, those comic 'intrusions' which have so exercised modern critics are unlikely to have disturbed the contemporary aesthetic sense, but even today many spectators and readers would bear witness to Marlowe's triumph in fusing apparently incongruous elements from his main source into a dramatic and conceptual totality. In large measure his skill lay in releasing the full potential for ambiguity, irony and tragic effect latent in the original tale.

If the conversion of P.F.'s blend of myth and jest-book into a major English tragedy constituted a more complex operation than is sometimes acknowledged, the demands made by *The Massacre at Paris* were altogether more exacting. Here Marlowe not only had an abundance of contemporary documentation to guide him but without doubt was also the recipient of a glut of gossip, reminiscence, hearsay and conjecture through which to pick his way. The events depicted and the figures involved stood only a mere twenty years distant, well within living memory, and he himself must have mingled in circles that possessed a good deal of 'inside information', perhaps curbing the writer's liberty of interpretation still further.

One method Marlowe employs to unify the disparate and frequently conflicting accounts on which he draws is through creating a series of continual but shifting polarities: Valois v. Bourbon, Catholic v. Protestant, loyalist v. traitor. Underpinning the mosaic of violent and self-seeking factions is one vital query: who will survive to rule in France? But the playwright endows what might otherwise be an academic question with a passionate intensity, by juxtaposing a multiplicity of relatively short interspersed scenes, which suggests a high degree of theatrical awareness, however mangled the surviving text.

The antecedents of *The Jew of Malta* constitute a rather special case in that the piece appears to stand independent of any known originals, and relies almost entirely on its author's powers of invention. If we need to seek real-life prototypes for Marlowe's powerful protagonist, then the historical figures cited in the main section dealing with the play are as plausible as any, but the claim that Barabas owes his genesis to an actual counterpart reflects a long discredited mode of approach to the personages of literature. However, it is perhaps the case that this piece in particular bears witness to both the breadth of Marlowe's reading and the width of his experiential range. Along with its obvious indebtedness to the data of contemporary history, *The Jew* owes something to the overall impression of the Orient sampled through books of travel, to dramatic tradition possibly going back to the Middle Ages, to various types of popular anecdotal narrative, even perhaps to controversy arising from Renaissance political theories. Here, if anywhere, the salient patterns of Marlowe's personal preoccupations may perhaps be best discerned.

Edward II offers one final instance of the way in which the presumed requirements of Elizabethan drama dictated the manner in which Marlowe shaped what he borrowed from his sources. Although his principal mentor was undoubtedly Holinshed, he nevertheless incorporated a miscellany of details from a range of chroniclers, enlivening and varying his main narrative by so doing. Marlowe was also aware of the appeal of topical allusions. 'The Wild O'Neill' and 'the haughty Dane' (II. 2. 163–4, 167) cannot be found in the chronicles, but Elizabethan audiences would have known of the Irish rebel family of O'Neill and of recurrent commercial disputes with Denmark. Yet just as, despite the presence of the notorious Guise, *The Massacre at Paris* (as we have it) tends to lack a true centre of interest, so the potential intensity of *Edward II* could also have become diffused, were it not for Marlowe's firm grasp on his source-materials. It is not simply that Marlowe's king provides the play with its centre, but it is notable that Marlowe streamlines the entire action, eliminating vast tracts of history to achieve a clean outline by which the successive phases of Edward's waxing and waning fortunes are clarified. It is only after scanning Holinshed's formidably exhaustive account that one realizes the skilful effectiveness with which Marlowe has wielded the pruning knife, marginalizing certain incidents and characters, foregrounding others, to create what for many remains his finest and most fluent theatrical achievement.

DIDO
QUEEN OF CARTHAGE

INTRODUCTION

The consensus of critical opinion is that *Dido Queen of Carthage* is probably Marlowe's first play. According to the title page of the earliest edition (1594), it was performed by the Children of Her Majesty's Chapel; this is one of several pointers to the date of composition, since by the time Marlowe left Cambridge in 1587 the popularity of the boys' troupes was already on the wane and it is unlikely that he would have written for them much later than this. The play is a dramatization of Books I, II and IV of the *Aeneid,* which on occasion keeps very close to Virgil's text; some passages are line-for-line translations and some of Virgil's most famous lines are quoted in the original Latin, a degree of fidelity to the original which suggests a certain immaturity in the dramatist. At the same time, a close comparison between the play and its source, as the studies by T.M. Pearce (1930), Mary Smith (1977) and Roma Gill (1977) have shown, reveals numerous differences in detail and in fundamental conception between the epic and the play.

Ethel Seaton (1959) and Mary Smith (1977) point out that Marlowe's reworking of the story owes a significant debt to medieval versions of the tale of Troy; the contribution of Ovid's Dido in the *Heroides* cannot be discounted, nor the possibility that Marlowe knew at least some previous dramatizations. Dido was a popular subject for sixteenth-century drama: there are Latin plays by John Rightwise (performed before Cardinal Wolsey in 1527), Edward Haliwell (performed at Cambridge in 1564), and William Gager (performed at Oxford in 1583). Of these Gager's is the only one to have survived; it was never printed or revived, and F.S. Boas, who gives a summary of it, concludes that it has no connection with Marlowe's play (1914: 189). In addition, there are plays in Italian by Alessandro Pazzi (1524), Giambattista Giraldi-Cinthio (1543?), and Lodovico Dolce (1547), and in French by Etienne Jodelle (155?). Marlowe is sufficiently close to the Italian plays to allow the tentative conclusion reached by Inna Koskenniemi (1972) and Mary Smith (1976) that he may have known Dolce at least. Marlowe's *Dido* is, however, formally very different from these strictly neo-classical versions. There is

17

a distinctively Elizabethan character to the play, especially in its lyricism, its moments of romantic comedy, and its adaptation of the material to the special talents of the troupe of boy actors for whom it was written, and all of these distance it from Virgil.

Marlowe was himself an accomplished translator of Latin and had no need to consult any previously published translation of Virgil. He certainly seems to owe nothing directly to Gavin Douglas's translation (1553) of all twelve books of the *Aeneid* into Scottish verse, or to Surrey's blank verse translation of Books II and IV (1554, 1557), and nothing at all to Richard Stanyhurst's hexameters (1582). There is some evidence, though, that he knew Thomas Phaer's translation in fourteeners, even if he did not make any systematic use of it, and this is why we have chosen to give some extracts from it here. It is interesting to note that Thomas Nashe's signature appears on the verso of the title page of the British Library copy of Phaer's translation of the first seven books of the *Aeneid* (1558). The extent of Nashe's collaboration (if any) with Marlowe on the play is uncertain; apart from his name on the title page (below Marlowe's and in smaller print), traces of Nashe's highly distinctive vocabulary can be detected in the text, but most commentators agree that the play is substantially Marlowe's. It is possible that Nashe revised it for publication in 1594. What is certain is that Nashe knew and approved of Phaer, whose translation he compares favourably with Stanyhurst's (Nashe 1958: III. 319).

R.B. McKerrow (who includes *Dido* in his edition of Nashe's works) and H.J. Oliver, in his edition of the play (1968), both note some resemblances to Phaer's translation, but McKerrow also stresses that Phaer 'cannot be regarded as the immediate source of the play' and that the author(s) went directly to the Latin (Nashe 1958: IV. 295). The latter point is indisputable, but Marlowe's knowledge of Phaer may be greater than has hitherto been acknowledged. Phaer is not the most accurate of translators; he omits and inserts a good deal in order to produce his long rhyming couplets. As McKerrow observes, one of Phaer's omissions is the leopard-skin tunic mentioned by Venus (*maculosae tegmine lyncis*, *Aen.* I. 323) when she appears to Aeneas in the guise of a huntress; Marlowe, correctly, has 'clothed in a spotted leopard's skin' (I. 1. 186), but a few lines later, 'And suit themselves in purple for the nonce' is closer to Phaer's vague 'purple weed' than to Virgil's *purpureoque . . . cothurno* ('purple buskin'). In some other instances, Phaer's translation follows that of Douglas; for example, Douglas's admirable translation of *revocate animos*, (*Aen.* I. 202) from Aeneas's speech of encouragement to his men, as 'Pluck up your hearts' is repeated in Phaer and in Marlowe (I. 1. 149), who is more likely to have taken it from Phaer than from Douglas. Laocoön's serpents are winged in Marlowe (II. 1. 166) and 'dragon-wise' (which implies wings) in Phaer; there is no mention of wings in the original (or in Douglas or Surrey). The turret from which in Marlowe Aeneas views the destruction of Troy (II. 1. 192) may have been suggested by the tower which in Phaer translates *summi fastigia tecti* (*Aen.* II. 302) and for which (in both cases more correctly) Surrey has 'house top' and Douglas 'howssis hed'. Again, only Phaer, not Douglas or Surrey, translates Virgil's *cadentia sidera* (*Aen.* IV. 81) as 'falling stars'; the passage is not directly translated by Marlowe but perhaps lies behind his 'the stars fall down / To be partakers of our honey talk' (IV. 4. 53–4).

The conversion of an epic, of which Dido's story is only a part, into a drama of which she is the centre inevitably results in the lessening of the importance of Aeneas as a man destined to found a second Troy; even Virgil's *pius Aeneas* appears at a disadvantage in a situation in which he must either disobey the divine behest or betray Dido. Marlowe includes a good deal of the epic material – most of Jove's speech outlining the future glories of Rome, for example – yet his Aeneas is remarkably unheroic. Ethel Seaton has pointed out that Marlowe must have been aware of the medieval view of Aeneas as a vile traitor (Seaton 1959: 27). He certainly knew Lydgate's *Troy Book* (1412–20), which derives, via the *Historia Destructionis Troiae* (1287) by Guido delle Colonne, from the supposedly eyewitness accounts of the spurious writers Dares Phrygius and Dictys Cretensis. According to this tradition, Aeneas, far from being preserved by the gods from the sack of Troy, together with Antenor betrays the city to the Greeks in return for a guarantee of his own safety, and hence in the story as told by Lydgate, and by Chaucer in *The House of Fame* and *The Legend of Good Women*, he has no shred of excuse for betraying Dido. That Marlowe was familiar with this tradition is made explicit in the play when Dido says 'Some say Antenor did betray the town' (II. 1. 110), but it is also clear that he did not base his play on this particular form of the legend. Marlowe's Aeneas is closer to the weak and vacillating Aeneas of Dolce's *Didone*, whose resolve to leave Carthage needs to be stiffened by his confidant, Achates. In Marlowe, Achates plays a similarly decisive role, and his contempt for 'dalliance [that] doth consume a soldier's strength / And wanton motions of alluring eyes / Effeminate our minds inur'd to war' (IV. 3. 34–6) echoes Mercury's words to Aeneas in Dolce: 't'hai fatto nido / Pien di lascivia, effeminato e molle' (II. ii, fol. 11 verso). In Virgil Achates is not mentioned in this context and the decision to leave Carthage is taken by Aeneas alone.

Marlowe's boldest departure from the story as told by Virgil occurs when Aeneas allows himself to be persuaded by Dido to ignore the divine command to depart that he has received in a dream. The waking encounter with Mercury occurs later, not because of Iarbas' prayer to Jove, as in Virgil, but because Aeneas has not obeyed the first message.

In Virgil too Mercury appears twice, but the dream vision comes later, when Aeneas has already embarked and its purpose is to warn him to flee Dido's revenge. Virgil's Aeneas responds at once to Jove's command, hard though he finds it; and he does at least intend to confront Dido, but she anticipates him. Marlowe's Aeneas accurately predicts that he will be unable to disentangle himself from Dido and tries to leave without seeing her, although he is aware that this is 'to transgress against all laws of love' (IV. 3. 48). This is precisely what he does in Lydgate and Chaucer; he is scarcely more admirable in Marlowe, when, caught in the act, he resorts to lies and half-truths: he went to take his farewell of Achates; he would not have left without Ascanius.

The Dido of the play is a far more dominant and impressive figure than her Aeneas, perhaps in part because Marlowe knew that the boy actors would be better able to cope with the demands of a female role than a male one. Although he drastically prunes the sequence in which, with Aeneas gone, she prepares for death, he gives her more to say and do in the earlier scenes than Virgil does. Initially, at any rate, her love for Aeneas is treated with a certain amount of humour, as when she chats about her suitors in a manner foreshadowing Shakespeare's Portia. It is all very different from the seriousness of Virgil's Dido. Her first meeting with Aeneas in the epic is immediately followed by the announcement of Venus's plan to make her fall in love with Aeneas, an episode which Marlowe delays until after the narration of the fall of Troy. Neither Dido can avoid destiny, but Marlowe's appears to co-operate with it, even to will it. Giving Sichaeus's robe to Aeneas is a symbolic gesture prophetic of Aeneas's future role; in Virgil it is Aeneas, as befits a guest, who fetches gifts from his ships to present to Dido.

Virgil does not describe the growing intimacy of Dido and Aeneas in any detail; Marlowe invents scenes in which Aeneas is almost absurdly passive and Dido is lyrically eloquent in a style which suggests a self-abandonment to passion unfitting in a ruler. One of these, Act IV Scene 4, in which she prevents Aeneas's departure, is followed by another invention, contrived by extending Cupid's impersonation of Ascanius, who so far has played a more prominent part than he does in Virgil. This second new scene introduces a typical feature of Elizabethan plays, a comic parody of the main plot, in which Dido's aged nurse, like her mistress, is struck by Cupid's arrows; her unjust punishment in Act V, however, is certainly not comic. The Nurse clearly has nothing to do with Virgil's Barce, who is mentioned only once, when Dido, about to commit suicide, sends her on a false errand to get her out of the way, nor is she anything like Dolce's 'nudrida', whose main function is to relate offstage action.

In the final scene of confrontation between Aeneas and Dido, Marlowe keeps many of Virgil's most famous lines, as do his Italian predecessors, but like one of them, Dolce, he adds an allusion to Scythia: 'But thou art sprung from Scythian Caucasus, / And tigers from Hyrcania gave thee suck' (V. 1. 158–9). A few lines later there is another verbal similarity to Dolce when Dido compares Aeneas to a serpent 'that came creeping from the shore / And I for pity harbour'd in my bosom'. The same image is used by Dolce at an earlier point in the play (see Text 5, p. 63). These parallels do not in themselves prove that Marlowe knew Dolce. The allusion to Scythia could have come from Seneca or from Ovid (who uses it frequently) and is just what one might expect from the author of *Tamburlaine*; the serpent image is proverbial. They do, however, acquire significance in the light of the other parallels between Marlowe's play and Dolce's.

In the *Aeneid*, Dido swoons and is carried out at the end of this speech of passionate denunciation, when Aeneas would have said more; in Marlowe, it is Aeneas who leaves, and the speech by that time has become one of passionate pleading. Virgil's Dido is at times poignant, at times magnificently angry; Marlowe is closer to Ovid in that pathos is more evident than fury, scorn and the desire for revenge. Virgil's Dido imagines herself rejoicing at Aeneas's death; Marlowe's Dido would weep over a drowned Aeneas (V. 1. 177), and Ovid's confesses that she doesn't really want him to drown at all (see Text 4, p. 62). Marlowe omits the lines in Virgil in which Dido regrets not having killed Ascanius and scattered his limbs on the sea; there is no need for Mercury to warn Aeneas to flee this Dido's revenge. If in her last speech Marlowe quotes in the original Latin Dido's vow of eternal enmity between Rome and Carthage, he also exploits the pathetic effect of the relics of Aeneas gathered on the pyre, especially with 'the sword that in the darksome cave / He drew, and swore by, to be true to me' (V. 1. 295–6). In Virgil, Aeneas swears no such oath.

Another, and more immediately striking, of Marlowe's variations on the story as told in Virgil is the plot complication involving Anna and Iarbas. In the epic, Iarbas is no more than a figure in the background; there is no suggestion that he is favoured by Dido and he is of importance to the story only when Jove answers his prayer by sending Mercury to Aeneas. In the three Italian plays, as in Marlowe, Iarbas acquires greater importance as a jealous rival of Aeneas. Marlowe keeps him in the picture throughout; in Dolce he does not actually appear on stage, but after Dido's death he invades Carthage and exacts a bloody revenge. In Marlowe's version, after his attempt to get rid of Aeneas by providing him with ships has resulted in catastrophe, his frustation and despair culminate in his suicide. The Virgilian commentator, Servius, notes that according to Varro, it was Anna, not Dido, who killed herself for love of Aeneas (Smith 1976: 231). Dolce too makes Anna kill herself – the only extant dramatist other than Marlowe to do so – but in this

21

case her motive is grief for her sister. Only Marlowe makes Anna hopelessly in love with Iarbas, enabling him to end his play with three on-stage deaths, in a testament to the power of love to torture and destroy. This is Dolce's theme too, but presented in neo-classical fashion by the messenger's speech describing the wholesale slaughter of Iarbas' invasion.

The opening dialogue, or induction, of the play has no connection with Virgil, apart from a passing reference to Juno's resentment of Ganymede. As so often, Marlowe invents freely on the basis of classical myth, but here in a spirit which is strongly satiric rather than Virgilian. In the *Aeneid*, Jove sadly ponders the plight of Aeneas' fleet and is addressed by Venus with the respect due to the father of the gods; in the play he is introduced as a doting pederast whose attention is fixed on a petulant Ganymede and who has to be reminded of his responsibilities by a sharp-tongued Venus. Marlowe extends the roles of the gods, especially that of Cupid, who does not have a speaking part in Virgil, but often in a way that diminishes them and which exploits the comic incongruity of using boy actors to play them. In their scenes with Aeneas, Venus and Mercury keep fairly close to their prototypes in Virgil, but Act III Scene 2, in which Juno and Venus quarrel, treats the source with more freedom. The equivalent scene in Virgil does not lack humour, but he certainly does not – unlike Marlowe – make Juno a would-be child killer or Venus a shrew.

The account of the fall of Troy in Act II contains a number of divergences from Virgil's narrative and some of Marlowe's most distinctive writing, together with some convincing evidence that he knew medieval versions of the story. To begin with, the departure of the Greeks from Troy is not a ruse, as in Virgil, and the account of Ulysses turning them back comes from Ovid (*Metamorphoses*, XIII, 223–7). In one of the most vividly realized passages describing the Greeks leaping down from the wooden horse: '. . . a thousand Grecians more, / In whose stern faces shin'd the quenchless fire / That after burnt the pride of Asia' (II. 1. 185–7), the stern faces, the thousand knights and the quenchless fire are not in Virgil, and 'stern face', as Ethel Seaton points out (Seaton 1959: 29) is a favourite expression of Lydgate. The thousand knights are also of medieval origin and are to be found in Caxton's *The Recuyell of the Histories of Troy* (II. 666). The speech is a masterpiece of compression (an entire book of the *Aeneid* in 168 lines) and this passage is an example; Virgil lists the names of eight Greeks, Marlowe names only Neoptolemus, who as 'the furious Pyrrhus' will be important later. He omits two long speeches by Sinon, but gives a vividly realized picture of him with his eyes turned up to heaven; the detail, which is not in Virgil, encapsulates Sinon's false piety. Laocoön's terrible end is dealt with summarily; in Virgil this is a prelude to horrors to come, but Marlowe concentrates on the sack of the city.

For Virgil's Aeneas the first event of the fateful night is the apparition of Hector in a dream, entrusting to him the city's household gods and the mission to found a new Troy – the great theme of the epic. This positive note of hope in destruction and despair is sounded again when Jove sends signs to convince Anchises that he must leave the city and when Aeneas meets the ghost of Creusa. Marlowe omits both incidents and divests the meeting with Hector of its significance in Virgil; in his version Hector makes no reference to Aeneas' destiny when he tells him to flee. By this time Marlowe's Aeneas, who is not asleep, has already witnessed dreadful scenes of carnage ('Young infants swimming in their parents' blood' (II. 1. 193)) which do not come from the *Aeneid* but which can be paralleled in Lydgate.

Virgil's Aeneas has some initial success against the Greeks, although he fails to rescue Cassandra; Marlowe's account moves swiftly to its climax, the death of Priam, postponing the Cassandra episode. Virgil describes the killing of Priam's son, Polites, before his parents' eyes. Marlowe abbreviates this episode to the single startling image of Polites' mangled head on Pyrrhus' spear. Virgil's Aeneas finds Priam struggling into his armour; deprived of courage and dignity, all Marlowe's Priam can do is beg for his life. This Priam is closer to the feeble and ineffectual king of the *Troy Book* than to Virgil, and as in Lydgate, it is he who bears responsibility for the foolish decision to break down the walls of Troy. His fate is to become yet another mutilated body, ripped open and with hands struck off; in Virgil, Pyrrhus simply runs him through. Hecuba's frenzied attack on Pyrrhus is Marlowe's own addition to the story, perhaps suggested by Lydgate's account of her reaction to Polyxena's death, although in one detail (tearing at Pyrrhus' eyes with her nails), it is closer to Ovid's story in *Metamorphoses* of how she tore out the eyes of King Polymestor in revenge for the death of her son, Polydorus (see Text 3, p. 59). Both these events occur after the fall of the city. In Virgil the killing of Priam takes place at the altar, but there is no mention of a statue. There is a statue in Lydgate (with the customary 'stern face') but it is of Apollo; Inna Koskenniemi points out that in pictorial representations of the scene there is often a prominent statue of Jove (1972: 152). Pyrrhus dipping his father's flag in Priam's blood has been seen as another medieval touch (Tucker Brooke 1930: 161), but it is also one which suggests the revenger of Elizabethan plays, with whom Shakespeare associates Pyrrhus in the Player's speech in *Hamlet*.

In Marlowe, Aeneas fails to save three women in succession in his flight from the city: not only Creusa, from whom, as in Virgil, he becomes separated, but Cassandra and Polyxena as well. The Cassandra episode is transferred from its earlier position in the *Aeneid*: Polyxena, who does not appear in the *Aeneid* at all, is another link with Ovid and with medieval versions of the story. Ovid recounts Polyxena's fate as a sacrifice to the shade of Achilles but does not link her with Aeneas; Lydgate and Caxton tell how, after the death of Priam, Hecuba begged Aeneas to save her daughter. The details of the story seem to be Marlowe's own; no other version has Aeneas swimming to Polyxena's aid, or mentions Myrmidons, or that she is killed at an altar. So too with Cassandra; in Virgil she is dragged from Minerva's temple, not Diana's fane, and there is no mention of her rape by Ajax. Marlowe's treatment of the loss of Creusa is especially curt. In the original the frantic search for her and the meeting with her ghost are movingly described; in the play she is given no special prominence, but is just another casualty of war. The collocation of these three incidents shows Aeneas in a rather equivocal light as a man who, although his intentions are good, abandons three women to their deaths – an unhappy omen for the woman whose interjections show how intently she listens to him.

TEXT 1

The Seven First Books of the 'Aeneidos' of Virgil

translated by Thomas Phaer
(1558)

[The text is based on the British Library copy (shelfmark C. 56. e. 2).]

FROM BOOK 1

[The *Aeneid* begins with Juno's anger against the Trojans, fuelled by her jealousy of Ganymede, a youth of the Trojan royal house. At her request, Aeolus, god of the winds, raises a storm to wreck the Trojan fleet, but Neptune calms the sea and the Trojans land on the coast of Africa.]

Then from the ship to walk aland Aeneas longed sore,
And chose of all the number seven and brought with him to
   shore.
There by a bank their weary limbs of salt sea did they stretch,
And first Achates from the flint a spark of fire did fetch,
Which he received in matter meet, and dry leaves laid about.
Then vittels [victuals] out they laid aland with seas well-near
   ymarred,
And corn to dry they set, and some with stones they bruised hard.
There whilst Aeneas up the rock was gone to walk on high,
To see where any ships of his astray he might espy,
If Caicus' arms upon the sail, or Capys haps to show.   10
No boat in sight, but on the shore three harts there stood a-row,
And after them the herd behind along the valley fed.
He stay'd, and of his bow and bolts Achates straight him sped.
The chief that highest bare their heads, adown with darts he kest
   [cast],
And to the woods he followed then with like pursuit the rest.
He left them not till seven of them were fall'n with bodies great,
To match the number of his ships that now had need of meat. . . .
And then to cheer their heavy hearts with these words he him bent
   [aimed]:

25

'O mates,' quoth he, 'that many a woe have bidden [endured]
   and borne ere this,
Worse have we seen, and this also shall end when God's will is.   20
Through Scylla rage, you wot, and through the roaring rocks we
   passed;
Though Cyclops' shore was full of fear, yet came we through at
   last.
Pluck up your hearts and drive from thence both thought and
   fear away;
To think on this may pleasure be, perhaps, another day.
With pains and many a danger sore by sundry chance we wend
To come to Italia, where we trust to find our resting end,
And where the dest'nies have decreed Troy's kingdoms eft
   [again] to rise.
Be bold, and harden now yourselves; take ease when ease applies.'
Thus spake he tho [then], but in his heart huge cares him had
   oppressed,
Dissim'ling hope with outward eyes, full heavy was his breast. . . .   30
                     (A 3 recto–A 3 verso)

[Venus makes a tearful protest to Jove about the plight of her son,
Aeneas.]

The maker of the gods and men to her all sweetly smiles
With count'nance such as from the skies the storms and clouds
   exiles,
And sweetly kiss'd his daughter dear and therewithal he speaks:
'Fear not,' quoth he, 'thy men's good hap, for none their fortune
   breaks.
Thy kingdom prosper shall, and eke [also] the walls I thee
   behight [promised]
Thou shalt see rise in Lavin land and grow full great of might.
And thou thy son Aeneas stout [brave] to heaven shalt bring at
   last,
Among the gods; be sure of this, my mind is fixed fast.
And now to thee disclose I shall (for sore I see thee doubt)
The long discourse of destinies that years shall bring about.   40
Great war in Italy have he shall, ere he the people wild
May undertread, and learn to live, and then the city build,
That summers three ere he shall sit as king them shall renew,
And winters three, before he can the Rutiles all subdue.
Then shall Ascanius, now a child, whose name Iulus hight
(Was Ilus call'd when Troy's estate and kingdom stood upright),
Till space of thirty years expire his kingdom shall obtain,

26

And he from Lavin shall translate the old state of the reign
And strongly fortify the town of Alba long [Alba Longa] shall he,
Where whole three hundred years the stock of Hector kings
   shall be, 50
Till Ilia queen, with child by Mars, two twins to light shall bring,
Whom wolves shall nurse, and proud thereof he grows that shall
   be king.
He, Romulus, shall take the rule and up the walls shall frame
Of mighty Rome, and Romans all shall call them of his name.
No end to their estate I set, ne [nor] terms of time or place,
But endless shall their empire grow. . . .'

                       (A 4 recto–A 4 verso)

[Mercury is sent to ensure that Aeneas will be kindly received by Dido.]

But good Aeneas all that night his mind about he tossed,
And in the morning went him out to search and see the coast,
To learn what land they were come to, what people dwelt
   thereon,
If men or savage beasts it holds, for till'd [cultivated land] he
   could see none. 60
This would he know, and to his men the truth of all to tell.
There whilst within a water cave his ships he made to dwell,
Whom trees and woods with shadows thick and eke the rock doth
   hide.
Then forth he goeth, and took but one, Achates, by his side,
And lances two they bare in hand of metal sharp and light,
And as they went amid the wood he met his mother right,
Most like a maid in maiden's weed, she maiden's armour bears,
As doth Harpalycee the queen that horses wild outwears,
So wight [fleet] of foot, that Heber stream so swift she leaves
   behind;
For hunterlike her bow she bare, her locks went with the wind 70
Behind her back, and tuck'd she was that naked was her knee.
She call'd to them and said, 'Good sirs, I pray you, did you see
To stray this way as ye have come, my sisters any one,
With quiver bound that in the chase of some wild beast are gone
Or with a cry pursueth apace the foamy boar to pain?'
   So Venus said, and Venus' son her answer'd thus again:
'None of thy sisters have I seen nor heard, I thee assure.
O maid, what shall I make of thee? Thy face I see so pure,
Not mortal like, ne like mankind thy voice doth sound. I guess
Some goddess thou art, and Phoebus bright thy brother is
   doubtless, 80
Or of the noble nymphs thou comest. Of grace we thee beseech

27

Whatever thou art, and help our need, and now vouchsafe to
 teach
What land is this? What coast of heaven be we come under here?
Where neither man nor place we know, so stray'd we have in fear;
Out of our course we have been cast, with winds and floods
 yshake.
Afore thine altars many a beast to offer I undertake.'
 'As for mine altars,' quoth she tho [then], 'no such estate I
 bear,
The manner is of virgins here this short array to wear;
In purple weed we use to walk with quiver light unbound.
The realm of Afric here thou seest, and men of Tyrus' ground.   90
Here is the city of Agenor; fierce be the lands about.
Queen Dido rules and wears the crown; from Tyrus she came out
And lately from her brother fled. The cause is long to lere [tell],
The story long, but touch I will the chief and leave it there. . . .'

[Venus then tells how when Dido fled from Tyre after the murder of her
husband, Sichaeus, by her brother, Pygmalion, she was offered as much
land as a bull's hide would cover; cut into strips, the hide covered a
large area. This story is not spelled out in the play, but Iarbas (IV. 2. 13)
recalls how Dido 'crav'd a hide of ground to build a town'.]

'But what are you, fain would I know, or what coast come ye fro?
Where would you be?' Demanding thus, he answer'd her unto,
With sighing deep, and from his breast his heavy tale he set.
 'O lady mine,' quoth he, 'to tell if nothing did me let
 [prevent],
And of our pains ye list to hear the stories out at large,
The day were short, and ere an end the sun would him discharge.   100
Of ancient Troy (if ever Troy beside your ears hath passed),
Of thence be we; by sundry seas and coasts we have been cast,
And now the tempest hath us brought to Lyby land by chance.
My name Aeneas cleped [called] is; my country gods to advance
In ships I bring; unto the stars well blazed is my fame.
Of Italy I seek the land, and Jove's offspring I am.
A Trojan fleet I took to sea with twenty vessels wide;
My mother goddess taught my way, as dest'ny did me guide.
Now seven thereof do scant [scarcely] remain, the rest with
 weathers gone,
And I unknown in wilderness here walk and comfort none.   110
From Asia and from Europa quite thus driven I am.' With that
She could no longer bide him speak, but brake his tale thereat.
 'Whatever thou art,' quoth she, 'for well I wot the gods above
Doth love thee much to save thy life to this place to remove,

28

Go forth to yonder palace straight, assay the queen to see,
For safe thy company aland be set, believe thou me. . . .
Now get thee forth, and where the way thee leads hold on thy
    pace.'
Scant had she said, and therwithal she turn'd aside her face,
As red as rose she gan to shine, and from her heavenly hair
The flavour sprang, as nectar sweet; down fell her kirtle there,   120
And like a goddess right she fled. When he his mother wist
    [knew],
He follow'd fast [close] and call'd, 'Alas, what mean you, thus to
    list
In feigned shapes so oft to me beguiling to appear?
Why hand in hand embrace we not, and jointly speak and hear?'
Thus plaining sore he still his pace unto the city holds. . . .

                      (A 4 verso–B 2 recto)

[Venus throws a cloud of invisibility over Aeneas and Achates. They
reach a grove in which stands a temple dedicated to Juno and decorated
with frescos depicting scenes from the Trojan war which move Aeneas
to tears. Dido arrives and after her a number of Aeneas's shipwrecked
companions.]

When they were in, and licence had before the queen to speak,
The greatest lord, Sir Ilionee [Ilioneus], thus gan the silence
    break:
'O queen, to whom is given of God to build this city new,
And for your justice peoples proud and savage to subdue,
We Trojans poor whom through the seas all tempests tossed have   130
Beseek your grace our silly ships from wicked fire to save.
Have mercy upon our gentle stock [noble race], and graciously
    relieve
Our painful case. We come not here with weapons you to grieve,
To spoil the coast of Lyby land, nor booties hence to bear.
We conquer'd men be not so bold, our pride need none to fear.
There is a place the Greeks by name Hesperia do call,
An ancient land and stout in war, and fruitful soil withal.
Out from Oenotria they came that first did till the same,
Now Italy men saith is call'd so of the captain's name.
To that our course was bent,   140
When suddenly there rose at south a wind and tempest wood
    [wild],
That toward shore enforc'd to fall and so took on the flood
That in the rocks we be dispers'd; we few this coast have caught.
What kind of men be these of yours? What manners wild ytaught
This country keeps? To lodge in sand we cannot suffer'd be.

They fight, and none to tread aland they can content to see.
If mortal men you do despise and care for none in fight,
Yet have respect to gods above that judge both wrong and right.
We had a king, Aeneas call'd, a juster was there none;
In virtue, nor in feats of war, or arms could match him one.   150
Whom if the dest'nies keeps alive (if breath and air of skies
He draws, nor yet among the ghosts of cruel death he lies)
There is no fear it shall be quit [requited] the favour now you
   show,
You first his kindness to provoke shall never repent, I know. . . .'
                             (B 3 verso–B 4 recto)

[The cloud concealing Aeneas and Achates is withdrawn. Dido welcomes
the Trojans and brings them to her palace.]

Aeneas then, for in his mind could love not let him rest,
His friend Achates for his son Ascanius hath him dressed
   [directed]
Unto the ships, and bade him tell the news, and bring him there
As fast as may, for in Ascanius fix'd was all his fear.
And gifts with him he bade to bring from Troy destroy'd yfet
   [fetched]:
A royal pall [robe], that all with gold and stones was overset   160
And eke [also] a robe with borders rich; sometime it was the
   weed [garment]
Of Helen bright when Paris her from Greece to Troy did lead. . . .
These things to fet Achates haste unto the navy makes.
   But Venus strange devices new and counsels new she takes,
That Cupid shall the face and hue of sweet Ascanius take,
And bear the presents to the queen, her heart afire to make
With fervent love, and in her bones to fling the privy flame.
Suspect she doth the Moors, that have of double tongue the name,
And Juno's wrath her frets, and in the night her care returns.
Therefore she thus exhorts her son Cupid, that lovers burns. . . .   170
'. . . Now go'th the child, my chiefest care, unto his father kind
Into the town, and from the seas the presents forth he brings,
That from the flames of burning Troy was kept as worthy things.
Him purpose I asleep to make, and into high Cythere
Or to my seats in Ida mount, all unaware to bear,
That from this craft he may be far, ne let [hindrance] herein
   do make.
Thou for a night, and not beyond, his form and figure take,
Her to beguile, and of a child thou, child, put on the face,
That when within her lap the queen thee gladly shall embrace,
Among the royal pomp of meat and wine of Bacchus' bliss,   180

30

And clips [embraces] thee sweet, and on thy lips doth press the
   pleasant kiss,
Disperse in her thy secret flame and poison sweet inspire.'
Love doth obey, puts off his wings, and after her desire
Puts on Ascanius' shape forthwith, and like the same he went.
But Venus on Ascanius sweet a restful slumber cast,
And in her bosom up she bears, and forth with him she passed
To Ida woods, where beds of thyme and marjoram so soft,
And lusty flowers in greenwood shade him breathes and
   comforts oft.

[The Trojans are entertained at a feast; Dido asks to hear their story.]

'And from the first', quoth she, 'my guest, vouchsafe, I pray,
   to tell
The treasons of the Greeks, and how your town and people fell;   190
And of your chance and travels all, for thus these seven year
About the lands and all the seas thou wand'rest, as I hear.'
(C 1 recto–C 2 verso)

FROM BOOK II

They whisted [fell silent] all, and fix'd with eyes intentive did
   behold
When lord Aeneas where he sat from high bench thus he told.
'A doleful work me to renew, O queen, thou dost constrain,
To tell how Greeks the Trojan wealth and lamentable reign
Did overthrow, which I myself have seen and been a part
No small thereof. But to declare the stories all: what heart
Can of the Greeks or soldier one of all Ulysses' rout
Refrain to weep? Now the night with high heaven go'th about
And on the skies the falling stars doth men provoke to rest;
But if such great desire to know, such longing have your breast   10
Of Troy the latter toil [strife] to hear, to speak or yet to think
For all that it my mind abhors, and sorrows make me shrink,
I will begin. Forsaken gods, and tir'd with wars at last,
The lords of Greeks, when all in vain so many years had passed,
A horse of tree [wood] by Pallas' art most like a mount they frame
With timber boards, and for a vow to leave they blow
   [proclaim] the same.
   There is an isle in sight of Troy and Tenedos it hight [is
   called],
A wealthy land while Priam's state and kingdom stood upright,
But now a bay and harbour bad for ships to lie at road [at
   anchor].

31

To that they went, and hid them close that none was seen abroad.   20
We thought them gone, and with the wind to Greece to have
    been fled.
. . . Till from the town Laocoön came in haste as he were wood
    [mad],
And after him a number great, and ere they gan to throng
He cried, 'O wretched citizens, what madness is you among?
Believe ye gone the Greeks? Or do you think that any gifts
Of them be good? So know you well that false Ulysses' drifts?
In this tree (for my life) is hid of Greeks an hideous rout
Or this is but an engine made to scale our walls without
And suddenly to slip them down and on the city fall,
Or other worse device there is; take heed, ye know not all.   30
Whatever it is, I fear the Greeks, and trust their gifts as small.'
He said, and with a courage good his mighty spear he drives
Against the side beneath the ribs, that where he hits it clives
    [cleaves].
It shakes aloft, and still it stood that through the belly round
The vaults within and crooked caves of noise did all rebound.
And if the will of gods had not, had not our hearts been blind,
Enough was done all up to break, and all the craft to find,
And Troy thou shouldst have stond [stood] as yet, and Priam's
    tow'rs have shined.
                    (C 3 verso–C 4 recto)

[The shepherds bring in a captive (Sinon), who pretends to have
escaped from a sentence of death by hiding 'in a slimy lake of mud'.]

Then pardon we for pity gave, this wailing smarts us so;
King Priam first his men commands to unbind him free to go.   40
'Whatever thou art, forget the Greeks; from hence thou need
    not care,
Thou shalt be ours. And now the truth of my request declare.
What mean they by this monster big, this horse who did invent?
Wherefore? Religion sake? Or for the wars some engine bent?'
Thus said, and he with Greekish wiles and treasons false
    yfreight,
His loosed hands to heavens above with great cry held on height.
'O everlasting fires of God, whose wrath no wight can bear,
You altars, and you swords also, whose force I fled, I swear,
And you to witness now I call, and by the garlands gay
That like a beast to slaughter brought,' quoth he, 'I bare that day: 50
Not by my will I am compell'd great secrets here to spread;
Not by my will my country I hate, but since their cruel deed
Hath forc'd me thus, it lawful is. All gods me pardon shall,

Though myst'ries high whom they conceal I blaze and utter
    all. . . .'

(D 1 verso)

[Sinon convinces Priam that the wooden horse is 'a sacrifice t'appease
Minerva's wrath' (II. 1. 163).]

By this deceit, and through the craft of Sinon false perjur'd,
This to believe us falsehead taught, and we with tears allur'd,
Whom neither all Tydides' force, nor fierce Achilles'.fame,
Not ten years' war, nor yet of Greeks a thousand ships could tame.
    Another monster worse than this, and worse to dread our eyes
Amazed made, and quite from doubt confounds our hearts so
    wise.   60
For as by chance that time, a priest to Neptune chosen new,
Laocoön, a mighty bull on the off'ring altar slew,
Beheld from Tenedos aloof [afar] in calm seas through the deep
(I quake to tell) two serpents great with foldings great doth sweep
And side by side in dragons' wise to shore their way they make.
Their heads above the stream they hold, their fire-red manes they
    shake.
The salt sea waves before them fast they shoven, and after trails
Their ugly backs, and long in links behind them drag their tails.
With rushing noise the foam upsprings, and now to land they
    passed
With blood-red looks, and glist'ring fires their sparkling eyes out
    cast,   70
Where hissing out with spurting tongues their mouths they lick'd
    for ire.
We dead almost for fear do flee; they straight with one desire
On Laocoön set, and first in sight his tender children twain
Each one they took, and winding wraps their tender limbs to
    strain,
And gnawing them with greedy mouths, poor wretches, feed they
    fast;
Then he himself to their defence with drawn sword making haste
In hold they caught, and writhing gripp'd his body about at twice,
And twice his throat with rolls they girt themselves in compass
    wise.
And then their heads and scalebright necks him over aloft they
    lift,
When from their knots himself to untwine with hands he sought
    to shift,   80
Their poisons rank all over him runs, and loathsome filth outflies;
Therewith a grisly noise he casts that mounts up to the skies. . . .

33

Then trembling fear through all our hearts was spread and
   wonder new;
We think how Laocoön for sin was paid with vengeance due
For hurting of that holy gift, whom he with cursed spear
Assailed had, and worthy was, men said, that plague to bear.
'Bring in the holy horse,' they cry, 'this goddess' wrath to
   appease,
And her of mercy great beseek.'
Then wide abroad we break the walls, a way through them we
   make.
With courage [eagerness] all men falls to work. Some sort doth
   undertake   90
His feet on sliding wheels to slip, some thwart his neck begin
The cables bind, and on the walls now climbs the fatal gin [trap]
With armour freight [laden]; about him runs of boys and girls
   the school
With songs and hymns, and glad go'th he that hand may put to
   pull.
It enters, and afront the town it slides with threat'ning sight.
O country soil, O house of gods, thou Ilion, O the might
Of doughty Trojan walls in war! For there four times aground
It sway'd, and four times through the womb was harness heard to
   sound.
Yet we went on, and blind with rage our work we would not let
   [leave],
But in this cursed monster brought, by Pallas' tower to set.   100
Then prophecies aloud to preach Cassandra nothing spares,
As god-inspir'd, but never of us believ'd who nothing cares.
And wretches we that never day beside that day should bide,
The temples shroud [deck], and through the town great feasting
   made that tide.
   This while the firmament doth turn, and dark night up doth rise,
And overhides with shadow great both lands and seas and skies,
And falsehead of the Greeks withal. And now along the walls
The weary Trojans laid at rest, the dead sleep on them falls,
When with their fleet in goodly array the Greekish armies soon
From Tenedos were come (for then full friendly shone the
   moon).   110
In silence great their wonted shore they took, and then a flame
Their am'ral [admiral] ship for warning showed, when, kept all
   gods to shame,
Sir Sinon out by stealth him stirs, and wide he sets abroad
His horse's paunch, and he disclosed straight lay'th out his load,
Thessander, Sthenelus, and false Ulysses, captains all,

And Acamas and Thoas eke; by long ropes down they fall.
Neoptolemus, Achilles' brood, Machaon chief of pride,
And Menelaus with numbers mo [more], full gladly forth they
    slide,
And he himself, Epeus there, this mischief first that found.
The town invade they do forthwith, in sleeps and drinking
    drowned.   120
They slew the watch, and then the gates broad up they break,
    and stands
Their fellows ready to receive, and thick they join their bands.
    That time it was when slumber first and dead sleep deep
    oppressed
On weary mortal men doth creep, through gods' gift sweet at rest.
Unto my sight (as dream I did) all sad with doleful cheer
Did Hector stand, and large him weep with sobs I might well hear,
With horses hal'd, as bloody drawn sometime he was in dust,
And all to swoln his worthy feet where through the thongs were
    thrust.
Alas, to think how sore beray'd [disfigured], how from that
    Hector sore
He changed was, that in Achilles' spoils came home before,   130
Or when among the ships of Greece the fires so fierce he flung.
But now in dust his beard bedabb'd, his hair with blood is clung,
With naked wounds, that in defence of Trojan walls sustain'd
He often had; and me to weep for pity woe constrain'd.
With heavy voice methought I spake, and thus to him I plain'd:
    'O light of Troy, O Trojan hope at need that never fail'd,
What country thee so long hath kept? What cause hath so
    prevail'd
That after slaughters great of men, thy town, thy people tir'd
With sundry pains and dangers past, thee long (so sore desir'd)
At last we see? What chance unkind thy face before so bright   140
Hath made so foul, alas? And why of wounds I see this sight?'
He nothing hereto spake, nor me with vain talk long delayed,
But heavy from his breast he set his deep sigh; then he said,
'Flee, flee, thou goddess' son; alas, thyself save from these flames.
The walls are won,' quoth he, 'the Greeks of Troy pull down the
    frames.
For Priam and our country dear our duty is done; if hand
Or man's relief might Troy have kept, by this hand had it stand.
And now religions all to thee with gods doth Troy betake
    [entrust],
New fortune thou and they must seek. Thou unto them shalt
    make

35

More mighty walls, when through the seas long journeys hast
    thou take.'   150
So said, and with his hands methought he from their altars drew
The mighty gods, and all their fires aye lasting out he threw.
    By this time divers noise abroad through all the town is steer'd,
And wailings loud, and more and more on every side appear'd.
And though my father Anchises' house with trees encompass'd
    round
Stood far within, yet brym [fierce] we hear the noise and
    armour's sound.
Therewith I woke, and up the tow'r I climb by stairs on high,
And laid mine ear, and still I stood about me round to spy. . . .
And now the great house down was fall'n by fire that wild doth fly,
Of Deiphobus first, and next his neighbour burns on high,   160
Ucalegon, and shores and stronds [strands] with blazings shines
    about,
And shrieking shouts of people rise and trumpets blown are out.
Amazed, I mine armour took, nor what to do I wust [knew],
But headlong ran, and through the throngs to fight I thought to
    thrust,
And to the castle ward I hied more aid to call me nigh,
With anger wood [furious], and fair methought in arms it was to
    die. . . .

                              (D 2 recto–D 3 verso)

[Aeneas meets several of his compatriots and encourages them to
fight.]

    Behold where hal'd by hair and head from Pallas' temple sure
King Priam's daughter drawn we see, Cassandra, virgin pure.
And up to heaven in vain for help her glist'ring eyes she cast;
Her eyes, for then her tender hands with bolts were fetter'd fast. 170
That sight Coroebus, raging wood, could not him hold to see,
But even among the midst he leapt, with will to die, and we
Him after sued [followed], and thick in throngs of arms ourselves we
    thrust. . . .

                              (E 1 recto)

[Aeneas and his companions fail to rescue Cassandra; they reach the
royal palace just as Pyrrhus enters it.]

    The fatal end of Priam now perhaps you will require.
When he the city taken saw and houses' tops on fire,
And buildings broke, and round about so thick his foes to rage,
His harness on his shoulders (long unworn till then) for age
All quaking, on, good man, he puts to purpose small, and then

His sword him girt, and into death and en'mies thick he ran.
   Amids the court right underneath the naked skies in sight   180
An altar huge of size there stood, and by the same upright
An ancient laurel tree did grow, that wide abroad was shed,
And it and all the carved gods with broad shade overspread.
There Hecuba and her daughters all, poor souls, at the altar's side
In heaps together afraid them drew, like doves when doth betide
Some storm them headlong drive, and clipping [embracing] fast
   their gods they hold.
But when she Priam thus beclad in arms of youth so bold
Espied, 'What mind, alas,' quoth she, 'O woeful husband, you
In harness dight [dressed]? And whither away with weapons run
   ye now?
Not men nor weapons us can save; this time doth axe [ask] to
   bear   190
No such defence, no, not if Hector mine now present were.
Stand here by me; this altar us from slaughters all shall shield,
Or die together at once we shall.' So said she, and gan to wield
Him, aged man, and in the sacred seat him set and held.
   Behold where 'scaping from the stroke of Pyrrhus fets [comes]
   in sight
Polites, one of Priam's sons, through foes and weapons pight
   [placed],
Through galleries along doth run, and wide about him spies;
Sore wounded then, but Pyrrhus after him sues with burning eyes
In chase, and now well-near in hand him caught and held with
   spear,
Till right before his parents' sight he came, then fell'd him there   200
To death, and with his gushing blood his life outright he shed.
There Priamus, though now for woe that time he half was dead,
Himself could not refrain, nor yet his voice nor anger hold.
'But unto thee, O wretch,' he cried, 'for this despite so bold,
The gods (if any justice dwells in heaven or right regard)
Do yield thee worthy thanks, and thee do pay thy due reward,
That here within my sight my son hast slain with slaughter vile,
And not asham'd with loathsome death his father's face to file
   [defile].
Not so did he whom falsely thou beliest to be thy sire,
Achilles, with his en'my Priam deal, but my desire   210
When Hector's corpse to tomb he gave for gold, did entertain
With truth and right, and to my realm restor'd me safe again.'
So spake he, and therewithal his dart with feeble force he threw,
Which sounding on his brazen harness hoarse, it backward flew,

And on his target side it hit, where dintless down it hing [hung].
Then Pyrrhus said, 'Thou shalt go now therefore and tidings
   bring
Unto my father Achilles' soul, my doleful deeds to tell.
Neoptolemus his bastard is, not I; say this in hell.
Now die.' And as he spake that word, from the altar self he drew
Him trembling there, and deep him through his son's blood did
   imbrue [stain],   220
And with his left hand wrapp'd his locks; with right hand
   through his side
His glist'ring sword outdrawn, he did hard to the hilts to
   glide. . . .

                      (E 2 recto–E 3 recto)

[Marlowe omits a good deal here, including Aeneas' meeting with
Venus and the signs sent by Jove to convince his father, Anchises, that
he must leave Troy.]

And under burden fast I fled, my child my right hand kept,
Iule, and after me with pace unlike in length, he stepped.
My wife ensued; through lanes and crooks [byways] and darkness
   most we passed. . . .
And now against the gates I came, which out of danger found,
I thought I well escaped had, when suddenly the sound
Of feet we hear to tread, and men full thick my father scanned.
'Flee, flee, my son,' he cried, 'lo, here they come; lo, here at hand
Their harness bright appears, and glist'ring shields I see to shine.' 230
There what it was I not [knew not], some chance or god, no
   friend of mine,
Amazed then my wit, for while through thick and thin I pass
And from the accustom'd ways I drew to seek to 'scape, alas,
My wife from me, most woeful man, Creusa beloved best,
Remain she did, or lost her way, or sat her down to rest,
Unknown it is, but after that in vain her all we sought. . . .
In vain I call'd and call'd, and oft again and yet I cried.
Thus seeking long with endless pain and rage all places tried.
At last, with woeful luck, her sprite and Creusa's ghost, alas,
Before mine eyes I saw to stand, more great than wonted was. 240
I stonied [was benumbed], and my hair upstood, my mouth for
   fear was fast.
She spake also, and thus fro me my cares she gan to cast:
'What mean you thus your raging mind with labours sore to move,
O husband sweet? These things without the powers of gods above
Hath not betid. . . .'

                      (F 1 recto–F 2 recto)

FROM BOOK IV

By this time pierced sat the queen so sore with love's desire,
Her wound in every vein she feeds, she fries in secret fire. . . .
The morning sun with shining beams all lands had overspread,
And from the skies the drooping shade of night away was fled,
When thus unto her sister dear she spake with vexed head:
'Dear sister Anne, what dreams be these that thus my sleeps
    affrights?
What wondrous guest is this that thus among us newly lights?
How like a lord! How valiant strong of heart and arms he seems!
I see right well no fables been that men of gods esteems.
Of kind [lineage] of gods he is doubtless; by dread are dastards
    [cowards] known.   10
Alas, what wars hath he gone through, what dest'nies him hath
    thrown!
If fixed in my mind I were not fast, and shall not flit [change],
That to no wight in wedlock band I would vouchsafe to knit,
Since first in vain my love I lost, and death did me deceive,
That comfort none in chamber deeds nor joys I can conceive,
Perhaps to this offence alone I might be made to slide.
For Anne, to thee confess I shall, nor truth I will not hide,
Since of my husband first the death and fatal end I knew,
And that my brother with his blood his altars did imbrue [stain],
This only man hath bent [touched] my heart, and sore my mind
    doth move.   20
I know the steps of old; I feel the flames of former love.
But rather would I wish the ground to gape for me below,
Or God himself with thunder dint to hell my soul to throw
To hell beneath in darkness deep, with ghosts and furies black,
O virtue, ere I thee refuse, or shamefastness forsake.
He that him first to me did knit, he took from me my love;
He keeps it, in his grave it lieth, from thence it shall not move.'
Thus speaking, in her bosom full the tears of water run.
    Then answer'd Anne, 'O sister mine, more dear to me than
    sun,
O sister whom I more regard than life or light of day,   30
Will you alone for evermore your youth thus mourn away?
Will you not seek for children sweet? Nor Venus' comfort crave?
Do dead men care, trow ye, for this? Or souls that sleep in grave?
What though sometime, when sickness sore and griefs oppress'd
    your mind,
Of worthy princes none to wed your heart was not inclined?
For husband none of Lyby land or lords you would elect,

Nor king Iarbas eke before whom Tyrus did reject,
Nor captains proud of Afric land of wide renown and fame,
When love that likes you shows himself, will you resist the
    same?. . .'

[Anna reminds Dido that she is surrounded by enemies against whom
Aeneas would be able to aid her.]

With this her burning mind incensed more began to flame,   40
And hope in doubtful heart she caught, and off she cast her
  shame. . . .
    Sometime about the walls she walks, Aeneas by her side,
And town already made she shows, and pomp of Tyrus' pride;
Begins to speak, and in the midst thereof her tale she stays.
Sometimes again, and towards night to banquets him she prays,
And Trojan toils again to tell she him beseeks and harks
With burning mind, and every word and count'nance all she
  marks.
Then when they parted were, and light of moon was down by
  west,
And on the skies the falling stars do men provoke to rest,
She then alone, as one forsaken, mourns, and in his place   50
She layeth her down, and thinks she hears and seeth him face to
  face,
Or on her lap Ascanius for his father's likeness sake
She holds, if haply so she might this irksome love aslake
  [allay]. . . .
                                  (I 1 verso–I 2 verso)
    Whom when dame Juno saw with plague so wood [fierce] to be
  dismay'd
(The mighty spouse of Jove), nor for no speech it could be stay'd,
To Venus first she came, and thus to her began to break:
'A goodly praise, indeed, and worthy conquest great to speak
Thy boy and thou do get! A gay renown you do obtain
If one poor woman trained [deceived] be by heavenly persons
  twain.
Nor think not but I know that thou my walls of Carthage high   60
Hast in suspect, and dreading still the worst, all things dost try.
But shall we never end? Or why do we so fiercely strive,
And do not everlasting peace and friendship fast contrive?
Why wedlocks join we not? Thou hast thyself thine own desire,
Now love in Dido's bones is bred; she fries in raging fire.
Two peoples now therefore in one let us conjoin and guide
With equal love. To Trojan husband, lo, she shall be tied
And Carthage all I give to thee for jointure [dowry] fast to bind.'

To her again (for well she knew she spake with feigned mind
That Rome she might reject, and Carthage kingdom empire
    make)   70
Then Venus answer'd thus: 'Who is so mad that will forsake
This thing? Or gladly would in war with thee so long contend,
If what thou speakest now will fortune bring to perfect end?
But dest'nies makes me doubt, and whether he that reigns above
One town of Troy and Tyrus made can be content to love,
Or will allow the peoples twain to mix and league to bind.
Thou art his wife; thou mayst be bold to frayne [ask] and feel his
    mind.
Begin; I will proceed.' Then said dame Juno, queen so stout,
    [proud],
'Let me alone for that! Now, how this thing shall come about,
Give ear to me, for now my mind thou shalt perceive outright.   80
A-hunting forth Aeneas go'th with Dido, woeful wight,
In woods and forest wide, when morning next begins to spring
And sun with glist'ring beams again to sight the world doth bring.
I from aloft a stormy cloud, and mix'd with sleet and hail,
A tempest dark as night on them to pour I will not fail.
While in the woods they walk, and while the youth enclose the
    toil [net]
The rain shall rise, and heavens with thunders all I will turmoil.
Their company from them shall flee, each one his head shall
    hide;
A cave the queen shall take, the Trojan duke with her shall bide.
I will be there, and if thy will accord unto my mind,   90
Forever I shall make them fast and wedlock steadfast bind.
There shall begin the day that sorrows all shall quite exile.'
Dame Venus granted that, and to herself she gan to smile;
She gave a nod, and glad she was she could perceive the guile.
    The morning rose, and from the sea the sun was comen about,
When to the gates assembleth fast of noble youth a rout
With nets and engines great, and hunter spears full large of
    length.
The horsemen rush with noise, and dogs are brought, a mighty
    strength,
The great estates of Moors before the doors await the queen. . . .
At last she comes, and forth with mighty train she doth proceed,   100
All brave with mantle bright, encompass'd fresh in glist'ring weed
    [garment].
Her quiver on her shoulder hangs, her hairs with knots of gold
Are truss'd, and gold about her breast her purple garments hold.
The Trojan peers also went on, Ascanius glad of cheer,

Aeneas eke [also] before them all that fairest did appear,
Advanceth forth himself, and with the queen he joineth band,
Most like unto Apollo clear [bright], when to his country land,
To Delos down he comes, and winter cold he doth forsake. . . .
When to the mountains out they came and haunts of beasts on
    high,
Behold, adown the rocks the deer with bouncing leaps do fly   110
And over launds [glades] they course, and many an herd of hart
    and hind
With feet through dust upthrown they scud, and hills they leave
    behind.
But in the vale his prancing steed Ascanius swift bestrides,
And sometime these, and sometime those, with swift course
    overrides.
With dastard [timid] beasts his mind is not content, but maketh
    vows
Some foamy boar to find, or lion ramping [rearing] red would
    rouse.
    By this time heaven with rumbling noise and clouds is overcast,
And thunders break the skies, and rain outrageous poureth fast,
And showers of hail and sleet so sharp that fast on every side
The Carthage lords and Trojan youth each one themselves doth
    hide.   120
In woods and houses, here and there they seek, both man and
    child
For fear, and down from hills the floods do fall with waters wild.
A cave the queen did take, the Trojan duke with her did bide.
The ground proclaimed mirth, and Juno self did give the bride.
The fire and air agreed, and to this coupling gave their light
In sign of joy, and overhead the mountain fairies shright
    [shrieked].
There first began the grief, that day was cause of sorrows all,
For nothing after that by fame she sets nor what may fall,
Nor longer now for love in stealth Queen Dido her provides,
But wedlock this she calls, with wedlock's name her fault she
    hides.   130
    Anon through all the cities great of Afric Fame is gone,
The blazing Fame, a mischief such, as swifter is there none. . . .
She then the people's mouths about with babbling broad did
    fill;
And things unwrought and wrought she told, and blew
    [proclaimed] both good and ill:
How one Aeneas of the blood of Troy was come to land,
Whom Dido fresh for wanton love full soon had caught in hand,

And now this winter season long in pleasure pass they must,
Regarding none estate, but give themselves to filthy lust.
These things in mouths of men this goddess vile full thick did
  thrust.
  Then turning, straight her way she took unto Iarbas King,   140
Whose mind with tales on fire she set, and sore his wrath did
  sting. . . .
He mad in mind, and through these bitter news incensed wood,
Men say, as he before his altars pray'd and humbly stood,
His hands to heaven upthrew, and thus he cried with vexed mood:
'Almighty Jove, whom duly Moors esteem for God and king,
And feasts on broid'red beds to thee and wines of joy do bring,
Beholdst thou this? And mighty father, thee with thunder dints
Despise we thus? And yet from us thy strokes of lightnings
  stints [spares]?
Nor quake we not when through the clouds thy sounding breaks
  above?
In vain thy voices run; will nothing us to virtue move?   150
A woman lately come to land, that bought of us the ground,
To whom the soil we gave to till, and city new to found,
And laws also we lent, my wedlock, lo, she hath forsake;
And now Aeneas lord of her and all her land doth make.
And now this pranking [preening] Paris fine with mates of
  beardless kind,
To dropping [oiled] hair and favours nice and vices all inclined,
With Greekish wimple pinked [decorated], womanlike – yet must
  the same
Enjoy the spoils of this, and we thy servants take the shame;
For all our off'ring gifts to thee we find no fruit but fame [idle
  words].'
Thus praying in his fervent mood, and altars holding fast,   160
Almighty Jove him heard, and to the court his eyes did cast
Where now these lovers dwell, forgetting life of better fame. . . .
                    (I 2 verso–I 4 verso)

[Jove sends Mercury to command Aeneas to leave for Italy.]

Straight unto him he steps and said, 'Thou now of Carthage high
Foundations new dost lay, and doting dost thy mind apply
To please thy lusty spouse, and city fair thou dost prepare,
Alas, and of thine own affairs or kingdoms hast no care.
Himself the mighty God doth me to thee on message send;
The king of heaven and earth, that all this world with beck [nod]
  doth bend [direct],
Himself hath bid me through the winds so swift these things to tell.

What go'st about? Why spendest time in Lyby land to dwell?   170
If glory none of things so great thy courage do not move,
Nor thou for praise to take the pain [trouble] wilt for thine own
    behove [sake],
Yet by Ascanius' rising now have some regard to stand,
And hope of heirs of him, to whom by right Italia land
And empire great of Rome is due.' So said this heavenly wight,
And in the midst his tale he brake, and fled from mortal sight,
And out of reach of eyes as thin as air he vanish'd quite.
    Aeneas then affrighted stood in silence dumb dismay'd,
His hair uprose for fear, his voice between his jaws it stay'd.
Fain would he flee, and of that country sweet his licence take,   180
Astonied [amazed] with so great commandment given, and god
    that spake.
Alas, what shall he do? How dare he now attempt to break
Unto the queen of this? Or where his tale begin to speak?
His doubtful mind about him swift he cast both here and there,
And sundry ways he weighed, and searcheth dangers everywhere.
Thus striving long, this last device him liked best of all.
Cloanthus and Serestus strong and Mnestheus he doth call,
And bids them rig their fleet, and close their people draw to shore,
And armours all prepare; and lest thereof might rise uproar,
Some causes else they should pretend. Himself when time shall
    serve,   190
When Dido least doth know, and least suspects his love to swerve,
He will assay to seek most pleasant time with her to treat,
And meetest mean to make (for craft is all, who can the feat).
They glad, without delay their lord's commandment did fulfil,
All things in order set, and close they kept their prince's will.
    Anon the queen had found the guile. What craft can
    compass love?
She did forecast no less, and first she felt their practice
    [deceit] move,
All things mistrusting straight. And Fame also, that monster wood,
Her fumes increased more, with news that ships in armour stood
And Trojans for their flight, she said, all things prepared had.   200
Her heart therewith did faint, and frantic, like a creature mad,
She rails with ramping [wild] rage, and through the streets and
    towns about
With noise she wanders wide, most like a guide of Bacchus' rout,
When shouting through the fields with trumpet sound they run
    by night
In freak [frenzy] of Bacchus' feast, and mountains high they
    fill with shright [shrieking].

At last unto Aeneas thus in talk her words she dight
[addressed]:
'To hide also from me this mischief great, hast thou the heart?
Thou traitor false! And from my land by stealth wouldst thou
    depart?
Nor my unfeigned love, nor thy remorse of promise plight,
Nor Dido, like to die with cruel death, can stay thy flight?   210
But in the midst of winter storm away thou wilt in haste
In these outrageous seas, and through the force of northern
    blast?
O caitiff most unkind! What if it were a country known,
The land thou go'st to seek, no strangy realm, but all thine own?
What if that Troy, sometime thy native town, did yet endure?
Should Troy through all these boistous [rough] seas this time
    thy ships allure?
And fleest thou me? Now by these weeping tears, and thy right
    hand,
(For nothing else I left me, miser [unhappy], now whereby to
    stand)
By our espousal first, and for the love of wedlock sought,
If ever well deserved I of thee, if ever aught   220
Of joy thou hadst of me, have mercy now I am untwined
    [undone];
Destroy not all my house; O be not so extreme unkind.
If prayers may prevail, let prayers yet relent thy mind.
    For thee alone the tyrants all and kings of Lyby land
Doth hate me now; for thee alone my people me withstand,
For thee also my shamefast life I brake, and evermore
My fame I lost, that to the stars exalted me before.
To whom, alas, shall I be left, O guest, since die I shall,
That surname [name] must remain (for husband thee I dare not
    call).
Why should I longer live? Should I abide the day to see   230
Mine en'mies overthrow this town for hate and spite of thee,
Or till that King Iarbas come and me his captive make?
Yet if I chanced had some fruit of thee before to take,
If yet before thy flight there were some young Aeneas small
Resembling me thy face, to play with me within this hall,
Then slave I should not count myself, nor yet forsaken all.'
    These things she spake, but he rememb'ring Jove's
    commandment, still
Did stand with fixed eyes, and couched [hidden] care his heart
    did fill.
Few words at last he spake. 'All that,' quoth he, 'and nothing less

45

But rather more, whatever tongue may tell I will confess,   240
For never, noble queen, shall I deny thy goodness kind,
Nor Dido's love on me bestow'd shall never out of mind,
While on myself I think, while life and breath these limbs do guide.
To purpose this I speak. I never thought nor hop'd to hide
(Do you not feign) this flight, nor did prepare from hence to
   steal;
Nor I for wedlock ever came, nor thus did mind to deal.
For as for me, my life to lead if dest'nies did not let [prevent],
As I could best devise, and all my charge in order set,
Mine ancient town of Troy for me and mine I would again
Restore with labour sweet, and Priam's tow'rs should yet remain,   250
For though they conquer'd be, their walls again I would advance.
But now Italia land to seek, and there to take our chance,
To Italy Apollo great, and mighty gods us calls.
There lieth our country love. If you delight in Carthage walls
And you, a Moor among the Moors, rejoice this town to see,
Why should the Trojans from their country land restrained be?
What reason is but we likewise may strangy countries take?
My father Anchises' soul to me, as oft as shadows black
By night doth hide the ground, as oft as light of stars do rise,
He warns me through my dreams, and me with fearful ghost doth
   grise [terrify].   260
My child Ascanius eke, to me most dear, I put to wrong,
Whom from Italia realm and fatal fields I keep so long.
And now the message great of God from high Jove down is sent,
I call to witness both, as swift as wind his warning went.
I saw the god myself as clear as day, when on the ground
He lighted first, and from the walls these ears did hear the sound.
Cease for my love with wailing thus to fret both me and thee,
Italia against my will I seek.'
      These things while he did speak, she him beheld with looking
   glum,
With rolling here and there her eyes, and still in silence dumb   270
His gesture [bearing] all she view'd, and musing long against
   him stood.
At last thus out she brake, and thus she spake with burning mood:
'No goddess never was thy dame, nor thou of Dardan's kind,
Thou traitor wretch, but under rocks and mountains rough
   unkind
Thou wert begot; some brood thou art of beast or monster wild.
Some tigress thee did nurse, and gave to thee their milk unmild.
For what should I regard? Or whereto more should I me keep
   [refrain]?

46

Did he lament my tears? Did once his eyes on water weep?
Did he not comfort show? Or turn his face to me for love?
What should I first complain? Now nor dame Juno great above,   280
Nor God himself on my mischance with equal eyes doth look.
No steadfast truth there is. This naked miser [wretch] up I took
Whom seas had cast on shore, and of my realm a part I gave,
His fleet I did relieve, and from their death his people save.
Alas, what furies drive me thus to rage? Lo, now anon
Apollo layeth his lots, to Phoebus now he must be gone,
Now Jove himself hath sent his fearful mandate through the skies.
The post of gods is come; here is a fetch of fine device! [a
    cunning trick]
What else? Be not the careless gods with these things cumber'd
    sore?
These labours vex them much; whoever heard this like before?   290
They cark [care] for this? I neither that defend, nor hold thee
    more.
Go, seek Italia through the winds, hunt kingdoms out at seas,
In midst thereof I hope thou shalt, if good gods may displease,
Upon the rocks be thrown, that vengeance due thy carcass tear.
On Dido shalt thou cry; with brands of fire I will be there,
And when the cold of death is come, and body void remains,
Each where my haunting sprite shall thee pursue to give thee
    pains.
Yea, thief, it shall be thus; and as I sit in limbo low,
These tidings when I hear I shall rejoice thy woe to know.'
    And in the midst of this her tale she brake, and from the light   300
She fled with heavy heart, and drew herself away from sight,
Him leaving there; perplexed sore in mind, and sore in fear,
He would have spoke. Her ladies lift her up, and up did bear;
To chamber her they brought, in precious bed they laid her
    there.
    But good Aeneas, though full fain he would her grief assuage,
And words of comfort speak to turn from her that heavy rage,
In heart he mourned much, and shaken sore with fervent love;
Yet to his ships he went to do the charge of gods above. . . .
                                      (K 1 recto–K 2 recto)
    What mind, alas, O Dido now? What grief was this to thee?
What wailing up thou fet'st [fetchest] when so on shore thou
    didst them see?   310
And when thou mightst behold before thy face from tow'rs on
    high
The seas on every side resound with such uproar and cry?
O love unmild, what dost thou not man mortal drive to seek?

Again to tears she goeth, again she falls to prayers meek;
She yields to him for love, nor nothing will she leave untried,
But practise all to prove [try], if aught will help before she died.
  'Lo, sister Anne, thou seest how swift to shore this people hies,
From every coast they come, their sails are set for wind to rise,
With garland crowns for joy their mariners their poops have
    dress'd.
If ever, sister, such a grief had come within my thought,   320
I would have borne the same, or else some other shift have
    wrought.
Yet one thing, sister, in this woeful plight do thou for me,
For this perjured wretch regarded none so much as thee.
To thee alone he would commit both secret thought and deed;
Thou knowest the man's good hours, and pleasant time with him
    to speed.
Go sister, and go tell my words to my disdainful foe:
I was not she that did conspire with Greeks to Troy to go,
Nor did subvert his towns, nor ships nor armour ever sent
To 'stroy the Trojan blood, nor to his foes assistance lent. . . .
Where now away to run will he remove in all this haste?   330
O let him yet have one respect to me for token last,
This one reward I crave, for duties all, most miser wight.
O let him bide a while till wind and seas may serve his flight.
I seek no more the wedlock old, which he hath now betray'd,
Nor from Italia goodly land he longer should be stay'd.
I seek no longer him to keep his kingdom to forbear.
A vacant time I ask, and respite small my woe to wear,
While fortune learn me to lament and brook [endure] my fatal
    fall.
For pity, sister, sue for me this pardon last of all,
Which when thou dost obtain, requite it with my death I shall.'   340
  Thus talked she with tears, and weeping thus, both to and fro
Her sister went and came, and bare and brought increase of woe.
For weeping none prevails, nor wailing none his mind doth move.
His breast so stiffly bent, entreatings all from him doth shove;
God worketh so, his gentle ears are stopp'd from heavens
    above. . . .
  Then Dido, woeful soul, with plagues of dest'nies foul affright,
Desires to die; she loatheth now of heaven to see the light. . . .
                              (K 3 verso–K 4 recto)
A time thereto she seeks, and what device is best to take
She studies fast, and to her heavy sister thus she spake:
'Lo, sister, now rejoice with me, for I have found a way,   350
That either I shall hold him still or else my love shall stay [cease].

There is a land in ocean sea, that furthest lieth of all,
Where Ethiops do dwell, and where the sun from us doth fall,
Where Atlas, mighty mount, on shoulders strong the heaven
  doth turn,
And underprops the pole that stars doth bear that ever burn.
From thence a virgin priest is come. . . .
The minds of men, she saith, from love with charms she can
  unbind. . . .
Go thou, therefore, and in mine inner court, in secret wise,
Prepare the pile of wood, and frame it large aloft in skies.
Then take his harness [armour] all, and everything that thou
  canst find   360
Which in my chamber yet this wicked thief hath left behind.
Then all his wearing weeds, and then my bed of wedlock woe
Where I was cast away, alas, lay that with them also.
All monuments and tokens where that sinful wretch hath
  passed
I will consume with fire; so doth my priest command in haste.'. . .

[Dido's preparations for death are described at length.]

The queen when she prepared had the pile in skies on high
With logs in pieces cut, and pitch and gums and timber dry,
With garlands them she decks, and boughs and herbs doth on
  them strow
In mourning guise; then all the robes thereon she doth bestow.
His sword also she laid, and fair on bed his picture new   370
She couched all herself, and well she wist what should
  ensue. . . .

                              (K 4 verso–L 1 recto)
    Her cares increasing rise, with raging love in breast she boils
Afresh, and surges wild of wrath within herself she toils;
Between them thus she strives, and thus her heavy heart
  turmoils.
'Lo, what shall I now do? Shall I again go seek with shame
My former suitors' love? Shall I go sue to wed the same
Whom I so oftentimes to take to me disdained have?
Or shall I in the Trojan fleet go serve and live a slave?
What else? For where they had before this time relief of me
They well remember that, and well they quite [requite] me now,
  you see.   380
Admit I would so do, what is he there will me receive
To their disdainful ships? O fool, thou dost thyself deceive.
O creature lost, dost thou not yet the falsehead understand
Of that perjured nation false of Laomedon's band?. . .'

[Mercury appears to Aeneas in a dream, warning him to escape from Dido's 'wicked craft'; she sees his ships sail away.]

Her golden hair she tare, and franticlike, with mood oppress'd,
She cried, 'O Jupiter, O God,' quoth she, 'and shalla [shall he]
    go
Indeed? And shalla flout me thus, within my kingdom so?
Shall not mine armies out? And all my peoples them pursue?
Shall they not spoil their ships, or burn them all with
    vengeance due?
Out people, out upon them, follow fast with fires and flames,   390
Set sails aloft, make out with oars, in ships, in boats, in frames!
What speak I? Or where am I? What furies me do thus enchant?
O Dido, woeful wretch, now dest'nies fell thy head doth haunt,
This first thou shouldst have done, when thou thy kingdom
    put'st from thee.
Lo, this it is to trust. This godly faith and troth hath he
That so devout, his country gods, men say, doth seek to rear
And he that on his shoulders did his aged father bear.
Could I not him by force have caught, and piece from piece
    have torn?
Or spread his limbs in seas, and all his people slain beforn?
Could I not of Ascanius chopping made? And dress for meat   400
His flesh? And then his father done thereof his fill to eat? . . .
O sun with blazing beams, that every deed on earth dost view,
And Juno, goddess great, that knowest what thing to this is due,
Diana deep [holy], whose name by night all towns in
    crosspaths cry,
And fiends of vengeance fell, and gods that Dido make to die,
Receive my words and turn from me the wreak [punishment]
    of sinner's pain.
Hear now my voice: if dest'nies do that wicked head constrain
To enter haven, and needs he must with mischief swim to land,
If God will needs dispose it so to be, there let it stand.
Yet let him vexed be, with arms and wars of peoples wild,   410
And hunted out from place to place, an outlaw still exiled. . . .
Then to their lineage all, O you my people, show despite;
O Moors, apply them still with strife, let hatred hate acquite.
This charge to you I leave, these off'ring presents send you me,
When dead I am; let never love nor league between you be.
Then of my bones arise there may some imp [descendant],
    revenger fell,
That shall the Trojan clowns [peasants] with force of fire and
    sword expel.

Now, then, and evermore, as time shall serve to give them
    might,
Let shore to shore, and stream to stream, be still repugnant right.
This I desire: let them in arms and all their offspring fight. . . .'   420
                              (L 2 recto–L 2 verso)

[Dido sends Barce, her nurse, to fetch Anna, supposedly to perform a
sacrifice.]

Anon to the inner court in haste she runs, and up the pile
She mounting climbs aloft, and on the top thereof a while
She stood, and naked from the sheath she draws the fatal blade,
A gift of Troy, that unto these effects [ends] was never made.
There, when she saw the Trojan weeds and couch acquainted laid,
With trickling tears awhile, and mourning heart herself she
    stayed.
Then flat on bed she fell, and these her last words then she said:
'O sweet remain of clothing left, and thou, O dulcet [sweet] bed,
While God and fortune would, and while my life with you I led,
Receive from me this soul, and from these cares my heart
    untwine.   430
A time of life I had, of fortune's race I ran the line,
And now from me my figure great goeth under ground to dwell.
My walls I raised have, and city rich that doth excel.
My husband's death, and on my brother false I wroke my tene
    [wrought my revenge].
O happy, welaway, and overhappy had I been,
If never Trojan ship, alas, my country shore had seen.'
This said, she wried [turned aside] her head. 'And unrevenged
    must we die?
But let us boldly die,' quoth she, 'thus, thus to death I ply.
Thus, under ground I gladly go; lo, thus I do expire.
Let yonder Trojan tyrant now with eyes devour this fire   440
As on the seas he sits, and with my death fulfil his ire.'
    Thus speaking, in the midst thereof she left, and therewithal
With breast on piercing sword, her ladies saw where she did
    fall. . . .
Lamenting loud begins, and wailings wide, and roarings high,
In every house they howl, and women cast a rueful cry;
The city shakes, the noise rebounding breaks the mighty sky. . . .
Her sister heard the sound, as dead for dread she stood
    undressed;
With nails her face she tore, and with her fists she beat her breast,
And ramping [wildly] through the midst of men she runs, and by
    her name

51

She calls her, now in death: 'O sister mine and lady dame,   450
Is this the cause that I from thee so far beguiled was?
Did I this pile of fire and altars build for this? Alas,
What should I now, forsaken, first complain? O sister sweet,
Hast thou despised me to take with thee a mate so meet?
Why didst thou me, thy sister, to this death disdain to call?
One weapon should us both dispatch at once from sorrows
  all. . . .'

(L 2 recto–L 3 verso]

TEXT 2

The History, Siege and Destruction of Troy (Troy Book)

John Lydgate
(1412–20)

[The text is taken from the Early English Text Society edition, published in 1910.]

And when this horse brought was to the gate,
It was so narrow that there was no space
For the steed into the town to pass,
Albe [although] that they assayed overall.
Wherefore Priam beat adown the wall
To make it large, right at their device [counsel of Antenor and
    Aeneas],
In which thing, alas! he was unwise:
For cause chief of his confusion
Was that this horse came into the town. . . .

(IV. 6206–14)

And when they had at leisure and good ease   6276
From Troy sailed unto Tenedon
With their navy, the false Greek Sinon
In Troy waker [vigilantly] gan to take keep [watch for]
The hour when men were in their first sleep;
And, in all haste, with his sleighty gin [cunning craft],
Many vice [screws] and many subtle pin [pegs]
In the steed he made about goon,
The crafty locks undoing everychone [everyone];
And out he go'th, and gan anon to call
Within the horse the worthy knights all,   6286
So secretly no man might espy;
And traitorly he gan him for to hie
Upon the walls, the self-same night,
And toward Greekis gan to show a light,
Whereas they lay tofore Tenedon,
Ready armed to fall upon the town.

And when they had the sudden light espied,
On horseback anon they han them hied
Toward Troy, armed clean at all;
And in they went by the same wall   6296
Which for the horse was but late broke;
And mortally, for to been awroke [avenged],
The knights eke [also] in the steed of brass
Han with them met, a full stern pace [fiercely],
And gan anon throughout the city
On every half for to kill and slee,
With bloody sword upon every side,
And made their wounds broad, large, and wide,
While they, alas! nothing adverting [noticing],
At midnight hour abed lay sleeping,   6306
Full innocent, and thought nought but good,
All forbathed in their own blood,
Both man and child, without exception,
The Greekis sparing no condition
Of old nor young, woman, wife, nor maid,
That with the cry Priamus abraid [started]
Out of his sleep, and suddenly awoke,
Which lay all night and none heed ne took
Of the slaughter and murder in the town;
But tho [then] he wist that there was treason   6316
Falsely compassed unto his city
By Antenor and also by Enee [Aeneas],
Of whose malice he was no more in doubt. . . .

(IV. 6276–319)

For now, alas! the wildfire is seen   6336
In towers high with the wind yblazed,
Whereof Priam, astonied and amazed,
All awaped [bewildered] stert [started] out of his bed,
And comfortless to the temple is fled
Of Apollo, to save him if he might. . . .
The Greekis aye with their swords naked
Murder and slay whereso that they go,
That twenty thousand thilke [that same] night and mo [more]
They killed han, long or [ere] it was day;
And in this slaughter and this great affray   6346
Spoil and rob, and take what they find,
Treasure and good, and left not behind,
By mighty hand and sturdy violence.
And the temples, without reverence
They han despoiled throughout the town,

54

And greedily rent and razed down
Of gold and silver the ornaments all
Tofore the gods – foul might them fall!
King Priam aye with a deadly cheer
To Apollo making his prayer   6356
Furiously, this heartly [exceedingly] woeful man,
As he, in sooth, that no rede ne can [knew no remedy]
But wait his death and his fatal eure [destiny].
And Cassandra, that holy creature,
Of inward woe desirous to sterve [die],
Complaining ran unto Minerve,
Making to her a lamentation
With other gentlewomen of the town. . . .

(IV. 6336–70)

And Pyrrhus after to the temple go'th   6404
Of Apollo, by great cruelty,
And fell on Priam kneeling on his knee,
And with his sword, furious and wood [fierce],
Tofore the altar shed there his blood,
That the streams of his wounds red
So high raught [reached], both in length and bred,
That the statue of gold borned [burnished] bright
Of this Apollo, for all his great might,
For all his power and his stern face,
Defouled was, and pollute all the place,   6414
Only by death of this worthy king,
By Pyrrhus slain while he lay kneeling,
Of old hatred and envious pride,
While Antenor and Enee stood beside,
That ruth was and pity to behold,
To see him lie on the stones cold,
So piteously toforn the altar bled.
Whereof, alas! when Hecuba took heed,
And her daughter, fair Polycene [Polyxena],
With hair to-rent, as any gold wire sheen [shining],   6424
Inly surprised with sorrow to the heart,
When they began consider and advert
The noble king, with bloody streams red
All foredrowned, his eyen dark and dead,
With Pyrrhus' sword girt through other side,
For mortal fear they durst not abide;
But inwardly through-darted [pierced] with the sight,
All in a rage took them to the flight.
And yet, in sooth, throughout the city

55

They wist never whitherward to fly;   6434
Rescue was none nor no remedy
Of kin nor friend, nor of none ally,
With Greekis sword the town was so beset.
And in her flight this woeful queen hath met
Aeneas, causer of all this wrack [destruction],
Unto whom, rebuking, thus she spake:
'O thou traitor, most malicious!
Thou false serpent, adder envious!
Crop [head] and root, finder [deviser] of falseness,
Source and well of unkindness,   6444
How mightest thou in thine heart find
Unto thy king to be so unkind [cruel]?. . .
Thou were not only traitor in this case,
But to his death conspiring and unkind,
Pyrrhus conveying where he should him find,
Toforn Apollo mid of this city,
Where thou shouldest of very duty
Rather have been his protection. . . .
Yet in thine heart if any drop be
Of gentleness, mercy or pity,   6454
In this deadly rage full of teen [affliction],
Rue on my daughter, young Polycene,
From Greekis sword her youth for to save. . . .'

                          (IV. 6404–75)

[Aeneas does hide Polyxena from the Greeks, but when Calchas says that they will not be able to sail from Troy unless Polyxena is sacrificed in reparation for the death of Achilles, Antenor finds her and hands her over.]

The death of whom when Hecuba the queen   6894
Hath seen, alas! as she beside stood,
For very woe gan to wax wood [mad],
And for sorrow out of her wit she went,
And her clothes and her hair she rent
All in a rage, and wot not what she doth,
But gan anon with hands and with tooth
In her fury cracchen [strike] and eke bite,
Stones cast, and with fists smite
Whom she met, till Greekis made her bind
And sent her forth, also as I find,   6904
Into an isle to Troy pertinent [belonging],
Where she was slain only by judgement
Of the Greekis, and stoned to the death. . . .

                          (IV. 6894–907)

[Aeneas is banished from Troy for hiding Polyxena.]

Again resorting to tellen of Enee,   1434
After how he hath his tyme spent,
Which is from Troy with many Trojan went.
His ships stuffed, he and his meinie [followers]
Be sailed forth by many strange sea.
Many danger and many strait [narrow] passage,
Toforn or he arrived in Carthage,
Leading with him his father Anchises,
That, by the way, I find that he les [lost]
His wife Creusa by fatal aventure.
But all the woe that he did endure,   1444
Whoso list seriously [in due course] to seen [discover],
And how that he falsed [deceived] the queen,
I mean Dido, of womanhead flower,
That gave to him her riches and treasure,
Jewels and gold, and all that might him please,
And everything that might do him ease,
But for all that, how he was unkind,
Read *Eneydos*, and there ye shall it find;
And how that he falsely stole away
By nighter time while she abed lay,   1454
And of his conquest also in Itaille,
Where he had many strong bataille,
His aventures and his works all,
And of the fine [end] that is to him fall,
Ye may all see, by full sovereign [pre-eminent] style
From point to point compiled in Virgil. . . .

                    (V. 1434–60)

TEXT 3

The XV Books of P. Ovidius Naso entitled Metamorphoses

translated by Arthur Golding
(1567)

[The text is taken from *The English Experience* facsimile edition
published in 1977.]

[In Ovid's version of the tale of Troy, Hecuba attacks not Pyrrhus, as in
Lydgate and Marlowe, but King Polymestor, the murderer of her
youngest and last-remaining son, Polydorus, who had been sent to
Polymestor for safe-keeping during the Trojan war.]

The Trojan ladies shrieked out. But she was dumb for sorrow.
The anguish of her heart foreclos'd as well her speech as eke
Her tears, devouring them within. She stood astonied
   [benumbed], leke [like]
As if she had been stone. One while the ground she star'd upon.
Another while a ghastly look she cast to heaven. Anon
She looked on the face of him that lay before her killed.
Sometimes his wounds (his wounds, I say) she specially beheld.
And therewithal she arm'd herself and furnish'd her with ire,
Wherethrough [whereby] as soon as that her heart was fully set
   on fire,
As though she still had been a queen, to vengeance she her bent
   [turned],
Enforcing all her wits to find some kind of punishment.
And as a lion robbed of her whelps becometh wood [furious],
And taking on the footing of her en'my where he stood,
Pursueth him though out of sight, even so Queen Hecubee,
Now having meynt [mixed] her tears with wrath, forgetting quite
   that she
Was old, but not her princely heart, to Polymestor went,
The cursed murderer, and desir'd his presence to th'intent
To show to him a mass of gold (so made she her pretence)
Which for her little Polydore was hid not far from thence.

10

58

The Thracian king, believing her, as eager of the prey,   20
Went with her to a secret place. And as they there did stay,
With flatt'ring and deceitful tongue he thus to her did say:
'Make speed, I pray thee, Hecuba, and give thy son this gold;
I swear by God it shall be his, as well that I do hold
Already, as that thou shalt give.' Upon him speaking so,
And swearing and forswearing too, she looked sternly tho [then],
And being sore inflam'd with wrath, caught hold upon him, and
Straight calling out for succour to the wives of Troy at hand,
Did in the traitor's face bestow her nails, and scratched out
His eyes; her anger gave her heart and made her strong and stout
  [resolute].   30
She thrust her fingers in as far as could be, and did bore
Not now his eyes (for why, his eyes were pulled out before)
But both the places of the eyes beray'd [defiled] with wicked
  blood.

> (Book XIII, fol. 166 recto–166 verso)

TEXT 4

The Heroical Epistles of the Learned Poet P. Ovidius Naso
VII (Dido to Aeneas)

translated by George Turbervile
(1567)

[The text is taken from the British Library copy (shelfmark STC. 1. 1837).]

Even so, when fates do call, ystretch'd in moisted spring,
Upon Maeander's winding banks the snowish swan doth sing.
Not for I think my words may aught prevail I write;
For why I know the haughty gods at this my purpose spite.
But since my fame, my corpse, and spotless mind are lost
By canker'd hap [malignant fortune], to waste my words I reck it
    little cost.
  Now art thou bent [resolved] to pass and leave poor Dido so,
And with the selfsame winds thy sails and fickle faith shall go.
Aeneas, now thou mindst [intendest] thy navy with thy vow
To lose, and seek Italia land – but where thou dost not know.   10
Not Carthage built anew, ne [nor] yet the rising wall,
No, not my stately sceptre may convert thy mind at all.
Thou fleest the thing achiev'd for those that are not done;
Thou hast been in one land, and now wilt to another run.
Suppose thou find an isle, who will give thee the place
To rule? Will any yield his soil to men of foreign race?
New love remains for thee; another Dido take,
With other troth to be impawn'd [pledged], which thou again
    mayst break.
When will it be that thou wilt build Carthago's peer?
Or view from turret's top a troop of such as sojourn here?   20
Though all these came to pass, and thou hadst wish at will,
Yet where wouldst thou have such a spouse to bear thee like
    good will?
  Even as a waxen torch with sulphur touch'd I burn;

Both day and night to Dido's thought Aeneas makes return.
Even that ungrateful guest that scorns the gifts I gave,
And he whom I might want [lack] full well, as wisdom's lore
    doth crave.
Yet hate I not the man, though he deserve despite [anger];
But make complaint of his untruth [disloyalty], and less
    embrace the wight.
O Venus, use her well, that married with thy son,
O Cupid, friend thy brother; let him in thy number run;   30
Or else let him (for why I ne [not] disdain to love)
Whom I began to fancy, force me greater cares to prove.
    I see I am deceiv'd; his image blear'd my sight;
He differs from his mother's trade, and swerves her manners
    quite.
Thee rocks and rugged hills and oaks in mountains bred
Begat, and thou of brutal beasts in desert hast been fed
Or of the gulf, which now thou seest turmoil'd with wind,
On whom, though waves rebel, to pass thou fixed hast thy mind.
Why? Whither fleest? The storms do rage; let storms have power
To aid my case. See how the seas do surge with Eurus' scour;   40
Let me indebted be to storms, for that which I
Had rather owe to thee, more just than whom the waves I try.
    I am not so much worth, though thy desert be small,
That fleeing me by walt'ring [rolling] seas thou lose thy life
    and all.
Thy hate is dear indeed, and of no slender price,
If whilst thou go from me, to die thou reck it but a trice.
Within a while the seas will cease their swelling tide,
And Triton with his grayish steeds on calmed waves will ride.
O that with winds thou wouldst exchange [change] thy ruthless
    mind!
And so thou wilt, unless of oaks thou pass the stubborn kind.   50
What if thou didst not know how raging seas could roar?
Yet thou that hast so often tried wilt travel on before.
Though waves were never so smooth when thou shouldst leave
    the bay,
Yet dure [hard] and doleful things, God wot, might happen by
    the way.
And further, they that false their faith in danger are
On perilous seas; the place with them for treason's guilt doth war.
And most when love is wrong'd, 'cause Venus hath been thought
T'have had her offspring of the waves that in Cytheris wrought.
    I fear lest I undone shall be thy cause of woe,
Or lest by wrack of ship I should endanger thee, my foe.   60

I pray thee live, for so I may revenged be
Far better than by death; thou shalt be said to murder me.
Put case, that thou were caught with sway of whirling wind –
But vain be this abodement [omen] fell! – what then would be
    thy mind?
Then wouldst thou oft revoke to thought the Phrygian [Trojan]
    tongue
That did pronounce the perjur'd talk which wrought poor Dido's
    wrong.
Before thine eyes the form and idol of thy fere [wife]
Deceiv'd would stand in saddest sort, with bloody felt'red
    [tangled] hair.
Thyself wouldst grant thou hadst deserv'd these torments all,
And think the thunder cast on thee what so should hap to fall.   70
    Wherefore give time to wrath and rage of roaring flood;
Great is the price of little stay; thy passage shall be good.
Hast no respect to me? Yet spare Iülus' breath;
Sufficeth thee to have been thought the author of my death.
What poor Ascanius hath or country gods deserved?
The sea shall sink the saints which were from Phrygian flame
    preserved.
But neither thou thy sire, ne private gods didst bear
Upon thy back: thy vaunting cracks [brags] these to Elissa were.
Thou li'st at every word; not now thy tongue doth 'gin
To gloze [flatter], ne I the first in trap and guileful snare hath
    bin.   80
If question were what of Iülus' dame became;
Her cruel husband her forsook to his eternal shame. . . .

                (pp. 41–3)

TEXT 5

Didone

Lodovico Dolce
(1547)

[The text is translated from the British Library copy
(shelfmark 11715. aa. 19).]

III. 5

[The messenger, who has overheard Aeneas and Achates planning their departure, compares Aeneas to a serpent. Cf. *Dido Queen of Carthage*, V. 1. 165–8.]

NUNCIO: Behold, we have nourished in our houses the serpent who came back to life, so that, in return for the good he received, he may now kill us with his poison. But this is how it goes, this is how it is right that he should weep who becomes a slave of barbarous people.

III. 7

[In the scene in which Aeneas takes his leave of Dido Dolce, like Marlowe (V. 1. 158), introduces an allusion to Scythia.]

DIDONE: O pitiless and faithless man, he is a fool who believes that your mother was the holy and gentle goddess, mother of love, and that your paternal lineage descends from Dardanus. On the contrary, in cold and hard stones, Caucasus itself or some other horrid mountain brought you forth in snowy Scythia and Hyrcanian tigers gave you their milk. . . .

V. 4

[The death of Anna (recounted by Bitia) and the invasion of Iarbas follow Dido's suicide in Dolce; Marlowe also ends his play with these two characters, although in a very different fashion.]

BITIA, NUNCIO, PREFETTO, CONSIGLIERE

BITIA: So that no support should be left to us, poor women, after the queen, death deprived us of her sister.

NUNCIO: Alas, what will happen? Alas, poor me, will our misfortune, our tragedy have an end?

PREF. Heaven does not set to work for small things when it strikes and brings low a mortal creature.

CONS. Since we must hear of cruel deaths, go on, Bitia, and to our ears tell of this new death after the first one.

BITIA: The tears that Anna poured out over the dead body of poor Dido would have put out any great fire. And the lamentations she made and uttered would have tamed cruel death if it had not first torn from her her fateful hair with its voracious hands. When her tongue became weary and the source of tears had dried up and her voice had grown hoarse, with great labour we took Anna from the body [of Dido] and put her in her room, on her bed. But, when the servants had gone elsewhere (for they were all gone where the lit flame was burning the beautiful limbs – not only the ladies-in-waiting and the other women, but the whole town had hastened there: each was throwing into the sacred fire sweet-smelling incense and rich gifts), returning to her we found (alas, how tragic, how cruel!) that the sorrowing old woman had hanged herself from the inside of a window with a cord tightly wound round her neck and the cord was the very girdle from which the sword was hung of that enemy [i.e. Aeneas], so that every one of our ills should come from him alone.

NUNCIO: O we unfortunates, what else is left us except seeing the lost city captured and looted by fierce Iarbas? And such cruelty used against our blood that would not be believed if told?

BITIA: You guess well our sufferings. One of our people has just now come – horrible to see and pitiful to behold. His hands, his ears, and his nose cut off, he was red all over with his own blood. He told us that the Getulians burn all over our fields and kill any man, woman, child, and feeble old man they find in the fields or in the houses. Having recounted this, pierced by grief, he fell dead before our feet. Already the ruin of Carthage and our scourge is very near. . . .

NOTES

1 *The seven first books of the 'Aeneidos' of Virgil* (pp. 25–52)

Book I (pp. 25–31)

5   *leaves laid about*: one of several unrhymed lines. Phaer omits *rapuitque in fomite flammam* (*Aen.* I. 176), 'and waved the flame amid the tinder'.

21   *Scylla*: a sailor-devouring monster opposite the whirlpool of Charybdis.

22   *Cyclops*: one-eyed giants.

36   *Lavin land*: Latium (Italy), from its capital, Lavinium.

44   *winters three*: *ternaque transierint Rutulis hiberna subactis* (*Aen.* I. 266), 'and three winters have passed in camp since the Rutulians were defeated'. Cf. 'Three winters shall he with the Rutiles war' (I. 1. 89).

51   *Ilia queen*: Marlowe's 'princess priest' (I. 1. 106) is a more accurate translation of *regina sacerdos* (*Aen.* I. 273).

68   *Harpalycee*: Harpalyce, an Amazon.

69   *Heber*: Hebrus, a river in Thrace.

80   *Phoebus*: Apollo, brother of Diana.

91   *Agenor*: a mythical king of Tyre.

104   *country gods*: Penates, hearth-gods, brought from Troy.

174   *Cythere*: Cythera, the island on which Venus landed after her birth in the sea.

175   *Ida mount*: for Idalium in Cyprus. Marlowe also says 'Ida' when he means Idalium (III. 2. 99; V. 1. 40–1).

Book II (pp. 31–8)

16   *proclaim the same*: three lines (*Aen.* II. 18–20) are omitted here (also in later editions) describing how the Greeks conceal armed soldiers in the wooden horse.

57   *Tydides*: Diomedes, son of Tydeus.

96   *Ilion*: Ilium (Troy) from Ilus its founder.

117   *Neoptolemus*: Pyrrhus, son of Achilles.

Book IV (pp. 39–52)

254   *our country love*: *hic amor, haec patria est* (*Aen.* IV. 347), 'there is my love, my homeland'.

273   *Dardan's kind*: Dardanus, son of Zeus and Electra, was the ancestor of the kings of Troy.

319   *poops have dress'd*: this line is supplied with a rhyme in later editions.

320–1   *If ever . . . have wrought*: Phaer, like Surrey, mistranslates *hunc ego si potui tantum sperare dolorem, /et perferre, soror, potero* (*Aen.* IV. 419–20), 'If I was able to foresee this great sorrow, sister, I shall be able to endure it.'

384   *Laomedon's band*: Laomedon, king of Troy, broke his promise to pay Apollo and Neptune for building the walls of the city.

406   *turn from me the wreak of sinner's pain*: *meritumque malis advertite numen* (*Aen.* IV. 611), 'and as is meet, incline your power to my wrongs'. Not a mistranslation; Phaer's text, like Surrey's, read *avertite* for *advertite*.

4 The Heroical Epistles of the Learned Poet P. Ovidius Naso VII (*Dido to Aeneas*) (pp. 60–2)

2	*Maeander*: a winding river in Asia Minor.
28	*But make complaint of his untruth, and less embrace the wight*: *sed queror infidum questaque peius amo* (*Heroides*, VII. 30), 'but only complain of his faithlessness and having complained, I love yet more madly'.
40	*Eurus*: east or south-east wind.
42	*more just than whom the waves I try*: *iustior est animo ventus et unda tuo* (*Heroides*, VII. 44), 'wind and wave are more just than your heart'.
48	*Triton*: a merman, son of Poseidon and Amphitrite.
78	*Elissa*: Dido's other name.

5 *Didone* (pp. 63–4)

12	*fateful hair*: in the *Aeneid*, Dido's soul cannot be released from her dying body until Proserpine cuts a lock of her hair.

TAMBURLAINE
THE GREAT

INTRODUCTION

There is good reason to believe that Marlowe embarked on his first major dramatic creation while still *in statu pupillari* at Cambridge. He may well have completed both parts of *Tamburlaine the Great* before receiving his MA in the summer of 1587, but if Part II was genuinely a response to 'the general welcome' received by its predecessor, then it seems probable that the public presentation of Part I was not long delayed following Marlowe's last exit from Cambridge. It remains uncertain as to when the play was first staged, either in its separate parts or as a totality, but an allusion contained in a letter written on 16 November 1587 by Philip Gawdy describes how in a piece recently presented by the Lord Admiral's Men an actor, called on to fire a gun at one of his fellows tied to a stake, missed his aim, killing a pregnant woman and a child in the audience and maiming others. This has often been taken to refer to Tamburlaine's execution of the Governor of Babylon in the final act of Part II, but the assumption cannot be verified. Certainly by 1588 Robert Greene, in the letter prefacing his *Perimedes the Blacksmith*, could allude to Marlowe 'daring God out of heaven with that Atheist Tamburlan', a far less ambiguous reference to the scene in which Tamburlaine follows the murder of the Governor by ordering the destruction of the Koran and defiantly daring Mahomet to come down and punish him for impiety. If the play was completed subsequent to the first performance of Part I, Marlowe must have penned his sequel sometime late in 1587 or early in 1588.

The only light Marlowe's borrowings throw on the issue of dating is that Paul Ive's *Practice of Fortification*, from which Tamburlaine quotes more or less verbatim in Part II, seems not to have been available in print until 1589, while the first three books of Spenser's *Faerie Queene*, also laid under debt in Part II, were not entered in the Stationers' Register until 1 December 1589 and not published until 1590. If one accepts 1588 as the latest possible date for the completion of *Tamburlaine the Great*, one explanation for the presence of the borrowed passages is that Marlowe may have been able to read both works in manuscript and

69

hence incorporate certain passages into his text. In the case of Ive there are some grounds for the notion, in that he and Marlowe were probably acquainted: both came from Kent – Ive as an engineer having worked on the Canterbury canal system – and were involved in the spy network organized by Sir Francis Walsingham. But another possibility is that Marlowe revised the play prior to its publication by Robert Jones in 1590, and hence was able to incorporate a number of loans into the text. But as Una Ellis-Fermor (1930) pointed out, the Ive passages deemed to have been thus included are of the kind more likely to be cut out than written in. As yet no definitive conclusion has won universal acceptance.

The chief events and incidents featured in Marlowe's blank-verse epic may have been embedded in the popular consciousness well before *Tamburlaine the Great* made its impact on Elizabethan audiences. Accounts of the fabled life and deeds of the redoubtable Tartar warrior (1336–1405) became widely disseminated throughout Western Europe during the century following his death: for Renaissance authors the cataclysmic phenomenon which was Tamburlaine supplied a graphic case-history through which to validate the legitimacy of relentless aspiration, deplore the vagaries of Fortune's favours, or regret the ruthlessness inseparable from outstanding martial prowess. By the time that Marlowe composed his drama late in the 1580s, numerous treatments of Tamburlaine were available for his purposes, even if he ignored the distended cargo of moral or political platitudes which they were often required to carry.

Allusions to Tamburlaine's achievements and personality are relatively frequent in both Latin and vernacular texts, and to identify particular accounts as having an exclusive claim to precedence among Marlowe's potential sources would be imprudent. As W.L. Godshalk (1974:105) summarizes the position:

> it must be remembered that this same story [i.e. that of Tamburlaine's career], or one of its variants, may be found in as many as one hundred Renaissance sources, told from varying points of view, and it is now impossible to know how many or how few of these sources Marlowe read. What we do know is that he took this inherited fable of an Eastern conqueror and molded it into a unified play.

Godshalk rightly draws attention to Marlowe's synthesizing skills, but we must also accept that while the major narratives differ from each other in points of detail, they retain a considerable element in common.

The semi-legendary exploits of the historical Timur the Lame (in Persian Timur-i-lang, in Turkish Timur Lank, and in English Tamerlane or Tamburlaine) offer for contemplation a potent image of 'perhaps the greatest artist in destruction known in the savage annals of mankind' (Fisher 1938: I.405). Born at Kesh or Karshi, near Samarkand in present-day Uzbekistan, where his tomb still stands surmounted by a blue-ribbed dome, Tamburlaine cast himself in the role of reviver of the fortunes of the Mongol Empire which, following the conquering exploits of Genghis Khan, had remained moribund for virtually a hundred years. The several traditional accounts of Timur's rise to power are often contradictory and unreliable, but he seems to have claimed lineal descent from Genghis himself, whose feats of arms he emulated. Through strategic alliances, military opportunism, oppressive severity, and brutal treachery, he made himself master of Transoxiana by about 1370, his sobriquet 'the Lame' immortalizing the legacy of numerous punitive campaigns to install himself on the throne of Samarkand; from hence he was to rule a prosperous and fiercely well-ordered kingdom, whose capital ultimately became one of the wonders of the late medieval world.

The next decade saw him primarily occupied with his enemies to the east, overrunning Kashgar by 1380; his earliest attempt to extend his influence further afield led him into the Kipchak Empire to the north-west, where he intervened in the power struggle engulfing the rival Russian princes of the Golden Horde in vassalage to the Mongol Khans. Their capital Sarai on the Volga formed the turning-point for this incursion, but in 1381 Timur shifted his gaze westward towards Persia (present-day Iran), and moved to capture Herat. Divided among themselves, the Persian leaders failed to unite to stem the oncoming Tartar hordes, and thus in a steady sequence of victories Timur was able to seize Khurasan province and eastern Persia, Fars province, Mesopotamia (modern Iraq), Georgia, Azerbaijan, and Armenia. Even his former protegé Toktamish, Khan of the Golden Horde, failed to unseat him, Timur turning the tables on his adversary in 1395; now he sacked Astrakan, Sarai and Bolgar, cities west of the Volga, although choosing to spare Moscow. However, during his absence on this campaign, many of Persia's conquered cities broke out in revolt, reprisals taking the form of ferocious massacres which inevitably accompanied the utter destruction of the offending communities.

His sway now extending from Sarai in the north to Baghdad in the west, and from Samarkand down to the northern shores of the Arabian Sea, in 1398 Timur struck into the north of India by way of the Punjab, crossing over the Indus and invading territories belonging to the Sultan of Delhi. Having defeated the Sultan at the Battle of Panipat, he proceeded to inflict such devastation on Delhi that the city took a century to recover from its ruined condition. With the Punjab annexed and stripped of its resources, Timur's word was now law between the Indus and Lower Ganges.

But at this juncture, the conqueror having returned to his capital loaded with booty, he resolved to make another foray to the west in order to visit retribution on the Mameluke ruler of Egypt, who had supported in their previous resistance to Timur's invading armies the Mongol Jala'irs who held sway in Baghdad and Tabriz. Also in Tamburlaine's sights, however, was the expanding Ottoman Empire reigned over at this date by as ruthless a tyrant as he, the Sultan Bayezid or Bajazeth I (1347–1403), who had succeeded to the Turkish throne on the death of Amurath or Murad I in 1389, following the latter's assassination by a Serb after the Battle of Kossovo ('The Field of Blackbirds'), which ended effective Christian resistance to the spread of Ottoman influence in the Balkans. Bajazeth stamped his character immediately on the new reign by having his brother Yakub put to death the day after Kossovo, notwithstanding his valorous conduct on the field of battle.

Bajazeth lost little time in extending the area of Ottoman control as far as the Danube and the Euphrates: in 1390 he invaded Serbia and then Hungary; he moved into Macedonia and Thessaly; in 1393 it was the turn of Bulgaria and Wallachia, to be swiftly succeeded by Anatolia (Asia Minor). The rapidity and success of his conquests soon earned him the title of *Yildirim* ('Lightning' or 'Thunderbolt'): even the strenuous efforts of Sigismund, King of Hungary (1368–1437) and later Holy Roman Emperor, to head a concerted crusade to relieve the Turkish threat to Constantinople ended in abject failure, the great army marching to lift the siege being annihilated at the Battle of Nicopolis on 28 September 1396. The result was not only a vast slaughter of Christian prisoners, but the blunting of Hungary as a weapon in the fight to resist ultimate Ottoman domination.

But although Christian rulers were exercised by the threatened collapse of Constantinople, Tamburlaine was more concerned at the continuation of Bajazeth's conquering presence in Anatolia. Having re-established his sovereignty in Azerbaijan on the west shore of the Caspian Sea, the Tartar invaded Syria, stormed and sacked Aleppo, destroyed the army of the Egyptian Sultan, and completed the operation with the conquest of Damascus in 1400. The next year saw him marching south-east to take Baghdad, where he exacted a terrible price for his victory from the inhabitants by way of an indiscriminate massacre, allegedly erecting a lofty pyramid constructed of his victims' skulls. As with Delhi all traces of the city were virtually obliterated.

Moving northwards into Georgia, Tamburlaine next invaded Anatolia, ready to challenge the Turkish Emperor, who at that moment was on the point of delivering the *coup de grâce* to Constantinople. In the event Bajazeth's plans were thwarted, and the capital of the Eastern Empire was kept out of Ottoman hands for virtually fifty more years.

The Turk was compelled to quit the siege, and, in a classic confrontation between Mongol overlord and Ottoman ruler near Angora (present-day Ankara) on 20 July 1402, the mighty Bajazeth was overthrown and captured. Christians came to regard Tamburlaine's victory over the infidel as an instance of providential intervention, and hence to enlist the invincible warrior as an unlikely ally in the struggle with Islam. Bajazeth was removed to Samarkand under armed guard, though not in the infamous iron cage of subsequent legend. Dying in captivity, the emperor did not survive to see the Mongol armies loot and pillage their way west towards the Aegean.

Having quelled all opposition and reached an accommodation with Egyptian Sultan and Byzantine Emperor, Timur retraced his steps to his sumptuous capital, where, as a venerable war-lord nearing seventy years of age, he planned one last military excursion in the form of an expedition to China, some 200 miles away. En route, at Otrar, near Chimkent on the north-western border with China, on 19 January 1405, the mighty Tamburlaine is said to have died of 'inflammation of the brain': tradition has it that his corpse was taken back to Samarkand in a wedding palanquin in order to prevent the news of his death becoming widely known. In 1941 the body was exhumed; archaeologists discovered the remains of a well-built man, lame and with a scarred forehead; the hair was red in colour. The height measured just 5 feet 5 inches.

The fascinating, but complicated and labour-intensive exercise of tracing the potential sources of Marlowe's two-part drama has its origins in the late nineteenth century, an endeavour complicated by those confusions and inconsistencies of identification and attribution to which early printed texts are subject. But despite occasional scholarly modifications of the main thesis over almost a century, the two lives of Tamburlaine first highlighted by Herford and Wagner (1883) remain the most probable principal sources for the major portions of Marlowe's diptych. Herford and Wagner argued in support of the central importance of a Spanish miscellany of narratives and moral reflections by Pedro Mexía (1497–1551) entitled *Silva de Varia Lección*, first published in Seville in 1540; and of a Latin life published by Petrus Perondinus, styled *Magni Tamerlanis Scytharum Imperatoris Vita*, which, drawing in part from Mexía, appeared in Florence in 1553.

Both narratives incorporate much of the information current concerning the Tartar leader, such originality as they possess consisting in their handling and rearrangement of what they gleaned from such earlier authorities as Pope Pius II (Aeneas Silvius Piccolomini), the Florentines Matthias Palmerius and Andreas Cambinus, the Vatican librarian Bartholomeus de Platina, and Baptista Fulgosius. Marlowe may have read both Mexía and Perondinus in the languages in which they were first composed, but the Spaniard was also accessible to him in two recent English adaptations, one Sir Thomas Fortescue's *The Forest or Collection of Histories* (1571), the other George Whetstone's *The English Mirror* of 1586. Salient features of Perondinus's *vita* too had found their way into vernacular accounts by the late 1580s; hence the exact route by which Marlowe gained access to the two major authorities remains problematic.

The *Silva*, one of the most popular compilations of its time, went through more than thirty Spanish editions by 1600, proving highly conducive to translation, the earliest being Mambrino da Fabriano's Italian rendering of 1544. In 1552 Claude Gruget published a French version, *Les Diverses Leçons de Pierre Messie*, and it was on this source that Fortescue based his abridged rendering of 1571. Thomas Izard (1943) argued that Marlowe was unlikely to have worked directly from *The Forest or Collection of Histories* of 1571, but even if he did, his account was twice removed from Mexía: Fortescue not only relied on Gruget as his intermediary, but considerably curtailed the Frenchman's version, reproducing only 67 of Gruget's 156 chapters.

By whatever means Marlowe obtained knowledge of it, Mexía's work provided an account of the career and defeat of Bajazeth (Book I, Chapter 14), followed later by a general portrait of Tamburlaine himself (II. 28). Since the latter chapter duplicated in some measure the previous account of Bajazeth's harsh treatment in captivity, Mambrino and Gruget had abbreviated it, and Fortescue went further, omitting Gruget's fullest treatment, which included the colourful detail that, among the various humiliations inflicted on Bajazeth, his back had to serve the triumphant Tartar as a footstool or mounting-block whenever he chose to mount his horse. Fortescue's omission is of little significance, and Marlowe could have found the incident preserved in many other accounts, including Mexía's original. However, Fortescue's version contains one vital alteration: for Mexía's account of Tamburlaine's legendary practice of pitching a sequence of white, red and black tents ('*tienda*') around towns under siege, the Englishman substituted 'ensigns', a detail which Izard employed to support his view that Whetstone's *English Mirror*, a kind of prose *Mirror for Magistrates* in which the blessings of the Elizabethan polity were extolled, provided Marlowe with a more probable point of departure, and that he might not even have known *The Forest* at all. The relevant passages in both Fortescue and Whetstone (Texts 1 (a) and (b)) will enable readers to adjudge the matter for themselves.

Mexía deserves credit for synthesizing into one not entirely streamlined but reasonably coherent account many of the variegated traits and deeds attributed to the Tartar warrior. The Spaniard is not entirely consistent in his view of 'the ire of god', tempering admiration with some recognition of the rapacity and cruelty such a career involved, and thus perhaps contributing to the ambivalence of the dramatic counter-part. But it is to Perondinus (Text 2) that Marlowe appears to have gone for the most fluent and cogent account of Tamburlaine's origins, career and character, albeit couched in somewhat laborious Latin. The *Vita Tamerlanis* owes a great deal to contemporary Italian humanistic histori-ography, with its fascinated obsession with the concept of *virtù* (Voegelin 1951; Ribner 1953), and arguments have been mounted for assuming that the inspiration for Marlowe's Tamburlaine resides in the political thought of Machiavelli as transmitted via Perondinus. But, as Cunning-ham (1981) concludes after a detailed analysis, the playwright's portrait of the brazenly defiant, generous-spirited, and at times even aesthetic-ally sensitive Mongol differs in many important respects from Machia-velli's ideal of a devious, furtive and ruthlessly pragmatic Prince.

There is little in Mexía and his predecessors that escapes Perondinus, but frequent touches of indisputable authority and artistic *finesse* argu-ably make the Italian's Tamburlaine a being far more instinct with theatrical potential, and to this the author responded. The distinguish-ing highlights of Marlowe's stage treatment of his theme – his hero's humble origins, the seemingly limitless ambition and rude physical vigour (despite the crippled leg which Marlowe firmly rejects), the gleeful but inexorable rise to power, the warm, generous capacity for *cameraderie*, the touches of sardonic violence and cruel ruthlessness, the ingenuity in overcoming foes, the effortlessly truculent superiority to Fortune and the gods, the apparent absence of moral reprobation – all find at least potential origin in the pages of the Italian chronicler, though Marlowe is never betrayed into reproducing his material slav-ishly: Perondinus seems to have fired his imagination, but not dictated his script word for word.

Thus by combining aspects of two mainstream contemporary accounts of the Tartar Emperor, Marlowe created his masterly drama of conquest and slaughter on a titanic scale. Beginning *in medias res* and thus unable to depict Tamburlaine's selection by his fellow-herdsmen as their king in sport, or their attacks on the merchant caravans, he creates from references to unspecified internal feuding at the Persian court the tense yet comic opening scenes of friction between Cosroe and Mycetes, of which his protagonist is able to take advantage; indeed, the frankness and loyalty of Tamburlaine's followers contrasts favourably with the sly treachery and backbiting of the Persian court. Tamburlaine's fabled liberality to his companions runs like a thread through much of the action; the contrast drawn by Mexía and Perondinus between those who enjoy Fortune's favour and those who suffer the results of her in-constancy dominates those scenes during which the imperious Bajazeth and his queen come to their ghastly humiliating ends. Even their somewhat casual references to the inability of Tamburlaine's two sons to hold his empire together following his death are incorporated to create the mounting sense of the protagonist's gradual loss of authority which becomes the *leitmotiv* of Part Two.

The precise extent to which Part One employed other sources must in part be a matter for speculation. In that much of what other possible influences contained had been assimilated into the work of Mexía and Perondinus, there is no reason to assume that Marlowe troubled to take much notice of the several rival versions which offered themselves. The paradox of Tamburlaine's combination of acceptable aspiration and overbearing pride had already been emphasized by Baptista Fulgosius in *De Dictis Factisque Memorabilis Collectanea* (Text 3), while Andreas Cambinus in his work on the origins of the Turks (Text 4) and Paulus Jovius in his *Elogia Virorum Bellica Virtute Illustrium* (Text 5) helped to give currency to the image of the imperturbable and invincible warrior Marlowe gloried in bringing to articulate life on the public stages of Elizabethan London. Jovius (Paolo Giovio) had already delivered himself of graphic accounts of Bajazeth and Tamburlaine in his *Commentarii della cose de Turchi* (1541) translated into English by Peter Ashton in 1546, and Marlowe may have known its account of the escape of the prototype of Callapine. But generally these accounts merely fleshed out what he gleaned from his two principal authorities.

In common with a majority of their immediate successors, both Cambinus and Jovius place a heavy emphasis on the defeat and degradation of Bajazeth at Tamburlaine's hands, but as William Brown (1971) points out, Marlowe's presentation of the debasement of the Turkish Emperor is far more thoroughgoing and radical than that of any of his putative sources. Bajazeth is shown to be 'pompous, tyrannical and prone to flattery', while most early accounts paint him as at least a courageous and honourable foeman worthy of his opponent. Various explanations for the decision to alter the emperor's heroic stature have been forthcoming (Spence 1926–7,1927; Ellis-Fermor 1930; Dick 1949), but Brown believes that John Foxe's *Acts and Monuments* in its 1570 version may have played a formative part in influencing Marlowe's dramatic characterization, since Foxe too presents a Bajazeth who is both cruelly tyrannical and a persecutor of Christians, and a Tamburlaine whose harsh treatment of his pagan foe is treated approvingly. Foxe, like Marlowe, treats the emperor as a victim of divine retribution for his attitude towards Christian believers, displaying no hint of compassion for the Turk, and devoting few words of condemnation to Tamburlaine. Bajazeth's valour in battle is underplayed, his humiliation carefully stressed in all its details. Marlowe's precise echoing of Foxe's reference to the Turk acting as the Tartar's 'footstool' may also be of significance (Text 6).

In the same way John Bishop's *Beautiful Blossoms* (Text 7), while containing little new information, may have determined at least one Marlovian departure from received opinion. Bishop's attractive and succinct account lays particular stress on Tamburlaine's physical disability, and this (if he knew the account) Marlowe chose to ignore, along with the reference to Tamburlaine's plausible but all-too-human fear of the King of India. As in his handling of most of his chronicle materials, Marlowe prefers to present his hero as a Superman in whom no suspicion of physical or moral weakness can be detected. In a similar vein, where Bishop dwells on Tamburlaine's anxious reaction to three portents which preceded his death (a detail derived from Perondinus possibly via *La Cosmographie* of 1575), Marlowe rejects the account of the apparition of Bajazeth's ghost which terrorizes Tamburlaine to death, and plays down the earthquake and the comet. Nevertheless, the sight of 'the ugly monster death' brandishing 'his murdering dart' (*2 Tamburlaine* V.3) may well derive from Bishop's 'man appearing in the air, holding in his hands a lance'.

Fortunately for those whose linguistic knowledge is finite, it has never been suggested that Marlowe had access to such contemporary Persian records as the *Mulfazāt Tīmūry*, often accepted as Timur's own autobiographical memoir, though possibly a forgery, in which Bakeless (1942) located the basis for the tradition that Timur originally acquired his beloved wife as one of the spoils of battle, much as Tamburlaine acquires Zenocrate. The memoir certainly contains an account of Timur's capture of Arzū Melk Aghā, a rival chieftain's pregnant wife whom he subsequently married, but the key to the close relationship between Marlowe's conqueror and his captive bride may lie in one of the several Greek accounts supplied by such fifteenth-century Byzantine historians as Laonicus Chalcocondylas (*c.* 1423 – *c.* 1490) whose work in Latin translation by Conrad Clauserus Marlowe may have known (Text 8). Even here the resemblances are not strong: Tamburlaine's spouse is portrayed as influential in her husband's incipient conflict with Bajazeth, but theirs is scarcely a romantic relationship. Tamburlaine's amorous exploits and the 'divine Zenocrate' may have been Marlowe's own invention from first to last, though he may also have picked up hints of a lost tradition.

It has been argued that Marlowe only created the second part of his drama after the success of Part I had been assured, and that as a result he was propelled into a feverish search for materials with which to 'eke out' his sequel, which is therefore held to lack the unity of Part I (Ellis-Fermor 1930; Kelsall 1981). While several critics, including Gardner 1942, Battenhouse 1941 and Cole 1962, reject this view as mistaken and derogatory, supporting evidence has been sought in the number of 'importations' which seem to have little direct relationship with the major accounts of the historical Tamburlaine. Of these, the most important is undoubtedly one of the classic narrative descriptions of the Battle of Varna fought between the forces of the Christian alliance headed by King Vladislaus III of Hungary and Poland, and the Turkish army under its sovereign the Emperor Amurath or Murad II on 10 November 1444 (Seaton 1921). The previous year Amurath's need to defend Natolia against the ravages of the King of Caramania had led to the conclusion of a treaty with Vladislaus sworn at Szegedin by the rival monarchs on the Koran and the Gospels respectively. Vladislaus's breaking of the truce at the urgent instigation of Cardinal Julian the papal legate, and his subsequent defeat and death at Varna, came to serve as a classic example of Christian perfidiousness, and developed into a recurrent feature of Protestant polemic against the Catholic Church (Battenhouse 1941, 1973). In particular, Martin Luther in his *Open Letter to the Christian Nobility of the German Nation* (1520) was to associate with Vladislaus's treachery before Varna the Emperor Sigismund's infamous breach of faith with John Huss and Jerome of Prague at the Council of Constance in 1415. John Foxe was one of those Protestant apologists who reflected this view, and it now seems likely that Marlowe was again influenced by Foxe in creating Act I Scene 1 and the first three scenes of Act II of *2 Tamburlaine*. Not only does the martyrologist reverse chronology by making Sigismund's defeat by Bajazeth at Nicopolis appear a consequence of his betrayal of Huss and Jerome of Prague, but in associating this disaster with a second inflicted on the Christians by Bajazeth's successor Callapine, and treating the sequel to Vladislaus's act of treachery before Varna as a parallel instance of perjury inflicted on infidels similarly visited with divine retribution, Foxe may have sown a seed in Marlowe's mind.

Thus it is more than likely that under Foxe's influence Marlowe decided to employ Sigismund, Tamburlaine's near-contemporary, as the central figure in events which actually involved the historical Vladislaus, and to substitute for Amurath II that Orcanes named by Foxe as Callepine's successor. The Hungarian king's 'popish' adviser, Cardinal Julian, is replaced by the unctuously righteous figures of Lord Frederick and Baldwin. As far as the facts go, as Seaton (1921) pointed out, the likeliest accounts from which Marlowe derived much of the detail of his main action in the opening acts of *2 Tamburlaine* are those of Callimachus in his *De Clade Varnensi*, and of Antonius Bonfinius's *Rerum Ungaricarum. . .* (1543), which contains nearly all the elements present in Marlowe's dramatic confrontation, including not merely the arguments advanced by Cardinal Julian in persuading the young king to break an oath taken on the Scriptures, but also the Turkish leader's invocation of the Christian God to avenge such perjury:

Can there be such deceit in Christians,
Or treason in the fleshly heart of man,
Whose shape is figure of the highest God?
Then if there be a Christ, as Christians say,
But in their deeds deny him for their Christ;
If he be son to ever-living Jove,
And hath the power of his outstretched arm;
If he be jealous of his name and honour
As is our holy prophet Mahomet,
Take here these papers as our sacrifice
And witness of thy servant's perfidy. . .

(II. 2. 36–46)

It is, moreover, just possible that the playwright was able to read the version of Bonfinius incorporated into his *General History of the Turks* by Richard Knolles, which, although not published until 1603, may have been in manuscript early enough for Marlowe to have had access to it before 1587–88 (Dick 1949). Both men were associated with the Kentish family of Manwood from Sandwich, so that the connection is by no means far-fetched. At all events, either in the Latin original or Knolles's rendition of it, Marlowe could have found an account of Varna and the events leading up to it graphic enough to allow almost direct transcription in *2 Tamburlaine* Acts I and II (Text 9).

Minor sources of *2 Tamburlaine* are less significant, but it has always been recognized that several important allusions derive from specific works which the dramatist must have known. The indefatigable Ethel Seaton (1929) identified part of Orcanes's fulmination against the perjured (and dying) Sigismund in Act II Scene 3 of Part 2 with the description of the pangs of the Mohammedan Hell in Philippus Lonicerus's *Chronicorum Turcicorum*, a work which Marlowe may well have recalled as being in John Gresshop's library (see Introduction) and consulted in the course of his general researches. The unfamiliar word 'zoacum' which features in the Turkish monarch's malediction certainly suggests a direct linkage which detailed comparison (Text 10) would tend to support.

Perhaps less felicitously integrated into the text of *2 Tamburlaine* is a passage from a contemporary treatise on the technicalities of Elizabethan warfare, written by Paul Ive (Danchin 1912), a possible acquaintance of Marlowe's (Nicholl 1992). Direct indebtedness to Ive's *Practice of Fortification* (Text 11), dedicated to Sir Francis Walsingham, is plainly demonstrated in the close correspondence of terms and phrases taken from its second and third chapters found in Tamburlaine's speech instructing his sons in the arts of war, found in Act III Scene 2:

I'll have you learn. . .
. . . the way to fortify your men;
In champion grounds what figure serves you best,
For which the quinque-angle form is meet,
Because the corners there may fall more flat
Whereas the fort may fittest be assail'd,
And sharpest where th'assault is desperate.
The ditches must be deep, the counterscarps
Narrow and steep, the walls made high and broad,
The bulwarks and the rampires large and strong,
With cavalieros and thick counterforts,
And room within to lodge six thousand men.
It must have privy ditches, countermines,
And secret issuings to defend the ditch;
It must have high argins and covered ways
To keep the bulwark fronts from battery,
And parapets to hide the musketeers,
Casemates to place the great artillery,
And store of ordnance, that from every flank
May scour the outward curtains of the fort,
Dismount the cannon of the adverse part,
Murder the foe, and save the walls from breach. . .
(III. 2. 55, 62–82)

However, it does not follow, as some have inferred (Ellis-Fermor 1930: 45), that because of the indebtedness the borrowing is inartistic, undramatic or unsuccessful. Tamburlaine, distressed beyond measure at the loss of Zenocrate, may legitimately be viewed here as reciting in semi-automatic fashion from a military textbook once learnt by rote.

The heterogeneous materials laid under debt in the second part of *Tamburlaine* must include Münster's *Cosmographia*, best known to Marlowe through the intermediary of Belleforest's *Cosmographie Universelle de tout le monde*, which doubtless provided a little of the background to *The Jew of Malta*. In reading from its account of the siege of Rhodes in 1522, Marlowe may have registered the anecdote of the faithful mistress of the island's governor (Text 12), and combining it with Ariosto's account of Isabel's deadly stratagem for avoiding seduction by Rodomont in Book 29 of his *Orlando Furioso* (Text 13), no doubt based on it those episodes involving the widowed Olympia and her successful resistance to the advances of the amorous Theridamas which form the substance of Act III Scenes 3 and 4, and Act IV Scene 2.

Ariosto's was not the only romantic epic to which Marlowe turned in composing *Tamburlaine*; in the 1590 edition of Edmund Spenser's *Faerie Queene* there are a variety of allusions of which Marlowe availed himself at sundry points (Bakeless 1942: I. 205–9). The most famous without doubt is adopted from the glowing description of Prince Arthur, the poem's hero, in Book I, and in particular the reference to the crest surmounting his helmet:

> Upon the top of all his loftie crest,
> A bunch of haires discolord diversly,
> With sprincled pearle, and gold full richly drest,
> Did shake, and seem'd to daunce for jollity,
> Like to an Almond tree ymounted hye
> On top of greene *Selinis* all alone,
> With blossomes brave bedecked daintily;
> Whose tender locks did tremble every one
> At every little breath, that under heaven is blowne.
>
> (Book I, Canto VII, stanza 32)

Some critics have regretted what they see as the incongruity of Marlowe's borrowing from the grand master of the Elizabethan epic in order to expand Tamburlaine's climactic self-portrait in Act IV Scene 3 of Part Two, but the Scythian is more than an eloquent thug. It is clear that in associating the splendours of his hero's magnificent vision of himself as 'emperor of the threefold world' with Spenser's presentation of his own chivalric ideal, Marlowe did not hesitate to align his grand diptych with the finest flowering of English Renaissance poetry. By contrast, Tamburlaine's brutal sadism, which reaches its climax in his entry drawn by the defeated kings in Act IV Scene 3, may owe something to its anticipation by the similar figure of Ambition in the dumbshow preceding Gascoigne and Kinwelmershe's tragedy of *Jocasta* (Text 14) staged at Gray's Inn in 1566.

TEXT 1

Silva de Varia Lección

Pedro Mexía
(1542)

(a) *taken from* The Forest or Collection of Histories . . .
by Thomas Fortescue
(1571)

[The text is based on the British Library copy (shelfmark 95.c.8).]

PART I CHAPTER 15

How for the most part cruel kings and bloody tyrants are the Ministers of God: and how notwithstanding they continually end in state most wretched and extreme misery.

Whoso hath, or lieth subject under any of these accursed Monsters [the cruel rulers cited in the previous chapter], must for his consolation or comfort consider that for the most part, though they be terrible and cruel, yet be they notwithstanding the Ministers of God. The Scriptures in many places, as we find still, termeth them by no worse title than the Servants of God, for that by them it hath pleased Him to chastise the wicked, perfecting and confirming to Himself [ratifying as his] such as love and fear Him. . . .

The accursed Totila [Attila], King of the Goths, was named the Scourge of God, and reputed for the same. The great Tamburlaine, that reigned not so many years hence, a captain no less bloody than valiant, which also subdued so many countries and provinces, being demanded why he so more than tyrannously used his captives, whereunto he answered, forwrapped [deeply suffused] in choler: 'Supposest thou me to be any other than the ire of God?' Whence we have in fine [to sum up] to conclude that all such cruel and incarnate devils are instruments wherewith God chastiseth sin, as also with the same approveth [proves] and trieth the just, and yet they notwithstanding are not hence held for [considered as] just, ne [nor] shall they escape the heavy judgement of God. For necessary is it that example of ill happen, but woe be unto him by whom it happeneth. Further in this life God assuredly at some time doth punish them, besides that in another world, Hell and damnation is certainly allotted. Neither at any time hath it almost been seen, as we have remembered in the forepassed chapter, but that such merciless and transubstantiate [transformed] Monsters have died of some violent and ignominious death. . . .

Let those therefore that rule and govern the world in any wise, leave to be bloody and cruel, leaning on the staff of compassion and clemency, to the intent they may live assured of the hearts of their vassals; for the best assurance of his state that the Prince may have is to be beloved of his people and subjects.

PART II CHAPTER 14

Of the renowned and great Tamburlaine, of the kingdoms and countries that he subdued, and finally of his practice and manner in war.

There hath been among the Greeks, Romans, the people of Carthage and others, infinite worthy and famous captains, which as they were right valiant and fortunate in war, so were they no less fortunate in that some others by writing commended their chivalry to the posterity for ever. But in our time we have had one, in no respect inferior to any of the others, in this one point notwithstanding less happy, that no man hath vouchsafed by his pen in any sort to commend him to the posterity following. So that I, who most desired something to speak of him, have been forced to gather here and there little pieces and pamphlets, scarce lending you any show [demonstration] of his conquerous exploits, the same also confusedly and without any order. This then of whom we speak was that great and mighty Tamburlaine, who in his tender years was a poor labourer or husbandman, or (as other some report) a common soldier. Howbeit, in the end he became lord of such great kingdoms and seigniories, that he in no point was inferior to that prince of the world Alexander; or if he were, he yet came next him of any other that ever lived. He reigned in the year of Our Lord God a thousand, three hundred and fourscore and ten.

Some suppose that he was a Parthian born, a people less honourable than dread [feared] of the Romans: his father and mother were very poor and needy. He, notwithstanding, was of honest and virtuous condition, well-featured, valiant, healthy, quick and nimble, sharp-witted also, of ripe and mature deliberation and judgement, imagining and devising haut [ambitious] and great

83

enterprises, even in that his most and extreme penury, as though he sometimes should be a master of many things. He was of a valiant and invincible courage, so that from his cradle and infancy, it seemed he was vowed to Mars and martial affairs only. Whereunto he gave himself with such painful endeavour that hardly a man might judge whether he were more happy indeed in advised [judicious] counsel or princely dexterity. By mean of which his virtues, and others that we shall hereafter remember, he in short time acquired such honour and reputation as is to be supposed man never shall do again.

His first beginning was, as writeth Baptista Fulgosius, that being the son of a poor man, keeping cattle in the field, living there with other boys of his age and condition, was chosen in sport by the others for their king, and although they had made indeed this their election in play, he whose spirits were ravished with great and high matters, forced them to swear to him loyalty in all things, obeying him as king where or when it should please him in any matter to command them. After this oath, then in solemn sort ministered, he charged each of them forthwith to sell their troop [herd] and cattle, leaving this servile and base trade of life, seeking to serve in war, accepting him for captain. Which indeed they did, being quickly assembled of other workmen and pastors [shepherds], to the full number at least of five hundred. With whom the first attempt that ever he took in hand was that they robbed all such merchants as anywhere passed nigh them, and after he imparted the spoil so justly that all his companions served him with no less faith than love and loyalty, which occasioned sundry others anew to seek and follow him.

Of which news in the end the King of Persia advertised [informed], sent forth under the conduct of one of his captains a thousand horses well appointed to apprehend and take him. At whose coming he so well knew in this matter how to bear him, that of his enemy he had soon made him his assured friend and companion, in such sort that they joined both their companies together, attempting than before enterprises much more great and more difficill [difficult]. In the meantime a certain discord or breach of amity grew betwixt the King of Persia and his brother, by occasion whereof Tamburlaine took part [sided] with the king's brother, where he so ordered the matter in such sort that he deposed the king and advanced the other. After this, by this new prince, in recompense of his service, he was ordained general of the greater part of his army, who under pretext that he would conquer and subdue other provinces to the Persians, mustered still and gathered more soldiers at his pleasure, with whom he so

30

40

50

60

practised [conspired] that they easily revolted like rebels following 70
him, subduing their liege and sovereign. Thus having now deposed
whom he before advanced, he crowned himself king and lord of
that country.

Now moved with compassion towards his own country, which
long times had been tributary to the Princes of Persia and to
the Saracens, did [caused] them to be free from all service and
exactions, lotting [allocating] to them for prince himself and none
other. After thus considering with himself that he presently [at that
time] had gathered a huge and great army, moved privy mutinies
and rebellions in other countries, by means whereof in process of 80
time he conquered Syria, Armenia, Babylon, Mesopotamia, Scythia
Asiatica, Albania and Media, with others, many teritories, rich also
and famous cities. And although we find written nothing of any his
wars whatsoever, yet is it to be presumed that he fought many a
battle in open field with the enemy before he had subdued so many
kingdoms and territories. For as much as all those that remember
of him anything commend to us the haut [lofty] exploits of this
most valiant personage, and further, that he so circumspectly
ordered his company, that in his camp was never known any brawl
or mutiny. He was very courteous, liberal; doing honour to all men 90
according to their demerits that would accompany or follow him;
feared therefore equally and loved of the people.

He so painfully [painstakingly] and with such care instructed his
soldiers, that in an instant always, if it were behoveful, either by
sound of trumpet or any other, one only sign given, every man was
found in his charge or quarter, yea, though his army were such, so
great and numerous, as never besides himself conducted any other.
In few [brief], his camp resembled one of the best and richest cities
in the world, for all kind of offices were there found in order, as
also great heaps of merchants to furnish it with all necessaries. He 100
in no case permitted any robberies, privy figging [filching], force,
or violence, but with severity and rigour punished whomsoever he
found thereof guilty or culpable, by means whereof his camp was
no worse of all provisions furnished than the best city in the world
in time of most safe and assured security. His desire was that his
soldiers should evermore glory in their martial prowess, their virtue
and wisdom only. He paid them their salary and wage without
fraud; he honoured, he praised, he embraced and kissed them,
keeping them notwithstanding in awe and subjection.

Thus being king now and emperor of sundry realms and countries 110
in Asia, great troops came to him still out of every quarter, besides
these that were in any respect his subjects, for the only fame [mere
reputation] of his honour and virtue. So that his camp grew in

short time to be greater than ever was that of Darius and Xerxes, for such as write of him report that he had four hundred thousand horsemen, but of footmen a greater number by two hundred thousand more, which all he led with him at the conquest of Asia the Less. Whereof the great Turk advertised [being informed], who then hight [was called] Bajaceth, Lord and Prince of that country, but present then in person at the siege of Constantinople, having a little before subdued sundry provinces and parts of Greece, with other territories adjacent and towns thereabout, thence grown to more wealth and more feared than any prince in the world, was nevertheless constrained to raise his siege incontinently [then and there], passing thence into Asia with all his army, taking up still by the way as many as was possible. So that, as some affirm, he had as many horsemen as had the great Tamburlaine, with a marvellous number of other soldiers, both old and of much experience, especially by means of the continual wars which he had still with the Christians.

This Bajaceth now, like a good and like an expert captain, seeing that he no way else might resist this puissant [mighty] emperor, determined to meet him and to give him present battle, having marvellous affiance [faith] in the approved [proven] manhood and virtue of his soldiers. Wherefore marching on within a few days, they met each with other upon the confines of Armenia, where both of them ordering as became good captains their people, began in the break of day the most cruel and most terrible battle that [on] earth was ever heard of, considering the number on both parts, their experience and policy [judgement], with the valiant courage and prowess of their captains.

Thus continued they in fight even almost until night, with marvellous slaughter on both sides, the victory yet doubtful, till in the end the Turks began to faint and to flee, more indeed oppressed with the multitude than that they feared or otherwise, the most part of them with honour dying manfully in the field. And as one reporteth, two hundred thousand were taken prisoners after the battle was ended, the residue slain and fled for their better safety. Which Bajaceth, of part perceiving before the end how it would weigh, to [en]courage his people and to withdraw them from flight, resisted in person valiantly the furious rage of the enemy. Howbeit, he thereby gained such and so many knocks that as he was in the end indeed unhorsed, so was he for lack of rescue presented to the great Tamburlaine, who incontinently closed him up in a cage of iron, carrying him still [always] with him whithersoever he after went, pasturing [feeding] him with the crumbs that fell from his table, and with other bad morsels, as he had been a dog.

Whence assuredly we may learn not so much to affy [trust] in riches, or in the pomp of this world, for as much as he that yesterday was prince and lord of all the world almost, is this day 160 fallen into such extreme misery that he liveth worse than a dog, fellow to them in company, and that by the means of him that was sometimes a poor shepherd or if you rather will, as some report, a mean soldier, who after as we see aspired to such honour that in his time none was found that durst or could abide [resist] him, the other that descended of noble race or lineage constrained to live an abject, in most loathsome and vile servitude. This tragedy might suffice to withdraw men from this transitory pomp and honour, acquainting themselves with Heaven and with heavenly things only.

Now this great Tamburlaine, this mighty prince and emperor, 170 overran all Asia the Less, to the Turk before subject, thence turning towards Egypt, conquered also Syria, Phoenicia and Palestina, with all other cities on their borders of what side soever, and besides these Smyrna, Antioch, Tripoli, Sebasta, and Damascus. Afterward, being come with all his army into Egypt, the Soldan and the King of Arabia with sundry other princes, assembled all together and presented him battle, but in the end to their unspeakable detriment discomfited, were slain and spoiled at the pleasure of the enemy, by mean whereof the Soldan saved himself by flight. Howbeit, Tamburlaine had easily taken from him all Egypt, had it not been for the 180 great and inaccessible deserts in that country, through which to pass with so puissant [mighty, powerful] an army was either impossible or at the least very difficill [difficult]. Notwithstanding, he subdued all such parts of the country as were next him.

Some report of him that he then him held best contented when he found his enemy most strong and best able to resist him, to the end that he might be occasioned to make profit of himself [demonstrate] what he was able to do, and how much in his necessity: that which well chanced him at the city of Damascus. For after he had taken the most honourable and valiant personages of the city, the 190 others retired into a certain castle or hold, such and so strong that all men accounted it impregnable, where, nevertheless, desirous to grow to some composition [agreement] with him, were utterly refused, no entreaty prevailing, so that in fine, they must needs fight it out or yield them to his mercy. And finding no place where he by any means might assault it, built fast by it another more high and strong than that, where he so painfully and in such sort despatched it, that the enemy by no means could or [either] let or annoy [hinder or injure] him, so that his fort, in the end or equal or rather higher than the other, began his battery such and so cruel 200 that it never ceased day nor night until at last he had taken it.

87

It is written of him that in all his assaults of any castle or city, he usually would hang out to be seen of the enemy an ensign white, for the space of one full day, which signified (as was then to all men well known) that if those within would in that day yield them, he then would take them to mercy without any their loss of life or goods. The second day he did to be hanged out another all red, letting them thereby again to understand that if they then would yield, he only then would execute the officers, magistrates, masters of households and governors, pardoning and forgiving all others whatsoever. The third day he ever displayed the third [ensign] all black, signifying thereby that he then had shut up his gates from all compassion and clemency, in such sort that whosoever were in that day taken or in any other then following should assuredly die for it, without any respect either of man or woman, little or great, the city to be sacked and burnt withal to ashes. Whence assuredly it cannot be said but that he was very cruel, though otherwise adorned with many rare virtues. But it is to be supposed that God stirred him up an instrument to chastise these princes, these proud and wicked nations.

For better proof whereof Pope Pius [II] which lived in his time or at least eight or ten years after him, reporteth of him, saying that on a time besieging a strong and rich city, which neither on the first or second would yield to him, which only days were days of mercy, as is above said; on the third day nevertheless, affying [trusting] on hope uncertain, to obtain at his hands some mercy and pardon, opened their gates, sending forth in order towards him all their women and children in white apparelled, bearing each in their hands a branch of olive, crying with haut [high-pitched] voices, humbly requesting and demanding pardon in manner so pitiful and lamentable to behold that besides him none other was but would have accepted their solemn submission. This Tamburlaine, notwithstanding that, beheld them afar off in this order issuing, so far then exiled from all kind of pity, that he commanded forthwith a certain troop of horsemen to overrun, to murder and kill them, leaving not one alive of what condition soever, and after sacking the city, razed it even unto the very foundations.

A certain merchant of Genoa was then in his camp, who had often recourse to him, who also used him in causes familiarly, and who, for that this fact [crime] seemed very bloody and barbarous, hardened himself to demand him the cause why he used them so cruelly, considering they yielded themselves, craving grace and pardon. To whom he answered in most furious wrath and ire, his face red and fiery, his eyes all flaming with burning sparkles, as it were blazing out on every side: 'Thou supposest me to be a man,

88

but thou too much abasest me, for none other am I but the wrath and vengeance of God, and ruin of the world. Wherefore advise thee well, that thou never again presume to be found in any place in my sight or presence, if thou wilt that I chastise thee not, according to thy desert and thy proud presumption.' This merchant 250 without more then suddenly retired, neither after that was at any time seen in the camp of Tamburlaine.

These things thus accomplished, this great and mighty personage having conquered many countries, subdued and done to death sundry kings and princes, nowhere finding any resistance in any part of all Asia, returned home again into his country, charged with infinite heaps of gold and treasure, accompanied also with the most honourable estates of all the countries subdued by him, which brought with them in like manner the greatest part also of their wealth and substance, where he did to be built a most famous and 260 goodly city, and to be inhabited of those, as we foresaid, that he brought with him, which all together no less honourable than rich, in very short time with the help of Tamburlaine, framed the most beautiful and most sumptuous city in the world, which by the multitude of the people, was also marvellously enlarged, abundant and full of all kind of riches.

But in the end this Tamburlaine, though he maintained his estate in such authority and honour, yet as a man in the end he payeth the debt due unto Nature, leaving behind him two sons, not such as was the father, as afterward appeared by many plain and 270 evident signs. For as well by their mutual discord, each malicing the other, as also by their insufficiency, with the lack of age and experience, they were not able to keep and maintain the empire conquered by their father. For the children of Bajaceth, whom they yet held as prisoner, advertised of this their discord and dissension, came into Asia with valiant courage and diligency; by the aid of such people as they found willing to assist them, recovering their possessions and territories [be]fore lost, which, in manner semblable did they other princes, which Tamburlaine before had also subdued. 280

So that this empire in process of time so declined, that in our age there remaineth now no remembrance at all of him, ne [nor] of his posterity or lineage, in what respect soever. Howbeit, true it is that Baptista Ignatius, a diligent searcher of ancient antiquities, reporteth that he left two sons, princes and protectors of all the countries subdued by him, reaching and extending even unto the river of Euphrates, as also their successors after them, even until the time of King Usancasan, against whom the Turk Mahomet waged sometimes battle. And the heirs of this Usancasan, as most

men surmise, advanced themselves to the honour and name of the 290
first Sophy, whence now is derived the empire of Sophy, which
liveth [flourishes] this day as sworn enemy to the Turk. Which,
howsoever it be, it is to be supposed that this history of Tamburlaine,
had it of any been written, would have been a matter worthy both of
pen and paper, for that great exploits no doubt were happily
achieved of him. But as for me, I never found more than I here
presently have written, neither suppose I that any other thing is of
any other man written, this only excepted, whereon all men accord,
that he never saw the back or frowning face of Fortune; that he
never was vanquished or put to flight of any; that he ne'er took 300
matter in hand that he brought not to the wished effect; and that
his courage and industry never failed him to bring it to good end.
By means whereof we may for just cause compare him with any
other whatsoever, though renowned in times past.

This then that I here give you, that all have I borrowed of Baptista
Fulgotius; Pope Pius; Platina upon the life of Boniface the Ninth; of
Matthew Palmier; and of Cambinus, a Florentine, writing the
history and exploits of the Turks.

(b) *taken from* The English Mirror. A Regard Wherein All Estates may behold the Conquests of Envy . . .

George Whetstone
(1586)

[The text is based on the British Library copy (shelfmark 231.l.18).]

BOOK I CHAPTER 3

Envy original of war, and capital [chief] cause of the destruction of the first monarchies.

[Whetstone locates the principal cause of warfare and its multiple
evils in the vice of envy, and cites instances of lawful sovereigns
deposed through the enmity of those intent on supplanting them.
Commenting on the uncertainty surrounding the selection of an heir
to succeed Alexander the Great, he digresses to introduce a familiar
anecdote of Tamburlaine.]

. . . for discontented (or rather dissentious) persons, howsoever the power of a settled prince keep them under, upon a change will discover [make known] their seditious hearts, as fire hid in ashes by the sprinkling of gunpowder bewrayeth [reveals] the heat. To quell which cunning dangerous people, though Machiavel prescribe a policy un[be]seeming a Christian prince, who is to refer hidden trespasses to the vengeance of God, and not to punish with death an intent without an attempt of evil. For untimely death only appertaineth either to God's secret vengeance, to open and lawful conviction [legal proof] of justice, or in lawful wars to the sword of   10
the soldier, for what human blood is otherwise shed is tyranny in a prince, and punishable in a private person. Yet princes, to bridle such close [covert] enemies of public peace may safely without reproach of tyranny follow the counsel of a Genoan merchant who was sometimes familiarly favoured of Tamburlaine the Great, surnamed *flagellum dei* [the scourge of God], who (worthy the name of vengeance), at what time as he after two assaults was peaceably possessed of a fair city, the citizens with their chief magistrates, wives and children clothed all in white, having olive branches in their hands, as assurances of peace, upon their knees   20
humbly beseeching him of grace, notwithstanding commanded his soldiers to kill them all like dogs. This Genoan, moved with pity to see this outrage, besought Tamburlaine to spare his cruelty for such as he conquered by force. 'And', quoth he, 'if ye fear that these dogs will another day bite, strike out their teeth. Their countenances, if need be, will help to fear [scare] wolves', meaning that he should spoil them of their armour, and if occasion served, he might make them fight, as King Astyages did his cowardly soldiers, either with enemies in their faces or friends at their backs. Which good counsel, though Tamburlaine in his fury   30
regarded not, yet other princes that have their passions more temperate may thereby learn how to keep under their own suspected subjects without dispeopling of their realms to animate foreign enemies. Upon which consideration William the Conqueror, when he entered this realm, straightly [firmly] commanded that no outrage should be done upon the common people, 'for', quoth he, 'though they obey me, I must reign by them'. . . .

[Whetstone moves on to contend that envy among the princes of Christendom was 'the first ground and sure foundation of the great Turks' Empire'.]

BOOK I CHAPTER 11

The puissant kingdom of the Turks, at this day so much renowned and feared, together with the lineage and family of their Ottomans and kings, are of late years sprung up, as a scourge sent and suffered [permitted] by God, for the sins and iniquities of the Christians. . .

[*The English Mirror* now describes events leading to the classic confrontation between Bajazeth and Tamburlaine.]

Now two of the mightiest princes of the world encountered each other in battle, where Bajazet was overcome and taken, who endured the most vile and hard prisonment that ever was heard of. Tamburlaine still carried him with his army in an iron cage, and always when he mounted upon his horse, he set his foot upon his shoulders. Moreover, at meals he tied him under his board, and like a dog fed him with fragments. In this sort [condition] ended this prince his life, who had been the most adventurous, the most renowned and the most feared prince of his time. The sons of Bajazet which escaped the battle where their father was overthrown, in their flight [were] taken upon the seas by certain galleys of the Christians, and certainly at that instant a fair occasion was offered the Christians to have kept under for ever their capital [chief] enemy the Turk, but their sins forbade so precious a blessing. The one of Bajazet's sons named Calapin was delivered, who, seeing the incapacities and contention of Tamburlaine's sons, and taking withal other advantages that time offered, proclaimed himself lord of his father's empire, and by strong hand kept Greece and Thracia. The Emperor Sigismund, both to keep Calapin under, and to be avenged of the overthrow which his [i.e. Callapine's] father gave him, offered him battle, in which Sigismund was overthrown, and narrowly escaped by flight. Calapin reigned six years, and died, leaving behind him two sons, the eldest named Orcan, and the other Mahomet. Orcan was slain by his uncle, who thought thereby to have had his kingdom, but Mahomet behaved [conducted] himself so well, as he slew the murderer of his brother and recovered the empire. He made cruel war upon the Christians in Wallachia, and reconquered the lands and provinces which Tamburlaine won from his grandfather in Turkey and Asia, in which conquest he spent fourteen years, and died in the year 1420. . . .

BOOK I CHAPTER 12

The wonderful conquest of Tamburlaine reconquered, and his large kingdom overthrown by the envy and discord of his two sons.

Among the illustrous captains Romans and Grecians, none of all their martial acts deserve to be proclaimed with more renown than the conquest and military disciplines of Tamburlaine. But such was the injury of [damage to] his fortune as no worthy writers undertook his history at large, although Baptista Fulgosius in his *Collection*, Campinus Florentin[us] in his history of the Turks, make some mention thereof about the year of the Lord 1390. Tamburlaine, being a poor labourer, or in the best degree a mean soldier, descended from the Parthians; notwithstanding the poverty of his parents, even from his infancy he had a [far-] reaching and an imaginative mind, the strength and comeliness of his body answered the haughtiness of his heart. This Tamburlaine, as Fulgosius reporteth, keeping beasts among other youths of his condition, his companions in a merriment chose him for their king, whereupon Tamburlaine, having a ruling desire, after an oath of obedience, commanded every man to sell his cattle [goods], and to contemn [despise] their mean estate, and to follow him as their captain, and in small time he assembled five hundred herdmen and labourers, whose first act was to rob the merchants that passed that way. He parted the spoil continually among his companions, and entertained them with such faithfulness and love, as the rumour thereof daily increased his strength.

The King of Parthia [i.e. Persia] understanding these matters, sent one of his captains with a thousand horse to take him, but Tamburlaine so behaved [conducted] himself, as he won this captain to be his companion and assistant with all his strength, who thus joined, did things of greater importance than before. These matters in question, envy had sown discord between the King of Persia and his brother. Tamburlaine joined with the king's brother, and so valiantly behaved himself, that he overthrew the king and seated his brother in the kingdom. The new king created Tamburlaine chief captain of his army, who, under colour [pretence] to enlarge his kingdom, raised many people, and found the means to make them revolt from their obedience, and so deposed the new king whom he lately aided to the kingdom, and then made himself king of Persia, redeeming by this industry and dexterity in arms his country from the servitude of the Saracens and kings of Persia.

Tamburlaine, having a puissant army, in process of time conquered Syria, Armenia, Babylon, Mesopotamia, Scythia, Asia,

93

Albania, and other provinces, with many goodly and invincible   40
cities. It is pity his policies and battles be not largely written [fully
described], which in these conquests could not but be famous, but
of his military discipline thus much writers commend: in his army
was never found mutiny. He was wise, liberal, and rewarded every
soldier with his desert. There is no remembrance of a greater army
than his. His government and order was such that his camp seemed
a goodly city wherein every necessary office was found. Merchants
without fear of robbing or spoiling repaired thither, with all
manner of necessary provision for his army. The reason was he
suffered no theft unpunished, and as lovingly honoured, praised   50
and paid the virtuous and valiant soldier; which favour joined with
justice, made him both feared and loved. He led a greater army
than King Darius, or Xerxes, for writers affirm that he had four
hundred thousand horsemen, and six hundred thousand footmen,
the which he led to conquer the less Asia.

Bajazet the great Turk, of whose worthiness and wonderful
prowess is sufficiently spoken in the former chapter, advertised
[informed] of Tamburlaine's proceedings, was driven to leave his
siege to Constantinople, and with all expedition, to enlarge his
power to the uttermost to encounter Tamburlaine: by estimation   60
he had as many horsemen as Tamburlaine, and a great number of
footmen. These two puissant captains, in whom wanted neither
valour, policy [skill] nor any advantage of war, with equal cour-
ages, mutually consented to abide the fortune of battle. And so
encountering on the confines [boundaries] of Armenia at the
dawning of the day, with all their power, they began the fiercest
battle that in any age was foughten, which by the huge number of
people and the experience of their captains, may be lawfully
supposed [legitimately accepted].

In fine [conclusion], the Turks, of whom two hundred thousand   70
were slain, vanquished by the multitude of their enemies, turned
their backs, which Bajazet perceiving, to encourage his army, with
an unappalled spirit resisted the fury of his enemies. But such was
God's will, for lack of rescue, by the overcharge of foes, he was
taken prisoner, and presented to Tamburlaine, who closed this
great emperor in an iron cage, and as a dog, fed him only with the
fragments that fell from his table (as in the former chapter is
shown), a notable example of the incertainty of worldly fortunes.
Bajazet, that in the morning was the mightiest emperor on the
earth, at night (and [for] the residue of his life), was driven to feed   80
among the dogs, and which might most grieve him, he was thus
abased by one that in the beginning was but a poor shepherd.

Tamburlaine thus possessed of Asia Minor which was before in the possession of the Turk, he speeded into Egypt, and by the way raised all Syria, Phenice, and the Palestine, he took many famous cities, and among others Smyrna, Antioch, Tripoli, Sebastia and Damas[cus]. In Egypt he encountered with the Soudan and the King of Arabia, and overthrew them. He was ever best at ease when he found a stout resistance in his enemy, that his policy and prowess might be the better known. As appeared at the city of 90 Damas, which after he had taken, the principal and most valiant men retired unto a tower, which was thought impregnable. Afterwards they offered him composition [a truce], but he refused unless they would fight or yield unto his mercy, and with diligence beyond expectation, he raised a tower level with theirs, from whence he battered them in such sort as they were unable to resist.

It is said that in his batteries and assaults he used the first day to raise a white tent, which gave knowledge that if that day the citizens yielded, they should have both their goods, lives and liberty. The second day he raised a red tent, which signified that if they did that 100 day yield, he would save all but the masters and chief of every house. The third day he raised a black tent, which signified that the gates of compassion were closed, and all that were that day and afterwards subjected were slain without respect of man, woman or child. It is written that Tamburlaine besieged a strong city which withstood the first and second days' assault. The third day the people, fed with a vain hope of mercy, set open the gates, and with their wives and children clothed all in white, having olive branches in their hands, they humbly beseeched grace. But Tamburlaine in place of compassion caused his squadrons of horsemen to tread 110 them under their feet, and not to leave a mother's child alive, and afterwards he levelled the city with the ground.

At that time there was a merchant of Genoa somewhat favoured of Tamburlaine [who,] pitying the cruelty, boldly demanded why he showed such cruelty to those that yielded and beseeched pardon. Whom Tamburlaine with a countenance fired with fury answered: 'Thou supposest that I am a man, but thou art deceived, for I am none other than the ire of God, and the destruction of the world. And therefore see thou come no more in my sight, lest I chasten thy overproud boldness.' The merchant made speed away, 120 and was never afterwards seen in the camp. And in truth Tamburlaine, although he was endued with many excellencies and virtues, yet it seemed by his cruelty that God raised him to chasten the kings and proud people of the earth.

In the end this great personage, without disgrace of fortune, after sundry great victories, by the course of nature died, and left behind him two sons, every way far unlike their father; between whom envy followed such dissension that through their incapacities to govern the conquests of their father, the children of Bajazet, whom they kept prisoner, stole into Asia, and so won the people to 130 disobedience, as they recovered the goods and possessions that their father lost. The like did other kings and princes whom Tamburlaine had spoiled [destroyed], insomuch as in small time this empire was so abased that many days ago there was no remembrance left, either of him or his lineage. . . .

TEXT 2

Magni Tamerlanis Scytharum Imperatoris Vita

Petrus Perondinus
(1553)

[The text is translated from the British Library copy (shelfmark 280.f.33); the dedicatory letter to Jacobus Cortesius, Patriarch of Alexandria, is omitted.]

CHAPTER 1

Of Tamerlane's ancestors

Tamerlane's ancestors came from Maracanda [Samarkand], an obscure village near the Jaxartes [Syr Darya] river in the land of Sogdiana, whose capital is Zagataia. His family was then so lowly and undistinguished as to persuade one that only by Fortune's decree could he have risen above their level and that of those who brought him up to become the ruler of virtually the entire East.

CHAPTER 2

Of Tamerlane's birth and youth

Tamerlane's father was a herdsman in the remote pastures and wastes of the mountains near Samarkand; in witness to this are the trophies, the plunder and the immense booty taken from his enemies with which he endowed it. For Tamerlane enriched it beyond all other cities of the East. Up till then, such fame as we know it had comes from the histories of Alexander the Great, another man guided by Fortune. It was the site of the battle he and a pitched force from his army fought to avenge the death of Menedemos who had been lured by Spitamenes into an ambush and killed along with two thousand infantry and three   10
hundred horse.

From earliest youth Tamerlane, mere shepherd and poorest of

97

the poor that he was, nevertheless gave evidence of such intelligence, genius, energy and exceptional ambition as to indicate truly royal qualities of bearing and full and obvious signs of a future great commander. Robust of physique, strong of mind, physically agile, he mastered the skill of leaping in every particular, as well as archery which is the Scythians' especial enthusiasm. His success in outclassing all the other shepherds of the region was so remarkable that he won the greatest respect and goodwill of almost all the 20 inhabitants of Sogdiana. His daily conduct showed none of that addiction to the allurements and opportunities for self-indulgence that usually have a hold on the minds of the young.

CHAPTER 3

Of the beginning of his rule and of other deeds

One writer on his youth tells us that before he was swept by Fate to domination of the entire East he had passed through every military rank, culminating in the command of the Grand Army, so emerging at the highest eminence of all, Empire. We can trust fully the writers of the time when they tell us that as a shepherd in the mountains of Sogdiana he used to join his contemporaries in sports common among shepherds; they report that he engaged in daring activities as well as in wrestling and archery contests. He always won the prizes and so was made the King of their Games; to this role he constantly devoted the greatest possible efforts. 10

It was his pleasure to bind to him all his companions in these sports by spoken oath, by which they vowed to act only on his will and wishes, pledging their faith not to desert him. By receiving their oaths he made himself their leader, and his first order was for them to collect their flocks together into one and to go to sell them. For herding was a lowly occupation, without prospects of glory or the accumulation of wealth; they preferred to carry arms under their leader's auspices. They would go out as an army; from their condition as the lowest of all men, in which they could experience only obscurity, they might attain that height of success to which 20 they all so strongly aspired.

In this way he formed from these rustics a disciplined company of men, who immediately prepared for themselves whatever weapons they thought would be effective; they then fell in behind Tamerlane, acclaiming him as their true leader and commander. His companions changed his name; he was now called Tamir Gutt, which in the Scythian language means *Sword of Fortune*.

Within a very short time he had gathered around him two

thousand men, so forming a large band out of these dispossessed
and lawless persons, united only in the joint winning of plunder. 30
So, for a start, he ordered them out on looting expeditions against
the villages and farms of the region, telling them to devastate
everything they encountered and then to share their plunder with
their fellow-warriors. It was his habit to take only a share equal to
those of the others, so that it would not seem that their efforts
served only his own greed, and thus they might all be the more loyal
to him, all having an equal interest in the outcome of their efforts.

From this start, their activities widened ; many people came to
join Tamerlane, from Sogdiana and the villages of Oxiana, as well
as from around Alexandria on the Tanais [Don], a city founded to 40
commemorate Alexander, joining him out of greed for plunder
and hope of freedom. Even the thickly populated and settled
villages as far as the Caucasian foothills surrendered their fields
and settlements and gave many further undertakings to him.

So, having now a great band committed to robbery, plunder and
slaughter, Tamerlane in his ambition was able to turn against
Persia, where he would be able to accumulate an even greater
hoard of spoils – for, as he reckoned, the Persians being masters of
the richest of all the farming countries of the East, their land would
be packed thick with the flourishingly wealthy treasuries of kings. 50

He and his forces accordingly crossed the Rha [Volga] river, to
make an easier passage to the Caspian Sea. Their route took
them through Iberia, Colchis and Albania, which are beyond the
Caucasus, and by means of the winding paths of the dense forests,
they came through the passes into Persia. They debouched into the
plains, which had many villages and farms, and plundered its large
population, taking possession for himself and his companions of a
vast quantity of loot. Any resistance met with death or maiming, but
those who surrendered were accepted as companions; the majority
of these remained loyal to him, for they were only safeguarding 60
their own interests. They learned from the foreigners' example
what their service under his banner should be, and joined him
in the raids that ravished the plain's inhabitants and destroyed
everything in their path.

The news reached the Persian king, who determined to crush
this banditry, establish some defence against it, and re-open the
passes Tamerlane had blocked; he despatched an energetic general,
whom he considered loyal, with a thousand horsemen to capture
Tamerlane. This man easily crossed the River Araxes [Araks], which
after a long course flows into the Caspian Sea, and soon came within 70
sight of Tamerlane. This in no way alarmed Tamerlane; he was
accustomed to taking risks, which used to stimulate his mind to ever

more burning eagerness for action. He rode out to meet him, and then insinuatingly suggested that, so far from killing or capturing Tamerlane, he was himself in need of avoiding the threat of envelopment, and that it would undoubtedly be to his advantage to make terms and become an ally. At one stroke, he not only increased the size of his own forces but also boosted his soldiers' morale and courage; with these additional cavalry squadrons, he was in a position to undertake new ventures far beyond his previous ones.   80

It happened that the Persian king's brother, who was his younger twin, in his ambition for power and envy for his lawful overlord, had started to gather large forces against the king and make strenuous preparations for a bitter war, to seize the crown for himself. Tamerlane, who had his own thoughts and designs on the government of Persia, heard of this and joined the king's brother with assurances of military support; he saw quite clearly how difficult it would be to sustain power as king without foreign support, or even to challenge the brother in war and prevail by his own resources, without disaster and great loss of life.   90

He therefore concentrated his forces and fell on the king's divisions with such speed and ferocity that he won a glorious victory, driving them back and with immense slaughter destroying them, and at the climax of the battle capturing the king. Once the latter was out of the way, his victorious brother assumed the kingship without opposition; he did not forget the benefits he had received, but entrusted Tamerlane with the command of the entire Persian army and the conduct of affairs at the highest level.

But Tamerlane was a man both cruel and shifty, and where his own advantage demanded he had regard for no one else; his sense   100 of rivalry led him to look for opportunities to remove this man from the throne and to take it for himself. He made out that he wished to annex new regions to this king's empire, but by means of this very large army was in reality looking only to betray him. He started to incite unrest and defection everywhere, and thoroughly prepared the first moves to make every city within the king's dominions rebel against him.

It was not long before he made his challenge for the throne of Persia, marching across the Kalderun Plain to the Taurus Palace, which is the Persians' capital, to take the king's throne and life. He   110 had already prepared for this by attaching seven of the most loyal generals to him under sworn bond. Meeting with no resistance (for how could a few, unarmed people stand up against the advance of so great an armed host?), he took possession of his objective, the kingdom, by force and fraud. He entered the palace, where the king was vainly bewailing and lamenting in misery at his loss, had him executed even as he begged and pleaded against the death that threatened, and also put to death his sons, along with all of the royal stock who remained.

Having removed them all at one stroke, he could now hope to 120 rule without fear of rivals, and the kingdom being won by these deceitful means, he proceeded to distribute vast bounties to win the gratitude and goodwill of the soldiers. He then marched from Persia into Parthia, to seize possession of those parts and to check the plundering raids of the Saracens.

CHAPTER 4

Of the provinces he subdued and took into his rule

He broke the Saracens in battle, crushing their bold spirit for raiding, and then returned to Parthia to set himself to the commission of crimes far and away greater, which were to open the way for his domination of the entire East. His insatiable appetite led him to campaign as far as the northern marches, where the Hyrcans, the Margians, the Amazons, the Bactrians, the Sogdians, the Sacae and countless other people who live this side of the Imaus [Pamir] mountains, and who are today collectively known as the Tartars, all submitted to him. He also forced the Seras [Chinese], the Aryans, the Drangians, the Arachosians, the Gedrosians and the 10 Parapamirids, who live beyond the Pamirs, to pay him tribute; these are people who live amid perennial snows and who, to survive the cold, build hut-like houses from blocks of ice, which have roof-ridges like keels but pierced with holes.

Using the Tartars as troops, he forced the Massagetae and Evergetae of Inner Asia, all of whom are descendants of the Scythians, to withdraw further to the East; he then reduced to subject status Sarmatia, Bithynia and Pontus, which of old was the kingdom of Mithridates the Great and today bears the name of Anatolia. He also subjected everything that was under their 20 control, all the lands lapped by the Euxine [Black] Sea, part of the Propontis [Sea of Marmara], Lake Maeotis [the Sea of Azov] and the Cimmerian Bosporus [Straits of Kerch]. Having defeated and reduced all their minor kings and chieftains, he could now gaze on an infinity of cities and provinces throughout the East, all conquered by himself.

Then, with his entire cavalry and infantry, he crossed the River Tigris and invaded Oxiana and Susiana, which he tamed by force; he took possession of the whole of the region through which that long river flows for so many miles, down to its mouth in the Persian 30

101

Gulf. Then with his huge army he crossed the Taurus mountains
[Toros Daglari] into Mesopotamia and brought this too under his
power; then across the Parcoatran mountains into Media, where he
received the surrender of many famous cities, and also of the
Cadusii, the Amardi, the Tapirdi and the Circassians, peoples who
used to migrate, with much plundering, among the Zagros and
Niphates mountains in the interior of Media.

He then turned south, through the wooded valleys of the Amanus
mountains, so scented with incense and balsam, and so down into
Syria and neighbouring Commagne. This was the same route to the   40
Euphrates that Pompey the Great took after he had defeated
Mithridates at Mount Stella, taken possession of Colchis, Albania
and Iberia, and then moved into Judaea, where he arbitrated in the
dispute between the twin brothers Hyrcanus and Aristobulus; he
ordered Hyrcanus to be made king, an arrangement which Aristobulus soon upset by putting his brother in chains and also
imprisoning several other leading men of Judaea.

This was the route that Tamerlane followed in carrying the
Tartar banners to Jerusalem and the frontiers of Arabia. Having
swallowed up Lydia's treasure he and his forces returned by cross-   50
ing the River Halys, which rises in the mountains of Armenia; they
forded the Halys by wading, for it is said that the river is so shallow
that both infantry and cavalry can wade across. In this way he
reduced Lydia, once the great Croesus's kingdom, to the status
of a province, together with the Phrygians, Mantieni, Cappadocians,
Paphlagonians, Mysians, Myriandini, Ionians, Dorians and Aeol-
ians, subduing them, one and all. He reduced to his service the
other peoples who live along the Halys, where it flows down to the
Black Sea.

By this time there was no nation between the Pamir Mountains,   60
the Red Sea, the Caspian and the [Indian] Ocean which was not
held in thrall and oppression under the Tartar banners.

CHAPTER 5

Of Manuel, the Emperor of Byzantium, and his plea to
Tamerlane for help against Bayazed, the King of the Turks

By right of war Bayazed dominated Epirus [Ipiro]; he had cam-
paigned further, to the far parts of Illyricum as well as in the heart
of Macedonia, bordering on Thrace, and had also ravaged the
population, with Thessaly and Thrace both reduced, right up to the
Bosporus. All this had elated and swelled his mind and so, with an
impressive war-train and vast numbers of warships, he sailed up the

Hellespont to assault Byzantium. First, he took the celebrated port of Velona [Vlore], although it was most strongly defended both by a garrison and by ships; this captured, he then moved to the other side of Greece and seized Salona [Amfissa], by means of the Bay of Panacum which provides an entry on the left [of the Gulf of Corinth]. Then, without delay, he moved on Byzantium with the fixed determination of besieging it and so extending his empire over the whole of Greece.

Byzantium, now called Constantinople, is a most rich and flourishing city of Thrace, sited on a plateau girt by the narrows of the Propontis [Sea of Marmara]. It is a city distinguished not just by the countless citizens who have settled there from the wide world over but also by its inhabitants of extremely illustrious and ancient descent. The majority of its population were then extremely affluent through their skills in trade and business; there were besides schools of Greek learning, which the young attended at public expense, to learn and to be taught.

The buildings, brothels and convents alike are of marble; it has the most august of royal halls and temples of the immortal gods, all built and adorned with the most wonderful craftsmanship, and also houses and pleasure-gardens for relaxation, all most beautiful. The distinction of this greatest of cities is reflected in the amazing construction of its fine buildings. There are also hostels where the sick are well looked after; servants and stewards have the markets, for which sellers come into the city with an unimaginable range of merchandise. There are shops which have every commodity for sale, and where merchants may be seen every day, gathering for trade and exchange and growing ever richer.

For the rest, to sum up as briefly as possible, there are sporting contests, with every game appropriate to the contests of the young, and a great number of theatres, where not only serious plays but also spectacles and farces are staged. The countryside around is spacious and fertile with every fruit, abundant in cattle, and with no shortage of trees for the delight of the beholder. . . .

Bayazed was elated by the many battles he had won in seeking so pugnaciously, avariciously and impiously to gain possession of Byzantium; he now sailed to press the war home on the Emperor and to blockade the city as closely as possible. Manuel [Emperor of the Greeks] realized that he could hardly sustain the onset of war, having no confidence in his resources, and so sent envoys to the great Tamerlane, then campaigning in Parthia, to beg aid.

These were the terms of his request: if his own forces were to be surrounded and the city besieged, he would wish him to advance as close as possible, for Bayazed's hostile force was already swarming

103

around, ravaging fiercely and destroying all those delightful areas
surrounding the city, inflicting destruction both by land and by sea.
Manuel was prepared to divest himself of the Byzantine Empire and
add it to Tamerlane's dominions, for he considered it better for the
common well-being of all and for the tranquillity of that most
renowned and wealthy city that it side with one who could uphold
the liberty of Greece, now so savagely oppressed by the tyranny of
the Turks; therefore he would hand it over to the most noble, most
just and best Emperor of the Tartars, for him to rule and administer,
rather than yield it to the most evil, monstrous and unjust tyrant   60
Turks, who would bring everything to pernicious and savage destruction, devastation and annihilation.

CHAPTER 6

Of the response Tamerlane gave to the Byzantine envoys

The embassy departed and carried out its duty by reporting
Manuel's instructions to Tamerlane. He gave his response with
a glad and calm countenance: he would willingly do everything
required to help Manuel, and expressed his opinion that the
coming war would result in nothing else but the elimination of
Bayazed. He therefore enjoined Manuel to be of stout heart and
hope, for he would bring his Asian campaign to as speedy a
close as possible and would then turn his entire Scythian army
on to the warpath against his principal enemy; help was coming.
Tartar arms would blunt the enemy's raging onslaught and would   10
strip him of his power. Hearing this, the envoys returned rejoicing
to Thrace.

CHAPTER 7

Of Tamerlane's preparations for war against Bayazed King
of the Turks

Tamerlane's ambitious and naturally pugnacious mind, now turned
against the Ottoman kingdom by the disasters that had befallen
Manuel, increasingly grew so incensed that it seemed to him that
no part of the entire Eastern world should escape his dominion,
least of all those parts of the European shore opposite, bounded by
the Aegean, the Propontis and Cariaquetanus, which the ancients
call Asia Minor but which is now called Turkey, so great has the
Turkish name grown and its empire expanded.

Despite his aim of attacking Bayazed, the Tartar was for the

moment constrained by what he had just started; this induced a false   10
hope in the enemy, for it was certain that he would bring the
promised aid to the Caesar Palaiologos, who was now under a wicked
and destructive siege. Tamerlane knew how the most excellent and
provident Emperor of the Greeks was being so unjustly afflicted by
Bayazed, and therefore made ready the largest and strongest army
he could. The affair aroused his sense of mercy more than any
inexorable slaughter could have done, and this made him prepare
his own dominions to bring effective help to that disaster-ridden
suppliant. For it is something deep in nature, that the afflictions of
the unfortunate often attract the minds of others towards a sense of   20
mercy, as if seeing in such suppliants a shared concern.

So Tamerlane was brought to have pity for the Emperor thus cast
on the waves of adverse fortune. He therefore came down from
Parthia, passing through the border-lands and peoples of his own
Empire and directing his march through Armenia, having first built
a bridge of rafts over the Euphrates, which provided a safe crossing
to the other side for all. On this entry into Armenia it was his
pleasure to cross first, leading the whole host of infantry and
cavalry in this invasion of Armenia and to the utter destruction of
that unyielding and senseless Ottoman. For it was his glorious and   30
fated destiny to subjugate all Asia.

Behind his banner there marched Archosians, Sogdians, Bactrians, Hyrcanians, Commagenes, Parthians, Medes and Massagetae
and also islanders from the Caspian and the Red Seas. According to
some writers' reports, this vast concourse, drawn from so many
nations, consisted of one hundred myriads of cavalry and infantry,
of which one hundred thousand were fully armoured. Each nation
had its own commander, and in the advance guard went Median
and Persian horsemen, with their towering helmets, their flowing
clothes all adorned with silver and gold, carrying short swords and   40
armoured with heavy link-mail, especially over the chest. These
were followed by long ranks of both light and heavy armed troops
from the Islands. Then could be seen advancing the famous units of
the Massagetae, mounted and foot, never defeated in either form of
combat; they were armed with sangars [battle-flails] and bronze
axes, their reins, chestplates, bosses and saddles all adorned with
gold. After them came the rest of the army, all mixed up, together
with the skirmishers armed with swords and javelins.

With this host, altogether beyond counting and comparable to
the armies of Darius and Xerxes, Tamerlane marched through   50
Anatolia. Every community was a witness to the horrible and
terrifying slaughters committed, for he had given especial orders to
the soldiers to lay waste everything in their path; this burning and

looting of towns and villages was intended to ensure that nothing
should be omitted that might serve in the elimination of the Turks.
No restrictions of sex were placed on the killings, and all were given
permission to rape or kill anything he could or wished to.

Through slaughter, arson and looting on this scale, he brought
almost the whole of Armenia under his control.

CHAPTER 8

Of the encounter of Tamerlane with the army of Bayazed

As we have just said, Tamerlane, after crossing the Euphrates in
order to subject ever more peoples to himself and to free Manuel
from his close siege, had invaded Armenia which he annexed to his
own dominions by a strategy of almost universal killings, plunder-
ings, burnings, even of sacred buildings, and by the removal of
livestock. The outcome was that to avoid bloodshed many of the
nearby regions and the peoples deserted to him, being seized by
great terror. Natives and strangers alike were amazed at his advance
but even more so by the very size of his army; they were paralysed by
fear and many of the peoples of Asia came forward to greet this
terrible Prince of the Tartars, welcoming him with acclamations,
wishing him good fortune and offering him great gifts.

The Turkish king received the news just as he was moving his
army forward for the siege of Byzantium. He showed no signs of
alarm at all, and his mind was unshaken by the rapid advance of so
large an army. Rather, he abandoned the siege of Byzantium and,
gathering his forces, marched to the foothills of Mount Stella
which, being on the Anti-Taurus range, would enable him to face
the enemy with the prospects of good fortune being added to his
own outstanding skill in generalship. He had the utmost confidence in the discipline of his troops, whom he had trained in
everything that might serve him in the future. With the greatest
care he deployed them, working them up to fight intrepidly.

Tamerlane appeared not to respond but, being a man whose
mind was set on violence, he was constantly giving thought to a
successful outcome for his own army and the annihilation of
the Turks. He encouraged them by reference to their intrepid
Scythian appearance and recalled to them their continuous good
fortune, now as in the past. Fortune had always been with him and
them as a faithful companion and their ally in the thousand
combats they had experienced.

So it came about that these two extremely powerful kings, more
warlike than all others, strenuously got their soldiers ready for the

106

battle by encouragement, working up the ranks to greater belli-
cosity. The result was that, after many sallies by the skirmishers and
injuries inflicted on both sides by both arrows and swords, a general
and bloody engagement developed; it was a long struggle whose
outcome remained uncertain, the fortunes of battle favouring now
one, now the other side.

But the Tartar prince had long developed his skill in so many   40
battles that now there remained no doubt but that Fortune was
leading him to a general mastery in all things, but especially in
warfare, and would lead him to prevail in victory. For now he saw
that the enemy's forces were weakening, partly through the continuous slaughter and partly through exhaustion at the constant
effort; many of their banners had fallen, while, as he could see, the
majority of his own army still retained its strength. So he ordered a
renewal of the fighting with a discharge of arrows, and commanded
that the archers should move forward to finish it off.

Bayazed, on the other hand, had now fully experienced the battle-   50
discipline of the Scythians; he therefore formed a column of fresh
infantry on his right, while on his left he ranged powerful squadrons
of cavalry, while in support he concentrated battalions of veterans.
The plan was that if, when battle was renewed, Fortune turned
against the front ranks, it might still be possible to snatch victory.
He gave orders for them to level their lances against the massed foe
and to charge all together; they were to guard against wounds from
the showers of arrows by raising their shields to protect their heads.

Between the long lances on the one side, anchored in the
ground, and the showers of arrows from the air on the other, there   60
broke out so bitter a slaughter to both armies that almost the whole
of that vast plain was flooded with blood, the Euphrates taking on
the appearance of a river of blood, like the Red Sea. Great were the
volleys of Tartar arrows from on high, hard the thrusting of the
Turkish lance-heads; these were matched by the shattering of
shields and the breaking open to death by sword and arrow of the
Turkish columns.

Those already wounded collapsed on top of others; many turned
back and dissolved in rout. Many more, wounded to the point of
death, fell into ditches or the river, where they gave up the ghost.   70
Some fled to the hill-tops and mountain-heights, making for the
steep Armenian crags, but were driven over the precipices by the
pursuing Tartars. Horses and riders fell together, overwhelmed by
the blades of weapons, and it came about that as the sun sank,
Bayazed's battle-line was dissolved and he himself fell, his horse
pierced by arrows. This was the final episode of that disaster and
slaughter to him and his; he fell alive into the power of Tamerlane.

The aftermath of so fierce a battle, so bloody a victory, so great a rout and flight among the Turkish armies, and of the capture of Bayazed, was that a great fear of Tamerlane took hold not only of all the peoples of Asia but also of those nations whom Tamerlane had never threatened nor could have threatened with war; even the Muscovites, protected from the Tartars as they were by the continuously flowing barrier of the Rha [Volga], offered tribute. So too did the whole of that wide steppe-land which is, they say, where Mithridates the Great, King of Pontus, fled from Gnaeus Pompeius after their great night-time battle; on hearing of Tamerlane's coming, of his ambition to conquer and of his rapid deprivation of Bayazed of both lordship over Asia and of life, these regions also submitted.

George [Scanderbeg], the son of the King of Upper Moesia (which is now called Serbia), and who had the title of Despot, had been received by Bayazed in friendship and alliance only a few days before, who had entrusted him with two of his sons, Celebinus and Mustapha, being anxious to preserve and remove them from the dangers of the imminent battle, so as not to expose his entire progeny at one stroke to the fall of Fortune's fickle and uncertain dice. He now brought back three hundred thousand cavalry and two hundred thousand infantry, together with a great host of camp-followers and cattle-drivers following under their own commanders; he did not hesitate, with this strong army that had been Bayazed's, to venture within sight of Tamerlane, although he engaged none of his troops with the Scythians, for he was alarmed at their boldness, strength, speed and spirit.

Tamerlane led his men in follow-up battles against many other peoples, especially the Cercetari, the Leucosyri, and the entire population that dwells between the Hercanian [Caspian] Sea and the Tanais [Don]. Among the other peoples who surrendered to him were the Khorassians, the Dacians, the Sagi who live across the Don, as well as the Nogaii and Sciabani, the most warlike of the inhabitants of Muscovy. Having taken possession of all these, Tamerlane ordered Bayazed to be led round the whole of Asia, his hands bound behind his back, so that the entire population might see their king a prisoner in chains, and that Tamerlane himself had gained the victory, and won supremacy over Asia.

CHAPTER 9A

[Both this and the succeeding chapter are numbered '9' in the original edition. However, there is no chapter numbered '11'.]

Of the numbers of the dead on either side and of other events

It is said that two hundred thousand Tartars were killed in that battle; of the Turks, more than one hundred and forty thousand, but they also had their camps destroyed by the Scythians, with a huge plunder of gold and silver taken. Many Turks were captured, and of these a majority were violently put to death. For three days continuously the victorious Scythians feasted on their gains, gorging wholeheartedly, for they had won in abundance all the materials required for their sort of feasting, namely the flesh of slain men and horses; it is the custom of the Massagetes, the Bactrians and of many Scythians to eat both human and horse flesh.

CHAPTER 9B

Of the degrading and vile punishment inflicted on Bayazed, and of his death

Even now the harsh mind of the victor Tamerlane was not satisfied or satiated by the vast slaughter and disaster inflicted on the miserable Turks; there still remained with him enough savagery to pour out on that most wretched of men, Bayazed. He would humiliate him by using him as a mounting-block, stepping on to his back as he crouched; when he ate, he kept him tied up like a dog under a three-legged table, to be the butt of all as he ate the crumbs and scraps. For the rest of the time he was kept in an iron cage like a wild animal, a pitiable spectacle, a prime example of human affairs and of the fickleness of Fortune. 10

His wife had also been captured with him. Before Bayazed's own eyes, Tamerlane forced her, clad insultingly only in sandals and an extremely short military cloak, to serve drinks to the Scythian chieftains as they reclined, obscenely naked. In this respect the Tartar was imitating the Roman Emperor Tiberius, who would never dine unless waited on by naked girls.

In this great shame that he was undergoing, Bayazed was pierced through by rage, seized by grief, and overwhelmed with insult; he begged for death, and, when in his right mind, made an inexorably determined vow to take his own life. By repeated blows 20 against the iron bars of his cage he smashed his head so that it broke open and the brains spilled out, and so brought about his unhappy, mournful fate.

On the one hand, Fate had handed him over, once the supreme King of Asia, to a shameful imprisonment, the kingdom he had inherited had been plundered by a former herdsman, and his great wealth had been engulfed by calamity. On the other hand, his rival was carried by Lady Fortune to such a peak of domination over the nations that he could make war against a king hitherto undefeated, distinguished by many victories and vast wealth, and with tre- 30 mendous power, enjoy an astounding outcome. That king and his wife were in sordid chains, and he himself was able to return to his own lands with vast booty and great glory.

CHAPTER 10

Of his severity, illustrated by his rebuke to a jewel-merchant

There was a jewel-merchant of Ligurian [Genoese] origin, who was a close confidant of Tamerlane, and also greatly attracted to pearls. He felt extremely unhappy on the king's [i.e. Bajazeth's] account, and begged Tamerlane, with the most urgent entreaties to show some sense of mercy and respect towards him, such as a king of such power and wealth could afford to display; for this was something that the greatest of kings had been pleased to grant. But Tamerlane glared threateningly at him and, it is said, replied in a truculent voice that this punishment was not being exacted from a king subdued by force of victorious arms but from a tyrant who had 10 been a terror to all, whose cruelty had led him to depose and kill his own elder brother Suleiman, and that the end he was suffering was therefore wholly appropriate.

[There is no chapter numbered '11'.]

CHAPTER 12

Of the liberality and generosity with which he treated Manuel

The liberal and munificent side of his nature is shown above all in the following episode:

When [Manuel] Palaiologos became Emperor, and Bayazed had been defeated in battle, he sent envoys to the victor Tamerlane, who was at that time campaigning against the Bithynian city of Bursa. These envoys first greeted him by name and in terms of the utmost admiration, then congratulated him on so great a victory over the common enemy. They then declared that it was his intention to place Byzantium, himself and all his resources under the authority and jurisdiction of Tamerlane, the great 10 Prince of the Tartars, to whom alone the immortal gods had

assigned the Empire of the entire East, and through whose bene-
ficence alone, as all men acknowledged, the freedom of Greece
was owed from that great tyranny which had almost overwhelmed
and dismembered it.

Tamerlane received these men graciously, giving them a friendly
hearing; he is reported to have replied in gentle terms, saying that
he was most reluctant to subject to servitude that most celebrated
and famous of all cities of renown, distinguished as it was by its
descent from the men of antiquity, so recently rescued as it was   20
from the clutches of the Turks. He is reported to have added that
he himself was by no means so puffed up with odious pride as to be
governed by insatiable greed for acquiring cities or for extending
dominions; the possession of many kingdoms in itself incited
further war. But he would assign further resources to the Emperor,
the city and the other Greek powers, and would safeguard Greece
from any harm. Finally, anything that related to defence was to be
referred to himself, for him to determine whether a war could justly
be undertaken, for this was the duty of a good and supremely fair
Emperor. None of the princes of Thrace was to exert any form of   30
pressure on him or his government; the defeated tyrant, now a
prisoner, was to pay the due penalty for his crimes and, as [their]
petition had requested, would be kept in chains until he met an
appropriate end to his life.

The ambassadors left Bursa in joy and astonishment at hearing
this; through God's aid the noblest of cities had escaped the hands
of the Turks, although later, when Christian princes had become
embroiled in domestic troubles, Bayazed's nephew Mohammed,
son of Maumathes [Amurath], was to defeat and destroy it, killing
Constantine Palaiologos amid great slaughter, to the harm of all   40
Christendom.

CHAPTER 13

Of the honours accumulated by Tamerlane from all the people of Parthia, and of other deeds

Loaded down with plunder and glory, he returned from Asia with
his army, having spent some time in reorganizing the state of
the provinces and appointing governors to them. In Parthia he
celebrated his triumph, wearing laurels given by the people of
every province, crowns made from their native flowers. There were
solemn dances and carnivals according to the traditions of each
race; in the prosperity he had brought them they acclaimed him,
and repeatedly expressed the joy such great victories carried with

them. Collectively, they welcomed the return of a prince who
brought such spoils with him; they revered and venerated him on   10
bended knees as he personally distributed abundant largesse to
the crowds. The routes of his entries were strewn with flowers and
crowns; all the peoples over whom he ruled dedicated monuments
to him, bronze or marble statues made by craftsmen, as well as
portraits, painted tableaux, panegyrics, all dedicated to his genius.
He himself could hardly conceal his delight at so great a victory;
he summoned all the Scythian chieftains to a vast and magnificent
banquet, at which he entertained them and his entire army to
Parthian delicacies, in a fashion more luxurious than warlike.
It would take many words to describe the equestrian games and   20
the spectacles the Scythians provided; these lasted for several
days, during which he presided from his throne, honouring the
contestants according to their merits and awarding especially large
prizes to the pentathletes.

CHAPTER 14

Of the wars he fought in Egypt and other parts

So much did he hold peace and tranquillity in abhorrence, that at
about the same time as he was gathering his banners to fight the
foolhardy Bayazed, he also launched himself on another campaign,
a great one, in the course of which he crossed the whole of Asia as
far as the marshy regions at the mouth of the Nile.

It took him only a very few days to capture Smyrna, Sebaste and
Tripoli by force; he then advanced with his entire army to the River
Orontes, which flows down from the mountains of Lebanon, and so
came up against Antioch, which is close to that river. He then
seized the famous city of Seleucia in Phoenicia, along with all its   10
suburbs and markets; then moved to the interior of Syria, where he
captured the cities of Galata and Rabbata, famous in the histories
of the royal Ptolomies and Seleucids, slaughtering their entire
populations.

He then struck camp and marched into Egypt to attack the
Sultan of Memphis, who had recently invaded Palestine; Palestine
itself he reduced, handing it over to his own troops for utter
devastation and destruction with all their Scythian cruelty. The
Sultan of Egypt and the King of Arabia received news of this but
although they gave orders for the invasion to be resisted, they   20
were self-centredly more concerned with their kingdoms' immense
wealth and their own escape. Their armies were dispersed at the
first attack and they both immediately fled.

The Sultan fled across to Pelusium, fearing that by Fortune's fluctuations that were engulfing him he might lose his life as well as kingdom. Tamerlane pursued him vigorously, driving him from his fatherland and throne, and adding to his own dominions all of Egypt that lies between the Nile and the western shore of the Red Sea, until at last the desert terrain and the sand-filled water-courses brought a halt to his planned movements.

CHAPTER 15

Of the city of Damascus and how he besieged and captured it

Nothing was more pleasing to him in his military strength and confidence in his good fortune than to undertake great and arduous enterprises, to subdue a stubborn province, to invade the most inaccessible regions or to attack those cities which were generally reckoned by the military experts to be the strongest and most insuperable. In every such enterprise he clearly showed himself as a paradigm of courage and vigour, for he was ever ready to undertake those ventures that were considered by others the hardest and most difficult.

As an example of this we may make particular note of his assault 10 on the city of Damascus, a very strong city, well garrisoned, with a strongly fortified citadel built after our own fashion; it was considered impregnable and impossible to capture through any human force or ingenuity. His siege and assault lasted an extremely long time; he cut off all the roads around it, so that the citizens grew so weary of his attacks and blockade, and so fearful of him that they agreed to send a herald to sue for peace.

These were the terms: that he should not allow so famous a city, that for so many ages past had been scarcely touched by the attacks of armed enemies, to be damaged or destroyed. Their offer was 20 that if Tamerlane lifted the siege and removed his forces from Damascus, they would pay him an annual tribute. He rejected this offer, and persisted in his implacable savagery, destroying any hope they had placed in this attempted pact. He reacted by renewing his assault on the city more fiercely and violently than ever before, using the most astounding engines to reduce it by setting it on fire.

In consequence the Megistanes and the Damascenes lost confidence in their strength and withdrew into the citadel, which was in the middle of the city, extremely strongly fortified and garrisoned 30 and well stocked with supplies. All the soldiers who had been defending the city and the countryside withdrew into the citadel, thinking it offered the safest defence; there they awaited whatever relief from the impending threat might appear.

Tamerlane carefully examined the citadel's position but could see no hope of taking it; he therefore had huge military engines quickly prepared in the Lebanese mountains, and ordered the building of a castle, which was to be higher than the citadel of Damascus and so would overlook it and thus allow his archers to shoot over the crown of the walls. The defenders of the citadel were pierced and knocked down, the Tartars engaged in this action fighting with ever greater ferocity and vehemence, maintaining the shooting by day and by night. But the castle was shattered and split open by numerous blows, weakened and collapsed, killing all its garrison. Enraged, Tamerlane ordered an immediate, full-scale assault on the city, which was successful but only at the cost of a great slaughter of his own men.

Then began a most barbaric looting.

CHAPTER 16

Of his subjection of Capha [Kerch], and of other deeds

He then declared war on the inhabitants of Kerch, a great city widely renowned as the most opulent of all and reputedly full of gold and silver. In antiquity it was called Theodosia, being a Ligurian colony established in the Tauric Chersonnese, by the Cimmerian Bosporus. It was well populated, indeed crowded, for many rich merchants used to trade there; a great concourse of people was daily drawn there from Bulgarian Thrace and Trapezus [Trebizond], and also from the Aegean, the Propontis and the Black Sea.

To capture this city, remove its wealth and subject it to his own empire and jurisdiction, Tamerlane thought out a new strategy for its destruction; he thought it possible that under threat of war its inhabitants might flee in order to protect their treasures from falling into enemy hands, or that they might bury in secret underground chambers the items they considered most precious. To prevent this happening the Tartar ordered all his own traders to take their entire available stocks of martens' skins and sables and sell them in Kerch, for he knew that, while treasure could be hidden away, skins could not be dug up again. These traders were to offer them to the people of Kerch at prices lower than usual, to encourage buyers to come all the more readily to market. Very many did so, with the result that the merchants of Kerch came in great hopes of making even bigger deals; they spent all their available money.

114

So, having by this trade removed all the ready money from Kerch's treasury, he promptly declared war; as soon as he had collected a large armed force he attacked the city, which he captured after battering it with many siege engines. He then seized all the wealth with which it was stuffed.

CHAPTER 17

Of the tents he used when attacking cities

This is the appropriate place to recall the preparations he used to make in besieging or assaulting towns:

– On the first day upon appearing before a city, he would instruct his camp marshal to erect a white tent for him. This was intended to give clear notice to the citizens that they should yield at once; if they opened their gates, they would receive pardon and be immune from any punishment;

– On the second day, he would order a red tent to be pitched as his headquarters, intending to indicate by this that he would impose the death penalty on all heads of households and these alone, the rest being allowed safe conduct;   10

– On the third day, a tent of the most funereal black would be pitched in sight of the whole city; this proclaimed that Tamerlane had shed every vestige of compassion from that moment on, that he would put everyone to death in the most inhumane way and that the city would be levelled to the ground.

CHAPTER 18

Of the savagery and cruelty he showed towards those he conquered and to suppliants

You will appreciate from this that he was a man of exceptionally savage and unrelenting disposition. For example, on one occasion he made an attempt against some very powerful city, which was well-populated and possessing a large force of defenders, which was girt around with ditches and abundantly equipped with everything deemed necessary for its protection and safety, and which had confidence in its own resources to fight a war successfully. When Tamerlane and his uncountable army came to besiege it, he first of all sent messengers to invite the citizens to surrender. If they rejected the Tartar's suggestion and refused to   10

115

surrender, they would have no alternative but to resist as strongly as they could and to fight as fiercely as possible. Two days would be allowed for this combat.

At dawn on the third day, that of the funereal tent, the day that by experience men knew would see the extremes of fire and slaughter inflicted on the citizens, and when he judged that it was feasible for his sappers to undermine the city by way of the ditch, then the siege engines were brought up. The engagement continued without respite, the inhabitants being allowed no rest by day or night. Then he gave the order for the ditch to be undermined, and this, in   20
conjunction with the repeated blows from battering-rams on the exposed walls, caused a large section to collapse, effecting an entry for his soldiers.

The citizens were in despair at this turn of events; their soldiers panicked and they considered the end to be inevitable. But in the hope of being able to influence the inexorable conqueror, they sent out from the city to Tamerlane a long procession of their boys and girls, a dearly cherished troop, all dressed in white and with olive branches in their hands, to beg and plead for pardon, salvation, amnesty and peace for the city, or else that they might be   30
allowed to evacuate it.

He saw them the moment that they emerged, and exploded into a more than Tartar-like rage; he then launched the strongest of his cavalry squadrons in a great charge against the column of children. Abandoning any sense of clemency or humanity, he subjected these undeserving innocents to being trampled under the hooves of his horsemen, to being crushed against the rocks, and so to perishing amid utter misery and grief.

He then gave the order for total destruction by fire and sword to ensue.

CHAPTER 19

Of his brutal and atrocious manner of speech

There was a man of Italian birth who had gained great favour with Tamerlane and who was also held in great respect by all the court treasurers, so that Tamerlane wanted to place him in charge of all the finance officers and merchants of Parthia; he had been a skilled merchant of some substance.

This man was moved to pity and compassion at the misfortunes and afflictions heaped on this city, and distressed at the funereal fate of that innocent troop of children. He therefore broached, but

indirectly, the topic of these cities for which he had so much
concern; he asked the tyrant why he permitted his soldiers to   10
wallow in such brutality against those who had been defeated and
were suing for pardon, when it might seem that the greatest glory of
the most excellent of kings was displayed rather in the splendour of
their clemency and humanity.

Tamerlane scowled and glared at him with flashing eyes:

'Remember, I am the Wrath of the greatest God, and Disaster
and Death to a depraved world. Therefore, unless you wish to
be plucked away by the great punishments you deserve, get out
of here.'

So terrified was the merchant by the harsh menace of the tyrant's   20
words that he left at once and never again dared to come within
Tamerlane's gaze.

CHAPTER 20

Of his strict disciplining of the camp

In order to present himself as a sharp and strict leader, one who
had emerged to be the most skilled of all Scythian chieftains in the
military arts, he treated his army extremely harshly. The perimeter
of his camp was patrolled, to prevent any mutiny among the troops,
or any theft or corruption in its supplies or finances, and to
stop men wandering beyond its gates to forage. He was also
notably careful to see that those who transported supplies should
experience no interference from soldiers compelled by suffering
and need to leave the camp to forage. All who offended through
theft, quarrels or armed disputes were punished, and he sup-   10
pressed all riotous behaviour or self-indulgence on the part of
his men. Because men going into market-places or shops were
liable to become disorderly, merchants would come to the camps
themselves, laying out their stock for inspection, great quantities of
food, clothing and footwear. Within the Tartar camp a specific
place was assigned to every single craft; it was a miracle of good
order, just as within walled towns you may see all manner of
commodities and manufactures filling the shops.

There was strict supervision of the various duties to be performed, and a check kept on any soldier who wanted to go out; he   20
would be asked where he wished to go. The consequence was that
by retaining supplies in abundance for both men and horses
everything needed was available within the camp.

117

CHAPTER 21

Of Tamerlane's appearance and manner of life

He was of noble bearing, heavily bearded, broad-shouldered, deep-chested; his limbs were well-formed and indicative of general good health, except for one of his feet, which was misshapen and caused him to limp visibly.

His mouth was truculent. He had deep-set and slanting eyes that glittered with all the savagery of some exceptionally ferocious beast, striking terror and awe into all who saw him. He was heavily muscled; in wrestling he could floor even the strongest Scythian and he could easily draw the strongest of the large Parthian bows back beyond his ear and drive a small spike through a bronze mortar.

Both physically and in other respects Tamerlane was very similar to Hannibal of Carthage as described by several ancient writers and also as shown on coins. His genius lay in cunning, the committing of atrocities and untrustworthiness. He was not a man given to reflection but relied on the use of savagery, both in the punishment of criminals and – but even more so – against his own soldiers. This was in order that they would keep their hands off the gold and other treasures, for fear of punishment; for he claimed everything for himself and disposed of everything arbitrarily.

For the rest, it was his wish to be seen as a brutal exponent of warfare, to be untiring in every enterprise he embarked on, to be able to impose his bestial yoke alike on those he attacked, on those against whom he stirred up the storms of war, or even against those who were enjoying undisturbed freedom.

CHAPTER 22

Of his training in the arts of war

It is legitimate to assume that Tamerlane was born and first saw the light under some favourable conjunction of the planets and an extremely beneficent constellation. It must be seen as an extraordinary wonder that, born of the humblest of parents, the lowest of his own clan, with no education in manners or the training normally exalted as the first path to glory and fame which hitherto humankind had been accustomed to associate with Mars's gifts of largeness of vision and a pertinacious spirit, he was nevertheless carried to the pinnacle of military achievement, to the point where the Scythian chieftains acclaimed him as their Emperor.

All those qualities we consider should be displayed in the highest generalship, we can have no doubt from what we have heard were displayed in Tamerlane: skill in military matters, an authoritative bearing, good fortune, a sharp cunning, endurance in tough activities, and boldness in undertaking the greatest of enterprises. These qualities were matched by others equally outstanding, gifts both of body and spirit; all these were splendidly manifest in him, constantly and in amazing degree, so much so that he was a prince who seemed to have received every aptitude given to mortal men, and to have earned every plaudit of the highest sort. No one ever, 20 throughout the long course of time, will rival or surpass this glory of the Tartar race, and none of the Scythians, I believe, has achieved his fame in this world.

CHAPTER 23

Of the religion which engaged his mind

Who could possibly maintain that instances of religious sentiment could be drawn from the profane and impious mind of a Tamerlane? For someone who destroyed the former Sultanate of Persia and so monstrously ravaged everything to the south and the west in inexorable savagery, who burnt cities and towns wherever they might be, was nevertheless touched by a sense of religion, or perhaps rather was inspired by some secret power (which I consider may be the same); for he always spared Muslim mosques, which can be seen to this day to be the most beautiful of buildings.

CHAPTER 24

Of Tamerlane's wife and children

He took as wife the daughter of a Bactrian chieftain, by whom, as all the authorities affirm, he was the father of two sons, neither of them to be compared to Tamerlane in personality or military skill, as we may see from the future development of events. For, once he was taken from the sphere of human activity, Tartar fortunes began to melt away, to the extent that the reputation of the Scythians, which he himself had made almost imperishable and had spread throughout the whole world, seemed with his death to become extinct and obliterated; for so it is that the waxings and wanings of sad Fortune dispose of affairs.

CHAPTER 25

Of other works that he did

He overthrew many kings in battle; he laid low virtually countless tyrants; he ground down and subdued so many peoples; he seized so many cities by fire and the sword. Then finally, burnt out after so many grievous wars and turmoils and having pacified the entire East and having surfeited his army with rich spoils taken from his enemies, he returned to his own native Scythia, that hearth whence he had come, dismissing his forces to carry out whatever savage ravaging they might and retaining only his praetorian cohort which he had always supported with monthly payments to be his bodyguard and supervisors of those who attended his court.   10

Thenceforth he devoted himself to the embellishment of Maracanda [Samarkand], his native town – and here the errors of Pius II and Cambinus are evident and their opinion is to be rejected, since they maintain that Tamerlane built it from its foundations up, whereas Quintus Curtius [Rufus] makes frequent mention of it.

He decreed that it should excel all other towns of the East in wealth, and devoted himself to providing it with new buildings, temples to the gods, all most beautifully decorated with carvings out of various kinds of marble, and ancient bronze statues of the famous kings of the East. Everything that was on the point of   20 collapse he restored, and gave orders for the whole to be provided with the strongest of watch-towers and gate-houses, as well as with a garrison and squadrons of ships, which were intended to keep the Caspian Sea clear of pirates and bandits for the sake of merchants and their cargo-ships.

He also gave orders to make the Jaxartes navigable for the largest of barges and lighters for the transport of agricultural produce and other necessary commodities to the city. He further instituted athletic games, after the model of the Roman Emperors, so that the young might be exercised in mock cavalry battles; the people of the   30 city were to be trained in the use of weapons by professional swordsmen, so that if ever occasion demanded they should not shrink from confronting any enemy.

Above all, he ensured that those who were closest to the hearts of the chieftains and the wealthiest citizens of the provinces he had subdued were transported to and established within Samarkand, so that whenever the people assembled on feast days it should be seen as the one city among those of the East which stood out among all others in splendour, nobility and wealth. He also decreed that these should be exempt from all official duties so that, having been   40 removed from their homelands and brought up among strangers, they should on return to their own land influence their own people to grow up in awe of his victories. It was here that he ordained the most lavish of his public works, establishd the seat of his Empire, issued laws according to his whim, and handled the reins of his good Fortune.

CHAPTER 26

Of Tamerlane's death and of the comet that announced it

There was one especially great, outstanding presage of the death of such a prince; a vivid comet which arose some months before his death, and which could forbode nothing but the death of so great a king. For he died through choking in his own bed-chamber while his guard slept. This was in the year since Our Lady gave birth 1402 [actually 1405], in the fiftieth year of his life, Pope Boniface IX at that time presiding over the Most Holy Commonwealth.

He left two sons as successors and heirs to his empire spread over so many kingdoms, and to such immense wealth. But these showed no desire to take up his dominion, nor did they maintain their father's inheritance, for they soon started to engage in recurrent mutual strife, each hoping to obtain for himself his rich inheritance, each inciting rebellion against the other amongst the subject peoples, with the result that they lost and were despoiled of the almost infinite populations conquered and subjected by their father by right of war, and in this were seen to have fallen far from their father's quality. So they became subject to foreign control, in the first instance to the Ottomans.

So Tamerlane came to his life's term. He was indisputedly pre-eminent in warrior-like attributes over all mortals who had gone before, and never did he encounter Fortune's hostility. No one would dare to compare with Tamerlane even the generals of Rome or those of the Greek emperors, who also distinguished themselves in warfare, achieved great feats on land and by sea, often engaged with the most powerful of enemies, and frequently returned in triumph with the trophies of victory. But he made war against the untamed and ferocious warriors from beyond the Pamir Mountains as far as the River Volga and, although by no means with ease, defeated and subdued them in arms. Whether provoking war or being provoked into it, he even prevailed over and reduced to servitude peoples who had never been defeated in open battle even by Darius, the greatest of the Persian kings with his many thousands of soldiers, or Alexander of Macedon himself, the terror of the East, or Cyrus King of the Medes, who led a vast army against Persia and Lydia and also performed outstanding deeds. Of these, the first ended up in discreditable flight and deposition; Zopirio, the general of the second, was destroyed with all his forces, and so too were Cyrus and his entire army, as ancient writers have recorded. Nor could any of these have escaped intact from any encounter with the Roman armies, the most formidable of those of any country in the world.

But indeed it is above all true that amid such great and amazing success in his affairs, in which Fortune was his ever-present, never-failing, and remarkably faithful companion, Tamerlane may seem in one aspect only to have been deficient in enjoying supreme good fortune. And that is that, although he would have prevailed over all the most glorious leaders in war now living and over those of antiquity as well, the passage of the ages would never have deprived him of his trophies and monuments, had he found a eulogist who was equal to the task of celebrating his sterling worth.

TEXT 3

De dictis factisque memorabilis collectanea . . .

Baptista Fulgosius (Battista Fregoso)
(1509)

[The text is translated from the British Library copy
(shelfmark 637.k.16).]

BOOK III CHAPTER 4

Concerning those who, sprung from lowly estate,
won for themselves an illustrious name

Just as merit incurs envy, so also, generally speaking, it tends to
be accompanied by fame, and so that it may show itself to be
unrestricted by any shackles, it does not always court high rank
and wealth. Just as it favours the whole of human nature, it
embraces those who seek it out; and very often it comes to those
of humble origin and makes them famous so that their name
becomes carried on the lips of men. Moreover, it gives everyone
cause to entertain, in full measure, a hope that is not unwelcome,
and to obtain fame and honour or dishonour and infamy according
to their manner of life, both during their lifetime and after   10
meeting their death. Therefore, taking certain men as examples,
we shall demonstrate that those born in lowly circumstances have
obtained very great fame. . . .

(fol. lxxxviii recto)

[The writer goes on to cite, among others, the examples of Virgil,
Horace, Theophrastus, Pythagoras, King David, Vespasian, the Apostle
Peter, and St John the Evangelist.]

Concerning Tamburlaine King of the Persians

In our grandfathers' time Tamburlaine was regarded as the equal
of old-time chieftains in armed strength and justice, but in respect
of the size of his kingdom and army he was the superior of Xerxes,

123

let alone his equal. As far as could be ascertained he hailed from
Scythia: he did not spring from a royal line nor any distinguished
stock – his father was a shepherd and extremely poor; he himself
was reared among shepherds, and having been made king by the
shepherds in the course of boyish games, by cunning and singular
assiduity he persuaded them to swear and promise that they would
do his bidding. Therefore he ordered them to sell their livestock   10
and, in order to free themselves from a life of poverty, to procure
weapons and horses. Up to five hundred others had joined him and
with this number he overcame by force of arms certain companies
of merchants who were accustomed to travel through those regions
in great numbers commonly called caravans for the sake of protection. In sharing out the booty he showed himself so fair and
generous among his companions that the shepherds not only did
not regret their changed condition, but also bound themselves to
him the more zealously in loyalty and love.

To curb the boldness of these bandits, the King of the Persians   20
sent a commander at the head of a thousand horsemen to the
borders of the region where these exploits against the merchants
had taken place. Summoned to a parley by the leader of the
robbers, the commander was charmed by the robber's crafty words
and became his comrade instead of his enemy. In the meantime a
dispute arose between the Persian king and his brother, and the
bandit chiefs espoused the brother's cause. After they had appropriated the kingdom for him, they requested and obtained the
greater part of his army, under the pretext of wishing to extend the
empire among foreign nations. But they incited the people to   30
rebel, and soon he who had previously been a bandit chief made
himself King of Persia.

Now because he was crippled in his hip-joints, the Persians added
to his name Temir (which in the Scythian language means 'the
thigh') the word 'lang' which in their ancient language indicates
someone crippled in the hip, and when the two words were combined he was called 'Temirlang'. But we, owing to the dissimilarity
of language, have corrupted the word, and he is called Tamburlanus
instead of Temirlang.

This man added to the Persian kingdom Armenia, Syria, Babylon   40
and other vast nations; and he also founded a commercial city
of vast circumference. The immense fame which he had won
for himself was such that anyone, though born in humble and
unfortunate circumstances, might by dint of physical and mental
courage and assiduity attain to any height of mighty kingship
and rule.

(fos. xc verso–xci recto)

BOOK IX CHAPTER 5

Concerning vain-gloriousness

The Persian king Tamburlaine, although in other respects apparently reacting temperately to what fortune sent him, nonetheless in
dealing with Bajazet the Turkish ruler, whom he captured in war,
behaved with undue presumption (as in the case of two of those
already discussed [perhaps Sesostris and Cambyses]), since, setting
no store by the ups-and-downs of fortune, he shut Bajazet up in a
cage, and in the same manner, placing the cage on a wagon he
transported him wherever he himself journeyed, using the king as
a footstool so that he might mount his horse with greater ease.

However, these kingly examples, of which we have spoken   10
recently, are not easy to adjudicate in absolute terms: perhaps those
who were defeated were over-zealous to preserve their lives, since at
all events they did not seek to free themselves in death, either on
the battlefield, or from so foul and miserable a form of servitude,
once they had been captured.

(fo. ccxcii verso)

TEXT 4

Libro . . . della origine de Turchi et imperio delli Ottomanni

Andreas Cambinus
(1529)
translated out of Italian into English by John Shute
(1562)

[The text is taken from the British Library copy (shelfmark G.4213).]

[Cambinus speaks of the rise of the Ottomans, and of the desperate straits to which Bajazeth's siege reduced the citizens of Constantinople.]

. . . there is no doubt that if God by extraordinary means had not provided for it, the city of Constantinople the which in time before, many hundred years past, had been the head, not only of Graecia, but also of the greatest part of the world, had at that time fallen into hands of the most cruel and barbarous nation of Turks, had not been Tamerlano, a Parthian born, who with a great power entered the lesser Asia and assailed it with such fury that he constrained Bajazith to abandon Constantinople, and to pass with his army into Asia, for the defence thereof.

And having now occasion to speak of the acts of Tamerlano and   10
his people, I have thought it not inconvenient to make some little digression, and to declare from whence this puissant captain had his original, and by what means he did attain to the high and supreme degree of honour, in the which he then was, when Bajazith was chief prince and King of the Turks. This Tamerlano was born in Parthia, of base and simple parents; he was exercised in arms even from his childhood, and did so profit therein that it was hard to say which had the greater place in him, either strength and lustiness of his body or else his wisdom and other virtues of the mind, so that among his soldiers he was had in great reputation and   20
honour, in such sort that a great multitude followed him, and chiefly those which were most experimented [tested, experienced]

126

in the wars, and thus in short time he became prince of a mighty army, both of horsemen and footmen, whom he had gained to follow him by his virtue, good disposition, and liberality, by whose aid he first delivered his country of Parthia from the bondage of the Saracens, and then became prince thereof. After that with great violence, he assailed the countries near unto him and in few years possessed them, and brought to his obedience Scythia Asyatyea, Iberia [in the Caucasus], the Albaneses [inhabitants of ancient Albania], the Persians, the Assyrians and Medes, and last of all he brought under his yoke Mesopotamia and the greater Armenia, and then passed over the flood Euphrates about the year of our Lord 1390 with a far greater army than was that of Dario [Darius], or that which Xerxes brought into Graecia, for it is said that he had in his camp 400,000 horsemen, and 600,000 footmen, with whom he assailed the lesser Armenia, upon whose confines Bajazith the Turk, King of Asia, encountered him with a mighty power, both of horsemen and footmen, and trusting in the virtue and discipline of his people, whose labour he had a long time used with great felicity, did not refuse to accept the battle, notwithstanding that he knew himself to be far inferior in number[s].

Then these two mighty princes approaching the one towards the other, so near as they might discern the one the other's order, omitted no time but joined in battle, in the which for the greater part of the day there were slain great numbers on both sides, and they fought with such assurance, neither part giving place to the other, that it was hard to say where the victory should incline, till at the last the Turks being weary and not able to endure the force of the Parthians (who continually supplied their squadrons with fresh bands) sought to retire themselves in order, fighting continually in their retreat, but the Prince, being ware hereof, commanded certain great troops of horsemen to give charge upon them, who charged them with such force that they disordered them, and then the Turks began to flee, leaving the victory to their enemies, and Bajazith fought valiantly a long time in person, till he had lost a great multitude of his people, and also last of all his horse was slain under him, and then [Bajazeth] was taken and presented to Tamerlano, who commanded him to be enchained, and led him with him throughout all Asia for a spectacle, and it is said that whilst he did dine and sup, he had him always tied under his table like a dog, and so fed him, and when he went to horse, he caused him to be brought, and to sit him down upon his knees and elbows, and thus used him instead of a block to go to his horse on. And thus he held him prisoner during his life in most miserable calamity.

All those which at any time have written of Tamerlano have

greatly commended him for the discipline and order which he
observed in the conducting of his armies, for they declare that
every occupation had his street appointed him in the camp, wherein he might use his exercise [practise his usual activity] even in   70
like order as it had been in a famous city, and there was in it
great abundance of all things for the commodity of man, which
proceeded of his severity and justice, for he would not leave
unpunished the least violence that was committed, not so much as
the taking away of one handful of grass against the owner's good
will, whereupon it followed that he had as great abundance of all
necessaries in his camp, as if it had been in great fairs and markets
brought thither voluntarily from the countries about him as he
passed. His severity also was such that it held his soldiers so within
the bands of modesty, that there was never seen nor heard any kind   80
of sedition among them, and they say further, which is greatly to be
marvelled at, that he never fought with man, but he had the victory
over him so that he never tasted of Fortune's bitterness. Thus when
he had spoiled and conquered all Asia, even to the flood Nilo,
and had taken by force Smyrna, Antiocha, Sebastia, Tripoli, and
Damasco, with a great number of other cities more, and put the
inhabitants of them to the sword, carried away their spoil, and
consumed them into ashes, leaving them desert and planed to the
ground, then entered he into Egypt, where he gave many overthrows to the Soldan's people, and constrained them to flee beyond   90
Pelusium, and would have followed them had not the scarceness of
victuals been, for it was not possible for him to provide carriage for
to transport sufficient of victual for the nourishing of so populous
an army as his was, through the sandy and desert countries.

His courage was such that he delighted chiefly in those enterprises which seemed most difficile [difficult] to be achieved in the
opinion of others, as it came to pass in the taking of Damasco,
where a number of the defendants conveyed themselves out of the
town into the castle where in their own opinion and in the common
opinion of others, they were safe, considering the natural force of   100
the seat, and also the artificial force of the place, notwithstanding
being desirous to avoid the misery and travail of a siege and to save
their lives, they gave out a token, signifying that they were desirous
to talk with him and upon condition to yield him the place, but he
refused utterly to hear of any appointment [agreement, capitul-
ation], although his captains would gladly have persuaded him
thereunto, but went and considered thoroughly the seat and force
of the place, and seeing the walls to be such that no ladder might
attain the height of them, he determined in any wise to have it by
force, whereupon he caused forthwith, near unto the same castle,   110

another castle to be builded, of far greater height than the first, from the height whereof he did so beat his enemies day and night without cease, that in the end with the loss of a great number of his people he took it of force.

After this, having intelligence that in the city of Capha, a garrison town of the Genoese, was great store of gold and silver in the hands of the merchants, he having already purposed to take that town by force, which standeth in the Cheronesso Taurico, not far from the Bosphoro and Strait Cimerico, and considering that the treasure (although he won the town) might easily be buried under the 120 ground and so saved, he determined to have both the town and the treasure by this mean: he called to him the skinners of his country, such as had most rich furs, as sables, ermines, genets [furs from civets], martens, and such like, and gave the commandment, for the more speedy dispatch of the matter, that they should not pass for [object to] the selling of them at a low price, to the end that the merchants might more greedily buy them. This matter being skilfully handled was soon dispatched, and immediately after that, he denounced [declared] wars against them, and forthwith pre-sented himself with his army to the town, and when he had 130 environed the town with his camp, he planted his batteries and continued them day and night without ceasing, in such sort that in short space he possessed the town, the merchants, the furs, and the money which was an inestimable [incalculable] treasure.

It is written also that this was his order in besieging of towns. The first day his own lodgings were white, and if in that day the inhabitants of the town did yield unto him, they received no hurt neither in body nor goods. The second day his lodgings were red, which signified to them of the town that if then they yielded, that he would put to death all the masters of the families [the heads of 140 households]. And the third day was his last change, which was into black pavilions and tents, and then refused he all appointments [terms of agreement], and when he had in this sort taken any city or town, he put all that were in it to the sword, not sparing any of whatsoever age or kind they were. When he had thus done, then would he command to sack the town, and when the goods were taken out of it, then would he cause fire to be set in the town and so consume it to ashes and leave it desert.

And there is a bruit [story] which continueth even to this day in those parts, that on a time a certain populous city defended 150 themselves till the third day, and then seeing a great space of the wall laid flat on the earth, and the enemy in battle ready to give the assault, they were discouraged, and thinking to pacify the wrath of this cruel, proud and victorious enemy by humbling themselves, sent forth all the women and children of the town in white clothing with olive branches in their hands, offering him the town, calling to him with loud voice for mercy, whom, when Tamerlano saw afar off coming toward him, he gave commandment to certain bands of his horsemen to charge upon them and to put them all to the sword; after this he took the city and sacked it, and then burned it.   160

It happened at that time, by means of traffic of merchandise, a certain merchant, a Genoese born, to be greatly in favour with Tamerlano, and being with him at that same present [moment], discoursing of sundry matters, asked him why he used so great cruelty towards those people which he overcame, but he turned to him with an exceedingly troublous [disturbed] countenance, with eyes flaming like fire, and said unto him, 'If thou dost think that I am a man, thou art much deceived, for I say to thee that I am the wrath of God sent to plague and punish the world, and I command thee that if thou wouldest not receive due punishment for thy   170 audacious and foolish demand, that thou get thee hence out of my sight, and that thou come less in my presence.' The poor merchant, being much feared [frightened] with the words of the tyrant, departed from him and was never seen after that by him.

They that have seen Tamerlano living have said that he resembled much, both in face and manners, Hannibal of Carthage, according to the opinion of divers ancient writers, and before all other offences he showed his severe justice against thefts, in punishing them sharply without any remission [forgiveness, pardon]. And it is thought that he did it to that end, that the fear of punishment should cause them   180 to refrain, to the end that he alone might rob and spoil [plunder] according to his own desire the whole world. And last of all, his delight was wholly set to govern, in so much that he employed himself continually, as in an exercise most virtuous, to molest and trouble other princes with wars, by the which he had subdued many kings, and utterly impoverished a great number of tyrants, made desert many countries, and converted into ashes an infinite number of cities and towns. And then last of all he returned into his country with his army, incredibly enriched with the spoil of those nations whom he had subdued, and also he used to take out of every town   190 that yielded unto him certain of the chief households with all their substances and riches, and to send them wholly into Parthia.

When he returned home he built a new city, very beautiful and of a great circuit [circumference], and placed therein all those households afore rehearsed, in so much that the new city being inhabited with these rich and noble men of divers nations, in short time increased so in wealth that it became the chief city of all the Orient.

And if it had happened that Tamerlano had had with him some man of excellent learning and wisdom, who might with his writings have celebrated the great enterprises that he did, there is no doubt 200 but that he might have been numbered among the chief and principal captains, either of the old world or else of this present age, but God giveth not all things to one man. And also it seemed that his great cruelty which he used toward those that he overcame did not deserve to have his fame celebrated by writing, ne [nor] yet that it might long remain to his posterity. When Tamerlano died, he left to succeed him in his empire, which he had thus gotten by the sword, two sons which after his death fell out and maintained civil wars between them, and were the cause that the old and ancient Parthic fame, clearly extinct and brought to oblivion, and afterward by 210 Tamerlano revived, could not continue nor increase . . . .

(fos. 3 recto–6 recto)

TEXT 5

Elogia virorum bellica virtute illustrium . . .

Paulus Jovius (Paolo Giovio)
(1551)

[The text is translated from the British Library copy
(shelfmark 613.l.2(2)).]

BOOK II

Tamerlane [was] the Emperor of the Scythians, who because
of his unheard-of ferocity and cruelty of spirit, along with his
fantastic strength, received the title of 'Terror of the Universe'
and 'Destroyer of the Orient'; he rose from the position of a
humble soldier through every rank of honour to enjoy an outstanding reputation for his military prowess, and subsequently climbed
to the highest command, being especially remarkable for the seal
set on his achievements by his applauding soldiers when with a
degree of flattery he was dubbed 'Temer Cuthlas', which utterance
in the Tartar tongue means 'Lucky Sword'.   10
    They say that he was of lowly origins, a native of the city of
Samarkand, which lies on the river Jaxartes adjoining the region
of Sogdiana. We know that this city was remarked on by Quintus
Curtius [Rufus] right from the time of Alexander the Great, and
that the Persians, men not lacking in historical knowledge with
whom we have spoken, bear witness that Samarkand was wonderfully enlarged and decorated by Tamerlane with riches and booty
which he pillaged from the whole of the Orient.
    Tamerlane was a grim-faced man, with sunken eyes that always
held a threatening look; his body was vast, with strong sinews and 20
such muscular upper arms that he would draw the bowstring of
the mighty Scythian bow to a point beyond his ear, a feat which
very few could surpass. Moreover, in sport he was accustomed to
pierce with the point of the arrow he released a copper bowl set
up as a target by his archers. But some authorities record that he
was lame in one leg, and therefore walked with a limping gait. As

132

for the rest, having been acclaimed as emperor with those sole particular powers associated with that title, he gathered together, out of countless tribes avid for booty and slaughter, such large contingents that, as they advanced, it was believed there would be   30
insufficient crops to feed his men or grassy pasture to meet the needs of his animals. . . .

(pp. 93–4)

[Giovio continues with his account of Tamburlaine's career, and recounts the history of the capture of Bajazeth.]

[The Turkish Sultan found himself] kept alive to serve for the amusement of another, and to sate his pride, except that the spirit of the ferocious Tamerlane was never sated with piling up insults upon this wretched man, so recently a monarch of great renown. For the defeated one was forced to make a mounting-block of himself by offering his back to the victor when he wished to ascend his horse. This may be made the more credible by an example: Sapor, the King of the Parthians [sic] who hauled the Roman Emperor Valerian off   40
to death, having shamefully loaded him with ignoble insults of the same kind. But fate by no means carried off Bajazet with the same force early on in the course of his tribulations, since in the first instance being carried around Asia in an iron cage for a long period, he presented a spectacle of his own ill-fortunes. But out of Tamerlane's inexorable and barbarous nature there emerged an exceptional instance of a remarkably even-handed severity. For when a Ligurian [a native of northern Italy], a renowned dealer in gemstones, and for that reason a friend of Tamerlane (who took great delight in jewels), conversing with him about Bajazet's   50
sufferings, gently admonished him by reminding him of the claims of humanity and compassion, telling him that he should recall that Bajazet was among the most notable of Mohammedan rulers both for his victories in battle and his wealth, then Tamerlane with frowning forehead and glaring eyes, rejecting his remarks, replied that he was imposing a fitting punishment not on a proud king who possessed nobility and power, but on a wicked and ungodly criminal, who had killed his own elder brother in a most cruel manner.

(pp. 95–6)

Of Tamerlane a Xerxes new, which did the East subdue,
And in all places that he came, the nations overthrew;
That fill'd the fields with Scythian troops, brought
         from those climates cold,
This was the feature and the shape which thou dost
         here behold.

133

At whose approach the strongest towns could small resistance
    make,
The earth itself under his feet seeming for fear to quake.
The mountains high, mating [vying with] the sky, and uncouth
    valleys low,
Unable were the force to bear, where he did come or go.
All Asia from Mount Caucasus unto the banks of Nile,
With valiant hand he vanquished and made his force to feel.   10
Euphrates, Tigris, and the swift Orontes gave him way,
With force, waste, and destruction great on what he
    list to prey.
And as in tempests great ofttimes, when all things go
    to wrack [ruin],
The fiery lightning flashing forth out of the clouds so black
Doth break down what it lights upon, and with a dreadful fall
Overthrows the temples with their towers and stately buildings
    all,
So that the earth dismay'd therewith doth lower down descend,
And fearful [terrified] wights wrapp'd up in woe are brought
    to their wits' end:
In like sort he with fire and sword seeking all to confound,
The strongest castles, towers and towns laid equal with the
    ground.   20
And like a whirlwind taking up great Bajazet away,
Coop'd up in cage, so carried him for his disport and play.
But whilst he rageth thus about and plotteth in his head
Such hard commands and heavy dooms as all the world should
    dread,
A little fever in three fits oppressed him with woe,
And closing up his vital spirits did lay his head full low,
So that for all the world of wealth and kingdoms he possess'd,
The small remainder of himself in simple grave doth rest.

                        (pp. 96–7)

[Translated in Richard Knolles, *The General History of the Turks*, 1603.]

TEXT 6

The Ecclesiastical History, containing the Acts and Monuments of things passed . . .

John Foxe
(Second edition 1570)

[The text is taken from the Bodleian Library copy
(shelfmark Mason F142).]

FROM *THE HISTORY AND TYRANNY OF THE TURKS*

The power of the Turks began to increase in Europe what time
Bajazetes, the first of that name, after the death of his father
entered the possession of the Turks' kingdom. This Bajazetes had
two brethren, Solimanus and Sauces; which Sauces had his eyes
put out by his father for striving for the kingdom. Solimanus was
slain of his brother. Thus Bajazetes, beginning his kingdom with
the murder of his brother, reduced [restored] his imperial seat
from Prusia, a city of Bithynia, unto Adrianople, intending with
himself to subdue both Asia and Europe to his own power. First he
set upon the Serbians and Bulgarians. . . . All Thracia, moreover,   10
he brought likewise under his yoke, only Constantinople and Pera
excepted. That done, he invaded the residue of Graecia, prevailing
against the countries of Thessalia, Macedonia, Phocides and Attica,
spoiling [plundering] and burning as he passed, without any
resistance; and so returning with innumerable spoil of the Christians unto Adrianople, laid siege to Constantinople the space of
eight years, and had expugned [overwhelmed] the same, but that
Paleologus, being brought to extremity, was driven to crave aid
of the Frenchmen and of Sigismund the Emperor. Who, being
accompanied with a sufficient power of Frenchmen and Germans,   20
came down to Hungaria, and toward Serbia, against the Turk.
Bajazetes, hearing of their coming, raised his siege from Constantinople, and with sixty thousand horsemen came to Nicopolis,
where he, encountering with them, overthrew all the Christian
army, took John the captain of the French power prisoner;

135

Sigismundus, which before in the Council of Constance had burned John Huss and Jerome of Prague, hardly escaped by flying. Bajazetes, after the victory got, carried away Duke John, with five other in bands, into Prusia [Bursa], where before his face he caused all the other Christian prisoners to be cut in pieces. . . .   30

Bajazetes, the cruel tyrant, after this victory won and tyranny showed upon the Christians, returned again to his siege of Constantinople, fully bending himself to conquer and subdue the same; which thing no doubt he had accomplished, but that the providence of God had found such a means that Tamerlanes King of Parthia, with an hundred thousand horsemen and swarms of footmen, like a violent flood overrunning Asia and pressing upon Syria and Sebastia, had taken Orthobules, the son of Bajazetes, prisoner, and afterward slew him, exercising the like cruelty upon his prisoners as Bajazetes had done before upon the Christians, insomuch that he   40
spared neither sex nor age of the Turkish multitude. Of whom he caused twelve thousand at one time to be overridden and trodden down under his horses' feet. By reason whereof, Bajazetes the tyrant was enforced to raise his siege from Constantinople and to return his power into Asia, where he, near the hill called Stella, pitched his tents there to encounter with Tamerlanes.

The fight between these two was long and great on both sides, which was in the year of our Lord 1397 [actually 1402], and the second year after the slaughter of our Christians at Nicopolis in Pannonia, but the victory of this battle fell to Tamerlanes at length.   50
In the which battle, as Munsterus writeth, were slain [two hundred] thousand Turks. Among whom Bajazetes the tyrant, having his horse slain under him, was taken prisoner; and to make a spectacle of his wretched fortune, was bound in golden fetters, and so being enclosed in an iron grate [cage] (whom before all Graecia could not hold), was led about and showed through all Asia, to be scorned and laughed at; and moreover, was used instead of a footstool to Tamerlanes, or a block, as often as he mounted upon his horse. Some add also that he was made like a dog to feed under Tamerlanes' table. The tyranny of which Bajazetes [used] against the   60
Christians, as it was not much unlike to the cruelty of Valerianus the Roman Emperor. . . so neither was the example of his punishment much discrepant; for as Sapores King of the Persians did then with Valerianus in time of the eighth persecution of the primitive church, so likewise was Bajazetes this persecutor worthily handled by Tamerlanes King of the Parthians, as in manner above said.

Tamerlanes, after this conquest, passed with his army into Mesopotamia, to Egypt, and all Syria, where he, victoriously subduing the cities and munitions [fortifications] of the Turks, at length also

conquered Damascus. In his sieges his manner was the first day to 70
go all in white attire, the second day in red, the third day in black:
signifying thereby mercy the first day to them that yielded; the
second day the sword; the third day fire and ashes. At last, after
great victories and spoils gotten of the Turks, he returned into his
country again, and there died anno. 1402 [actually 1405].

Seb[astianus] Munsterus, writing of this Tamerlanes, recordeth
that he had in his army [one million two hundred thousand] men,
and that he overcame the Parthians, Scythians, Hiberians [Georg-
ians], Albans, Persians, Medes, and conquered all Mesopotamia,
and after he had also subdued Armenia, passing over the river 80
Euphrates with six hundred thousand footmen, and four hundred
thousand horsemen, he invaded all Asia Minor, conquering and
subduing from the flood Tanais unto Nilus in Egypt, and was called
terror orbis, the terror of the world. He left behind him two sons,
who, falling in discord for their possessions, lost all again that
their father got.

In the meantime Bajazetes in the second year of his captivity
died, leaving behind him divers sons: Jesus or Josua the eldest;
Mulsumanes; Moses; Celebinus or Calepinus; Jesus the younger;
Mustaphas; and Hali. Of whom first Jesus the eldest was overcome 90
and slain by Mulsumanes; which Mulsumanes afterward was delivered to Moses his brother, and by him was slain likewise. Which
Moses had also the like end by his brother Calepinus, having his
neck broken with a bowstring, which was then the usual manner
among the Turks in killing their brethren. The same Calepinus,
sparing only the life of Mustaphas his other brother, condemned
him to perpetual prison. Jesus the younger was baptized, and
shortly after departed [died] at Constantinople. In these such
discords and divisions among the Turks, what occasions [oppor-
tunities] were given to the Christians to have recovered again of 100
the Turks that they had lost, if they had not been either negligent,
or in their own private wars otherwise occupied with themselves!

Calepinus or Celebinus was the son of Bajazetes, and of seven
brethren the eldest; who, being all taken captives of the Parthians,
he only [alone] escaped and obtained his father's kingdom. This
Calepinus, encouraged by the sloth and negligence of the princes
of Europe, and by the discord of the Grecians amongst themselves
and other nations near about them, long troubled and vexed
the Bulgarians, Serbians, and Macedonians, even to the time of
Sigismundus. Which Sigismundus, seeing now Bajazetes to be 110
overcome and taken of Tamerlane, and the power of the Turks
weakened in Europe, and having such occasion offered him, as it
were from heaven, to destroy and utterly to root out, not only out

of Asia but also all Europe, that barbarous nation and cruel
enemies to the name and religion of Christ; and also to revenge
the great slaughter and discomfiture of his army fighting before
with Bajazetes at Nicopolis, a city in Mycea, with great power made
war against Calepinus at Columbatium, a town in Serbia. . . but
as unluckily and with as little success as he did before against
Bajazetes his father. For in that battle were slain of the Christians 120
to the number of twenty thousand, and the rest utterly discomfited,
the king himself escaping so hardly [with such difficulty] that he
entered not again into his kingdom for the space of eighteen
months after. Some write that this was done under Bajazetes,
other some refer this battle to Amurathes [i.e. Amurath III], but
howsoever it was, most pernicious was it to the Christians. . . .

(I. 875–6)

TEXT 7

Beautiful Blossoms, gathered by John Bishop, from the best trees of all kinds . . .

(1577)

[The text is taken from the British Library copy
(shelfmark C.117.b.55).]

CHAPTER 46

Of Tamburlaine the Tartar

Among these rogue kings will I enrol Tamerlane the Tartar.

This man, whom Thevet calls Tamirrhan and Tamerlanque, Sigismundus Liber Themirassacke, and Chalco[co]ndylas Temer, was son unto a poor man called Sangalis, a Massaget, says Chalcondylas, but a Parthian affirms Thevet, born at Samarkand. At the first he was a herdman of a town for horses, but afterward conspiring together with other herdmen, he became a strong [flagrant] thief, stealing horses and other cattle [livestock]. But climbing one night a wall to enter into a stable, and being espied of the goodman of the house, he was forced to leap down from the wall, and brake   10
his leg. Campofulgoso [Baptista Fulgosius] says that he brake his thigh, whereof he had his name; for in his country['s] language, 'Temer' is a thigh and 'Lang' is lame or maimed, the which two words being put together make 'Temerlang', but the Latins, keeping the propriety of their own tongue, corruptly call him Tamerlan.

But Sigismundus Liber says that one whose sheep he was about to steal brake his leg with a great stone, and because he bound the bones together with a hoop of iron, he was called Themerassacke, or 'iron and halting': for 'Themer' in the Tartarian tongue is 'iron' and 'assacke' 'halting'. But whether he had his name of the one   20
thing or the other, herein they do both agree that he could not when he came to be Lord of all the Orient and a terror unto the whole world step forth one foot but he felt his infirmity, nor record

139

his own name, but that he was put in mind of his infortunity [misfortune]. But after this mishap, he waxing wiser fortified a place where he and his might have safe refuge when that they were pursued.

At length he being marvellously enriched by robbing of all men that travelled within his walk ['beat', 'patch'], and also by stealing of all kind of cattle, he gathered together a fair band of soldiers, and associating himself with two captains called Chardanes and Myrxes, did set upon a power of enemies which spoiled the country, and gave them a great overthrow, the like whereunto he also oftentimes did afterward, whereby he became so famous that the King of the Massagetes made him Captain-general over his armies, the which office he administered both valiantly and fortunately, and namely [especially] a little before the king's death, having driven his enemies into the cities of Babylon and Samarkand, and the king dying, he married the queen and took Samarkand or also Babylon; yea, and then with continued course, conquered Iberia, Albania, Persia, Media, both Armenias, Mesopotamia, Syria, Damascus, Egypt even unto Nilus, and Capha upon the coast of the Euxine Sea, Cilicia, Asia the Less, where he discomfited [routed] in battle Bajazet the Turk with ten hundred thousand Turks, neither was his own ordinary army anything inferior in number.

But while he was busied in those parts about taking of Turkish towns, heavy news was brought him, that one of his confederates, a King of India called the King of Tzachataa, passing over the River Araxis, had subdued a great part of the country thereabouts, which were subject unto Tamerlane, and among all other manifold detriments, had miserably defaced the city of Cheria, and had taken Tamerlane his treasure, and returned home; but yet so that he still threatened that he would be his confederate no longer.

This sorrowful message did put Tamerlane in great fear lest that the King of India would return again and sweep him out of all his dominions at home, while he was busied abroad with foreign wars. And herewithal the cursed condition also of human affairs and man's tickle [insecure] state, the which doth not suffer any man long to enjoy here on earth the blissful blast of friendly Fortune, appalled his heart; wherefore he hasted homeward, and whereas before he injuried all men, now did he not only put up [suffer] cowardly the Indian wrong, but also made great suit to recover his ancient friendship.

But after that Tamerlane had thus recovered his countries lost, and quieted them, and built that renowned city of the world Samarkand in the village where he was born, which he beautified and enriched with the spoils of the whole Orient, and had throughly [completely] peopled it, he prepared a voyage against the Turks and Christians, from the going forward wherewith he was stayed both by a mighty earthquake, and also two celestial signs and prodigies; the one of a man appearing in the air, holding in his hands a lance; and the other of a blazing star, terrible for his greatness, the which stood directly over the city by the space of fifteen days.

He, consulting with the soothsayers and astrologians about these wonders, was told by them and namely by one Bene-jaacam, a man of greatest authority and credit among them, that they were tokens, either of his own death shortly after to ensue, or else of the utter ruin and bringing to naught of his empire.

But much more was he in short time after amazed by a vision that he had one night, the which was the cause of his fatal sickness, and in the end of his death. For he dreamed one night that Bajazeth, the Turk whom he had made to die miserably in an iron cage, came unto him (or else the Devil in his likeness) with a countenance stern and terrible to behold, and said unto him: 'Now it shall not be long, villain, but that thou shalt worthily be paid for thy manifold outrages, and I too shall be revenged for the wearisome wrong that thou diddest to me, making me to die like unto a beast in mine own dung.'

And when he had thus said, Tamerlane thought that Bajazeth did beat him very grievously and trod and trampled upon him with his feet, sore bruising his belly and bowels, in so much that the next morning, when he thought to have risen, he remained still attainted [affected] with the apprehension conceived in his sleep, the which did near quite bereave him of his wits, and so raving always upon Bajazeth died, leaving his large empire unto his two sons begotten of divers venters [different wombs], who, consuming themselves with civil wars one upon another, left an easy way for all those princes and countries whom their father had spoiled [plundered] and conquered, to recover all that which they had before lost.

(fos. 146 verso–148 verso)

TEXT 8

De origine et rebus gestis Turcorum . . .

Laonicus Chalcocondylas

translated by Conrad Clauserus
(1556)

[The Latin text is translated from the British Library copy
(shelfmark C.80.f.8).]

LIBER SECUNDUS

[Bajazeth's oppressive policies in Asia compel a number of Muslim
princes to travel in disguise to Tamburlaine's court at Samarkand where
they hope for support in seeking revenge for the wrongs done them.
Tamburlaine dispatches an ambassador to the Ottoman monarch,
requesting more lenient treatment for the Asian rulers. To sweeten his
request, he presents gifts, including costly garments, to Bajazet who
loftily advises him not to interfere in matters not his concern, and
rejects the proferred clothing as beneath contempt.]

. . . When this was reported to King Timur at Samarkand, it is said
that he was greatly incensed at the insult arising from the rejection
of his gift of raiment. He immediately sent a herald with orders that
Bajazet should not hesitate to restore their power to the Asian
leaders as soon as possible, for so he had decreed. If he refused to
obey, Timur would regard him as an enemy: he had pronounced
judgement on that case, and gave it as his opinion that the
Turcoman leaders had suffered injury at Bajazet's hands; therefore
for as long as he lived he would not neglect the rights of men
wandering about Asia deprived of their kingdoms.   10

   Bajazet sent back the messenger with an answer in these terms: 'If
he will not come against us with an army, I urge him to take back
again, once and for all, his wife from whom he has separated on
three occasions.' (Among the Turks it amounts to a humiliating
insult to take back your wife three times, unless you are forced to do
so. For the Turks have a law which decrees that anyone who
repudiates his wife must declare that he will no longer admit her

142

into his household. Hence it is scarcely felt proper for a husband to resume the same marriage after he has declared before three arbitrators [?] that he has withdrawn from it and refused to resume the relationship. The only exception is if someone makes a deposition on three occasions before an arbitrator so that a husband is forced through his own adultery with another to cohabit once more with a polluted woman.)

Having received these instructions, the messenger hastened on his journey to King Timur. They say that Timur's wife was very superstitious with regard to important matters, and that she would not allow Timur to take the offensive against Bajazet, a praiseworthy man who had fought with great glory against the Christian faith in defence of the religion of Mohammed. Indeed she advised the king to leave so great a man in peace and not to make trouble for him, since he had not deserved to suffer any harm at the hands of those who supported the same religion.

As soon as the messenger explained Bajazet's demands to Timur, the latter summoned his wife and bade the messenger recount those demands in her hearing. When the man had obeyed this instruction and made Bajazet's orders clear, they say that Timur asked his wife whether she still thought it right to treat Bajazet with forbearance, even though he provoked attack through his insulting behaviour. Was it justifiable to allow him to inflict such harm with impunity? Indeed it was clear that Timur was in favour of making war on Bajazet, even though his wife was still inclined to adhere to her former opinion. Thus he argued that he was legally bound to his wife, and that as a result he was obliged to avenge the injuries inflicted upon her, no matter what he might have to endure for all that.

At that point his wife is said to have answered as follows: 'It is true, O King, that this man has been in the grip of such a disease for so long that he no longer enjoys the benefits of sanity; others know that as well I do, who have just heard his response. Undoubtedly, if you were to wreak just vengeance on Bajazet, you would be regarded as acting prudently, and in that way show him what kind of a man you are, and to what kind of man he sends so vile a message. However, I want to make this fact perfectly clear to you: I should not consider it right to make war on this man who battles on behalf of our god against the Greeks [i.e. the Christians of Constantinople] and against other nations of Epirus. But on the other hand, if he has foolishly held me up to ridicule, I do not take the view that it would be proper for us to suffer those insults to go unavenged. Therefore declare war on that man. . . .'

(p. 3)

143

TEXT 9

Rerum Ungaricarum decades quattuor Cum dimidia . . .

Antonius Bonfinius
(1543)
taken from Richard Knolles, *The General History of the Turks* . . . (1603)

[The text is found in the third edition (1621);
British Library shelfmark 9135.h.5.]

[Bonfinius describes how the Christian powers led by the Hungarian general Janós Hunyady, having won several victories over the Turks, and the Albanians under George Castriotis or Scanderbeg having rebelled against Ottoman rule, force the Turkish Sultan Amurath (or Murad) II to seek for terms.]

Amurath, having received two so great overthrows, first from Huniades and the Hungarians and now from Scanderbeg, and seeing himself elsewhere beset with so many mischiefs as that he could not tell which way to turn himself, tormented with despair and desire of revenge (whereof he saw small possibility), fell into such a melancholy passion that, overcome with the dark conceits [fancies, imaginings] thereof, he was about to have become the bloody executioner of himself, had not Cali Bassa [Pasha] by his grave advice comforted up his dying spirits; by whose persuasion, contrary to his haughty nature, he yielded by his ambassadors   10
sent for the same purpose, to desire peace of Vladislaus King of Hungary, using the exiled Despot of Serbia, his father-in-law, then present with the king, as a mean [intermediary] therein. Who at the first gave small credit unto the ambassadors or unto such things as they told him, until that at length better persuaded of the true meaning of the Turk, he so wrought the matter both with the king and the rest of the nobility, and especially with Huniades, that . . . a peace for ten years was forthwith on both parts concluded, and the same by solemn oath confirmed, King Vladislaus taking his oath

144

upon the Holy Evangelists, and Amurath (by his ambassadors) by   20
their Turkish Alcoran [the Koran]. This was the most honourable
peace that ever Christian Prince had before that time made with
any of the Turkish kings, and most profitable also, had it been with
like sincerity kept as it was with solemnity confirmed . . . .

Old Amurath, thoroughly wearied with continual wars and other
troubles incident unto restless rooms [stressful positions], resolved
now to retire himself to a more private and quiet kind of life, and
therefore sent for his son Mahomet, being then but fifteen years
old, to whom he voluntarily resigned his kingdom, appointing Cali
Bassa his tutor, with one Chosroe, a learned doctor of their law, to   30
be his trusty counsellors and chief directors. And so taking with
him Hamze-Beg, one of his noblemen in whom he took greatest
pleasure, departed to Magnesia and there, as a man weary of the
world, gave himself to a solitary and monastical kind of life, in the
company of certain religious Turkish monks, as they accounted of
them [reckoned them to be].

Many great kings and princes, as well Mahomedans as Christians,
glad before of the Hungarian victory, were now no less sorry to hear
of the late concluded peace betwixt King Vladislaus and the old
Sultan Amurath, as being of opinion that the prosecution of what   40
was so happily begun would have been the utter ruin and destruction of the Turkish kingdom. Wherefore they sought by all possible
means to induce the young king Vladislaus to break the league he
had so lately and so solemnly made with the Turk; especially John
Palaeologus the Emperor of Constantinople did by letters im-
portune the king to remember the confederation he had made
with the other Christian princes for the maintenance of the wars
against the common enemy of Christianity, which princes were now
pressed [prepared] and ready (as he said) to assist him with their
promised aid; adding moreover that, whereas Amurath had divers   50
times sought to join with him in amity and friendship, he had
utterly rejected that offer of peace, preferring the universal profit
(like to ensue to all Christendom by that religious war) before his
own proper security and profit, being for his part in readiness to
join his forces with the king's, if he would presently [immediately]
enter into arms, which he could never do in better time than now
whilst Amurath, terrified with his late overthrow and still beset with
doubtful [dubiously poised] war, had drawn his greatest forces out
of Europe into Asia, in such disordered haste, as that it should seem
he rather fled for fear of his enemies in Europe than marched to   60
encounter his enemies in Asia, and now being weary of all, had
betaken himself unto a private kind of life. To conclude, he
requested the king not to leave him and the other Christian

145

princes of small power as a prey unto the Turk, who would assuredly with all hostility invade them so soon as he thought himself safe from the danger of the Hungarians.

At the same time also, and upon the departure of the Turks' ambassadors for the performance of such things as they had promised, letters came from Francis the Cardinal of Florence, Captain-General of the Christian fleet, declaring how that Amurath having left almost none in Europe, was with all the power he could make gone over into Asia against the Caramanian King, leaving a most fair occasion [opportunity] for the Christians easily to recover whatsoever they had before lost in Europe, and that he was in good time come with his fleet unto the straits of Hellespontus, according unto promise, and there lay ready to embar the Turks' passage back again out of Asia.

Both these letters being read in the Council so much moved the king with all the rest of the nobility of Hungary there present, as that they were never more sorry or ashamed for anything they had done in their lives than for the league so lately with Amurath concluded: for why, they saw that all the plot they had laid for their immortal glory was by now by this hasty peace that they had made with the Turk without the good liking or knowledge of their confederates [allies] brought to nought; and that they had thereby most shamefully deceived the general expectation that the Christian commonweal had conceived of them; and that they, of so long time called the protectors of the Christian faith, the defenders of true religion, the revengers of Christ His name, and deliverers of the faithful nations, should now be accounted the breakers of the Christian league, men forgetful of their confederation both with the Latins and the Greeks, contemners [scorners] of immortality, and lovers of their own profit only.

In this doubtfulness of minds whilst they stood yet thus wavering, Julian the Cardinal and Legate, always an enemy unto the peace, and by reason of his place a man in greatest authority next unto the king, took occasion to dissuade the same as followeth . . . .

'. . .Consider, I pray you, into what miseries his hasty resolution hath cast us. We have entered into league with the Turk, an infidel, to violate our faith with the Christians and to break the holy league before made with the great Bishop [the Pope] and the other Christian princes our confederates. And that for what, for what profit, I say? Forsooth, so that we might again recover Serbia, long before destroyed. Verily a small and woeful profit, which may again in short time be cut off, and depriveth us of others far greater and of much longer continuance. For what can be more fond or inconsiderate than in our consultations to have regard to our private profit only and not the public, without respect of religion, honesty or conscience? It is not demanded of you at this present, right honourable, what you owe unto the perjured Turk, but you   110 are by me, Julian the great Bishop's and the confederate princes' legate and agent, before the tribunal seat of your own consciences accused of breach of faith, breach of league, and breach of promise; and thereof even by your own judgement, rather than by the judgement of God or other men, I will condemn you . . . .'

[Julian reminds the Hungarians of their solemn league with the Pope and the other Christian opponents of Islam, accusing them of betraying their erstwhile allies in a most inconsistent manner; what are they to tell the Emperor of Constantinople, the Pope, the Venetians, the Genoans, the Burgundians now?]

'Who is so partial an esteemer of men's actions that would not easily judge that in [a] case where faith were given to both, it were rather to be kept with a Christian than with a Turk; with a believer than an infidel? Against a perfidious enemy it is lawful (as they say) for a man to use all cunning, force and deceit, deluding craft with   120 craft and fraud with fraud. By craft the Turk first passed over into Europe; by little and little he crept into that kingdom; he never kept faith with any; he grew to this height rather by cunning than by strength: and are you become so blind as to think it better to keep your promise with the Turk, devoid of all faith and humanity, rather than with the faithful Christians, and especially the most holy Bishop? All great things are done by device and policy. . . . It is sometime lawful for the commonweal's sake, neither to keep our faith with them that be themselves faithless. Lawful it is to break unlawful oaths, and especially such as are thought to be against   130 right, reason and equity . . . . Wherefore a just and lawful oath is in the judgement of all men to be religiously kept, but such an oath as tendeth not only unto private but public destruction, that ought to be vain and frustrate . . . .

. . . make no conscience of the league you have made with the infidel, but think it a great impiety and wickedness to violate the holy league made with the great Bishop and the other Christian princes: thinking that if you should do otherwise, God (which He of His mercy forbid) would become of that your falsified faith a most severe and sharp revenger, and that you can do nothing more   140 acceptable unto our Saviour Christ, or more glorious to yourselves, than to deliver the oppressed Christian countries from the cruel slavery and bondage of the Turk. . . .'

[After sundry diplomatic exchanges Vladislaus sets forth to give battle

to the Turkish armies, crossing the Danube, and invading those territories held by Ottoman forces. Amurath is persuaded out of retirement,
and finding the fleet blocking his passage over the Hellespont, journeys
by way of the straits of Bosporus, and eventually confronts the combined
armies at Varna on the West coast of the Black Sea. Although surprised
by the Turks' sudden presence, the Hungarian King resolves to engage
his troops.]

Vladislaus, understanding by his espials [spies] that Amurath the
night before encamped within four miles, was now putting his army
in order of battle; committed the ordering of all his forces unto the
valiant captain Huniades, who with great care and industry disposed
the same, guarding the one side of the battle with a fen or marish
[marsh], and the other side with carriages, and the rearward of his
army with a steep hill, therein politicly [shrewdly] providing that   150
the Christian army, being far less than the Turks in number, could
not be compassed about with the multitude of their enemies,
neither anyway charged but afront [frontally]. The Turks' army,
approaching, began to skirmish with the Christians, which manner
of fight was long time with great courage maintained, and that
with divers [variable] fortune, sometime one party prevailing, and
sometime the other; but with such slaughter on both sides that the
ground was covered and stained with the dead bodies and blood of
the slain. At length the battle being more closely joined, the victory
began to incline to the Christians, for Huniades had most valiantly   160
with his Transylvanian and Wallachian horsemen put to flight both
the wings of the Turkish army and made great slaughter wheresoever he came. Insomuch that Amurath, dismayed with the flight
of his soldiers, was about to have fled himself out of the main battle,
had he not been stayed by a common soldier, who laying hands
upon the reins of his bridle stayed him by force, and sharply
reproved him of cowardice. The captains, and prelates about the
king (whom it had better beseemed to have been at devout prayers
in their oratories than in arms at that bloody battle), encouraged by
the prosperous success of Huniades and desirous to be partakers of   170
that victory, foolishly left their safe stations, where they were
appointed by him to stand fast, and disorderly pursued the chase,
leaving that side of the battle where they stood open unto the
Turks, but they were not gone far before they were hardly [stal-
wartly] encountered by a great part of the Turks' army, for such
purpose placed in a valley fast by . . . .
  The Cardinal [i.e. Julian], with some other of the expert captains
retiring toward their former standings, were hardly assailed by the
Turks, who by the coming in of the king and Huniades, were with

great slaughter forced to retire and even ready to fly. Amurath, 180
seeing the great slaughter of his men and all brought into extreme
danger, beholding the picture of the Crucifix in the displayed
ensigns of the voluntary [i.e. non-conscripted] Christians, plucked
the writing out of his bosom wherein the late league was comprised,
and holding it up in his hand with his eyes cast up to heaven, said:

'Behold, thou crucified Christ, this is the league thy Christians
in thy name made with me, which they have without cause violated!
Now, if thou be a God, as they say thou art and as we dream,
revenge the wrong now done unto thy name and me, and show thy
power upon thy perjurious people who in their deeds deny thee, 190
their God!'

... A great while the victory stood doubtful insomuch that at
length the Turks began to shrink back in that part of the battle
where the king and Huniades fought. But in the left side they
prevailed so upon the Christians that they were even ready to have
fled. Which when Huniades, having a vigilant eye unto every part of
the army, perceived, he with speed made thither, and there again
with his presence restored the battle almost before lost. Which
done, he returned again towards the king, who in the meantime
had most valiantly repulsed a great number of the Turks, and now 200
was come unto the Janissaries, Amurath his last hope.

There was to be seen a thousand manners of death, whilst both
the armies fought more like wild beasts in their rage and fury than
wary and politic [astute] soldiers. In this confused medley the young
King Vladislaus with greater courage than care of himself brake into
the battle [-line] of the Janissaries; at which time Amurath himself
was by a valiant Frenchman, a Knight of the Roads [i.e. a Knight
Hospitaller of Rhodes?], first wounded with a pike and after
assailed with his sword, and had there ended his days but that he
was speedily rescued by his guard, by whom this worthy knight after 210
great proof of his valour was there slain in the midst of his enemies.
Vladislaus, being got in also amongst them, valiantly performed all
the parts of a worthy soldier until such time as his horse being slain
under him, he was forthwith oppressed with the multitude of his
enemies and slain. His head being struck off by Ferizes, one of
the old Janissaries, was by him presented unto Amurath who
commanded it presently [immediately] to be put upon the point of
a lance, and proclamation to be made that it was the head of
the Christian King, which was afterwards so carried through the
principal cities of Macedonia and Graecia as a trophy of the Turks' 220
victory . . . .

Julian the Cardinal, flying out of the battle, was found by that
worthy man Gregory Sanose lying in the desert [desolate] forest by

149

the wayside, mortally wounded and half stripped; by whom he was in few words sharply reproved as the wicked author of that perfidious war, and there left giving up the ghost. Many of the Christians which fled out of that battle fell into the enemies' hands and so were slain, but greater was the number of them which were drowned in the fens or that by hunger and cold perished in the woods, or else after long and miserable travail, finding no passage 230 over Danubius, fell at length into the Turkish slavery . . . This bloody battle was fought near unto Varna (in ancient time called Dionisiopolis, a place fatal unto many great warriors and therefore of them even yet abhorred) the tenth day of November in the year of our Lord Christ 1444.

(pp. 288–99)

TEXT 10

Chronicorum Turcicorum . . .

Philippus Lonicerus
(1578)

[The text is taken from the British Library copy (shelfmark 434.i.17).]

CHAPTER XXIII

Concerning the punishments of damned souls

[Marginal note: The punishments for wicked souls ordained by Mahomet]

As the Koran has it, as many as are damned in accordance with divine justice because of the crimes they have committed, are distinguished by their own names which are inscribed on the foreheads of each one of them. Burdens consisting of their sins are placed upon the shoulders of each; loaded with the burden of their own sins they proceed into Tartarus through a pass between two mountains. A horrible serpent guards the entrance to Hell.

They will be compelled to cross a bridge which is called 'Sera cuplissi', that is, 'the Bridge of Justice' and which is made of very sharp iron. On one side of that bridge those who have been completely sunk in wickedness will forthwith be cast headlong into the eternal torments of Hell, where having been consumed by fire they will then be reborn to suffer new torments which will endure forever. But on the other side those who have not been altogether hardened in wickedness will fall into the fire of Purgatory from which they will be delivered, either quickly or slowly, according to the nature of their sins, and then they will be admitted to the joys of Paradise.

Moreover, it is believed that there is a tree planted as it were in the middle of Hell, and flourishing in spite of the fire: it is called 'Zoacum agacci', that is, the Tree of Bitterness. Every single one of its fruits resembles the heads of devils. The damned feed on the bitter fruit of that tree, hoping to receive therefrom some cooling refreshment. But not only do they not receive coolness from that

151

source, but they suffer greater and greater torture from the bitter and poisonous taste, so that they are affected by the more grievous tortures of death. Moreover, the devils themselves, fettering them in fiery chains, keep continually rolling them about, thus ensuring that not merely one form of punishment is meted out. . . .

(p. 122)

TEXT 11

The Practice of Fortification . . .

Paul Ive
(1589)

[The text is taken from the copy reproduced in facsimile in
The English Experience series (1962).]

THE FIRST CHAPTER

[The necessary placing of a fort]

The reason that moved men first to enclose their cities and other
habitations with walls was to be assured [secure] from enemies, and
that a small number might defend themselves from the violence
and oppressions of the great. Wherein their first practice extended
no farther than the preservation of private estates, until such time
as it was considered that not only particular places, but also the
general estate of a kingdom, province or country, might be defended by placing of walled towns, castles and fortresses, upon the
edge and borders of the same, of such sufficient strength and
greatness, as that in time of peace, they might be kept with a few   10
men, and upon a surmise [suspicion] of war, receive a greater
number by whom the enemy borderer should not only be annoyed
[molested] in his country, and hindered to enter upon the lands
of his neighbours so frontiered with any small power upon the
sudden, but bringing any great army, be constrained not to pass the
fort without subduing it, for avoiding the great mischief [harm] he
might receive of so noisome [harmful] an enemy left behind him,
which to invade, would ask great charge, time, travail, besides the
danger that might happen. In placing of which fortresses, two
things are chiefly to be considered of: the necessity and the   20
situation. For as a fort not placed where it were needful, might
scantly be accounted for frontier, so having no benefit of the place
it standeth in, it might hardly be reckoned for fortress, so that one
must help the other to the best effect that may be.

A fort therefore that shall serve for a frontier must be set near the
walled towns, castles and frontiers of the enemy borderer, or near

other places where an enemy may make any sudden assembly of people in his country, having the way from thence commodious to enter upon the lands of his neighbours, and the retreat good, and upon the sea-coasts, at havens and roads, where a fleet of ships may be harboured, and have commodious landing. In which places, because the grounds may be of diverse natures for this purpose, I will show the manner of fortifying in all sorts of grounds, and the commodities and discommodities that a fort may have of the place where it standeth in.

THE SECOND CHAPTER

[The manner of fortifying in all sorts of grounds, and the commodities and discommodities a fort may have of its situation.]

Whoso shall fortify in plain [level] ground, may make the fort he pretendeth [designs] of what form or figure he will, and therefore he may with less compass of wall enclose a more superficies [greater surface-area] of ground, than where that scope may not be had. Also it may be the perfecter, because the angles that do happen in it may be made the flatter or sharper. Moreover, the ground in plains is good to make ramparts of, and easy for carriage, but where water wanteth, the building is costly and chargeable, for that a fort situated in a dry plain must have deep ditches, high walls, great bulwarks, large ramparts, and cavalieros [gun platforms]. Besides, it must be great to lodge five or six thousand men, and have great place in it for them to fight ranked in battle. It must also have countermines [intercepting excavations], privy ditches, secret issuings out to defend the ditch, casemates [niches] in the ditch, covered ways round about it, and an argine [earthwork] or bank to impeach [hinder] the approach; will require great garrison, much artillery, powder, victuals, and other things necessary for the keeping and maintaining of it; is subject to mines and to cavalieros; may be surprised, scaled, battered, and assaulted on every side, and may be kept besieged with forts, men, horse, and artillery.

Where water may be found, the fort may be the less, and needeth not the ditches so deep as in dry ground, for it will be free from surprise, scale [scaling] and mining, and being battered, the assault will be troublesome, for that one man standing upon firm ground, may resist five upon a bridge, boat, float [raft], or suchlike. Moreover, the fort standing near unto any river, may receive great commodities of [by means of] it for the bringing of things necessary unto it, both for making and maintaining of it, and it may have

154

the river turned into the ditch, to scour the ditch of anything that
may be cast into it, and the same may also be kept up with sluices   30
within the fort to drown the ground about it, and in those low
places which abound with water, an enemy can hardly cover himself
from the fort.

Betwixt these two situations, there are diverse opinions held,
some commending dry ditches, alleging them that by a dry ditch a
fort may receive relief, the ruin that a battery maketh may be taken
away, and anything that an enemy may cast into the ditch to fill it
may be burnt, and by the sallies that may be made out of a dry ditch,
an enemy may be charged in his trenches on every part, which may
serve the turn for a while. But these consider not, the counterscarp   40
[outer slope of the ditch] being won, the benefit and use of the
ditch will be taken away by the artillery and harquebusery [small-
arms' fire] of the enemy, nor that of those three means wherewith
a wall may be breached – to wit, the cannon, mine, and men's hands
– water hindereth the putting in practice of two of them. The
discommodities that proceed of water are these: in hot countries
standing water engendereth infective airs, and in cold countries, it
freezeth [so] that men, horse and artillery may pass over. . . .

[Ive goes on to consider next the advantages and disadvantages of
siting forts among hills and mountains, on a lake or a river, and finally
in the sea.]

A fort situated in the sea is not only free from battery and assault,
because the battery that may be made at sea is feeble, weak and   50
uncertain, by reason of the sea's continual motion, but also is free
from besieging, not only for that those enemies are few that can put
any great army to sea, but also because the wind and sea's alteration
is such that an assiege [siege] at sea cannot be continued. Moreover, it may be maintained with merchant trade, and with its
shipping occupy [seize] things appertaining to other men. But a
fort that standeth in the sea cannot serve the land it standeth near
unto for frontier, but at sea only, because it may put not men and
horse ashore, and serve them for retreat.

A fort that must serve for frontier upon the sea-coast, at havens,   60
roads and suchlike landing-places, must be set part within the sea,
or at least so near unto the sea, that an enemy must make no fort,
trench or other coverture, how little so ever it be, to save himself
from the violence of the fort betwixt the sea and it, nor may use any
artillery within one or two hundred paces on neither side of the
port or haven, to impeach the free entering and going out of ships.
And being so placed for the benefit it hath of the sea, it may be the
greater, and both in time of war and peace be kept and defended

with less number of men and provision, because it may be succoured
at all times, and may serve itself with the commodities both of sea   70
and land, and may serve for frontier unto both, for that it may keep
shipping, men and horse. And to besiege a fort so placed, an enemy
that dwelleth upon the same main [ocean] the fort standeth, shall
be enforced to have two armies, the one by sea, and the other by
land, and coming from any other part, shall be constrained to bring
in so great an army by sea, as that may carry men, horse, artillery
and other things for the maintaining of an army, to put ashore, and
yet must keep the seas also. But how hard a matter it is to land an
army, and troublesome to continue an assiege at sea, and of what
value those towns are that have this situation, Flushing, Rochelle   80
and Ostend do and will bear witness, but the discommodity that
those forts have that stand by the seaside where great ebbs do run,
is [that] they are subject unto surprise at low water.

THE THIRD CHAPTER

[The manner of the lining-out of a fort, and the considerations to be used therein.]

In the delineation of a fort that shall serve for a royal frontier, the
figure triangular is not to be used at all, nor the quadrant, but only
in those watery grounds where it cannot be approached. Neither is
the cinqueangle to be chosen for any perfection that is in the
figure, for this purpose (although that many fortresses are made in
that form, of the castle of Antwerp, the citadel of Turin, and
others) but rather for sparing of charges in building and maintaining the fort. For the exterior angles of the bulwarks, placed upon
the angles of those figures, do fall out sharp, and therefore are
weak to resist a battery, and hard to be defended. But in other   10
figures they become flatter, and the more bulwarks a fort hath,
from the more places it may travail [harass] and offend [injure] an
enemy; but then it will require the greater garrison, provision and
artillery, the more cost in making and care in keeping. All which
being considered, line out the fort you pretend [plan], if nothing
do hinder the delineation, nor that any part may be less approach-
able than others with equal sides and angles. But if any part may be
better assured [secured] of the situation than the rest, on that side
lay out the longer sides and sharper angles, or both, to the intent
that the other part more easy to be approached, may be the more   20
defensible. Yet herein there must be a foresight that the fort may
fall out as circular as possible it may. . . .

(pp. 1–7)

156

TEXT 12

La cosmographie Universelle de tout le monde . . . beaucoup plus augmentée, ornée, et enrichie, par François de Belleforest (1575)

[The text is translated from the British Library copy (shelfmark 568.h.5).]

[In 1522 the Turkish Sultan Suleiman I mounted a costly campaign in a further attempt to wrest the island of Rhodes from the protective grasp of the Knights Hospitallers of St John of Jerusalem, who after lengthy resistance had to evacuate their fortress home. Belleforest describes a notable action in which the defenders repelled a major attack with conspicuous gallantry, highlighting an incident described in a marginal gloss as 'Histoire fort Tragique'.]

Some maintain that in that assault the Turkish power suffered a remarkable loss, to such an extent that in the six hour period that they found themselves confronted in five distinct places [in the defences], more than 15,000 Turks were killed, although not without the Knights Hospitallers themselves losing several of their company, of whom I am sorry that I do not have the names and the numbers, so that I could honour the memory of those who by their virtue merited everlasting glory.

    I am sorry not to be familiar with the name of a certain Greek woman, despite the fact that she was not conspicuous for her chastity. This lady was mistress to the governor of the fort of Rhodes, who, as soon as she heard that her lord and lover had died fighting valiantly, and as he was also a man of honour, took the two children she had had by the said lord, and kissing and hugging them, imprinted the sign of the cross on their foreheads, and then cut their throats and threw their bodies on the fire, stating that there was no good reason why such lovely children sprung from such a distinguished father should serve for the amusement of infidels. After this action had been done (I do not know whether

157

one ought to call it savage rather than great-hearted), she rushed to [20] the place where lay the body of her lover, put on her lord's coat of mail and hoqueton [padded jerkin] which were still covered in blood, and taking his short sword in her hand, made her way into the midst of the enemy, where doing the kind of deeds that the bravest of men perform, she was killed by the Turks, whom she believed would shortly take the town by assault. That Christian victory astonished Suleiman quite forcibly. . . .

(II. cols 749–50)

TEXT 13

Orlando Furioso in English Heroical Verse

Sir John Harington
(1591)

[The text is based on the reprinted edition published by
the Centaur Press in 1962.]

[Ariosto's romantic epic was published in 40 cantos in 1516, as a sequel
to Boiardo's *Orlando Innamorato* of 1495; a final definitive version in 46
cantos appeared in 1532. Harington's translation of 1591 was the
earliest English rendering to be produced, although significantly it was
preceded by twelve French versions.]

[Earlier in the poem Isabel, Princess of Galicia, has fallen in love with
Zerbin, son of the King of Scotland, and he with her. Captured by
bandits, she is rescued by Orlando, and reunited with her lover, who is
shortly slain by the Saracen King Mandricard in a dispute over the
sword Durindana. Isabel subsequently conveys Zerbin's body to Provence, where she encounters the African king Rodomont, the principal
pagan champion. He slays her companion, a pious friar, and proceeds
with his efforts to seduce Isabel.]

Thus cruel Rodomont that had remov'd
The babbling friar that did him so much spite;
The fearful damsel's love to win he prov'd [attempted],
By all kind words and gestures that he might;
He calls her his dear heart, his sole belov'd,
His joyful comfort and his sweet delight,
His mistress and his goddess, and such names
As loving knights apply to lovely dames.

Her reasons he doth courteously confute
(Love soon had made him such a learned clerk),
In phrases mannerly he moves his suit,   10
And still his suit was levell'd at one mark,

159

And though he might by force have pluck'd the fruit,
Yet for that time he doth but kiss the bark:
He thinks it will more sweet and pleasing make it,
If she do give him leave before he take it.

Wherefore awhile he is content to pause,
In hope by time to win her love and grace;
She deems herself like mouse in cat's sharp claws,
In stranger's hands, and in as strange a place;   20
She sees he fear'd not God's nor human laws,
Nor had no pity of her woeful case,
That only for his lust would her persuade
To break the vow that she to God had made.

Her heart and eyes oftimes to heav'n she lifts,
And prays the blessed Virgin and her son
To save her from this pagan's filthy drifts [schemes],
That unto her no villainy be done:
She doth bethink her of a hundred shifts,
How she his beastly lust may safely shun [avoid],   30
That like an open gulf on her did gape,
So as it seem'd unpossible to scape.

She finds out many 'scuses and delays,
That to prolong which she would fain prevent;
Sometime in humble manner him she prays
That to release her he would be content;
But being still repuls'd at all assays [attempts],
At last she doth a way and means invent,
Not only how to shun that present shame,
But merit to herself eternal name [fame].   40

Unto the cruel Turk that now began
From all good course of courtesy to swerve,
She cometh in the meekest sort [manner] she can,
And saith, if he her honour will preserve,
(Which is the part of each true valiant man),
She would of him that favour well deserve
And give him such a gift as in due measure
Should far surpass this momentary pleasure.

'But if you needs will me deflower, I wis,'
She said, 'when you have done, you will repent   50

160

To think how fondly [foolishly] you have done amiss,
And lost that might have bred you true content;
As for your carnal love, you need not miss
More fair than I, and fitter for your bent,
But in ten thousand, one you shall not know
That such a gift upon you can bestow'.

'I know', quoth she, 'an herb, and I have seen
A little since the place whereas it grew,
That boil'd upon a fire of cypress clean,
And mix'd with elderberries and with rue,   60
And after strained harmless hands between,
Will yield a juice that who [whoever], in order due
Anoint therewith, shall never damage [injury] feel,
By flame of fire nor yet by dint of steel'.

'I say, if one therewith anoint him thrice,
These strange effects thereof will straight ensue,
Provided always that in any wise
He must each month the liquor's strength renew:
I have the way to make it in a trice,
And you shall see by proof that it is true;   70
This thing I think should joy you more to gain
Than if you conquer'd had all France and Spain.'

'And now for my reward of you, I pray
Let me obtain this favourable meed;
To swear that you henceforth will not assay [try]
My chastity, by either word or deed.'
Fell Rodomont thinks this a blessed day,
And hopes he now shall never armour need,
And swears he will her honour safe defend,
Though to perform it he doth not intend.   80

Yet still she might this work bring to effect,
He doth himself against his mind [intention] enforce,
And that she might no violence expect,
He doth not offer any sign of force;
But that once done, his oath he will neglect,
For of an oath he never had remorse;
But specially he thought it least disgrace,
His oath to violate in such a case.

161

He makes to her a solemn protestation,
And with most damned oaths the same doth bind,   90
That he will never do her molestation,
If she procure a juice of such a kind:
This sinks so deep in his imagination,
Of Cygnus and Achilles runs his mind,
For by this means he doth himself assure
Such privilege as they had to procure.

Poor Isabella, glad of this delay,
By which awhile her chastity she shields,
Receiving this his promise, go'th straightway
To seek these herbs amid the open fields;   100
In ev'ry bank and grove and hedge and way,
She gathers some, such as the country yields;
And all the while the pagan walketh by,
And to the damsel casteth still an eye.

And lest she should want cypress wood to burn,
He with his sword cuts down whole cypress trees,
And in all other things to serve her turn,
That each thing may provided be he sees.
Now with her herbs she made her home return;
The cauldrons are on fire (no time to leese [lose]);   110
She boils and parboils all those herbs and flowers,
In which he thought there were such hidden powers.

At all these ceremonies he stands by,
And what she doth he many times doth look;
The smoke and heat at last made him so dry
That want of drink he could no longer brook [endure];
Greek wines there were, and those he doth apply [use]:
Two firkins late from passengers he took,
He and his men by drinking both that night,
Their heads full heavy made, their hearts full light.   120

Though by their law they are forbidden wine,
Yet now that here they did the liquor taste,
They thought it was so sweet and so divine,
That nectar and that manna far it pass'd [surpassed];
At that restraint they greatly do repine,
That did debar them of so sweet repast,
And at their own law and religion laughing,
They spend that night carousing and in quaffing.

162

Now had fair Is'bell' finish'd that confection,
Which this gross pagan doth believe to be   130
Against both steel and fire a safe protection;
'Now, sir,' she said, 'you shall the trial see,
And that you may be sure that no infection
Is in these drugs, you first shall prove by me:
I shall you show thereof so perfect trial,
As you shall see the proof past all denial'.

'Myself,' quoth she, 'mind first to take th'essay [test],
That you may see I do not feign nor lie;
Then after on yourself you prove it may,
When you have made a witness of your eye: 140
Now therefore bid your men to go away,
That none be present here but you and I'.
And thus, as with herself she had appointed [arranged],
Her neck and breasts and shoulders she anointed.

Which done, in cheerful sort [manner] she open laid
Her naked neck before the beastly Turk,
And bade him strike, for she was not afraid,
She had such skill and trust in this rare work.
He, unadvis'd and haply overlaid
With wine that in his idle brain did work,   150
Was with her speech so undiscreetly led,
That at one blow he quite cut off her head.

The head where love and all the graces dwelt
By heedless hand is from the body sever'd:
Alas, whose heart at such hap could not melt?
Yea, that is more, the head cut off endeavour'd
To show what pleasure of her death she felt,
And how she still in her first love persever'd:
Thrice from the floor the head was seen rebound;
Thrice was it heard Zerbino's name to sound.   160

His name to whom so great love did she bear
As she to follow him would leave her life,
To whom 'tis hard to say if that she were
A truer widow or a kinder wife;
O soul that did'st not death or danger fear –
A sample [example] in these latter times not rife –
To save thy chastity and vowed truth,
Ev'n in thy tender years and greenest youth!

Go, soul, go, sweetest soul forever blest,
So may my verse please those whom I desire,   170
As my poor Muse shall ever do her best,
As far as pen can paint and speech aspire,
That thy just praises may be plain express'd
To future times. Go, soul, to heaven or higher;
And if my verse can grant to thee this charter,
Thou shalt be call'd of chastity the martyr.

(Book XXIX, stanzas 8–29)

TEXT 14

Jocasta

A Tragedy written in Greek by Euripides, translated and digested into Act

George Gascoigne and Francis Kinwelmershe
(1566)

[The extract is taken from J.W. Cunliffe's edition of
the works of Gascoigne, published 1907–10.]

The order of the dumbshows and musics before every Act.

First, before the beginning of the first Act, did sound a doleful and
strange noise of viols, cittern [early lutes], bandurion [bass guitars],
and suchlike, during the which there came in upon the stage a king
with an imperial crown upon his head, very richly apparelled, a
sceptre in his right hand, a mound [orb] with a cross in his left
hand, sitting in a chariot very richly furnished, drawn in by four
kings in their doublets and hosen, with crowns also upon their
heads. Representing unto us Ambition, by the history of Sesostris
King of Egypt, who being in his time and reign a mighty conqueror,   10
yet not content to have subdued many princes, and taken from
them their kingdoms and dominions, did in like manner cause
those kings whom he had so overcome, to draw in his chariot like
beasts and oxen, thereby to content his unbridled ambitious desire.
After he had been drawn twice about the stage and retired, the
music ceased, and Jocasta the queen issued out of her house,
beginning the first Act, as followeth. . .

(I. 246)

NOTES

1 Silva de Varia Leción

(a) Taken from *The Forest* (pp. 82–90)

Part I Chapter 15 (pp. 82–3)

9   *Totila*: Attila, King of the Huns (c. 406–53) defeated near Châlons in AD 451.

Part II Chapter 14 (pp. 83–90)

82   *Albania*: the country lying between the Caspian Sea and the Caucasus.

221   *Pope Pius*: Aeneas Silvius Piccolomini (1405–64), Pope (Pius II) from August 1458 to August 1464.

306   *Platina*: Vatican librarian whose life of Pope Boniface IX, incorporated in his lives of the Popes down to Sixtus IV (1479), contains an account of Tamburlaine.

307   *Matthew Palmieri*: Florentine historian who published (1475) a continuation of Eusebius's *Chronicon* to 1449 containing a description of Tamburlaine's career.

(b) Taken from *The English Mirror* (pp. 90–6)

Book I Chapter 3 (pp. 90–1)

28   *Astyages*: last king of Media (reigned 584–550 BC), reported by Herodotus erroneously to be grandfather of Cyrus, founder of the Persian Empire, who dethroned him.

Book I Chapter 11 (p. 92)

24   *The Emperor Sigismund*: son of the Emperor Charles IV, crowned King of Hungary in 1387, he was defeated by Bajazeth at Nicopolis in 1396. He became King of Germany in 1411, and Holy Roman Emperor in 1433, dying in December 1437. Among early Protestants he became infamous for his treatment of John Huss (see Text 6).

Book I Chapter 12 (pp. 93–6)

6   *Campinus Florentinus*: i.e. Andreas Cambinus (see Text 4).

85   *Phenice*: ancient Phoenicia, the western coastal areas of modern Syria, Lebanon, and Israel.

86   *Sebastia*: Sebaste, now Sabastiya, near modern Nablus in Jordan.

2 *Magni Tamerlanis Scytharum Imperatoris Vita* (pp. 97–122)

Chapter 1 (p. 97)

2   *Jaxartes*: the river Syr Darya in Soviet Central Asia (though Samarkand lies some distance from the river).

Chapter 5 (pp. 102–4)

44   *Manuel*: Manuel II Palaeologus (1350–1423), Emperor of Byzantium 1391–1425; he visited England and France, and made a treaty with the Turks in 1403, following the death of Bajazeth I.

Chapter 26 (pp. 121–2)

7   *Pope Boniface IX*: Boniface (formerly Pietro Tomacelli) held the Papacy from November 1389 to October 1404.

4 *Libro . . . della origine de Turchi et imperio delli Ottomanni* (pp. 126–31)

29   *Scythia Asyatyea*: the region around and beyond the Jaxartes.
91   *Pelusium*: city at eastern mouth of the Nile.
115   *Capha*: Panticapaeum, now Kerch, at the mouth of the Sea of Azov.

5 *Elogia virorum bellica virtute illustrium* . . . (pp. 132–4)

13   *Quintus Curtius [Rufus]*: author of a Latin life of Alexander the Great, *c.* AD 43.
39   *Sapor*: sometimes known as Sapores, Sassanid king of Persia, reigning AD 241–72, and warring successfully against Rome.
40   *Valerian*: Roman Emperor from AD 253–60, captured, imprisoned and tormented by the Persians in 260.

6 *The Ecclesiastical History,* containing the Acts and Monuments of things passed . . . (pp. 135–8)

76   *Sebastianus Munsterus*: Sebastian Münster (1489–1552), German Hebraist, mathematician, cartographer, and compiler of the *Cosmographia*, published first in Basel in 1544.
83   *flood Tanais*: the river Don.

7 *Beautiful Blossoms* . . . (pp. 139–41)

2   *Thevet*: André Trevet was editor of the first French edition of *La Cosmographie Universelle* (1552), improved and expanded by François de Belleforest for the 1575 version.

42   *Capha*: see under Text 4 above.

9 *Rerum Ungaricarum decades quattuor Cum dimidia . . .*
(pp. 144–50)

2   *Huniades*: Janós Corvinus Hunyady (*c.* 1387–1456), statesman and re-doubtable warrior against the Turks; Regent or Governor of Hungary from 1446 until 1453.
11   *Vladislaus*: Vladislaus III, King of Poland from 1434, and of Hungary from 1440, killed at Varna (1444).

14 *Jocasta* (p. 165)

3   *bandurion*: a bass guitar-like instrument often employed as an accompaniment to the cittern.
9   *Sesostris* (or Sensurit): legendary Egyptian king whose conquests were alleged to extend from Libya to India, and from Ethiopia to Scythia. Baptista Fulgosius (Text 3) also mentions Sesostris in connection with Tamburlaine.

DOCTOR FAUSTUS

INTRODUCTION

Doctor Faustus is a highly problematic play in regard to matters of date, authorship, text, and interpretation, but it can at least be stated with certainty that it was inspired by a prose narrative entitled *The History of the Damnable Life and Deserved Death of Doctor John Faustus*, an English translation of a German original, the *Historia von D. Johann Fausten*, published at Frankfurt am Main in 1587. (The former is often known as the *English Faust-book* and will be referred to hereafter as *EFB*.) Marlowe himself did not make extensive use of any other source for this play; most scholars are now agreed that the scenes in Act III with the Pope and Saxon Bruno, which appear to have been suggested by a passage in John Foxe's *Acts and Monuments*, are not by him, although he does draw on Foxe in some of his other plays. Greatly as he transforms the original, enriching and complicating it with a wide range of literary and theological allusions, the detailed correspondences between *EFB* and the play suggest that he set out to dramatize it chapter by chapter, with the book before him, frequently echoing its very words.

The *Historia* is the first printed collection of tales that had accumulated about the partly historical, partly legendary figure of Johann Faust. Contemporary allusions dating from 1507 to 1540 show that such a man did indeed exist, but the anecdotes told about him are largely fictitious, incorporating elements of the stories of earlier legendary magicians and mountebanks and numerous folk-tale motifs, such as the transformation of a horse into a bundle of hay. An outstandingly successful bestseller throughout Europe, the *Historia* owes its appeal primarily to the fearful fascination of the idea of occult or forbidden knowledge. It provides much pious exhortation, together with lurid descriptions of hell and of Faustus's terrible end; on another level, it trades on the popular appeal of the many comic tales in which Faust is a successful trickster rather than a soul in danger of damnation.

The English translator, who calls himself simply P.F., and whose identity remains unknown, produced a very free, not always accurate, and highly individual version of the original. He omits one entire

chapter (chapter 65), in which Mephostophiles taunts Faustus with a
barrage of proverbs, and in chapter 19 he leaves out Mephostophiles's
unbiblical account of the creation of the world, possibly as a result of
censorship in both cases; the visitation of devils in P.F.'s version of
chapter 19 becomes a terrifying punishment, rather than the friendly
call of the original German. In chapter 18, however, he makes magical
powers seem far more exciting than they had in the *Historia,* and on a
number of occasions he adds emphasis to Faustus's desire for knowledge; only in the translation, for example, does Faustus call himself 'the
insatiable speculator' (chapter 22). In chapter 21, he introduces his
own thoughts on cosmology and in the description of Faustus's terres-
trial travels which follows, he enthusiastically adds further details of his
own. Some of these variations make it possible to state with certainty
that Marlowe used the translation rather than the original; he follows
P.F.'s version of events in chapter 19, for example, and he includes a
description of St Mark's church in Venice (III. 1. 17–20) and a number
of details about Rome, all of which are P.F.'s additions.

The date of the translation is clearly of the greatest importance for
determining the date of the play. The earliest surviving edition of it,
printed for Thomas Orwin and dated 1592, claims to be an amended
version, implying the existence of an earlier edition. An entry in the
Court Book of the Stationers' Company (18 December 1592) concerning a copyright dispute over 'the book of Doctor Faustus' shows
that there was such an earlier edition, published by Abel Jeffes. W.W.
Greg, in his edition of the play, argues that the latter did not precede
Orwin's by more than a few months and hence that the play must
belong to the last year of Marlowe's life (Greg 1950: 2–4). Recent
bibliographical research by J.H. Jones (1991, 1994), however, estab-
lishes that Marlowe did not in fact use Orwin but one of several earlier
editions, now lost. There is no record of performance before 30
September 1594, but a number of allusions suggest that the play must
have been produced much earlier than this; MacDonald P. Jackson
(1971) has demonstrated that 'A ballad of the life and death of Doctor
Faustus', which shows knowledge of both *EFB* and the play, was in
existence in February 1589.

The likelihood that *Doctor Faustus* was written in late 1588 or early
1589 suggests that it is Marlowe, rather than Robert Greene, who should
be credited with pioneering the vogue for plays about magicians in the
early 1590s. In *Friar Bacon and Friar Bungay* (probably written 1590,
published 1594), Greene like Marlowe seized on the opportunity to
dramatize a popular prose narrative of magical feats. Dr Jones argues in
his edition of *EFB* (1994) that Greene's source is represented by a
version of *The most famous history of the learned Friar Bacon,* the earliest
surviving edition of which belongs to *c.* 1715; the original, however, can

be dated to March 1590. In its turn *The most famous history* leans heavily on *EFB*, providing clear evidence that an edition of the latter must have existed prior to March 1590. There is no reason to suppose that Marlowe would have delayed in capitalizing on the popularity of *EFB*; it is highly probable, therefore, that *Doctor Faustus* preceded both the prose and the dramatic versions of *Friar Bacon*. Greene's play, with its large admixture of romance, is very different from *Doctor Faustus*; on the other hand, there are some close parallels between Marlowe's play and *The most famous history*, of which perhaps the most significant is the conjuring of the comic servants, Miles and Robin/Rafe. The problem is to establish the direction of such borrowings; Dr Jones concludes that the author of *The most famous history*, who is an imitative writer, is the borrower and that these scenes are Marlowe's original conception.

The relationship of *Doctor Faustus* to its source is complicated by the fact that the play exists in two distinct versions, that of 1604 and that of 1616 (usually referred to as the A- and B-texts respectively). The B-text is the longer of the two, containing material that is not present in A, notably in the middle section of the play, where the B-text has the Saxon Bruno episode and the revenge of Benvolio, and in Act V, where the devils and the Good and Evil Angels return to the stage, as they do not in A. The payment of £4 in 1602 by Philip Henslowe, theatre manager at the Rose, to William Birde and Samuel Rowley 'for ther adyciones in docter fostes' (Henslowe 1961: 206) points to the most likely explanation for these passages. Critical opinion as to the relative merits of the two texts has swung first one way, then the other, but it is now generally accepted that the A-text is the more authentic and aesthetically coherent of the two. The latest editors of the play, David Bevington and Eric Rasmussen, who print both A- and B-texts, giving the reader the opportunity to compare them, point out that the A-text is also sometimes the more faithful of the two to the wording of *EFB*, for example when it refers correctly to four bridges over the Tiber (III. 1. 37) where B has two (Bevington and Rasmussen 1993: 65).

In either of its versions, the play contains a good deal of comedy of various kinds, to the dissatisfaction of many critics. Greg could not believe that Marlowe wrote any of the comic scenes (except for Act I Scene 2) or the Seven Deadly Sins episode, or indeed anything in the play that might be considered humorous, wherever it occurs. The prose comedy he assigns tentatively to Thomas Nashe, a theory earlier proposed by Paul H. Kocher (1942) currently supported by Roma Gill (1987–90, II). A good many judgements of this kind are merely subjective, depending on the individual critic's idea of what is or is not Marlovian. It is probable, however, that the text has acquired accretions over the years; Roma Gill argues that the prose comic scenes contain a good deal of improvisation, much of which was pruned in accordance with changing theatrical tastes when the play was updated in 1602 (Gill 1987–90: II, xxi) and Thomas Pettitt (1988) has pointed out the 'formulaic' nature of this material. The play's latest editors point to stylistic tests which suggest that Greg was right in his suggestion of a collaborator, to whom they assign even Act I Scene 2 (Bevington and Rasmussen 1993: 70–2). In what follows, however, it will be assumed for the sake of convenience that Marlowe is the author except where there is clear evidence to the contrary.

To read the source is to appreciate that the tragicomic nature of the legend dictates, to a great extent, the mixture of modes in the play. *EFB* is essentially tripartite in structure, with a first section (chapters 1–16) containing the conjuration, the signing of the bond and numerous dialogues between Faustus and Mephostophiles, culminating in the latter's revelations about hell. In the middle section, Faustus, despairing of salvation, appears determined to enjoy the fruits of his bargain and blot out the thoughts of his ultimate fate which overshadow the first part; the visit of the nameless old man, his neighbour, revives his fears, but only temporarily. The 'third and last part' containing both his 'merry conceits' and his 'fearful and pitiful end' begins at chapter 29, but the real break comes at chapter 53 when Faustus 'called to mind that his time from day to day drew nigh'. The enormous proliferation of incidents in chapters 16–53 indicates the popularity of the lighter side of the legend; any contemporary play about Faustus, in order to succeed on the public stage, was bound to include at least some of them. The tripartite stucture of *EFB* is evident in the play, but so too is the structural pattern of English morality plays, in which traditionally the momentous issue of the soul's eternal destiny is combined with a humour which is often coarse, but is also essentially serious. Hence in the play, humour is more pervasive, and more integrated, than in the source; comic elements appear in serious scenes, and conversely. In addition, the play draws on the more recently established English dramatic tradition of a comic subplot in which servants burlesque the main action, and this, as E.M. Butler (1952: 47) points out, amounts to a significant modification of the original story, in which neither Faustus himself nor his pact with the devil is the subject of mockery and the laughter is directed against his dupes.

The Prologue shows how close the play can be to the original at times, in this case giving Faustus's early history very much as it is recounted in chapter 1 of *EFB*, even to adopting the narrator's morally disapproving tone. Nevertheless, crucial differences begin to appear. In a characteristically homiletic manner, *EFB* uses Biblical quotations as a yardstick by which to condemn Faustus. These are not repeated in the Prologue, although R.M. Cornelius (1984) has detected echoes of other Biblical passages. More obviously, Marlowe introduces a classical allusion to the fall of Icarus, perhaps in part suggested by the introduction of the motif of flight in *EFB* chapter 2: 'taking to him the wings of an eagle, [Faustus] thought to fly over the whole world'. Marlowe does make frequent use of Biblical allusion elsewhere in the play, but, as Sara Deats (1981) has shown, in an oblique and often ironic manner which is very far removed from the admonitory simplicities of *EFB*.

The last line of the Prologue is the starting point for an imaginative leap into Faustus's mind which goes far beyond the scope of the prose tale. *EFB* is not greatly concerned with the process of Faustus's decision to conjure, but rather with the results of that decision. Very little in the soliloquy comes from *EFB*, although the latter may have provided some suggestions. For example, in *EFB* (chapter 1), Faustus is observed to throw the Scriptures from him; the note of reckless impatience is echoed in 'Divinity, adieu!' (I. 1. 48). The syllogism on which Faustus bases his rejection of religion, and the second of his quotations from the Bible (1 John 1: 8) as Kocher (1946: 106–7) has pointed out, also occur in a theological tract by Thomas Becon (chaplain to Archbishop Cranmer), called *The Dialogue between the Christian Knight and Satan*. In Becon, Satan tries to persuade the Christian Knight to despair of God's forgiveness:

> *Satan.* Ask thy conscience. Even that doth accuse thee, and evidently showeth that thou art a sinner, and that thou hast not kept the precepts of God. Daily also dost thou confess the same in the Lord's prayer, when thou sayest: 'Forgive us our debts or trespasses'; and in the epistle of John it is read: 'If we say we have no sin, we deceive ourselves, and the truth is not in us.'
>
> (*Works*, 1560, II, No. 7, fol. cxlvii recto)

It cannot be proved that Marlowe read Becon, but it is not unlikely, and it is interesting to note how apposite the reply of the Christian Knight is to Faustus's case:

> For if perchance at any time thou allegest any truth out of the Scriptures, yet, according to thine old wont and malicious crafty and false quarrelling wit, either thou dost not speak altogether whole, or the things that thou allegest hang not together. For some things thou rehearsest, some things again subtly thou dost omit and leave clean out, or else thou corruptest and depravest the Scripture.

Faustus too quotes selectively, leaving out the verses (in each case immediately following) that promise God's forgiveness to the repentant sinner; in the case of the quotation from 1 John 1, the two verses together form one of the Sentences to be read out at the beginning of the Anglican service of Morning Prayer, as Helen Gardner (1948: 49) and D.E. Dreher (1983) have noted, and as the more devout members of Marlowe's audience would have been well aware.

Faustus's dissatisfaction with traditional learning is expressed in terms which occasionally echo the contempt for pedantry of Marlowe's contemporary, Giordano Bruno; Roy T. Eriksen (1985) draws attention to a number of parallels with Bruno's writings, including the latter's allusion to those who '*voglion vivere e morire per Aristoteles*'. This motive is not made explicit in *EFB* until later: 'sithence I began to study and speculate the course and order of the elements, I have not found through the gift that is given me from above, any such learning and wisdom, that can bring me to my desires' (chapter 6). What chiefly distinguishes Marlowe's hero from his prototype is the nature of their ambitions. The *EFB* Faustus's desire for knowledge at any cost is his principal motive, though he is certainly not averse to the worldly rewards that magic can bring in the form of public recognition and access to bishops' wine cellars. What Marlowe's Faustus wants is above all power: godlike power over all things that move between the quiet poles, as well as political power over kings and emperors. Beatrice Daw Brown (1939) argues that such titanic ambitions are explained by the superimposition on the Faust story of the legendary first-century magician Simon Magus, who is described in the fourth-century *Clementine Recognitions* as wishing 'to be believed to be an exalted power, which is above God the Creator' (quoted in Palmer and More, 1936: 12). There is no real proof, however, that Marlowe did make use of the Apochryphal and patristic texts in which he might have read about him. Kocher's thesis that the supernatural powers that witches were believed to possess – to make the moon drop from her sphere, for example – are superimposed on *EFB* here, is more convincing (Kocher 1946: 138–72). Such powers are compellingly described both by Faustus and by Valdes and Cornelius; the two latter characters do not appear in *EFB*, although they are perhaps suggested by a passing reference to 'divers that were seen in those devilish arts' (chapter 1). In the source it is only much later (chapter 18) that magic begins to seem exciting.

In the most detailed study of the relationship of the play to *EFB* to appear so far, Sara Deats takes a highly critical view of the pretensions of Marlowe's hero, arguing that he is more foolish, more self-deceived, and more worldly than his counterpart and that the exalted nature of his ambitions only serves to emphasize the paltriness of his reward. She is certainly justified in rejecting the common view of *EFB* Faustus as a mere braggart rogue, who is quite overshadowed by Marlowe's more heroic character, but it is surely an overstatement to say that Marlowe's Faustus retains only 'some shrunken vestiges of the keen curiosity of the *EFB* original' (Deats 1976: 6). The relative lack of emphasis on the desire for knowledge in the play is at least in part the consequence of the process of dramatization; long discussions have to be curtailed and the chapters (24–8) in which Faustus is deferred to as an authority on astronomy are likewise undramatic and understandably omitted. Elizabethan stage conditions may well have restricted what could be made visible of his more ambitious exploits.

Faustus's soliloquy in Scene 1 is followed by the first entry of the Good and Evil Angels, who derive ultimately from the morality plays and have no place in the source. *EFB* Faustus, though initially reluctant to accept the terms of the pact proposed by Mephostophiles, shows little sign of internal conflict until after signing the bond; Marlowe's Faustus is much less cautious, recklessly offering his soul before it is asked for, but the promptings of his conscience are given dramatic embodiment from the start. Angels do not often appear in morality plays after the early fifteenth-century *Castle of Perseverance* and their use may be a deliberate archaism on Marlowe's part; it is also possible that they reflect contemporary theological discussions of the nature of angels. Michael G. Brennan has drawn attention, in particular, to a translation by Richard Robinson of *An Homily . . . of good and evil angels* by Urbanus Rhegius (1583), in which it is said that both kinds of angel perform a divinely appointed ministry, the good angels as messengers from heaven, the bad as tempters, a point which throws some light on the question of whether the Angels in the play are anything more than externalizations of Faustus's conscience (Brennan 1991: 467). Morality plays and moral interludes were going out of fashion by the late 1580s, but they were still familiar, and Marlowe may have known a more recent example, *The Conflict of Conscience* (probably written early 1570s, published 1581), by Nathaniel Woodes, which dramatizes the true story of Francesco Spira, as recounted by Matteo Gribaldi and translated by Edward Aglionby (*A notable and marvellous Epistle*, 1550; 1570). Spira's struggle to repent and inability to believe that God will forgive him presents, as Lily B. Campbell (1952) has argued, a very similar 'case of conscience' to that of Faustus.

The Faustus of the opening chapters of *EFB* is a solitary figure. The students who are his most frequent associates are not introduced until chapter 41, Wagner, his 'boy' or *famulus* not until chapter 8. The students in Act I Scene 2 who fear for Faustus's welfare are used to increase a sense of foreboding, offset by the undergraduate humour of Wagner's cheeky replies. The character of Wagner is developed from hints in *EFB*, where we are told that he is 'an unhappy wag' (chapter 8) and that he too had studied at Wittenberg (chapter 56). In chapter 10 we are told that he 'afterward found' the magic book which Mephostophiles gives Faustus; at the end he inherits not only Faustus's property, as in the play, but his magic books and a familiar spirit as well. In the play the possibilities of Wagner's finding a magic book are expanded into at least the beginning of a parodic subplot (Act I Scene 4); the book is then transferred to Robin the ostler and his companion (Rafe in A; Dick in B). Thereafter it is this pair of less distinctive clowns, neither of whom has any connection with *EFB*, whose flirtation with magic provides a grotesque lowlife version of Faustus's dealings with the supernatural. Marlowe's Wagner, however, is also a serious character; according to the A-text, he is the speaker of the Prologue, and, it may be deduced, of the Chorus to Act III; he also fulfils the role of chorus or presenter at the beginning of Act V, this time *in propria persona*. He is not consistent; rather he is a dramatic expedient whose several aspects illustrate the range of styles and points of view in the play.

The conjuration scene is a masterly distillation of several chapters of *EFB*. The latter does not supply an incantation for Faustus to speak; the publisher of the *Historia*, Johann Spies, evidently feared that some of his readers might be tempted to try it for themselves. On stage, however, Faustus has to be provided with 'heavenly words' with which to summon the devil. The resonant Latin of the incantation, together with the accompanying ritual actions, such as the sprinkling of holy water, are drawn from the stock-in-trade of the witch, as described by Reginald Scot in *The Discovery of Witchcraft* (1584): 'say: "*Per crucis hoc signum + fugiat procul omne malignum; Et per idem signum + salvetur quodque benignum*", and make suffumigations to thyself . . . with frankincense . . . bless the circle with holy water' (XV. 13). *EFB*'s long description of frightening sights and sounds in the wood (chapter 2) is recalled in the stage directions 'thunder' and 'dragon', but the highly charged atmosphere at the beginning of the scene, set by its magnificent opening lines, does not derive from *EFB*; rather, as Johannes Birringer (1984: 318) suggests, it has much in common with the expansive rhetoric and 'strange aura of the supernatural' which Marlowe would have found in Lucan's *Pharsalia*.

In *EFB* the appearance of the dragon is succeeded by Mephostophiles in the guise of a grey friar; only later does Faustus request that his spirit shall always appear thus and at this first meeting there is no extended dialogue. Marlowe's Faustus immediately orders his Mephostophiles to go away and return as a grey friar, and the demonstration of his apparent power over the spirit gives rise to a series of complacent reflections that appear heavily ironic in the light of the ominous disclosures that follow. The irony is visually underlined in the B-text by the presence on stage of four devils even before Faustus begins to conjure. A few lines later, Mephostophiles denies that it was only the conjuration that brought him: 'For when we hear one rack the name of God, / Abjure the scriptures and his saviour Christ, / We fly in hope to get his glorious soul' (I. 3. 47–9). *EFB* makes a similar point about the inefficacy of conjuring, but much later, when Mephostophiles tells

Faustus in chapter 14 that 'so soon as we saw thy heart, even then did we enter into thee'.

In *EFB*, Faustus has very little conversation with his spirit until after the signing of the bond. At this point, before the bond is signed, Marlowe's Faustus receives, but wilfully chooses to ignore, an astounding revelation of the reality of hell. In *EFB* Faustus receives no such warning; Mephostophiles does not deliver his hellfire sermon (chapter 15) until it seems too late to retreat. In Marlowe's version, the roles are reversed, and it is Faustus's questions about hell that 'strike terror' to the 'fainting soul' of Mephostophiles. In *EFB*, hell is unequivocally a place of crudely physical torment; the more spiritual idea of hell as separation from God which Marlowe's Mephostophiles describes with such poignancy may derive from St John Chrysostom. John Searle (1936: 139) has pointed out the striking parallel between 'Think'st thou that I. . . / Am not tormented with ten thousand hells, / In being depriv'd of everlasting bliss?' (I. 3. 77–80) and *Si decem mille gehennas quis dixerit, nihil tale est quale ab illa beata visione excidere.* The more common notion of hell as physical punishment does appear in the play, but chiefly in the Act V passage unique to B of which the authorship remains in doubt. Marlowe's significant modifications to his source here (as elsewhere in the play) reflect the fact that he had studied a good deal of theology during his six years at Cambridge, even if he did not take Holy Orders.

In the *Historia*, the invocation in the wood is not directed to any particular devil; the use of the name Mephostophiles at this point is one of the many indications that Marlowe is following P.F.'s adaptation rather than the German original. But the sophisticated and complex character Marlowe creates is very different from that in *EFB*. The latter never regrets his exclusion from the joys of heaven, although in chapter 16, when he is asked what he would do were he in Faustus's case, he sighs and says that he would turn to God. *EFB* Mephostophiles bludgeons his victim with the horrors of hell; Marlowe's indulges in some ironic humour at Faustus's expense. It is tempting to speculate that Marlowe may have known another literary devil, Astarotte, who appears in Canto XXV of Luigi Pulci's epic romance, *Il Morgante Maggiore* (1482). Pulci, like Marlowe, was labelled an atheist, and certainly wrote ridiculing the Scriptures, for example accusing Moses of being a cheap conjuror, an accusation also made by Marlowe, according to Baines's report. Astarotte is erudite, urbane and witty, and he too expresses an ardent wish for a reunion with God which he knows to be impossible: 'if after a million and a thousand centuries we could hope to see even the least of the flames of that love, every burden would be light. . .' (XXV. 285). A further parallel is Astarotte's willingness to assist his human masters to reach Roncesvalles because he has

179

foreknowledge that a great bloodbath will take place there, and 'as you know, it is comforting for the unfortunate to see others afflicted like them' (XXV. 209). The sentiment, which is traceable back to Seneca's *De Consolatione*, is a common one, but it may be more than a coincidence that it also occurs on the lips of Marlowe's Mephostophiles ('*Solamen miseris socios habuisse doloris*' (II. 1. 43).

The theme of conscience, with the accompanying symbolism of the Good and Evil Angels, is again prominent in the bond-signing scene, as it is not in chapters 5 and 6 of *EFB*. There the signing of the bond is a very businesslike affair; even the appearance of the words '*O homo fuge*' on his hand do not seem to deter this Faustus. Marlowe's use of the congealing of Faustus's blood to create another supernatural warning sign turns a mere hint in the heading to chapter 6 into an intensely dramatic moment; in the source, Faustus himself, not Mephostophiles as in the play, provides a saucer of warm ashes in case his blood should congeal, but nothing more is made of this. The bond signed, Marlowe's Faustus is given 'somewhat to delight his mind'. *EFB* Faustus is also rewarded with an entertainment. Although very different from Marlowe's crowns and rich apparel, it includes 'ravishing music'; in the next scene, Marlowe's Faustus discloses that he has heard the 'ravishing sound' of Amphion's harp. At the end of the bond-signing scene, Marlowe's Faustus asks for a wife; so does *EFB* Faustus in chapter 9, but fares no better than his counterpart. As often, *EFB* is more explicit than the play, explaining that Faustus cannot benefit from a Christian sacrament; it is also more informative on Faustus's sexual exploits thereafter, which include the enjoyment of an entire harem (chapter 22). Marlowe omits this episode, but a faint trace of it appears when the clowns summon Mephostophiles from Constantinople (Act III Scene 3).

Act II Scene 2 opens with Faustus sinking deeper into the despair which eventually overtakes his counterpart in *EFB* also. There the narrator attempts to explain Faustus's state of soul in terms of simple Lutheran piety: 'the devil had so blinded him, and taken such deep root in his heart, that he could never think to crave God's mercy' (chapter 15). In the play the emphasis on Faustus's agonized struggle to repent unmistakably reflects Marlowe's interest in one of the great religious controversies of the age, that of predestination and free will. The issue is also prominent in *The Conflict of Conscience*; Philologus (Spira) is convinced that he is, in Calvinist terms, 'reprobate' (rejected by God), but Woodes disapproves of his despair and even devises an alternative happy ending in which his hero is able to repent after all. In Marlowe the theological problem is not spelled out, as it is in Woodes's play, but is all the more terrible and mysterious for being implicit. Like Philologus, Faustus feels that his heart is hardened and that he cannot repent; yet later in this scene, when he appeals to Christ to save his soul,

180

he perhaps comes closer to repenting than either of his counterparts. At the equivalent moment in *EFB* (chapter 19), there is no crisis of conscience. *EFB* Faustus weeps not for his sins, but because 'the devil was parted from him in such a rage'. He is frightened by Lucifer's visitation, but that is nothing like as disturbing or shocking as the appearance of the infernal trinity as if in answer to the prayer of Marlowe's Faustus. The play abandons the unstageable phantasmagoria which follows in *EFB* in favour of the pageant of the Seven Deadly Sins, perhaps suggested in part by the fact that in the original there are seven principal devils. Marlowe, or perhaps Nashe, draws on a longstanding and popular literary tradition here, for which many analogues may be cited, from morality plays to Nashe's own prose pamphlet, *Piers Penniless* (1592).

The discussions that lead up to this climax are very different. Marlowe simply discards the exuberant if confusing cosmology of *EFB* chapters 18 and 21, substituting astronomical questions and answers of his own. In chapter 21, P.F. adds a substantial passage in which he adopts a compromise position between the Ptolemaic and Copernican theories: the sun is fixed in relation to the earth's diurnal movement, but it is moved with the annual revolution of the whole firmament. As F.R. Johnson (1946) explains, Marlowe is clearly aware of current astronomical controversies when he makes Mephostophiles expound an unorthodox, though still Ptolemaic concept of the universe, lacking the conventional crystalline sphere and the elementary sphere of fire. The subdued manner in which Faustus receives this not very exciting or revolutionary information reinforces the sense of disillusion with his bargain which is felt so much more keenly by the Faustus of the play than by his counterpart, who has a very enjoyable time in chapter 21.

The middle section of the play (Acts III and IV) begins with Faustus's travels, deprived of the important place they occupy in *EFB* by the physical limitations imposed by an Elizabethan public playhouse stage. The play concentrates on the Roman episode, which is handled with considerable freedom in both texts, as indeed it has to be if its potential for farce and spectacle is to be released. The B-text, however, adds incidents which have no counterpart in *EFB* and which make Faustus's Roman adventure more substantial. L.M. Oliver (1945) suggests that these passages (which may well be Samuel Rowley's additions) marry the *EFB* motif of pope-baiting with material very loosely derived from John Foxe's *Acts and Monuments* (see Text 2, pp. 239–41). There is nothing in Foxe that exactly resembles the play's wish-fulfilling fantasy; Raymond King of Hungary is not known to history, nor was there a Pope Julius in the time of the Emperor Sigismund (1368–1437). The pope of the play is called Adrian; in Foxe, Pope Adrian IV (1154–59), who is of course far removed in time from the historical Faustus, is the proud and aggressive enemy of Emperor Frederick Barbarossa. It is this Adrian's

181

successor, however, Alexander III (1159–81), who more closely resembles the pope in the play, since in his time the emperor did set up another pope, Victor IV (but not Bruno). The incident in the play in which the pope mounts to his throne on the back of his rival was perhaps suggested by Foxe's account of Alexander placing his foot on the neck of the defeated emperor, with a cross-reference to Tamburlaine using Bajazeth as a footstool. Certainly Bruno's words 'But thus I fall to Peter, not to thee' (III. 1. 94) echo those of the emperor: '*Non tibi sed Petro*: That is, not to thee but to Peter'.

In these scenes Faustus is given power to intervene in affairs of state, but in a way that denies him the public recognition he enjoys at the court of the Emperor Charles V. In the play he does rather better in terms of status than in *EFB*, at least in the B-text, where he is received as a principal and honoured guest; in *EFB* he is unexpectedly singled out of the throng by the emperor and invited to display his powers. The A-text begins abruptly at this point, leaving out any preliminaries, and then follows the source almost word for word. B's version is much freer and fuller, offering a more elaborate dumbshow and expanding the story of the injurious knight, who acquires the name of Benvolio and two companions. B makes all it can of Benvolio's abortive revenge, although here he does not get two attempts at it, as he does in *EFB*. *EFB*'s version of the fight in the wood does not include the grotesque incident of Faustus's apparent decapitation, but there is an instance of decapitation and (would-be) resurrection in chapter 47, not used in the play, in which Faustus prevents a rival magician from completing the beheading trick and so causes his death. Perhaps also, as Thomas Pettitt (1980) argues, the traditional folk-lore beheading motif as used in the mummers' plays underlies the scene.

Disconnected farcical episodes proliferate in *EFB*'s third section; the dramatization has to be selective and to find ways of integrating the chosen material. The B-text retains more of the original than does A; besides the horse-courser incident, common to both texts, B includes the stories about Faustus eating a load of hay (chapter 35) and striking the revellers dumb (chapter 37), gathering all three into a final sequence at the Duke of Vanholt's court. In both texts, the horse-courser scene combines farce with reminders of the play's serious concerns which are absent in *EFB*. The presence of Mephostophiles (who has a speaking role in the A-text, but does not appear at all in *EFB*) also helps to establish links with the beginning and end of the play.

In Act V the selection and rearrangement of episodes from *EFB* develops the latter's considerable potential for tragedy. Wagner in his choric role and as Faustus's heir sets the scene, with his master carousing with the students in the background; in *EFB*, Faustus's will is not mentioned until chapter 56, when his revelling days are almost over.

There is a sense of gathering tragic momentum in *EFB* too, achieved by means of fairly frequent time references from chapter 51 onwards but there are interruptions, like that of the knight's second attempt at revenge. In the play, the first raising of Helen takes place under the shadow of Wagner's opening announcement; the positioning throws greater emphasis on what in *EFB* is simply one incident among others. Marlowe's Helen is a dazzling and sinister creation, at least on her second appearance, but in *EFB* the effect of the detailed physical description of her is to reduce her to ordinariness.

It is several years later in the source that Faustus's neighbour, 'an honest and virtuous old man', invites him to dinner and tries to save his soul. In the play this encounter and the two appearances of Helen are drawn together, each acquiring a new depth of meaning from the juxtaposition. The A- and B-texts diverge markedly in this scene, with the B-text on this occasion much closer to *EFB*. As in the source, the old man of the B-text is a gentle admonisher, concerned that his words may seem harsh and unpleasant; in A he is a powerful and stern preacher whose theology has a strongly Calvinist flavour. Faustus's reaction of suicidal despair is not in the original nor is Mephostophiles on hand with a dagger. Faustus does attempt suicide in *EFB*, but much earlier on, during his visit to hell (chapter 20), when he tries to throw himself from a height. In G.R. Widman's *Wahrhafftige Historia* (published 1599 but written 1587/8) however, he does twice attempt suicide by stabbing himself in the last few months of his life, and on both of these occasions his arm becomes paralysed as soon as he grasps the dagger. Marlowe may have used a verbally transmitted tradition here, although it is more likely that the episode is a reminiscence of a typical feature of morality plays, in which the hero is often offered the means of suicide. Unlike most morality play heroes, though, Faustus is not saved from his ultimate fate, even if he does not use the dagger. In *EFB*, Mephostophiles's assault on Faustus for his apostasy takes place later that night; in the play, it is terrifyingly immediate and Faustus's collapse yet more abject. Unlike the *EFB* Faustus, he offers to sign a new deed of gift without any infernal prompting.

The play links this incident with the reappearance of Helen, which does not take place in *EFB* until six chapters later. In the play this second appearance is greatly enhanced by the struggle to repent that precedes it and the old man's heroic resistance that follows (the latter preserved from *EFB* only in the A-text). The ecstatic lyricism of Faustus's speech to Helen, with its wide-ranging allusions to classical legend and medieval romance, is a vivid contrast to the Christian drama of good and evil that surrounds it, although it is often alleged that its images are predominantly allusions to disaster. In *EFB* the episode simply offers a last chance to enjoy 'voluptuous pleasures' and Helen is only one among other women demanded by Faustus in his last years, although she is also the only one who steals away his heart, or who bears his child. *EFB* paints a picture of almost normal domesticity here.

Both A- and B-texts handle the final chapters of *EFB* very freely, but only B has the reappearance of the infernal trinity of Lucifer, Beelzebub and Mephostophiles and of the Good and Evil Angels. There is no precedent for this in *EFB*, although Mephostophiles does appear in the penultimate chapter to give Faustus cynically false assurances that he will not be in hell for ever. In the *Historia*, however, Mephostophiles is given a whole chapter (65) in which he gleefully taunts his doomed victim; in the B-text, the devils come to gloat, the Good and Evil Angels to reproach. The resemblance between the missing (or cancelled) chapter and the play seems more than coincidental; whoever wrote the B-text passages (which are now generally believed to be further additions to Marlowe's play) may have known more of the Faust legend than appears in the 1592 edition of *EFB*.

EFB allows Faustus an elaborate and highly moralistic lamentation, three chapters long, some of which is recalled in the last soliloquy of Marlowe's Faustus; for example, *EFB* Faustus's wish to be a beast and die 'without soul' (chapter 61) must have suggested Marlowe's line 'Why wert thou not a creature wanting soul?' (V. 2. 173). These resemblances, however, are less striking than the differences in the treatment of Faustus's last hours in the play and in the narrative. One crucial difference is in timing: in *EFB*, Faustus's monologue precedes the last scene with the students; in the play the order is reversed, increasing tension and emphasizing Faustus's final isolation. Marlowe's version of the dialogue with the students has much in common with a similar scene in *The Conflict of Conscience* (see Text 3, pp. 242–5), where Philologus is visited in his despair by friends who urge him to repent and to pray, but he is convinced that he can never be forgiven and, like Faustus, sees a devil (invisible to his companions on stage): 'See, where Beelzebub doth come' (line 105). The vision of devils is not in *EFB*, nor is Faustus's conviction that the devils prevent him from raising his hands in prayer. The fact that Faustus cannot weep is another instance of Marlowe supplementing *EFB* with witch lore; usually an indication of a witch's guilt, in this context it adds considerably to the poignancy of the scene.

There is no final soliloquy in *EFB*; the reader remains with the students outside the hall in which Faustus spends his last night. In the play the audience crosses the threshold to share Faustus's terror; as at the beginning of the play, Marlowe's technical mastery of the soliloquy allows him to transform the original. In the monologue in *EFB*, everything is static; time is suspended while Faustus develops his theme at length. In the soliloquy, nothing is more important than the sense of time rapidly passing, conveyed by the chiming of the clock and by the restless energy of the language. Among the many elements that coalesce in this extraordinary speech is another reminiscence of Spira's predicament, in the latter's own words as translated by Edward Aglionby, rather than as versified by Woodes:

> but so that I could conceive never so little hope or trust of the mercy of God, I would most gladly choose to live ten thousand years and more, in all the pains and torments of hell, so that at length I might hope for some end.
>
> (*A notable . . . Epistle*, 1570: C 1 recto)

Other additions to *EFB* are strikingly original; as in the speech to Helen, Marlowe's imagination seizes on the implications of the source story to create something entirely his own. There is no equivalent in *EFB* to the visionary line, 'See, see, where Christ's blood streams in the firmament' (V. 2. 147), still less to the quotation from Ovid's *Amores*: '*O lente lente currite noctis equi*', which is ironically incongruous in its context and yet entirely typical of Faustus as Marlowe conceives him.

At this point, the B-text reverts to *EFB* with the scene in which the students find Faustus's dismembered body. The A-text wisely avoids the descent to purely physical horrors and the somewhat banal remarks of the students. Both versions of the play follow the example of the source by providing a moralizing epilogue, but the play's version strikes an elegiac note lacking in the original, derived in part from an unexpected echo, pointed out by Alwin Thaler (1923), of a line in Thomas Churchyard's poem *Shore's Wife* (1563): 'And bent the wand that might have grown full straight'. The equivocal final lines, which have tempted many readers to side with the forward wits against the restraints of heavenly power, are very different in tone from the pious exhortation and prayer with which *EFB* ends.

TEXT 1

The History of the Damnable Life and Deserved Death of Doctor John Faustus

translated by P.F., Gent.
(1592)
[The English Faust-book]

[The text is based on the unique copy in the British Library,
shelfmark C.27.b.43. There are also unique copies of the editions
of 1608 and 1610; in some cases a 1608 reading has been adopted.]

*A Discourse of the most famous Doctor John Faustus of Wittenberg in Germany,
Conjuror, and Necromancer, wherein is declared many strange things that he
himself hath seen and done in the earth and in the air, with his bringing up, his
travels, studies, and last end.*

CHAPTER 1

Of his parentage and birth.

John Faustus, born in the town of Rohde [Stadtroda], lying in the
province of Weimar in Germany, his father a poor husbandman, and
not able well to bring him up, but having an uncle at Wittenberg, a
rich man, and without issue, took this John Faustus from his father
and made him his heir, insomuch that his father was no more
troubled with him, for he remained with his uncle at Wittenberg,
where he was kept at the university in the same city to study divinity. But Faustus being of a naughty [wicked] mind and otherwise
addicted, applied not his studies, but took himself to other exercises,
the which his uncle oftentimes hearing, rebuked him for it, as Eli oft-   10
times rebuked his children for sinning against the Lord; even so this
good man laboured to have Faustus apply his study of divinity, that
he might come to the knowledge of God and His laws. But it is
manifest that many virtuous parents have wicked children, as Cain,
Reuben, Absalom and suchlike have been to their parents; so this
Faustus having godly parents, and seeing him to be of a toward wit,

186

were very desirous to bring him up in those virtuous studies, namely,
of divinity, but he gave himself secretly to study necromancy and conjuration, in so much that few or none could perceive his profession.

But to the purpose. Faustus continued at study in the university,   20
and was by the rectors and sixteen masters afterwards examined how
he had profited in his studies, and being found by them, that none
for his time were able to argue with him in divinity, or for the
excellency of his wisdom to compare with him, with one consent they
made him doctor of divinity. But Doctor Faustus within short time
after he had obtained his degree, fell into such fantasies and deep
cogitations that he was marked of many, and of the most part of the
students was called 'the speculator'; and sometime he would throw
the Scriptures from him as though he had no care of his former
profession, so that he began a very ungodly life, as hereafter more at   30
large may appear. For the old proverb saith, 'Who can hold that will
away?' So, who can hold Faustus from the devil, that seeks after him
with all his endeavour? For he accompanied himself with divers that
were seen [well-versed] in those devilish arts, and that had the
Chaldean, Persian, Hebrew, Arabian, and Greek tongues, using
figures, characters, conjurations, incantations, with many other ceremonies belonging to these infernal arts, as necromancy, charms,
soothsaying, witchcraft, enchantment, being delighted with their
books, words, and names so well, that he studied day and night
therein, insomuch that he could not abide to be called doctor of   40
divinity, but waxed a worldly man, and named himself an astrologian,
and a mathematician, and for a shadow [as a blind] sometimes a
physician, and did great cures, namely, with herbs, roots, waters,
drinks, receipts [prescriptions], and clysters [enemas]. And without
doubt he was passing wise, and excellent perfect in the Holy
Scriptures; but he that knoweth his master's will and doth it not, is
worthy to be beaten with many stripes. It is written, 'No man can
serve two masters', and 'Thou shalt not tempt the Lord thy God'; but
Faustus threw all this in the wind, and made his soul of no estimation,
regarding more his worldly pleasure than the joys to come. Therefore   50
at the Day of Judgement there is no hope of his redemption.

CHAPTER 2

**How Doctor Faustus began to practise in his devilish art,
and how he conjured the devil, making him to appear and
meet him on the morrow at his own house.**

You have heard before, that all Faustus's mind was set to study
the arts of necromancy and conjuration, the which exercise he

followed day and night, and taking to him the wings of an eagle, thought to fly over the whole world, and to know the secrets of heaven and earth; for his speculation was so wonderful, being expert in using his *vocabula*, figures, characters, conjurations, and other ceremonial actions, that in all the haste he put in practice to bring the devil before him. And taking his way to a thick wood near to Wittenberg, called in the German tongue *Spisser [Spesser] Waldt*, that is in English the Spisser's Wood (as Faustus would oftentimes   10 boast of it among his crew being in his jollity), he came into the same wood towards evening into a crossway, where he made with a wand a circle in the dust, and within that many more circles and characters. And thus he passed away the time, until it was nine or ten of the clock in the night; then began Doctor Faustus to call for Mephostophiles the spirit, and to charge him in the name of Beelzebub to appear there personally without any long stay. Then presently the devil began so great a rumour [tumult] in the wood, as if heaven and earth would have come together with wind, the trees bowing their tops to the ground. Then fell the devil to blare   20 [roar] as if the whole wood had been full of lions, and suddenly about the circle ran the devil as if a thousand wagons had been running together on paved stones. After this at the four corners of the wood it thundered horribly, with such lightnings as if the whole world, to his seeming, had been on fire. Faustus all this while half amazed at the devil's so long tarrying, and doubting whether he were best to abide any more such horrible conjurings, thought to leave his circle and depart. Whereupon the devil made him such music of all sorts, as if the nymphs themselves had been in place, whereat Faustus was revived and stood stoutly [resolutely] in his   30 circle aspecting [holding to] his purpose, and began again to conjure the spirit Mephostophiles in the name of the prince of devils to appear in his likeness; whereat suddenly over his head hanged hovering in the air a mighty dragon. Then calls Faustus again after his devilish manner, at which there was a monstrous cry in the wood, as if hell had been open, and all the tormented souls crying to God for mercy. Presently not three fathom above his head fell a flame in manner of a lightning, and changed itself into a globe; yet Faustus feared it not, but did persuade himself that the devil should give him his request before he would leave. Oftentimes   40 after to his companions he would boast that he had the stoutest [proudest] head (under the cope of heaven) at commandment, whereat they answered, they knew none stouter than the Pope or Emperor; but Doctor Faustus said, 'The head that is my servant is above all on earth', and repeated certain words out of St Paul to the Ephesians to make his argument good: 'The prince of this world is upon earth and under heaven.' Well, let us come again to his conjuration where we left him at his fiery globe: Faustus, vexed at the spirit's so long tarrying, used his charms with full purpose not to depart before he had his intent, and crying on Mephostophiles 50 the spirit, suddenly the globe opened and sprang up in height of a man; so burning a time, in the end it converted to the shape of a fiery man. This pleasant beast ran about the circle a great while, and lastly appeared in manner of a grey friar, asking Faustus what was his request. Faustus commanded that the next morning at twelve of the clock he should appear to him at his house, but the devil would in no wise grant. Faustus began again to conjure him in the name of Beelzebub that he should fulfil his request, whereupon the spirit agreed, and so they departed each one his way.

CHAPTER 3

The conference of Doctor Faustus with the spirit Mephostophiles the morning following at his own house.

Doctor Faustus having commanded the spirit to be with him, at his hour appointed he came and appeared in his chamber, demanding of Faustus what his desire was. Then began Doctor Faustus anew with him to conjure him that he should be obedient unto him, and to answer him certain articles, and to fulfil them in all points.

1 That the spirit should serve him and be obedient unto him in all things that he asked of him from that hour until the hour of his death.
2 Further, anything that he desired of him he should bring it to him. 10
3 Also, that in all Faustus his demands or interrogations, the spirit should tell him nothing but that which is true.

Hereupon the spirit answered and laid his case forth, that he had no such power of himself until he had first given his prince (that was ruler over him) to understand thereof, and to know if he could obtain so much of his lord.

'Therefore speak further that I may do thy whole desire to my prince, for it is not in my power to fulfil without his leave.'

'Show me the cause why,' said Faustus.

The spirit answered, 'Faustus, thou shalt understand that with us 20 it is even as well a kingdom, as with you on earth; yea, we have our rulers and servants, as I myself am one, and we name our whole number the legion; for although that Lucifer is thrust and fallen out of heaven through his pride and high mind, yet he hath notwithstanding a legion of devils at his commandment, that we call the oriental princes, for his power is great and infinite. Also there is an host in *Meridie* [south], in *Septentrio*, [north], in *Occidente* [west], and for that Lucifer hath his kingdom under heaven, we must change and give ourselves unto men to serve them at their pleasure. It is also certain, we have never as yet opened unto any man the truth of our dwelling, neither of our ruling, neither what our power is, neither have we given any man any gift, or learned him anything, except he promise to be ours.' 30

Doctor Faustus upon this arose where he sat and said, 'I will have my request, and yet I will not be damned.'

The spirit answered, 'Then shalt thou want thy desire, and yet art thou mine notwithstanding; if any man would detain thee, it is in vain, for thine infidelity hath confounded thee.'

Hereupon spake Faustus: 'Get thee hence from me, and take St Valentine's farewell and chrism with thee! Yet I conjure thee that thou be here at evening, and bethink thyself on that I have asked thee, and ask thy prince's counsel therein.' 40

Mephostophiles the spirit, thus answered, vanished away, leaving Faustus in his study, where he sat pondering with himself how he might obtain his request of the devil without loss of his soul; yet fully he was resolved in himself, rather than to want his pleasure, to do whatsoever the spirit and his lord should condition upon.

CHAPTER 4

The second time of the spirit's appearing to Faustus in his house, and of their parley.

Faustus continuing in his devilish cogitations, never moving out of the place where the spirit left him (such was his fervent love to the devil), the night approaching, this swift flying spirit appeared to Faustus, offering himself with all submission to his service, with full authority from his prince to do whatsoever he would request, if so be Faustus would promise to be his.

'This answer I bring thee, and an answer must thou make by me again; yet will I hear what is thy desire, because thou hast sworn me to be here at this time.'

Doctor Faustus gave him this answer, though faintly (for his soul's sake) that his request was none other but to become a devil, or at the least a limb of him, and that the spirit should agree unto these articles as followeth: 10

1 That he might be a spirit in shape and quality.
2 That Mephostophiles should be his servant and at his commandment.
3 That Mephostophiles should bring him anything, and do for him
whatsoever.
4 That at all times he should be in his house, invisible to all men,
except only to himself, and at his commandment to show himself.   20
5 Lastly, that Mephostophiles should at all times appear at his
command, in what form or shape soever he would.

Upon these points the spirit answered Doctor Faustus that all this
should be granted him and fulfilled, and more if he would agree
unto him upon certain articles as followeth:

First, that Doctor Faustus should give himself to his lord Lucifer,
body and soul.

Secondly, for confirmation of the same, he should make him a
writing, written with his own blood.

Thirdly, that he would be an enemy to all Christian people.   30

Fourthly, that he would deny his Christian belief.

Fifthly, that he let not any man change his opinion, if so be any
man should go about to dissuade, or withdraw him from it.

Further, the spirit promised Faustus to give him certain years to
live in health and pleasure, and when such years were expired, that
then Faustus should be fetched away, and if he should hold these
articles and conditions, that then he should have all whatsoever his
heart would wish or desire; and that Faustus should quickly perceive
himself to be a spirit in all manner of actions whatsoever. Hereupon
Doctor Faustus his mind was so inflamed that he forgot his soul,   40
and promised Mephostophiles to hold all things as he had mentioned them; he thought the devil was not so black as they use to
paint him, nor hell so hot as the people say, etc.

CHAPTER 5

The third parley between Doctor Faustus and Mephostophiles
about a conclusion.

After Doctor Faustus had made his promise to the devil, in the
morning betimes [early] he called the spirit before him and
commanded him that he should always come to him like a friar,
after the order of St Francis, with a bell in his hand like St Antony,
and to ring it once or twice before he appeared, that he might know
of his certain coming. Then Faustus demanded the spirit, what was
his name?

The spirit answered, 'My name is as thou sayest, Mephostophiles, and I am a prince, but servant to Lucifer; and all the circuit from *Septentrio* to the Meridian, I rule under him.'

Even at these words was this wicked wretch Faustus inflamed to hear himself to have gotten so great a potentate to be his servant, forgot the Lord his maker, and Christ his redeemer, became an enemy unto all mankind, yea, worse than the giants whom the poets feign to climb the hills to make war with the gods: not unlike that enemy of God and His Christ that for his pride was cast into hell. So likewise Faustus forgot that the high climbers catch the greatest falls, and that the sweetest meat requires the sourest sauce.

After a while, Faustus promised Mephostophiles to write and make his obligation, with full assurance of the articles in the chapter before rehearsed. A pitiful case (Christian reader) for certainly this letter or obligation was found in his house after his most lamentable end, with all the rest of his damnable practices used in his whole life. Therefore I wish all Christians to take an example by this wicked Faustus, and to be comforted [strengthened] in Christ, contenting themselves with that vocation whereunto it hath pleased God to call them, and not to esteem the vain delights of this life, as did this unhappy Faustus, in giving his soul to the devil. And to confirm it the more assuredly, he took a small penknife, and pricked a vein in his left hand, and for certainty thereupon were seen on his hand these words written, as if they had been written with blood, '*O homo fuge*'; whereat the spirit vanished, but Faustus continued in his damnable mind, and made his writing as followeth.

CHAPTER 6

How Doctor Faustus set his blood in a saucer on warm ashes, and writ as followeth.

I, Johannes Faustus, Doctor, do openly acknowledge with mine own hand, to the greater force and strengthening of this letter, that sithence [since] I began to study and speculate the course and order of the elements, I have not found through the gift that is given me from above, any such learning and wisdom that can bring me to my desires; and for that I find that men are unable to instruct me any further in the matter, now have I, Doctor John Faustus, unto the hellish prince of Orient and his messenger Mephostophiles given both body and soul, upon such condition that they shall learn me and fulfil my desire in all things, as they have promised and vowed unto me, with due obedience unto me, according unto the articles mentioned between us.

192

Further, I covenant and grant with them by these presents, that at the end of twenty-four years next ensuing the date of this present letter, they being expired, and I in the meantime, during the said years be served of them at my will, they accomplishing my desires to the full in all points as we are agreed, that then I give them full power to do with me at their pleasure, to rule, to send, fetch, or carry me or mine, be it either body, soul, flesh, blood, or goods, into their habitation, be it wheresoever; and hereupon, I defy God   20
and His Christ, all the host of heaven, and all living creatures that bear the shape of God, yea, all that lives; and again I say it, and it shall be so. And to the more strengthening of this writing, I have written it with mine own hand and blood, being in perfect memory, and hereupon I subscribe to it with my name and title, calling all the infernal, middle, and supreme powers to witness of this my letter and subscription.

John Faustus, approved in the elements, and the spiritual doctor.

CHAPTER 7

How Mephostophiles came for his writing and in what manner he appeared and his sights he showed him; and how he caused him to keep a copy of his own writing.

Doctor Faustus sitting pensive, having but one only boy with him, suddenly there appeared his spirit Mephostophiles, in likeness of a fiery man, from whom issued most horrible fiery flames, insomuch that the boy was afraid, but being hardened by his master, he bade him stand still and he should have no harm; the spirit began to blare [roar] as in a singing manner. This pretty sport pleased Doctor Faustus well, but he would not call his spirit into his counting-house until he had seen more. Anon [at once] was heard a rushing of armed men and trampling of horses; this ceasing, came a kennel of hounds, and they chased a great hart in the hall, and   10
there the hart was slain. Faustus took heart, came forth, and looked upon the hart, but presently before him there was a lion and a dragon together fighting so fiercely that Faustus thought they would have brought down the house, but the dragon overcame the lion, and so they vanished.

After this came in a peacock with a peahen, the cock brustling [bristling] of his tail, and turning to the female, beat her, and so vanished. Afterward followed a furious bull, that with a full fierceness ran upon Faustus, but coming near him, vanished away. Afterward followed a great old ape; this ape offered Faustus the   20
hand, but he refused; so the ape ran out of the hall again.

193

Hereupon fell a mist in the hall, that Faustus saw no light, but it lasted not, and so soon as it was gone, there lay before Faustus two great sacks, one full of gold, the other full of silver.

Lastly was heard by Faustus all manner instruments of music, as organs, clarigolds [clavichords], lutes, viols, citterns [wire-stringed instruments], waits [oboes], hornpipes, flutes, anomes [wind instruments?], harps, and all manner of other instruments, the which so ravished his mind that he thought he had been in another world, forgot both body and soul, insomuch that he was minded never to change his opinion concerning that which he had done. Hereat came Mephostophiles into the hall to Faustus, in apparel like unto a friar, to whom Faustus spake: 30

'Thou hast done me a wonderful pleasure in showing me this pastime; if thou continue as thou hast begun, thou shalt win my heart and soul, yea, and have it.'

Mephostophiles answered, 'This is nothing; I will please thee better. Yet that thou mayst know my power and all, ask what thou wilt request of me, that shalt thou have; conditionally hold thy promise, and give me thy handwriting.' 40

At which words, the wretch thrust forth his hand, saying, 'Hold thee, there hast thou my promise.'

Mephostophiles took the writing, and willing Faustus to take a copy of it, with that the perverse Faustus, being resolute in his damnation, wrote a copy thereof, and gave the devil the one, and kept in store the other. Thus the spirit and Faustus were agreed, and dwelt together; no doubt there was a virtuous housekeeping.

CHAPTER 8

The manner how Faustus proceeded with his damnable life, and of the diligent service that Mephostophiles used towards him.

Doctor Faustus having given his soul to the devil, renouncing all the powers of heaven, confirming this lamentable action with his own blood, and having already delivered his writing now into the devil's hand, the which so puffed up his heart that he had forgot the mind of a man, and thought rather himself to be a spirit. This Faustus dwelt in his uncle's house at Wittenberg, who died, and bequeathed it in his testament to his cousin Faustus. Faustus kept a boy with him that was his scholar, an unhappy [unlucky] wag, called Christopher Wagner, to whom this sport and life that he saw his master follow seemed pleasant. Faustus loved the boy well, hoping to make him as good or better seen [versed] in his devilish exercise than himself, and he was fellow with Mephostophiles; otherwise 10

Faustus had no more company in his house but himself, his boy, and his spirit, that ever was diligent at Faustus' command, going about the house clothed like a friar, with a little bell in his hand, seen of none but Faustus. For his victual and other necessaries, Mephostophiles brought him at his pleasure from the Duke of Saxony, the Duke of Bavaria, and the Bishop of Salzburg, for they had many times their best wine stolen out of their cellars by Mephostophiles; likewise their provision for their own table, such meat as Faustus wished for, his spirit brought him in. Besides that, Faustus himself was become so cunning [skilful] that when he opened his window, what fowl soever he wished for, it came presently flying into his house, were it never so dainty. Moreover, Faustus and his boy went in sumptuous apparel, the which Mephostophiles stole from the mercers at Nuremberg, Augsburg, Frankfurt and Leipzig, for it was hard for them to find a lock to keep out such a thief. All their maintenance was but stolen and borrowed ware; and thus they lived an odious life in the sight of God, though as yet the world were unacquainted with their wickedness. It must be so, for their fruits be none other; as Christ saith through John, where he calls the devil a thief and a murderer; and that found Faustus, for he stole him away both body and soul.

CHAPTER 9

How Doctor Faustus would have married, and how the devil had almost killed him for it.

Doctor Faustus continued thus in his epicurish [voluptuous] life day and night, and believed not that there was a God, hell, or devil; he thought that body and soul died together, and had quite forgotten divinity or the immortality of his soul, but stood in his damnable heresy day and night. And bethinking himself of a wife, called Mephostophiles to counsel; which would in no wise agree, demanding of him if he would break the covenant made with him, or if he had forgot it.

'Hast not thou,' quoth Mephostophiles, 'sworn thyself an enemy to God and all creatures? To this I answer thee, thou canst not marry; thou canst not serve two masters, God, and my prince: for wedlock is a chief institution ordained of God, and that hast thou promised to defy, as we do all, and that hast thou also done, and moreover thou hast confirmed it with thy blood; persuade thyself, that what thou dost in contempt of wedlock, it is all to thine own delight. Therefore Faustus, look well about thee, and bethink thyself better, and I wish thee to change thy mind; for if thou keep

not what thou hast promised in thy writing, we will tear thee in
pieces like the dust under thy feet. Therefore sweet Faustus, think
with what unquiet life, anger, strife, and debate thou shalt live in   20
when thou takest a wife; therefore change thy mind.'

Doctor Faustus was with these speeches in despair, and, as all that
have forsaken the Lord can build upon no good foundation, so this
wretched Faustus, having forsook the rock, fell in despair with
himself, fearing if he should motion [propose] matrimony any
more, that the devil would tear him in pieces.

'For this time,' quoth he to Mephostophiles, 'I am not minded
to marry.'

'Then you do well,' answered his spirit.

But shortly, and that within two hours after, Faustus called his   30
spirit, which came in his old manner like a friar. Then Faustus said
unto him, 'I am not able to resist nor bridle my fantasy; I must and
will have a wife, and I pray thee give thy consent to it.'

Suddenly upon these words came such a whirlwind about the
place that Faustus thought the whole house would come down. All
the doors in the house flew off the hooks; after all this, his house
was full of smoke, and the floor covered over with ashes, which
when Doctor Faustus perceived, he would have gone up the stairs;
and flying up, he was taken and thrown into the hall, that he was
not able to stir hand nor foot. Then round about him ran a   40
monstrous circle of fire, never standing still, that Faustus fried as he
lay, and thought there to have been burned. Then cried he out to
his spirit Mephostophiles for help, promising him he would live in
all things as he had vowed in his handwriting. Hereupon appeared
unto him an ugly devil, so fearful and monstrous to behold, that
Faustus durst not look on him.

The devil said, 'What wouldst thou have, Faustus? How likest
thou thy wedding? What mind art thou in now?'

Faustus answered, he had forgot his promise, desiring him of
pardon, and he would talk no more of such things.   50

The devil answered, 'Thou were best so to do,' and so vanished.

After appeared unto him his friar Mephostophiles with a bell in
his hand, and spake to Faustus, 'It is no jesting with us; hold thou
that which thou hast vowed, and we will perform as we have
promised, and more than that, thou shalt have thy heart's desire of
what woman soever thou wilt, be she alive or dead, and so long as
thou wilt, thou shalt keep her by thee.'

These words pleased Faustus wonderful well, and repented
himself that he was so foolish to wish himself married, that might
have any woman in the whole city brought to him at his command;   60
the which he practised and persevered in a long time.

CHAPTER 10

Questions put forth by Doctor Faustus unto his spirit Mephostophiles.

Doctor Faustus living in all manner of pleasure that his heart could desire, continuing in his amorous drifts, his delicate fare and costly apparel, called on a time his Mephostophiles to him, which being come, brought with him a book in his hand of all manner of devilish and enchanted arts, the which he gave Faustus, saying, 'Hold, my Faustus, work now thy heart's desire.'

The copy of this enchanting book was afterward found by his servant, Christopher Wagner.

'Well,' quoth Faustus to his spirit, 'I have called thee to know what thou canst do if I have need of thy help.'   10

Then answered Mephostophiles and said, 'My lord Faustus, I am a flying spirit, yea, so swift as thought can think, to do whatsoever.'

Here Faustus said, 'But how came thy lord and master Lucifer to have so great a fall from heaven?'

Mephostophiles answered, 'My lord Lucifer was a fair angel, created of God as immortal, and being placed in the seraphim, which are above the cherubim, he would have presumed unto the throne of God, with intent to have thrust God out of His seat. Upon this presumption, the Lord cast him down headlong, and where before he was an angel of light, now dwells he in darkness, not able   20
to come near his first place, without God send for him to appear before him as Raphael; but unto the lower degree of angels that have their conversation with men he may come, but not unto the second degree of heavens that is kept by the archangels, namely, Michael and Gabriel, for these are called angels of God's wonders; yet are these far inferior places to that from whence my lord and master Lucifer fell. And thus far Faustus, because thou art one of the beloved children of my lord Lucifer, following and feeding thy mind in manner as he did his, I have shortly resolved thy request, and more I will do for thee at thy pleasure.'   30

'I thank thee, Mephostophiles,' quoth Faustus. 'Come, let us now go rest, for it is night.'

Upon this they left their communication.

CHAPTER 11

How Doctor Faustus dreamed that he had seen hell in his sleep, and how he questioned with his spirit of matters as concerning hell, with the spirit's answer.

The night following, after Faustus his communication had with Mephostophiles as concerning the fall of Lucifer, Doctor Faustus dreamed that he had seen a part of hell, but in what manner it was, or in what place he knew not; whereupon he was greatly troubled in mind, and called unto him Mephostophiles his spirit, saying to him, 'My Mephostophiles, I pray thee resolve me in this doubt: what is hell, what substance is it of, in what place stands it, and when was it made?'

Mephostophiles answered, 'My Faustus, thou shalt know that before the fall of my lord Lucifer there was no hell, but even then 10 was hell ordained. It is of no substance, but a confused thing; for I tell thee, that before all elements were made and the earth seen, the spirit of God moved on the waters, and darkness was over all, but when God said 'Let it be light,' it was so at His word, and the light was on God's right hand, and God praised the light. Judge thou further: God stood in the middle, the darkness was on His left hand, in the which my lord was bound in chains until the Day of Judgement; in this confused hell is naught to find but a filthy, sulphurish, fiery, stinking mist or fog. Further, we devils know not what substance it is of, but a confused thing. For as a bubble of 20 water flieth before the wind, so doth hell before the breath of God. Further, we devils know not how God hath laid the foundation of our hell, nor whereof it is; but to be short with thee Faustus, we know that hell hath neither bottom nor end.'

[In chapter 12, Faustus asks how many kingdoms there are in hell, and what are the names of their rulers.]

CHAPTER 13

Another question put forth by Doctor Faustus to his spirit concerning his lord Lucifer, with the sorrow that Faustus fell afterwards into.

Doctor Faustus began again to reason with Mephostophiles, requiring him to tell him in what form and shape, and in what estimation his lord Lucifer was when he was in favour with God. Whereupon his spirit required him of three days' respite, which Faustus granted. The three days being expired, Mephostophiles gave him this answer:

'Faustus, my lord Lucifer (so called now, for that he was banished out of the clear light of heaven) was at the first an angel of God; he sat on the cherubim, and saw all the wonderful works of God; yea, he was so of God ordained, for shape, pomp, authority, worthiness, and dwelling, that he far exceeded all other the creatures of God, yea, our gold and precious stones, and so illuminated, that he far surpassed the brightness of the sun and all other stars. Wherefore God placed him on the cherubim, where he had a kingly office, and was always before God's seat, to the end he might be the more perfect in all his beings. But when he began to be high-minded, proud, and so presumptuous that he would usurp the seat of His majesty, then was he banished out from amongst the heavenly powers, separated from their abiding into the manner of a fiery stone that no water is able to quench, but continually burneth until the end of the world.'

Doctor Faustus, when he had heard the words of his spirit, began to consider with himself, having divers and sundry opinions in his head; and very pensively (saying nothing unto his spirit), he went into his chamber, and laid him on his bed, recording the words of Mephostophiles, which so pierced his heart that he fell into sighing and great lamentation, crying out, 'Alas, ah, woe is me! What have I done? Even so shall it come to pass with me. Am not I also a creature of God's making, bearing His own image and similitude, into whom He hath breathed the spirit of life and immortality, unto whom He hath made all things living subject? But woe is me, mine haughty mind, proud aspiring stomach [temper], and filthy flesh hath brought my soul into perpetual damnation; yea, pride hath abused my understanding, insomuch that I have forgot my maker; the spirit of God is departed from me. I have promised the devil my soul, and therefore it is but a folly for me to hope for grace, but it must be even with me as with Lucifer, thrown into perpetual burning fire. Ah, woe is me that ever I was born!'

In this perplexity lay this miserable Doctor Faustus, having quite forgot his faith in Christ, never falling to repentance truly, thereby to attain the grace and Holy Spirit of God again, the which would have been able to have resisted the strong assaults of Satan. For although he had made him a promise, yet he might have remembered through true repentance sinners come again into the favour of God; which faith the faithful firmly hold, knowing they that kill the body are not able to hurt the soul; but he was in all his opinions doubtful, without faith or hope, and so he continued.

CHAPTER 14

**Another disputation betwixt Doctor Faustus and his spirit of
the power of the devil and of his envy to mankind.**

After Doctor Faustus had a while pondered and sorrowed with
himself of his wretched estate, he called again Mephostophiles
unto him, commanding him to tell him the judgement, rule,
power, attempts, tyranny, and temptation of the devil, and why he
was moved to such kind of living.

Whereupon the spirit answered, 'This question that thou demandest of me will turn thee to no small discontentment; therefore thou
shouldst not have desired me of such matters, for it toucheth the
secrets of our kingdom, although I cannot deny to resolve thy
request. Therefore know thou Faustus, that so soon as my lord   10
Lucifer fell from heaven, he became a mortal enemy both to God
and man, and hath used (as now he doth) all manner of tyranny to
the destruction of man, as is manifest by divers examples: one falling
suddenly dead, another hangs himself, another drowns himself,
others stab themselves, others unfaithfully despair, and so come to
utter confusion. The first man Adam, that was made perfect to the
similitude of God, was by my lord his policy, the whole decay of man;
yea, Faustus, in him was the beginning and first tyranny of my lord
Lucifer used to man. The like did he with Cain, the same with the
children of Israel, when they worshipped strange gods, and fell to   20
whoredom with strange women; the like with Saul; so did he by the
seven husbands of her that after was the wife of Tobias. Likewise
Dagon our fellow brought to destruction 30,000 men, whereupon
the ark of God was stolen, and Belial made David to number his
men, whereupon were slain 60,000; also he deceived King Solomon
that worshipped the gods of the heathen. And there are such spirits
innumerable that can come by men and tempt them, drive them to
sin, weaken their belief; for we rule the hearts of kings and princes,
stirring them up to war and bloodshed, and to this intent do we
spread ourselves throughout all the world, as the utter enemies of   30
God and His son Christ, yea, and all those that worship them; and
that thou knowest by thyself, Faustus, how we have dealt with thee.'

To this answered Faustus, 'Why, then thou didst also beguile me.'

'Yea,' quoth Mephostophiles, 'why should not we help thee
forwards? For so soon as we saw thy heart, how thou didst despise
thy degree taken in divinity, and didst study to search and know the
secrets of our kingdom, even then did we enter into thee, giving
thee divers foul and filthy cogitations, pricking thee forward in
thine intent, and persuading thee that thou couldst never attain to

thy desire, until thou hadst the help of some devil. And when thou 40
wast delighted with this, then took we root in thee, and so firmly,
that thou gavest thyself unto us, both body and soul, the which
thou, Faustus, canst not deny.'

Hereat answered Faustus, 'Thou sayest true, Mephostophiles, I
cannot deny it. Ah, woe is me, miserable Faustus; how have I been
deceived? Had not I desired to know so much, I had not been in this
case. For having studied the lives of the holy saints and prophets, and
thereby thought myself to understand sufficient in heavenly matters,
I thought myself not worthy to be called Doctor Faustus, if I should
not also know the secrets of hell and be associated with the furious 50
fiend thereof. Now therefore must I be rewarded accordingly.'

Which speeches being uttered, Faustus went very sorrowfully
away from Mephostophiles.

CHAPTER 15

**How Doctor Faustus desired again of his spirit to know
the secrets and pains of hell, and whether these damned
devils and their company might ever come into the favour
of God again or not.**

Doctor Faustus was ever pondering with himself how he might get
loose from so damnable an end as he had given himself unto, both
of body and soul, but his repentance was like to that of Cain and
Judas; he thought his sins greater than God could forgive: hereupon rested his mind. He looked up to heaven, but saw nothing
therein, for his heart was so possessed with the devil that he could
think of nought else but of hell, and the pains thereof. Wherefore
in all the haste he calleth unto him his spirit Mephostophiles,
desiring him to tell him some more of the secrets of hell: what pains
the damned were in, and how they were tormented, and whether 10
the damned souls might get again the favour of God and so be
released out of their torments or not.

Whereupon the spirit answered, 'My Faustus, thou mayst well
leave to question any more of such matters, for they will but
disquiet thy mind. I pray thee, what meanest thou? Thinkest thou
through these thy fantasies to escape us? No, for if thou shouldest
climb up to heaven, there to hide thyself, yet would I thrust thee
down again; for thou art mine, and thou belongest unto our
society. Therefore sweet Faustus, thou wilt repent this thy foolish
demand, except thou be content that I shall tell thee nothing.' 20

Quoth Faustus ragingly, 'I will know, or I will not live; wherefore
dispatch and tell me.'

To whom Mephostophiles answered, 'Faustus, it is no trouble unto me at all to tell thee, and therefore sith [since] thou forcest me thereto, I will tell thee things to the terror of thy soul, if thou wilt abide the hearing. Thou wilt have me tell thee of the secrets of hell, and of the pains thereof. Know Faustus, that hell hath many figures [images], semblances, and names, but it cannot be named nor figured in such sort unto the living that are damned, as it is unto those that are dead, and do both see and feel the torments thereof. For hell is said to be deadly, out of the which came never any to life again but one, but He is as nothing for thee to reckon upon; hell is bloodthirsty, and is never satisfied; hell is a valley, into the which the damned souls fall; for so soon as the soul is out of man's body, it would gladly go to the place from whence it came, and climbeth up above the highest hills, even to the heavens, where being by the angels of the first *mobile* denied entertainment (in consideration of their evil life spent on the earth) they fall into the deepest pit or valley which hath no bottom, into a perpetual fire which shall never be quenched. For like as the flint thrown into the water loseth not his virtue, neither is his fire extinguished, even so the hellish fire is unquenchable, and even as the flint-stone in the fire, being burned, is red hot, and yet consumeth not, so likewise the damned souls in our hellish fire are ever burning, but their pains never diminishing. Therefore is hell called the everlasting pain, in which is neither hope nor mercy; so is it called utter darkness, in which we see neither the light of sun, moon, nor star; and were our darkness like the darkness of the night, yet were there hope of mercy, but ours is perpetual darkness, clean exempt from the face of God.

Hell hath also a place within it called Chasma, out of the which issueth all manner of thunders, lightnings, with such horrible shriekings and wailings, that ofttimes the very devils themselves stand in fear thereof; for one while it sendeth forth winds with exceeding snow, hail, and rain congealing the water into ice, with the which the damned are frozen, gnash their teeth, howl and cry, and yet cannot die. Otherwhiles, it sendeth forth most horrible hot mists or fogs, with flashing flames of fire and brimstone, wherein the sorrowful souls of the damned lie broiling in their reiterated torments. Yea, Faustus, hell is called a prison wherein the damned lie continually bound; it is also called *Pernicies* and *Exitium*, death, destruction, hurtfulness, mischief, a mischance, a pitiful and an evil thing, world without end. We have also with us in hell a ladder, reaching of an exceeding height, as though it would touch the heavens, on which the damned ascend to seek the blessing of God; but through their infidelity, when they are at the very highest degree, they fall down again into their former miseries, complaining of the heat of that unquenchable fire; yea, sweet Faustus, so must thou understand of hell, the while thou art so desirous to know the secrets of our kingdom. And mark, Faustus, hell is the nurse of death, the heat of all fire, the shadow of heaven and earth, the oblivion of all goodness, the pains unspeakable, the griefs unremovable, the dwelling of devils, dragons, serpents, adders, toads, crocodiles, and all manner of venomous creatures, the puddle of sin, the stinking fog ascending from the Stygian lake, brimstone, pitch, and all manner of unclean metals, the perpetual and unquenchable fire, the end of whose miseries was never purposed by God; yea, yea Faustus, thou sayst I shall, I must, nay I will tell thee the secrets of our kingdom, for thou buyest it dearly, and thou must and shalt be partaker of our torments that (as the Lord God said) never shall cease; for hell, the woman's belly, and the earth are never satisfied. There shalt thou abide horrible torments, trembling, gnashing of teeth, howling, crying, burning, freezing, melting, swimming in a labyrinth of miseries, scalding, burning, smoking in thine eyes, stinking in thy nose, hoarseness of thy speech, deafness of thine ears, trembling of thy hands, biting thine own tongue with pain, thy heart crushed as in a press, thy bones broken, the devils tossing firebrands upon thee, yea, thy whole carcass tossed upon muck-forks from one devil to another; yea, Faustus, then wilt thou wish for death, and he will fly from thee; thine unspeakable torments shall be every day augmented more and more, for the greater the sin, the greater is the punishment. How likest thou this, my Faustus, a resolution [explanation] answerable to thy request?

Lastly, thou wilt have me tell thee that which belongeth only to God, which is, if it be possible for the damned to come again into the favour of God, or not. Why, Faustus, thou knowest that this is against thy promise. For what shouldst thou desire to know that, having already given thy soul to the devil to have the pleasure of this world, and to know the secrets of hell? Therefore art thou damned, and how canst thou then come again to the favour of God? Wherefore I directly answer, no; for whomsoever God hath forsaken and thrown into hell, must there abide His wrath and indignation in that unquenchable fire, where is no hope nor mercy to be looked for, but abiding in perpetual pains, world without end; for even as much it availeth thee Faustus, to hope for the favour of God again, as Lucifer himself, who indeed although he and we all have a hope, yet is it to small avail, and taketh none effect, for out of that place God will neither hear crying nor sighing; if He do, thou shalt have as little remorse, as Dives, Cain, or Judas had. What helpeth the emperor, king, prince, duke, earl, baron, lord, knight, squire or gentleman, to cry for mercy being there? Nothing; for if on the earth they would not be tyrants, and self-willed, rich with covetousness, proud with pomp, gluttons, drunkards, whoremongers, backbiters, robbers, murderers, blasphemers, and suchlike, then were there some hope to be looked for; therefore my Faustus, as thou comest to hell with these qualities, thou must say with Cain, 'My sins are greater than can be forgiven'; go hang thyself with Judas, and lastly, be content to suffer torments with Dives. Therefore know, Faustus, that the damned have neither end 120 nor time appointed in the which they may hope to be released, for if there were any such hope, that they but by throwing one drop of water out of the sea in a day, until it were all dry, or if there were an heap of sand as high as from the earth to the heavens, that a bird carrying away but one corn in a day, at the end of this so long labour, that yet they might hope at the last, God would have mercy on them, they would be comforted; but now there is no hope that God once thinks upon them, or that their howlings shall ever be heard. Yea, so impossible, as it is for thee to hide thyself from God, or impossible for thee to remove the mountains, or to empty the 130 sea, or to tell the number of the drops of rain that have fallen from heaven until this day, or to tell what there is most of in the world, yea and for a camel to go through the eye of a needle; even so impossible it is for thee Faustus, and the rest of the damned, to come again into the favour of God. And thus Faustus, hast thou heard my last sentence, and I pray thee, how dost thou like it? But know this, that I counsel thee to let me be unmolested hereafter with such disputations, or else I will vex thee every limb, to thy small contentment.'

Doctor Faustus departed from his spirit very pensive and sorrow- 140 ful, laid him on his bed, altogether doubtful of the grace and favour of God, wherefore he fell into fantastical cogitations; fain he would have had his soul at liberty again, but the devil had so blinded him, and taken such deep root in his heart that he could never think to crave God's mercy. Or if by chance he had any good motion [impulse], straightways the devil would thrust him a fair lady into his chamber, which fell to kissing and dalliance with him, through which means he threw his godly motions in the wind, going forward still in his wicked practices, to the utter ruin both of his body and soul.

CHAPTER 16

Another question put forth by Doctor Faustus to his spirit Mephostophiles of his own estate.

Doctor Faustus, being yet desirous to hear more strange things, called his spirit unto him, saying, 'My Mephostophiles, I have yet another suit unto thee, which I pray thee deny not to resolve me of.'

'Faustus,' quoth the spirit, 'I am loth to reason with thee any further, for thou art never satisfied in thy mind, but always bringest me a new.'

'Yet I pray thee this once,' quoth Faustus, 'do me so much favour, as to tell me the truth in this matter, and hereafter I will be no more so earnest with thee.'

The spirit was altogether against it, but yet once more he would abide [hear] him.

'Well,' said the spirit to Faustus, 'what demandest thou of me?'

Faustus said, 'I would gladly know of thee, if thou wert a man in manner and form as I am, what wouldest thou do to please both God and man?'

Whereat the spirit smiled saying, 'My Faustus, if I were a man as thou art, and that God had adorned me with those gifts of nature as thou once hadst, even so long as the breath of God were by and within me, would I humble myself unto His majesty, endeavouring in all that I could to keep His commandments, praise Him, glorify Him, that I might continue in His favour, so were I sure to enjoy the eternal joy and felicity of His kingdom.'

Faustus said, 'But that have not I done.'

'No, thou sayest true,' quoth Mephostophiles, 'thou hast not done it, but thou hast denied thy lord and maker, which gave thee the breath of life, speech, hearing, sight, and all other thy reasonable [rational] senses that thou mightest understand His will and pleasure, to live to the glory and honour of His name, and to the advancement of thy body and soul. Him, I say, being thy maker hast thou denied and defied, yea, wickedly thou hast applied that excellent gift of thine understanding, and given thy soul to the devil. Therefore give none the blame but thine own self-will, thy proud and aspiring mind, which hath brought thee into the wrath of God and utter damnation.'

'This is most true,' quoth Faustus. 'But tell me, Mephostophiles, wouldst thou be in my case as I am now?'

'Yea,' saith the spirit (and with that fetched a great sigh) 'for yet would I so humble myself, that I would win the favour of God.'

'Then,' said Doctor Faustus, 'it were time enough for me if I amended.'

'True,' said Mephostophiles, 'if it were not for thy great sins, which are so odious and detestable in the sight of God that it is too late for thee, for the wrath of God resteth upon thee.'

'Leave off,' quoth Faustus, 'and tell [answer] me my question to my greater comfort.'

CHAPTER 17

Here followeth the second part of Doctor Faustus his life and practices, until his end.

Doctor Faustus having received denial of his spirit to be resolved any more in suchlike questions propounded, forgot all good works, and fell to be a calendar-maker by help of his spirit, and also in short time to be a good astronomer or astrologian. He had learned so perfectly of his spirit the course of the sun, moon, and stars, that he had the most famous name of all the mathematics [astrologers] that lived in his time, as may well appear by his works dedicated unto sundry dukes and lords; for he did nothing without the advice of his spirit, which learned him to presage of matters to come, which have come to pass since his death. The like praise won he with his   10 calendars and almanacs-making, for when he presaged upon any change, operation, or alteration of the weather or elements, as wind, rain, fogs, snow, hail, moist, dry, warm, cold, thunder, lightning, it fell so duly out, as if an angel of heaven had forewarned it. He did not like the unskilful astronomers of our time, that set in winter cold, moist, airy, frosty, and in the dog-days, hot, dry, thunder, fire, and suchlike, but he set in all his works, day and hour, when, where, and how it should happen. If anything wonderful were at hand, as death, famine, plague, or wars, he would set the time and place in true and just order, when it should come to pass.

CHAPTER 18

A question put forth by Doctor Faustus to his spirit concerning astronomy.

Doctor Faustus falling to practise, and making his prognostications, he was doubtful in many points; wherefore he called unto him Mephostophiles his spirit, saying, 'I find the ground of this science very difficult to attain unto; for that when I confer [compare] *Astronomia* and *Astrologia*, as the mathematicians and ancient writers have left in memory, I find them to vary and very much to disagree; wherefore I pray thee to teach me the truth in this matter.'

To whom his spirit answered, 'Faustus, thou shalt know that the practitioners or speculators, or at least the first inventors of these arts, have done nothing of themselves certain whereupon thou mayst attain to the true prognosticating or presaging of things concerning the heavens, or the influence of the planets; for if by chance some one mathematician or astronomer hath left behind him anything worthy of memory, they have so blinded [obscured] it with enigmatical words, blind characters, and such obscure figures, that it is impossible for an earthly man to attain unto the knowledge thereof without the aid of some spirit, or else the special gift of God, for such are the hidden works of God from men; yet do we spirits that fly and fleet in all elements know such, and there is nothing to be done, or by the heavens pretended [portended], but we know it, except only the day of doom.

Wherefore, Faustus, learn of me; I will teach thee the course and recourse of ♄ ♃ ♂ ☉ ♀ ☿ and ☾ , the cause of winter and summer, the exaltation and declination of the sun, the eclipse of the moon, the distance and height of the poles, and every fixed star, the nature and operation of the elements, fire, air, water, and earth, and all that is contained in them; yea, herein there is nothing hidden from me, but only the fifth essence [quintessence], which once thou hadst Faustus, at liberty, but now Faustus, thou hast lost it past recovery. Wherefore, leaving that which will not be again had, learn now of me to make thunder, lightning, hail, snow, and rain, the clouds to rent, the earth and craggy rocks to shake and split in sunder, the seas to swell and roar, and over-run their marks.

Knowest not thou that the deeper the sun shines, the hotter he pierces? So, the more thy art is famous whilst thou art here, the greater shall be thy name when thou art gone. Knowest not thou that the earth is frozen, cold and dry; the water running, cold and moist; the air flying, hot and moist; the fire consuming, hot and dry? Yea, Faustus, so must thy heart be inflamed like the fire to mount on high. Learn, Faustus, to fly like myself, as swift as thought from one kingdom to another, to sit at princes' tables, to eat their daintiest fare, to have thy pleasure of their fair ladies, wives, and concubines, to use their jewels and costly robes as things belonging to thee, and not unto them; learn of me, Faustus, to run through walls, doors, and gates of stone and iron, to creep into the earth like a worm, to swim in the water like a fish, to fly in the air like a bird, and to live and nourish thyself in the fire like a salamander. So shalt thou be famous, renowned, far-spoken of, and extolled for thy skill: going on knives, not hurting thy feet; carrying fire in thy bosom, and not burning thy shirt; seeing through the heavens as through a crystal, wherein is placed the planets, with all the rest of the presaging comets, the whole circuit of the world from the east to the west, north and south. There shalt thou know, Faustus, wherefore the fiery sphere above ♄ and the signs of the zodiac doth not burn and consume the whole face of the earth, being hindered by placing the two moist elements between them, the airy clouds and the wavering waves of water.

Yea, Faustus, I will learn thee the secrets of nature: what the causes that the sun in summer being at the highest, giveth all his heat downwards on the earth; and being in winter at the lowest, giveth all his heat upward into the heavens; that the snow should be of so great virtue as the honey, and the lady Saturnia ♓ in *Occulto*, more hotter than the sun in *Manifesto*. Come on, my Faustus, I will make thee as perfect in these things as myself; I will learn thee to go invisible, to find out the mines of gold and silver, the fodines [mines] of precious stones, as the carbuncle, the diamond, sapphire, emerald, ruby, topaz, jacinth, garnet, jasper, amethyst. Use all these at thy pleasure, take thy heart's desire. Thy time, Faustus, weareth away; then why wilt thou not take thy pleasure of the world? Come up, we will go visit kings at their own courts, and at their most sumptuous banquets be their guests; if willingly they invite us not, then perforce we will serve our own turn with their best meat and daintiest wine.'

'Agreed,' quoth Faustus, 'but let me pause a while upon this thou hast even now declared unto me.'

CHAPTER 19

**How Doctor Faustus fell into despair with himself;
for having put forth a question unto his spirit, they
fell at variance, whereupon the whole rout of devils
appeared unto him, threatening him sharply.**

Doctor Faustus revolving with himself the speeches of his spirit, he became so woeful and sorrowful in his cogitations, that he thought himself already frying in the hottest flames of hell, and lying in his muse [meditation], suddenly there appeared unto him his spirit, demanding what thing so grieved and troubled his conscience, whereat Doctor Faustus gave no answer. Yet the spirit very earnestly lay upon him to know the cause, and if it were possible, he would find remedy for his grief and ease him of his sorrows.

To whom Faustus answered, 'I have taken thee unto me as a servant to do me service, and thy service will be very dear unto me; yet I cannot have any diligence of thee further than thou list thyself, neither dost thou in anything as it becometh thee.'

The spirit replied, 'My Faustus, thou knowest that I was never against thy commandments as yet, but ready to serve and resolve thy questions; although I am not bound unto thee in such respects as concern the hurt of our kingdom, yet was I always willing to answer thee, and so I am still. Therefore, my Faustus, say on boldly; what is thy will and pleasure?'

At which words, the spirit stole away the heart of Faustus, who spake in this sort: 'Mephostophiles, tell me how and after what sort God made the world, and all the creatures in them, and why man was made after the image of God.'

The spirit hearing this, answered, 'Faustus, thou knowest that all this is in vain for thee to ask. I know that thou art sorry for that thou hast done, but it availeth thee not, for I will tear thee in thousands of pieces, if thou change not thine opinions.' And hereat he vanished away.

Whereat Faustus, all sorrowful for that he had put forth such a question, fell to weeping and to howling bitterly, not for his sins towards God, but for that the devil was departed from him so suddenly, and in such a rage. And being in this perplexity, he was suddenly taken in such an extreme cold, as if he should have frozen in the place where he sat, in which the greatest devil in hell appeared unto him, with certain of his hideous and infernal company in the most ugliest shapes that it was possible to think upon, and traversing the chamber round about where Faustus sat. Faustus thought to himself, 'Now are they come for me, though my time be not come, and that because I have asked such questions of my servant Mephostophiles.'

At whose cogitations, the chiefest devil, which was his lord, unto whom he gave his soul, that was Lucifer, spake in this sort:

'Faustus, I have seen thy thoughts, which are not as thou hast vowed unto me, by virtue of this letter,' and showed him the obligation that he had written with his own blood. 'Wherefore, I am come to visit thee and to show thee some of our hellish pastimes, in hope that will draw and confirm thy mind a little more steadfast unto us.'

'Content,' quoth Faustus; 'go to, let me see what pastime you can make.'

At which words, the great devil in his likeness sat him down by Faustus, commanding the rest of the devils to appear in their form as if they were in hell. First entered Belial in form of a bear, with curled black hair to the ground, his ears standing upright; within the ear was as red as blood, out of which issued flames of fire. His teeth were a foot at least long, as white as snow, with a tail three ells long (at the least), having two wings, one behind each arm. And

209

thus one after another they appeared to Faustus in form as they
were in hell. Lucifer himself sat in manner of a man, all hairy, but
of a brown colour like a squirrel, curled, and his tail turning
upwards on his back as the squirrels use; I think he could crack nuts   60
too like a squirrel. After him came Beelzebub in curled hair of
horse-flesh colour, his head like the head of a bull; with a mighty
pair of horns, and two long ears down to the ground, and two wings
on his back, with pricking stings like thorns; out of his wings issued
flames of fire; his tail was like a cow's. . . .

[A number of other devils, in similarly fantastic forms, are described.]

. . . everyone at his entry into the hall made their reverence unto
Lucifer, and so took their places, standing in order as they came,
until they had filled the whole hall; wherewith suddenly fell a most
horrible thunder-clap, that the house shook as though it would
have fallen to the ground, upon which every monster had a muck-   70
fork in his hand, holding them towards Faustus as though they
would have run a tilt at him, which when Faustus perceived, he
thought upon the words of Mephostophiles, when he told him how
the souls in hell were tormented, being cast from devil to devil
upon muck-forks; he thought verily to have been tormented there
of them in like sort.

But Lucifer perceiving his thought, spake to him, 'My Faustus,
how likest thou this crew of mine?'

Quoth Faustus, 'Why came you not in another manner of shape?'

Lucifer replied, 'We cannot change our hellish form; we   80
have showed ourselves here, as we are there. Yet can we blind
men's eyes in such sort, that when we will we repair unto them
as if we were men or angels of light, although our dwelling be
in darkness.'

Then said Faustus, 'I like not so many of you together.'

Whereupon Lucifer commanded them to depart, except seven of
the principal. Forthwith they presently vanished, which Faustus
perceiving, he was somewhat better comforted, and spake to
Lucifer, 'Where is my servant Mephostophiles? Let me see if he can
do the like.'   90

Whereupon came a fierce dragon, flying and spitting fire round
about the house, and coming towards Lucifer, made reverence, and
then changed himself to the form of a friar, saying, 'Faustus, what
wilt thou?'

Saith Faustus, 'I will that thou teach me to transform myself in
like sort as thou and the rest have done.'

Then Lucifer put forth his paw, and gave Faustus a book, saying,
'Hold, do what thou wilt,' which he looking upon, straightways

changed himself into a hog, then into a worm, then into a dragon, and finding this for his purpose, it liked him well. 100

Quoth he to Lucifer, 'And how cometh it that all these filthy forms are in the world?'

Lucifer answered, 'They are ordained of God as plagues unto men, and so shalt thou be plagued,' quoth he.

Whereupon came scorpions, wasps, emmets [ants], bees, and gnats, which fell to stinging and biting him, and all the whole house was filled with a most horrible stinking fog, insomuch that Faustus saw nothing, but still was tormented.

Wherefore he cried for help, saying, 'Mephostophiles, my faithful servant, where art thou? Help, help, I pray thee.' 110

Hereat his spirit answered nothing, but Lucifer himself said, 'Ho ho ho Faustus, how likest thou the creation of the world?'

And incontinent [immediately] it was clear again, and the devils and all the filthy cattle were vanished, only Faustus was left alone, seeing nothing, but hearing the sweetest music that ever he heard before, at which he was so ravished with delight that he forgot the fears he was in before, and it repented him that he had seen no more of their pastime.

CHAPTER 20

How Doctor Faustus desired to see hell, and of the manner how he was used therein.

Doctor Faustus bethinking how his time went away, and how he had spent eight years thereof, he meant to spend the rest to his better contentment, intending quite to forget any such motions as might offend the devil any more.

Wherefore on a time he called his spirit Mephostophiles, and said unto him, 'Bring thou hither unto me thy lord Lucifer, or Belial.'

He brought him (notwithstanding) one that was called Beelzebub, the which asked Faustus his pleasure.

Quoth Faustus, 'I would know of thee if I may see hell and take a view thereof?' 10

'That thou shalt,' said the devil, 'and at midnight I will fetch thee.' . . .

[At midnight 'a great rugged black bear' appears on whose back Faustus is transported to 'a place which burneth continually'. In a nightmarish sequence he finds himself stranded on a high rock and casts himself off it intending suicide, but is unharmed and is carried back to his home by the devil in the shape of a bear.]

CHAPTER 21

**How Doctor Faustus was carried through the air up to the
heavens to see the world, and how the sky and planets ruled;
after the which he wrote one letter to his friend of the same to
Leipzig, how he went about the world in eight days.**

This letter was found by a freeman and citizen of Wittenberg, written
with his own hand, and sent to his friend at Leipzig, a physician
named Jonas Victor, the contents of which were as followeth:

Amongst other things (my loving friend and brother) I remember
yet the former friendship had together, when we were school-
fellows and students in the University at Wittenberg; whereas you
first studied physic, astronomy, astrology, geometry, and cosmog-
raphy, I to the contrary (you know) studied divinity. Notwithstanding, now in any of your own studies I am seen [advanced] (I am
persuaded) further than yourself, for sithence [since] I began I   10
have never erred, for (might I speak it without affecting my own
praise) my calendars and other practices have not only the commendations of the common sort, but also of the chiefest lords and
nobles of this our Dutch [German] nation; because (which is
chiefly to be noted) I wrote and presaged of matters to come, which
all accord and fall out so right, as if they had been already seen
before. And for that (my beloved Victor) you write to know my
voyage which I made into the heavens, the which (as you certify me)
you have had some suspicion of, although you partly persuaded
yourself that it is a thing impossible. No matter for that, it is as it is,   20
and let it be as it will, once it was done, in such manner as now
according unto your request I give you here to understand.

I being once laid on my bed, and could not sleep for thinking on
my calendar and practice, I marvelled with myself how it were
possible that the firmament should be known and so largely written
of men, or whether they write true or false, by their own opinions,
or supposition, or by due observations and true course of the
heavens. Behold, being in these my muses [meditations], suddenly
I heard a great noise, insomuch that I thought my house would
have been blown down, so that all my doors and chests flew open,   30
whereat I was not a little astonied [astonished], for withal I heard a
groaning voice which said, 'Get up! The desire of thy heart, mind,
and thought shalt thou see.'

At the which I answered, 'What my heart desireth, that would I
fain see, and to make proof, if I shall see I will away with thee.'

'Why then,' quoth he, 'look out at thy window; there cometh a
messenger for thee.'

That did I, and behold, there stood a wagon, with two dragons before it to draw the same, and all the wagon was of a light burning fire [ablaze], and for that the moon shone, I was the willinger at that time to depart. 40

But the voice spake again, 'Sit up and let us away!'

'I will,' said I, 'go with thee, but upon this condition, that I may ask after all things that I see, hear, or think on.'

The voice answered, 'I am content for this time.'

Hereupon I got me into the wagon, so that the dragons carried me upright into the air. The wagon had also four wheels, the which rattled so, and made such a noise as if we had been all this while running on the stones; and round about us flew out flames of fire, and the higher that I came, the more the earth seemed to be 50 darkened, so that methought I came out of a dungeon. And looking down from heaven, behold, Mephostophiles my spirit and servant was behind me, and when he perceived that I saw him, he came and sat by me, to whom I said, 'I pray thee Mephostophiles, whither shall I go now?'

'Let not that trouble thy mind,' said he, and yet they carried us higher up.

And now will I tell thee, good friend and schoolfellow, what things I have seen and proved [experienced]; for on the Tuesday went I out, and on Tuesday seven-nights following I came home 60 again, that is, eight days, in which time I slept not, no, not one wink came in mine eyes, and we went invisible of any man. And as the day began to appear, after our first night's journey, I said to my spirit Mephostophiles, 'I pray thee, how far have we now ridden? I am sure thou knowest. For methinks that we are ridden exceeding far, the world seemeth so little.'

Mephostophiles answered me, 'My Faustus, believe me, that from the place from whence thou camst, unto this place where we are now, is already forty-seven leagues right in height.'

And as the day increased, I looked down upon the world; there 70 saw I many kingdoms and provinces. . . . Then looked I up to the heavens, and behold, they went so swift that I thought they would have sprung in thousands. Likewise it was so clear and so hot, that I could not long gaze into it, it so dimmed my sight, and had not my spirit Mephostophiles covered me as it were with a shadowing cloud, I had been burnt with the extreme heat thereof, for the sky the which we behold here when we look up from the earth, is so fast [firm] and thick as a wall, clear and shining bright as a crystal, in the which is placed the sun, which casteth forth his rays or beams over the universal world, to the uttermost confines of the earth. But 80 we think that the sun is very little; no, it is altogether as big as the world. Indeed the body substantial is but little in compass, but the rays or stream that it casteth forth, by reason of the thing wherein it is placed, maketh him to extend and show himself over the whole world. And we think that the sun runneth his course, and that the heavens stand still; no, it is the heavens that move his course, and the sun abideth perpetually in his place. . . . It is the axle of the heavens that moveth the whole firmament, being a chaos or confused thing, and for that proof, I will show thee this example: like as thou seest a bubble made of water and soap blown forth of a quill is in form of a confused mass or chaos, and being in this form, is moved at pleasure of the wind. . . even so is the whole firmament or chaos, wherein are placed the sun and the rest of the planets, turned and carried at the pleasure of the spirit of God, which is wind.

Yea, Christian reader, to the glory of God, and for the profit of thy soul, I will open unto thee the divine opinion touching the ruling of this confused chaos, far more than any rude German author, being possessed with the devil, was able to utter; and to prove some of my sentence before to be true, look into Genesis unto the works of God, at the creation of the world. There shalt thou find that the spirit of God moved upon the waters before heaven and earth were made. Mark how He made it, and how by His word every element took his place. . . and like as I showed before of the bubble or confused chaos made of water and soap [which] through the wind and breath of man is turned round, and carried with every wind, even so the firmament wherein the sun and the rest of the planets are fixed [is] moved, turned, and carried with the wind, breath, or spirit of God, for the heavens and firmament are moveable as the chaos, but the sun is fixed in the firmament.

And further, my good schoolfellow, I was thus nigh the heavens, where methought every planet was but as half the earth, and under the firmament ruled the spirits in the air, and as I came down I looked upon the world and the heavens, and methought that the earth was enclosed in comparison within the firmament, as the yolk of an egg within the white, and methought that the whole length of the earth was not a span long, and the water was as if it had been twice as broad and long as the earth. Even thus at the eight days' end came I home again, and fell asleep, and so I continued sleeping three days and three nights together. And the first hour that I waked, I fell fresh again to my calendar[s], and have made them in right ample manner as you know, and to satisfy your request, for that you writ unto me, I have in consideration of our old friendship had at the University of Wittenberg, declared unto you my heavenly voyage, wishing no worse unto you, than unto

90

100

110

120

myself, that is, that your mind were as mine in all respects. *Dixi* [I have said].

Doctor Faustus the Astrologian.

CHAPTER 22

How Doctor Faustus made his journey through the principal and most famous lands in the world.

Doctor Faustus having overrun fifteen years of his appointed time, he took upon him a journey with full pretence [intention] to see the whole world, and calling his spirit Mephostophiles unto him, he said, 'Thou knowest that thou art bound unto me upon conditions, to perform and fulfil my desire in all things, wherefore my pretence is to visit the whole face of the earth, visible and invisible when it pleaseth me; wherefore I enjoin and command thee to the same.'

Whereupon Mephostophiles answered, 'I am ready, my lord, at thy command.'

And forthwith the spirit changed himself into the likeness of a 10 flying horse, saying, 'Faustus, sit up, I am ready.'

Doctor Faustus loftily sat upon him, and forward they went. Faustus came through many a land and province. . . . [There follows a list, considerably expanded by P.F., whose additions include 'all America'.] All these kingdoms, provinces and countries he passed in twenty-five days, in which time he saw very little that delighted his mind. Wherefore he took a little rest at home, and burning in desire to see more at large, and to behold the secrets of each kingdom, he set forward again on his journey upon his swift horse Mephostophiles, and came to Trier, for that he chiefly desired to 20 see this town, and the monuments thereof. But there he saw not many wonders, except one fair palace that belonged unto the bishop, and also a mighty large castle that was built of brick, with three walls and three great trenches, so strong, that it was impossible for any prince's power to win it. . . . From whence he departed to Paris, where he liked well the academy. And what place or kingdom soever fell in his mind, the same he visited. He came from Paris to Mainz, where the river of Main falls into the Rhine; notwithstanding, he tarried not long there, but went to Campania in the kingdom of Naples, in which he saw an innumerable sort of 30 cloisters, nunneries, and churches, great and high houses of stone, the streets fair and large, and straight forth from one end of the town to the other as a line. And all the pavement of the city was of brick, and the more it rained in the town, the fairer the streets were. There saw he the tomb of Virgil, and the highway that he cut through that mighty hill of stone in one night, the whole length of an English mile. . . . From thence he came to Venice, whereas he wondered not a little. . . at the fairness of St Mark's place, and the sumptuous church standing therein called St Mark's; how all the pavement was set with coloured stones, and all the rood or loft of the church double gilded over. Leaving this, he came to Padua, beholding the manner of their academy, which is called the mother or nurse of Christendom. There he heard the doctors, and saw the most monuments in the town, entered his name into the university of the German nation, and wrote himself, 'Doctor Faustus, the insatiable speculator'. Then saw he the worthiest monument in the world for a church, named St Antony's cloister, which for the pinnacles thereof, and the contriving of the church, hath not the like in Christendom. . . .

Well, forward he went to Rome, which lay, and doth yet lie, on the river Tiber, the which divideth the city in two parts. Over the river are four great stone bridges, and upon the one bridge, called Ponte S Angelo, is the castle of S Angelo, wherein are so many great cast pieces [cannons] as there are days in a year, and such pieces that will shoot seven bullets off with one fire. . . . The city hath eleven gates, and a hill called Vaticanum, whereon St Peter's church is built. . . . Hard by this he visited the churchyard of St Peter's, where he saw the pyramid that Julius Caesar brought out of Africa. It stood in Faustus his time leaning against the church wall of St Peter's, but now Pope Sixtus hath erected it in the middle of St Peter's churchyard. It is 24 fathom long and at the lower end six fathom four square, and so forth smaller upwards; on the top is a crucifix of beaten gold, the stone standeth on four lions of brass. Other monuments he saw, too many to recite, but amongst the rest he was desirous to see the Pope's palace, and his manner of service at his table, wherefore he and his spirit made themselves invisible, and came into the Pope's court and privy chamber where he was. There saw he many servants attendant on His Holiness, with many a flattering sycophant carrying of his meat, and there he marked the Pope and the manner of his service, which he seeing to be so unmeasurable and sumptuous, 'Fie,' quoth Faustus, 'why had not the devil made a pope of me?'

Faustus saw notwithstanding in that place those that were like to himself, proud, stout [arrogant], wilful, gluttons, drunkards, whoremongers, breakers of wedlock, and followers of all manner of ungodly exercises. Wherefore he said to his spirit, 'I thought that I had been alone a hog or pork of the devil's, but he must bear with me yet a little longer, for these hogs of Rome are already fattened, and fitted to make his roast meat. The devil might do well now to

216

spit them all and have them to the fire, and let him summon the 80
nuns to turn the spits; for as none must confess the nun but the
friar, so none should turn the roasting friar but the nun.'

Thus continued Faustus three days in the Pope's palace, and yet
had no lust to his meat, but stood still in the Pope's chamber, and
saw everything whatsoever it was. On a time the Pope would have a
feast prepared for the Cardinal of Pavia, and for his first welcome
the Cardinal was bidden to dinner; and as he sat at meat, the Pope
would ever be blessing and crossing over his mouth. Faustus could
suffer it no longer, but up with his fist and smote the Pope on the
face, and withal he laughed that the whole house might hear him, 90
yet none of them saw him nor knew where he was. The Pope
persuaded his company that it was a damned soul, commanding a
mass presently to be said for his delivery out of purgatory, which
was done. The Pope sat still at meat, but when the latter mess
[course] came in to the Pope's board, Doctor Faustus laid hands
thereon, saying 'This is mine'; and he took both dish and meat and
fled unto the Capitol or Campidoglio, calling his spirit unto him
and said, 'Come, let us be merry, for thou must fetch me some wine,
and the cup that the Pope drinks of, and here upon Monte Cavallo
[the Quirinal] will we make good cheer in spite of the Pope and all 100
his fat abbey-lubbers.'

His spirit hearing this, departed towards the Pope's chamber,
where he found them yet sitting and quaffing; wherefore he took
from before the Pope the fairest piece of plate or drinking goblet,
and a flagon of wine, and brought it to Faustus. But when the Pope
and the rest of his crew perceived they were robbed, and knew not
after what sort, they persuaded themselves that it was the damned
soul that before had vexed the Pope so, and that smote him on the
face. Wherefore he sent commandment through all the whole city
of Rome, that they should say mass in every church, and ring all the 110
bells for to lay the walking spirit, and to curse him with bell, book,
and candle, that so invisibly had misused the Pope's Holiness, with
the Cardinal of Pavia, and the rest of their company. But Faustus
notwithstanding made good cheer with that which he had beguiled
the Pope of, and in the midst of the order of St Bernard's
barefooted friars, as they were going on procession through the
market-place, called Campo dei Fiori, he let fall his plate dishes and
cup, and withal for a farewell he made such a thunderclap and a
storm of rain, as though heaven and earth should have met together, and so he left Rome. . . . 120

[A very long and detailed account follows of Faustus's travels in
Europe and the Near East. In Turkey he contrives to enjoy the ladies

217

of the Emperor's harem; finally, he is granted a sight of Paradise from 'the hill of Caucasus'. In the remaining chapters in this section, he displays his knowledge by answering a series of questions, chiefly concerning astronomy.]

The third and last part of Doctor Faustus his merry conceits, showing after what sort he practised necromancy in the courts of great princes, and lastly of his fearful and pitiful end.

CHAPTER 29

How the Emperor Carolus Quintus requested of Faustus to see some of his cunning, whereunto he agreed.

The Emperor Carolus, the fifth of that name, was personally with the rest of his nobles and gentlemen at the town of Innsbruck where he kept his court, unto the which also Doctor Faustus resorted, and being there well known of divers nobles and gentlemen, he was invited into the court to meat, even in the presence of the Emperor. Whom when the Emperor saw, he looked earnestly on him, thinking him by his looks to be some wonderful fellow, wherefore he asked one of his nobles whom he should be, who answered that he was called Doctor Faustus.

Whereupon the Emperor held his peace until he had taken his repast, after which he called unto him Faustus into the privy chamber, whither being come, he said unto him, 'Faustus, I have heard much of thee, that thou art excellent in the black art, and none like thee in mine empire, for men say that thou hast a familiar spirit with thee and that thou canst do what thou list. It is therefore,' saith the Emperor, 'my request of thee that thou let me see a proof of thine experience [skill], and I vow unto thee by the honour of mine imperial crown, none evil shall happen unto thee for so doing.'

Hereupon Doctor Faustus answered His Majesty, that upon those conditions he was ready in anything that he could, to do His Highness's commandment in what service he would appoint him.

'Well, then hear what I say,' quoth the Emperor. 'Being once solitary in my house, I called to mind mine elders and ancestors, how it was possible for them to attain unto so great a degree of authority, yea so high, that we, the successors of that line, are never able to come near. As for example, the great and mighty monarch of the world Alexander Magnus was such a lantern and spectacle to all his successors, as the chronicles make mention of so great riches, conquering and subduing so many kingdoms, the which I and those that follow me (I fear) shall never be able to attain unto. Wherefore, Faustus, my hearty desire is that thou wouldst vouchsafe to let me see that Alexander, and his paramour, the which was praised to be so fair, and I pray thee show me them in such sort that I may see their personages, shape, gesture and apparel, as they used in their lifetime, and that here before my face, to the end that I may say I have my long desire fulfilled, and to praise thee to be a famous man in thine art and experience.'

Doctor Faustus answered, 'My most excellent lord, I am ready to accomplish your request in all things, so far forth as I and my spirit are able to perform; yet Your Majesty shall know that their dead bodies are not able substantially to be brought before you, but such spirits as have seen Alexander and his paramour alive, shall appear unto you in manner and form as they both lived in their most flourishing time. And herewith I hope to please Your Imperial Majesty.'

Then Faustus went a little aside to speak to his spirit, but he returned again presently, saying, 'Now, if it please Your Majesty you shall see them, yet upon this condition, that you demand no question of them, nor speak unto them.' Which the Emperor agreed unto.

Wherewith Doctor Faustus opened the privy chamber door, where presently entered the great and mighty Emperor Alexander Magnus, in all things to look upon as if he had been alive, in proportion a strong thickset man, of a middle stature, black hair, and that both thick and curled, head and beard, red cheeks, and a broad face, with eyes like a basilisk; he had on a complete harness [armour], burnished and graven, exceeding rich to look upon. And so passing towards the Emperor Carolus, he made low and reverent courtesy, whereat the Emperor Carolus would have stood up to receive and greet him with the like reverence, but Faustus took hold of him and would not permit him to do it.

Shortly after, Alexander made humble reverence and went out again, and coming to the door his paramour met him; she coming in, she made the emperor likewise reverence. She was clothed in blue velvet, wrought and embroidered with pearl and gold; she was also excellent fair, like milk and blood mixed, tall and slender, with a face round as an apple, and thus she passed certain times up and down the house, which the Emperor marking, said to himself, 'Now have I seen two persons which my heart hath long wished for to behold, and sure it cannot otherwise be,' said he to himself, 'but that the spirits have changed themselves into these forms, and have not deceived me,' calling to his mind the woman that raised the prophet Samuel. And for that the Emperor would be the more

219

satisfied in the matter, he thought, 'I have heard say that behind her neck she had a great wart or wen.' Wherefore he took Faustus by the hand without any words, and went to see if it were also to be seen on her or not, but she perceiving that he came to her, bowed down her neck, where he saw a great wart, and hereupon she vanished, leaving the Emperor and the rest well contented. 80

CHAPTER 30

How Doctor Faustus in the sight of the Emperor conjured a pair of hart's horns upon a knight's head that slept out of a casement.

When Doctor Faustus had accomplished the Emperor's desire in all things as he was requested, he went forth into a gallery, and leaning over a rail to look into the privy garden, he saw many of the Emperor's courtiers walking and talking together, and casting his eyes now this way, now that way, he espied a knight leaning out at a window of the great hall, who was fast asleep (for in those days it was hot), but the person shall be nameless that slept, for that he was a knight, although it was done to a little disgrace of the gentleman. It pleased Doctor Faustus, through the help of his spirit Mephostophiles, to firm [fix] upon his head as he slept an huge pair of hart's horns. And as the knight awaked thinking to pull in his head, he hit his horns against the glass that the panes thereof flew about his ears. Think here how this good gentleman was vexed, for he could neither get backward nor forward; which when the Emperor heard all the courtiers laugh, and came forth to see what was happened, the Emperor also when he beheld the knight with so fair a head, laughed heartily thereat, and was therewithal well pleased. At last Faustus made him quit of his horns again, but the knight perceived how they came, etc. 10

CHAPTER 31

How the above-mentioned knight went about to be revenged of Doctor Faustus.

Doctor Faustus took his leave of the Emperor and the rest of the courtiers, at whose departure they were sorry, giving him many rewards and gifts; but being a league and a half from the city he came into a wood, where he beheld the knight that he had jested with at the court with other in harness, mounted on fair palfreys, and running with full charge towards Faustus. But he, seeing their intent, ran towards the bushes, and before he came amongst the bushes he returned again, running as it were to meet them that chased him. Whereupon suddenly all the bushes were turned into horsemen, which also ran to encounter with the knight and his company, and coming to them, they enclosed the knight and the rest, and told them that they must pay their ransom before they departed. Whereupon the knight seeing himself in such distress, besought Faustus to be good to them, which he denied not, but let them loose. Yet he so charmed them that everyone, knight and other, for the space of a whole month did wear a pair of goat's horns on their brows, and every palfrey a pair of ox horns on their head, and this was their penance appointed by Faustus, etc.

[There follows an account of some of Faustus's 'merry conceits' (chapters 32 and 33); in one, Faustus transports three young dukes from Wittenberg to Munich on his cloak; in the next, he deceives a Jewish money-lender by appearing to pawn his leg for a loan of sixty dollars.]

CHAPTER 34

How Doctor Faustus deceived an horse-courser.

In like manner he served an horse-courser at a fair called Pheiffering [a village near Munich], for Doctor Faustus through his cunning had gotten an excellent fair horse, whereupon he rid to the fair, where he had many chapmen that offered him money; lastly, he sold him for forty dollars, willing him that bought him, that in any wise he should not ride him over any water. But the horse-courser marvelled with himself that Faustus bade him ride him over no water.

'But', quoth he, 'I will prove [find out],' and forthwith he rid him into the river. Presently the horse vanished from under him, and he sat on a bundle of straw, insomuch that the man was almost drowned. The horse-courser knew well where he lay that had sold him his horse; wherefore he went angerly to his inn, where he found Doctor Faustus fast asleep and snorting on a bed, but the horse-courser could no longer forbear him, took him by the leg and began to pull him off the bed. But he pulled him so, that he pulled his leg from his body, insomuch that the horse-courser fell down backwards in the place. Then began Doctor Faustus to cry with an open throat [loudly], 'He hath murdered me.'

Hereat the horse-courser was afraid, and gave the flight, thinking none other with himself, but that he had pulled his leg from his body. By this means Doctor Faustus kept his money.

221

CHAPTER 35

How Doctor Faustus ate a load of hay.

Doctor Faustus being in a town of Germany called Zwickau, where he was accompanied with many doctors and masters, and going forth to walk after supper, they met with a clown [peasant] that drove a load of hay.

'Good even, good fellow,' said Faustus to the clown; 'what shall I give thee to let me eat my bellyfull of hay?'

The clown thought with himself, 'What a mad man is this to eat hay?' Thought he with himself, 'Thou wilt not eat much.'

They agreed for three farthings he should eat as much as he could, wherefore Doctor Faustus began to eat, and that so raven-   10
ously, that all the rest of his company fell a-laughing, blinding [deceiving] so the poor clown that he was sorry at his heart, for he seemed to have eaten more than the half of his hay, wherefore the clown began to speak him fair, for fear he should have eaten the other half also. Faustus made as though he had had pity on the clown, and went his way. When the clown came in place where he would be, he had his hay again as he had before, a full load.

[In chapter 36 Doctor Faustus strikes blind a group of brawling students; the students continue to fight, to the amusement of the spectators, but recover their sight on being led home.]

CHAPTER 37

How Faustus served the drunken clowns.

Doctor Faustus went into an inn, wherein were many tables full of clowns, the which were tippling can after can of excellent wine, and to be short, they were all drunk, and as they sat, they so sung and hallooed, that one could not hear a man speak for them.

This angered Doctor Faustus; wherefore he said to those that had called him in, 'Mark, my masters, I will show you a merry jest.'

The clowns continuing still hallooing and singing, he so con-jured them that their mouths stood as wide open as it was possible for them to hold them, and never a one of them was able to close his mouth again. By and by [at once] the noise was gone, the clowns   10
notwithstanding looked earnestly one upon another, and wist not what was happened; wherefore one by one they went out, and so soon as they came without, they were as well as ever they were; but none of them desired to go in any more.

[Chapter 38 repeats the trick played on the horse-courser with swine and a swine-driver, but the latter does not return to complain about his purchase.]

CHAPTER 39

How Doctor Faustus played a merry jest with the Duke of Anholt [Anhalt] in his court.

Doctor Faustus on a time came to the Duke of Anholt, the which welcomed him very courteously. This was in the month of January, where sitting at the table, he perceived the Duchess to be with child, and forbearing himself until the meat was taken from the table, and that they brought in the banqueting dishes, said Doctor Faustus to the Duchess, 'Gracious lady, I have alway heard that the great-bellied women do always long for some dainties. I beseech therefore Your Grace hide not your mind from me, but tell me what you desire to eat.'

She answered him, 'Doctor Faustus, now truly I will not hide   10
from you what my heart doth most desire, namely, that if it were now harvest, I would eat my bellyfull of ripe grapes and other dainty fruit.'

Doctor Faustus answered hereupon, 'Gracious lady, this is a small thing for me to do, for I can do more than this.' Wherefore he took a plate, and made open one of the casements of the window, holding it forth, where incontinent [immediately] he had his dish full of all manner of fruits, as red and white grapes, pears, and apples, the which came from out of strange countries.

All these he presented the Duchess, saying, 'Madame, I pray you   20
vouchsafe to taste of this dainty fruit, the which came from a far country, for there the summer is not yet ended.' The Duchess thanked Faustus highly, and she fell to her fruit with full appetite. The Duke of Anholt notwithstanding could not withhold to ask Faustus with what reason there were such young fruit to be had at that time of the year.

Doctor Faustus told him, 'May it please Your Grace to understand that the year is divided into two circles over the whole world; that when with us it is winter, in the contrary circle it is notwithstanding summer, for in India and Saba [the Yemen] there falleth or setteth   30
the sun, so that it is so warm that they have twice a year fruit. And, gracious lord, I have a swift spirit, the which can in the twinkling of an eye fulfil my desire in anything, wherefore I sent him into those countries, who hath brought this fruit as you see.'

Whereat the Duke was in great admiration.

[Chapter 40 describes the creation of the enchanted castle for the Duke of Anhalt which is alluded to briefly in the B-text (IV. 6. 3) at the beginning of the scene. In the next chapters, Faustus spends Shrovetide feasting and making merry at home with his students.]

CHAPTER 45

How Doctor Faustus showed the fair Helena unto the students upon the Sunday following.

The Sunday following came these students home to Doctor Faustus his own house, and brought their meat and drink with them. These men were right welcome guests unto Faustus, wherefore they all fell to drinking of wine smoothly [freely], and being merry, they began some of them to talk of the beauty of women, and everyone gave forth his verdict on what he had seen and what he had heard.

So one among the rest said, 'I never was so desirous of anything in this world as to have a sight (if it were possible) of fair Helena of Greece, for whom the worthy town of Troy was destroyed and razed down to the ground.' Therefore, saith he, that in all men's   10
judgement she was more than commonly fair, because that when she was stolen away from her husband, there was for her recovery so great bloodshed.

Doctor Faustus answered, 'For that you are all my friends and are so desirous to see that famous pearl of Greece, fair Helena, the wife of King Menelaus, and daughter of Tyndareus and Leda, sister to Castor and Pollux, who was the fairest lady in all Greece, I will therefore bring her into your presence personally, and in the same form of attire as she used to go when she was in her chiefest flower and pleasantest prime of youth. The like have I done for the   20
Emperor Carolus Quintus; at his desire I showed him Alexander the Great and his paramour. But,' said Doctor Faustus, 'I charge you all that upon your perils you speak not a word, nor rise up from the table so long as she is in your presence.'

And so he went out of the hall, returning presently again, after whom immediately followed the fair and beautiful Helena, whose beauty was such that the students were all amazed to see her, esteeming her rather to be a heavenly than an earthly creature. This lady appeared before them in a most sumptuous gown of purple velvet, richly embroidered; her hair hanged down loose as   30
fair as the beaten gold, and of such length that it reached down to her hams; with amorous coal-black eyes, a sweet and pleasant round face, her lips red as a cherry, her cheeks of roseal [roseate] colour, her mouth small, her neck as white as the swan, tall and slender of personage, and in sum, there was not one imperfect

part in her. She looked round about her with a rolling hawk's eye, a smiling and wanton countenance, which near hand [well-nigh] inflamed the hearts of the students, but that they persuaded themselves she was a spirit, wherefore such fantasies passed away lightly with them, and thus fair Helena and Doctor Faustus went out again one with another.   40

But the students at Doctor Faustus his entering again into the hall, requested of him to let them see her again the next day, for that they would bring with them a painter and so take her counterfeit; which he denied, affirming that he could not always raise up her spirit, but only at certain times.

'Yet,' said he, 'I will give you her counterfeit [portrait], which shall be always as good to you as if yourselves should see the drawing thereof.' Which they received according to his promise, but soon lost it again.   50

The students departed from Faustus home everyone to his house, but they were not able to sleep the whole night for thinking on the beauty of fair Helena. Wherefore a man may see that the devil blindeth and inflameth the heart with lust oftentimes, that men fall in love with harlots, nay even with furies, which afterward cannot lightly be removed.

[In the play the first appearance of Helen is followed immediately by that of the Old Man. In *EFB*, two more of Faustus's exploits intervene: in one he plays a trick on a churlish clown by removing the wheels from his wagon (chapter 46); in the second, out of jealousy, he causes the death of a juggler at Frankfurt fair by preventing him from completing a beheading trick (chapter 47).]

CHAPTER 48

How an old man, the neighbour of Faustus, sought to persuade him to amend his evil life and to fall unto repentance.

A good Christian, an honest and virtuous old man, a lover of the Holy Scriptures, who was neighbour unto Doctor Faustus, when he perceived that many students had their recourse in and out unto Doctor Faustus, he suspected his evil life. Wherefore like a friend he invited Doctor Faustus to supper unto his house, unto the which he agreed, and having ended their banquet, the old man began with these words:

'My loving friend and neighbour Doctor Faustus, I have to desire of you a friendly and Christian request, beseeching you that you will vouchsafe not to be angry with me, but friendly resolve me in   10
my doubt, and take my poor inviting in good part.'

To whom Doctor Faustus answered, 'My loving neighbour, I pray you say your mind.'

Then began the old patron to say, 'My good neighbour, you know in the beginning how that you have defied God, and all the host of heaven, and given your soul to the devil, wherewith you have incurred God's high displeasure, and are become from a Christian far worse than a heathen person. Oh, consider what you have done! It is not only the pleasure of the body, but the safety of the soul that you must have respect unto, of which if you be careless, then are you cast away, and shall remain in the anger of almighty God. But yet is it time enough, Doctor Faustus, if you repent and call unto the Lord for mercy, as we have example in the Acts of the Apostles, the eighth chapter, of Simon in Samaria, who was led out of the way, affirming that he was *Simon homo sanctus*. This man was notwithstanding in the end converted, after that he had heard the sermon of Philip, for he was baptized, and saw his sins and repented.

Likewise I beseech you, good brother Doctor Faustus, let my rude sermon be unto you a conversion, and forget the filthy life that you have led, repent, ask mercy, and live, for Christ saith, 'Come unto me all ye that are weary and heavy laden, and I will refresh you.' And in Ezekiel, 'I desire not the death of a sinner, but rather that he convert and live.' Let my words, good brother Faustus, pierce into your adamant heart, and desire God for His son Christ His sake to forgive you. Wherefore have you so long lived in your devilish practices, knowing that in the Old and New Testament you are forbidden, and that men should not suffer any such to live, neither have any conversation with them, for it is an abomination unto the Lord, and that such persons have no part in the kingdom of God?'

All this while Doctor Faustus heard him very attentively, and replied, 'Father, your persuasions like me wondrous well, and I thank you with all my heart for your good will and counsel, promising you so far as I may to follow your discipline.'

Whereupon he took his leave. And being come home, he laid him very pensive on his bed, bethinking himself of the words of the good old man, and in a manner began to repent that he had given his soul to the devil, intending to deny all that he had promised unto Lucifer.

Continuing in these cogitations, suddenly his spirit appeared unto him, clapping him upon the head, and wrung it as though he would have pulled the head from his shoulders, saying unto him, 'Thou knowest, Faustus, that thou hast given thyself body and soul unto my lord Lucifer, and hast vowed thyself an enemy unto God and unto all men, and now thou beginnest to hearken to an old doting fool which persuadeth thee as it were unto God, when indeed it is too late, for that thou art the devil's, and he hath good power presently to fetch thee. Wherefore he hath sent me unto thee, to tell thee, that seeing thou hast sorrowed for that thou hast done, begin again and write another writing with 60 thine own blood; if not, then will I tear thee all to pieces.'

Hereat Doctor Faustus was sore afraid and said, 'My Mephostophiles, I will write again what thou wilt.'

Wherefore he sat him down, and with his own blood he wrote as followeth, which writing was afterward sent to a dear friend of the said Doctor Faustus, being his kinsman.

CHAPTER 49

How Doctor Faustus wrote the second time with his own blood and gave it to the devil.

I, Doctor John Faustus, acknowledge by this my deed and handwriting, that sith [since] my first writing, which is seventeen years, that I have right willingly held, and have been an utter enemy unto God and all men, the which I once again confirm, and give fully and wholly myself unto the devil both body and soul, even unto the great Lucifer, and that at the end of seven years ensuing after the date of this letter, he shall have to do with me according as it pleaseth him, either to lengthen or shorten my life as liketh him; and hereupon I renounce all persuaders that seek to withdraw me from my purpose by the word of God, either ghostly or bodily. And 10 further, I will never give ear unto any man, be he spiritual or temporal, that moveth any matter for the salvation of my soul. Of all this writing, and that therein contained, be witness my own blood, the which with mine own hands I have begun, and ended.

Dated at Wittenberg the 25th of July.

And presently upon the making of this letter, he became so great an enemy unto the poor old man that he sought his life by all means possible, but this godly man was strong in the Holy Ghost, that he could not be vanquished by any means. For about two days after that he had exhorted Faustus, as the poor man lay in his bed, 20 suddenly there was a mighty rumbling in the chamber, the which he was never wont to hear, and he heard as it had been the groaning of a sow, which lasted long.

Whereupon the good old man began to jest and mock, and said, 'Oh, what barbarian cry is this? Oh fair bird, what foul music is this of a fair angel, that could not tarry two days in his place? Beginnest thou now to run into a poor man's house, where thou hast no power, and wert not able to keep thine own two days?'

With these and suchlike words the spirit departed. And when he came home Faustus asked him how he had sped with the old man; to whom the spirit answered, the old man was harnessed [spiritually armed], and that he could not once lay hold upon him, but he would not tell how the old man had mocked him, for the devils can never abide to hear of their fall. Thus doth God defend the hearts of all honest Christians, that betake themselves under his tuition.

[Chapter 50 shows Faustus playing the benevolent role of a marriage-broker, in contravention of his renewed oath to be an enemy to all men; in chapter 51 he entertains guests at Christmas by conjuring up fruit and flowers in his garden.]

CHAPTER 52

How Doctor Faustus gathered together a great army of men in his extremity against a knight that would have injured him on his journey.

Doctor Faustus travelled towards Eisleben, and when he was nigh half the way, he espied seven horsemen, and the chief of them he knew to be the knight to whom he had played a jest in the Emperor's court, for he had set a huge pair of hart's horns upon his head. And when the knight now saw that he had fit opportunity to be revenged of Faustus, he ran upon him, himself and those that were with him, to mischief him, intending privily to shoot at him, which when Doctor Faustus espied, he vanished away into the wood which was hard by them. But when the knight perceived that he was vanished away, he caused his men to stand still, where as they remained they heard all manner of warlike instruments of music, as drums, flutes, trumpets, and suchlike, and a certain troop of horsemen running towards them. Then they turned another way, and there also were assaulted on the same side; then another way, and yet they were freshly assaulted, so that which way soever they turned themselves he was encountered, insomuch that when the knight perceived that he could escape no way, but that they his enemies laid on him which way soever he offered to fly, he took a good heart and ran amongst the thickest, and thought with himself better to die than to live with so great an infamy.

Therefore, being at handy-blows with them, he demanded the cause why they should so use them, but none of them would give him answer, until Doctor Faustus showed himself unto the knight,

228

wherewithal [whereupon] they enclosed him round, and Doctor Faustus said unto him, 'Sir, yield your weapon, and yourself, otherwise it will go hardly with you.'

The knight, that knew none other but that he was environed with an host of men (where indeed they were none other than devils), yielded; then Faustus took away his sword, his piece [gun], and horse, with all the rest of his companions'.

And further he said unto him, 'Sir, the chief general of our army hath commanded to deal with you according to the law of arms; you shall depart in peace whither you please.'

And then he gave the knight an horse after the manner [according to custom], and set him thereon. So he rode, the rest went on foot, until they came to their inn, where being alighted, his page rode on his horse to the water, and presently the horse vanished away, the page being almost sunk and drowned, but he escaped. And coming home, the knight perceived his page so bemired and on foot, asked where his horse was become?

Who answered that he was vanished away; which when the knight heard, he said, 'Of a truth, this is Faustus his doing, for he serveth me now as he did before at the court, only to make me a scorn and a laughing-stock.'

CHAPTER 53

How Doctor Faustus caused Mephostophiles to bring him seven of the fairest women that he could find in all those countries he had travelled in, in the twentieth year.

When Doctor Faustus called to mind that his time from day to day drew nigh, he began to live a swinish and epicurish [sensual] life, wherefore he commanded his spirit Mephostophiles to bring him seven of the fairest women that he had seen in all the time of his travel; which being brought, first one, and then another, he lay with them all, insomuch that he liked them so well that he continued with them in all manner of love, and made them to travel with him in all his journeys. These women were two Netherlanders, one Hungarian, one English, two Walloons, one Franconian [Bavarian]; and with these sweet personages he continued long, yea even to his last end.

[In chapter 54, which the heading assigns to the twenty-second of Faustus's twenty-four years, the devil directs him to a hoard of silver and gold, guarded in traditional fashion by a serpent. The money is found after Faustus's death by his servant.]

CHAPTER 55

How Doctor Faustus made the spirit of fair Helena of Greece his own paramour and bedfellow in his twenty-third year.

To the end that this miserable Faustus might fill the lust of his flesh, and live in all manner of voluptuous pleasures, it came in his mind after he had slept his first sleep, and in the twenty-third year past of his time, that he had a great desire to lie with fair Helena of Greece, especially her whom he had seen and showed unto the students of Wittenberg, wherefore he called unto him his spirit Mephostophiles, commanding him to bring him the fair Helena, which he also did. Whereupon he fell in love with her, and made her his common concubine and bedfellow, for she was so beautiful and delightful a piece that he could not be one hour from her, if he should therefore have suffered death, she had so stolen away his heart. And to his seeming, in time she was with child, and in the end brought him a man child, whom Faustus named Justus Faustus. This child told Doctor Faustus many things that were to come, and what strange matters were done in foreign countries; but in the end when Faustus lost his life, the mother and the child vanished away both together. 10

CHAPTER 56

How Doctor Faustus made his will, in the which he named his servant Wagner to be his heir.

Doctor Faustus was now in his twenty-fourth and last year, and he had a pretty stripling to his servant, the which had studied also at the University of Wittenberg. This youth was very well acquainted with his knaveries and sorceries, so that he was hated as well for his own knaveries, as also for his master's, for no man would give him entertainment into his service because of his unhappiness [wickedness], but Faustus. This Wagner was so well beloved with Faustus that he used him as his son; for do what he would his master was always therewith well content. And when the time drew nigh that Faustus should end, he called unto him a notary and certain masters, the which were his friends and often conversant with him, in whose presence he gave this Wagner his house and garden. Item, he gave him in ready money 1600 guilders; item, a farm; item, a gold chain, much plate, and other household stuff. This gave he all to his servant, and the rest of his time he meant to spend in inns and students' company, drinking and eating, with other jollity; and thus he finished his will for that time. 10

CHAPTER 57

How Doctor Faustus fell in talk with his servant touching his testament and the covenants thereof.

Now, when this will was made, Doctor Faustus called unto him his servant, saying, 'I have thought upon thee in my testament, for that thou hast been a trusty servant unto me and a faithful, and hast not opened my secrets; and yet further,' said he, 'ask of me before I die what thou wilt, and I will give it unto thee.'

His servant rashly answered, 'I pray you, let me have your cunning [skill in magic].'

To which Doctor Faustus answered, 'I have given thee all my books, upon this condition, that thou wouldst not let them be common, but use them for thine own pleasure, and study carefully 10 in them. And dost thou also desire my cunning? That mayest thou peradventure have, if thou love and peruse my books well. Further,' said Doctor Faustus, 'seeing that thou desirest of me this request, I will resolve [answer] thee. My spirit Mephostophiles his time is out with me, and I have naught to command him as touching thee, yet will I help thee to another, if thou like well thereof.'

And within three days after he called his servant unto him saying, 'Art thou resolved? Wouldst thou verily have a spirit? Then tell me in what manner or form thou wouldst have him?'

To whom his servant answered that he would have him in the 20 form of an ape, whereupon presently appeared a spirit unto him in manner and form of an ape, the which leaped about the house.

Then said Faustus, 'See, there hast thou thy request, but yet he will not obey thee until I be dead, for when my spirit Mephostophiles shall fetch me away, then shall thy spirit be bound unto thee, if thou agree; and thy spirit shalt thou name Akercock, for so is he called. But all this is upon condition that thou publish my cunning and my merry conceits, with all that I have done (when I am dead) in an history; and if thou canst not remember all, thy spirit Akercock will help thee; so shall the great acts that I 30 have done be manifested unto the world.'

CHAPTER 58

How Doctor Faustus having but one month of his appointed time to come, fell to mourning and sorrow with himself for his devilish exercise.

Time ran away with Faustus as the hour-glass, for he had but one month to come of his twenty-four years, at the end whereof he had given himself to the devil body and soul, as is before specified. Here was the first token, for he was like a taken murderer or a thief, the which findeth himself guilty in conscience before the judge have given sentence, fearing every hour to die; for he was grieved, and wailing spent the time, went talking to himself, wringing of his hands, sobbing and sighing; he fell away from flesh and was very lean, and kept himself close; neither could he abide to see or hear of his Mephostophiles any more.

CHAPTER 59

How Doctor Faustus complained that he should in his lusty time and youthful years die so miserably.

This sorrowful time drawing near so troubled Doctor Faustus that he began to write his mind, to the end he might peruse it often and not forget it, and is in manner as followeth:

'Ah, Faustus, thou sorrowful and woeful man, now must thou go to the damned company in unquenchable fire, whereas thou mightest have had the joyful immortality of the soul, the which thou now hast lost. Ah, gross understanding and wilful will, what seizeth on my limbs other than a robbing of my life? Bewail with me, my sound and healthful body, wit and soul, bewail with me, my senses, for you have had your part and pleasure as well as I. O envy and disdain, how have you crept both at once into me, and now for your sakes I must suffer all these torments. Ah, whither is pity and mercy fled? Upon what occasion hath heaven repaid me with this reward by sufferance to suffer me to perish? Wherefore was I created a man? The punishment that I see prepared for me of myself now must I suffer. Ah, miserable wretch, there is nothing in this world to show me comfort; then woe is me, what helpeth my wailing?'

CHAPTER 60

Another complaint of Doctor Faustus.

'O poor, woeful and weary wretch; O sorrowful soul of Faustus, now art thou in the number of the damned, for now must I wait for unmeasurable pains of death, yea far more lamentable than ever yet any creature hath suffered. Ah, senseless, wilful and desperate forgetfulness! O cursed and unstable life! O blind and careless wretch, that so hast abused thy body, sense and soul! O foolish pleasure, into what a weary labyrinth hast thou brought me, blinding mine eyes in the clearest day? Ah, weak heart! O troubled soul, where is become thy knowledge to comfort thee? O pitiful weariness! O desperate hope, now shall I nevermore be thought upon! O care upon carefulness, and sorrows on heaps! Ah, grievous pains that pierce my panting heart, whom is there now that can deliver me? Would God that I knew where to hide me, or into what place to creep or fly! Ah, woe, woe is me, be where I will, yet am I taken.'

Herewith poor Faustus was so sorrowfully troubled, that he could not speak or utter his mind any further.

CHAPTER 61

How Doctor Faustus bewailed to think on hell, and of the miserable pains therein provided for him.

'Now, thou Faustus, damned wretch, how happy wert thou if as an unreasonable beast thou mightest die without soul, so shouldest thou not feel any more doubts. But now the devil will take thee away both body and soul, and set thee in an unspeakable place of darkness; for although others' souls have rest and peace, yet I, poor damned wretch, must suffer all manner of filthy stench, pains, cold, hunger, thirst, heat, freezing, burning, hissing, gnashing, and all the wrath and curse of God; yea, all the creatures that God hath created are enemies to me. And now too late I remember that my spirit Mephostophiles did once tell me there was a great difference amongst the damned, for the greater the sin, the greater the torment; for as the twigs of the tree make greater flame than the trunk thereof, and yet the trunk continueth longer in burning, even so the more that a man is rooted in sin, the greater is his punishment. Ah, thou perpetual damned wretch, now art thou thrown into the everlasting fiery lake that never shall be quenched; there must I dwell in all manner of wailing, sorrow, misery, pain, torment, grief, howling, sighing, sobbing, blubbering, running of eyes, stinking at nose, gnashing of teeth, fear to the ears, horror to the conscience, and shaking both of hand and foot.

Ah, that I could carry the heavens on my shoulders, so that there were time at last to quit me of this everlasting damnation! Oh, who can deliver me out of these fearful tormenting flames, the which I see prepared for me? Oh, there is no help, nor any man that can deliver me, nor any wailing of sins can help me, neither is there rest to be found for me day nor night. Ah, woe is me, for there is no help for me, no shield, no defence, no comfort. Where is my hold? Knowledge dare I not trust, and for a soul to Godwards that have I not, for I shame to speak unto Him; if I do, no answer shall be

made me, but He will hide His face from me, to the end that I   30
should not behold the joys of the chosen. What mean I then to
complain where no help is? No, I know no hope resteth in my
groanings. I have desired that it should be so, and God hath said
Amen to my misdoings; for now I must have shame to comfort me
in my calamities.'

CHAPTER 62

Here followeth the miserable and lamentable end of Doctor Faustus, by the which all Christians may take an example and warning.

In the twenty-fourth year, Doctor Faustus, his time being come,
his spirit appeared unto him, giving him his writing again, and
commanding him to make preparation, for that the devil would
fetch him against a certain time appointed. Doctor Faustus
mourned and sighed wonderfully, and never went to bed, nor
slept wink for sorrow.

Wherefore his spirit appeared again, comforting him and saying,
'My Faustus, be not thou so cowardly minded; for although that
thou losest thy body, it is not long unto the Day of Judgement, and
thou must die at the last, although thou live many thousand years.   10
The Turks, the Jews, and many an unchristian emperor, are in the
same condemnation; therefore (my Faustus) be of good courage,
and be not discomforted, for the devil hath promised that thou
shalt not be in pains as the rest of the damned are.'

This and suchlike comfort he gave him, but he told him false,
and against the saying of the Holy Scriptures. Yet Doctor Faustus,
that had none other expectation but to pay his debts with his
own skin, went on the same day that his spirit said the devil would
fetch him, unto his trusty and dearest beloved brethren and companions, as masters and bachelors of art, and other students more,   20
the which had often visited him at his house in merriment. These
he entreated that they would walk into the village called Rimlich,
half a mile from Wittenberg, and that they would there take with
him for their repast part of a small banquet, the which they all
agreed unto; so they went together, and there held their dinner in
a most sumptuous manner. Doctor Faustus with them (dissembling-
ly) was merry, but not from the heart; wherefore he requested them
that they would also take part of his rude supper, the which they
agreed unto.

'For,' quoth he, 'I must tell you what is the victualler's due.'   30

And when they slept (for drink was in their heads) then Doctor

234

Faustus paid and discharged the shot [bill], and bound the students and the masters to go with him into another room, for he had many wonderful matters to tell them. And when they were entered the room as he requested, Doctor Faustus said unto them as hereafter followeth.

CHAPTER 63

An oration of Faustus to the students.

'My trusty and well-beloved friends, the cause why I have invited you into this place is this: forasmuch as you have known me this many years, in what manner of life I have lived, practising all manner of conjurations and wicked exercises, the which I have obtained through the help of the devil, into whose devilish fellow-ship they have brought me, the which use the like art and practice; urged by the detestable provocation of my flesh, my stiff-necked and rebellious will, with my filthy infernal thoughts, the which were ever before me, pricking me forward so earnestly that I must perforce have the consent of the devil to aid me in my devices. And to the end I might the better bring my purpose to pass, to have the devil's aid and furtherance, which I never have wanted in mine actions, I have promised unto him at the end and accomplishing of twenty-four years, both body and soul, to do therewith at his pleasure; and this day, this dismal day, those twenty-four years are fully expired, for night beginning my hour-glass is at an end, the direful finishing whereof I carefully expect; for out of all doubt this night he will fetch me, to whom I have given myself in recompense of his service, both body and soul, and twice confirmed writings with my proper blood.

Now have I called you, my well-beloved lords, friends, brethren, and fellows, before that fatal hour to take my friendly farewell, to the end that my departing may not hereafter be hidden from you, beseeching you herewith, courteous, and loving lords and brethren, not to take in evil part anything done by me, but with friendly commendations to salute all my friends and companions wheresoever, desiring both you and them, if ever I have trespassed against your minds in anything, that you would all heartily forgive me; and as for those lewd practices the which this full twenty-four years I have followed, you shall hereafter find them in writing. And I beseech you let this my lamentable end to the residue of your lives be a sufficient warning, that you have God always before your eyes, praying unto Him that He would ever defend you from the temptation of the devil and all his false deceits, not falling altogether from God, as I wretched and ungodly damned creature have done, having denied and defied baptism, the sacraments of Christ's body, God Himself, all heavenly powers, and earthly men; yea, I have denied such a God, that desireth not to have one lost. Neither let the evil fellowship of wicked companions mislead you as it hath done me; visit earnestly and oft the church, war and strive continually against the devil with a good and steadfast belief on God, and Jesus Christ, and use your vocation in holiness.

Lastly, to knit up my troubled oration, this is my friendly request, that you would to rest, and let nothing trouble you; also, if you chance to hear any noise or rumbling about the house, be not therewith afraid, for there shall no evil happen unto you; also I pray you arise not out of your beds. But above all things I entreat you, if you hereafter find my dead carcass, convey it unto the earth, for I die both a good and bad Christian: a good Christian, for that I am heartily sorry, and in my heart always pray for mercy, that my soul may be delivered; a bad Christian, for that I know the devil will have my body, and that would I willingly give him so that he would leave my soul in quiet. Wherefore I pray you that you would depart to bed, and so I wish you a quiet night which unto me notwithstanding will be horrible and fearful.'

This oration or declaration was made by Doctor Faustus, and that with a hearty and resolute mind, to the end he might not discomfort them; but the students wondered greatly thereat, that he was so blinded [deceived], for knavery, conjuration, and suchlike foolish things, to give his body and soul unto the devil, for they loved him entirely, and never suspected any such thing before he had opened his mind to them.

Wherefore one of them said unto him, 'Ah, friend Faustus, what have you done to conceal this matter so long from us? We would by the help of good divines, and the grace of God, have brought you out of this net, and have torn you out of the bondage and chains of Satan, whereas now we fear it is too late, to the utter ruin of your body and soul.'

Doctor Faustus answered, 'I durst never do it, although I often minded to settle myself unto godly people, to desire counsel and help, as once mine old neighbour counselled me, that I should follow his learning, and leave all my conjurations. Yet when I was minded to amend, and to follow that good man's counsel, then came the devil and would have had me away, as this night he is like to do, and said, so soon as I turned again to God, he would dispatch me altogether. Thus, even thus (good gentlemen, and my dear friends) was I enthralled in that satanical band, all good desires

drowned, all piety banished, all purpose of amendment utterly
exiled, by the tyrannous threatenings of my deadly enemy.'   80

But when the students heard his words, they gave him counsel to
do naught else but call upon God, desiring Him for the love of His
sweet son Jesus Christ's sake, to have mercy upon him, teaching
him this form of prayer: 'O God, be merciful unto me, poor and
miserable sinner, and enter not into judgement with me, for no
flesh is able to stand before Thee. Although, O Lord, I must leave
my sinful body unto the devil, being by him deluded, yet Thou in
mercy mayest preserve my soul.'

This they repeated unto him, yet it could take no hold, but even as
Cain he also said his sins were greater than God was able to forgive,   90
for all his thought was on his writing; he meant he had made it too
filthy [heinous] in writing it with his own blood. The students and
the other that were there, when they had prayed for him, they wept,
and so went forth, but Faustus tarried in the hall; and when the
gentlemen were laid in bed, none of them could sleep, for that they
attended to hear if they might be privy of his end.

It happened between twelve and one o'clock at midnight, there
blew a mighty storm of wind against the house, as though it would
have blown the foundation thereof out of his place. Hereupon the
students began to fear, and got out of their beds, comforting one   100
another, but they would not stir out of the chamber; and the host of
the house ran out of doors, thinking the house would fall. The
students lay near unto that hall wherein Doctor Faustus lay, and
they heard a mighty noise and hissing, as if the hall had been full of
snakes and adders. With that the hall door flew open wherein
Doctor Faustus was; then he began to cry for help, saying, 'Murder,
murder,' but it came forth with half a voice hollowly; shortly after
they heard him no more.

But when it was day, the students, that had taken no rest that
night, arose and went into the hall in the which they left Doctor   110
Faustus, where notwithstanding they found no Faustus, but all
the hall lay besprinkled with blood, his brains cleaving to the
wall; for the devil had beaten him from one wall against another.
In one corner lay his eyes, in another his teeth, a pitiful and
fearful sight to behold. Then began the students to bewail and
weep for him, and sought for his body in many places; lastly they
came into the yard where they found his body lying on the horse
dung, most monstrously torn and fearful to behold, for his head
and all his joints were dashed in pieces.

The forenamed students and masters that were at his death have   120
obtained so much that they buried him in the village where he
was so grievously tormented. After the which, they returned to

Wittenberg, and coming into the house of Faustus, they found the servant of Faustus very sad, unto whom they opened all the matter, who took it exceeding heavily. There found they also this history of Doctor Faustus, noted and of him written as is before declared, all save only his end, the which was after by the students thereto annexed; further, what his servant had noted thereof was made in another book. And you have heard that he held by him in his life the spirit of fair Helena, the which had by him one son, the which 130 he named Justus Faustus; even the same day of his death they vanished away, both mother and son. The house before was so dark that scarce anybody could abide therein. The same night Doctor Faustus appeared unto his servant lively [as if alive], and showed unto him many secret things the which he had done and hidden in his lifetime. Likewise there were certain which saw Doctor Faustus look out of the window by night as they passed by the house.

And thus ended the whole history of Doctor Faustus his conjuration and other acts that he did in his life; out of the which example every Christian may learn, but chiefly the stiff-necked and 140 highminded may thereby learn to fear God and to be careful of their vocation and to be at defiance with all devilish works, as God hath most precisely forbidden, to the end we should not invite the devil as a guest, nor give him place as that wicked Faustus hath done; for here we have a fearful example of his writing, promise, and end, that we may remember him, that we go not astray, but take God always before our eyes, to call alone upon Him, and to honour Him all the days of our life, with heart and hearty prayer, and with all our strength and soul to glorify His holy name, defying the devil and all his works, to the end we may remain with Christ in all 150 endless joy. Amen, amen, that wish I unto every Christian heart, and God's name to be glorified. Amen.

FINIS

TEXT 2

The Ecclesiastical History, containing the Acts and Monuments of things passed . . .

John Foxe
(Second edition 1570)

[The text is taken from the Bodleian Library copy
(shelfmark Mason F 142).]

[The following passages recounting the disputes of Emperor Frederick I
('Barbarossa') with Popes Adrian IV (1154–9) and Alexander III
(1159–81) occur during Foxe's account of the reign of Henry II.]

Then followed Anastasius IV, and after him Hadrianus IV, an
Englishman, by his name called Breakspear, belonging once to St
Albans. This Hadrianus kept great stir in like sort with the citizens
of Rome for abolishing their consuls and senate, cursing, ex-
communicating, and warring against them with all power he could
make, to the time he removed the consuls out of their office, and
brought them all under his subjection. The like business and rage
he also stirred up against Apulia, and especially against the Empire,
blustering and thundering against Fredericus the Emperor, as (the
Lord granting) you shall hear anon. . . .   10

(I. 259)

    Although this Adrian was bad enough, yet came the next much
worse, one Alexander the third of that name, who yet was not
elected alone, for besides him the Emperor with nine Cardinals . . .
did set up another Pope, named Victor IV. Between these two
Popes rose a foul schism and great discord, and long continued.
Insomuch that the Emperor, being required to take up the matter,
sent for them both to appear before him, that in hearing them
both he might judge their cause the better. Victor came, but
Alexander (disdaining that his matter should come in controversy)
refused to appear. Whereupon the Emperor, with a full consent   20
of his bishops and clergy about him, assigned and ratified the

239

election of Victor to stand, and so brought him into the city, there to be received and placed. Alexander flying into France, accursed them both, sending his letters to all Christendom against them, as men to be avoided and cast out of all Christian company. Also to get him friends at Rome, by flattery and money [he] got on his side the greatest part of the city, both to the favouring of him, and to the setting up of such consuls as were for his purpose. After this, Alexander coming from France to Sicily, and from thence to Rome, was there received with much favour, through the help of Philip the French king.   30

[In margin: Anno 1164] The Emperor, hearing this rebellion and conspiracy in Rome, removed with great power into Italy, where he had destroyed divers great cities. Coming at length to Rome, he required the citizens that the cause betwixt the two Popes might be decised [decided], and that he which had the best right might be taken. If they would so do, he would restore again that which he took from them before. Alexander, mistrusting his part and doubting the wills of the citizens (having ships ready prepared for him from William, Duke of Apulia) fetched a course   40 about to Venice.

. . . the Pope being at Venice, and required to be sent of the Venetians to the Emperor, they would not send him. Whereupon Fredericus the Emperor sent thither his son Otho, with men and ships well appointed, charging him not to attempt anything before his coming. The young man, more hardy than circumspect, joining with [attacking] the Venetians, was overcome; and so taken, was brought into the city. Hereby the Pope took no small occasion to work his feats.

The father, to help the captivity and misery of his son, was   50 compelled to submit himself to the Pope, and to entreat for peace. So the Emperor coming to Venice, at St Mark's church, where the bishop was, there to take his absolution, was bid to kneel down at the Pope's feet.

[At this point there is a splendid woodcut illustration of the Pope treading on the prostrate Emperor's neck.]

The proud Pope, setting his foot upon the Emperor's neck, said the verse of the psalm, '*Super aspidem et basiliscum ambulabis, et conculcabis leonem et draconem*': that is, 'Thou shalt walk upon the adder and the basilisk, and shalt tread down the lion and the dragon.' To whom the Emperor answering again, said, '*Non tibi sed Petro*': that is, 'Not to thee but to Peter.' The Pope again, '*Et mihi et*   60 *Petro*': 'Both to me and to Peter.' The Emperor, fearing to give any occasion of further quarrelling, held his peace, and so was absolved, and peace made between them. The conditions whereof were these: first, that he should receive Alexander for the true Pope. Secondly, that he should restore again to the Church of Rome all that he had taken away before, And thus the Emperor, obtaining again his son, departed.

(I. 263)

TEXT 3

The Conflict of Conscience . . .

Nathaniel Woodes
(1581)

[The text is taken from the Malone Society reprint published in 1952.]

V. 3

[Philologus appears for the last time, with his sons Gisbertus and Paphinitius, and his friends Theologus and Eusebius. The two latter try to persuade him to pray, but Philologus is convinced that he is damned. There is only one edition of the play, but it exists in two issues; in the first Philologus hangs himself, in the second he repents and is saved. The guilt and despair of his real-life counterpart, Francesco Spira (who had recanted his Protestant faith under persecution), were so great that he starved himself to death in 1548.]

THEOLOGUS: Then pray with us, as Christ us taught, we do you all
    desire.
PHILOLOGUS: To pray with lips unto your God you shall me soon
    entreat;
My spirit to Satan is in thrall, I can it not thence get.
EUSEBIUS: God shall renew your spirit again; pray only as you can,
    And to assist you in the same we pray each Christian man.
PHILOLOGUS: O God, which dwellest in the heavens and art our
    Father dear.
    Thy holy name throughout the world be ever sanctified;
    The kingdom of Thy Word and Spirit upon us rule might bear;
    Thy will in earth, as by Thy saints in heaven be ratified;
    Our daily bread, we Thee beseech, O Lord for us provide;   10
    Our sins remit Lord unto us, as we each man forgive;
    Let not temptation us assail, in all evil us relieve. Amen.
THEOLOGUS: The Lord be prais'd, who hath at length thy spirit
    mollified.
    These are not tokens unto us of your reprobation.
    You mourn with tears and sue for grace, wherefore be certified
    That God in mercy giveth ear unto your supplication.

242

Wherefore despair not thou at all of thy soul's preservation,
And say not with a desperate heart that God against thee is;
He will no doubt, these pains once past, receive you into bliss.
PHILOLOGUS: No, no my friends, you only hear and see the outward part,   20
  Which though you think they have done well, it booteth not at all;
My lips have spoke the words indeed, but yet I feel my heart
With cursing is replenished, with rancour, spite, and gall;
Neither do I your Lord and God in heart my Father call,
But rather seek His holy name for to blaspheme and curse.
My state therefore doth not amend, but wax still worse and worse;
I am secluded clean from grace, my heart is harden'd quite,
Wherefore you do your labour lose, and spend your breath in vain.
EUSEBIUS: O say not so, Philologus, but let your heart be pight [fixed]
  Upon the mercies of the Lord, and I you ascertain   30
Remission of your former sins you shall at last obtain.
God hath it said, who cannot lie, at whatsoever time
A sinner shall from heart repent, I will remit his crime.
PHILOLOGUS: You cannot say so much to me as herein I do know,
That by the mercies of the Lord all sins are done away,
And unto them that have true faith abundantly it flow;
But whence do this true faith proceed to us, I do you pray?
It is the only gift of God, from Him it comes alway.
I would therefore He would vouchsafe one spark of faith to plant
Within my breast; then of His grace I know I should not want.   40
  But it as easily may be done as you may with one spoon
At once take up the water clean which in the seas abide
And at one draught then drink it up; this shall ye do as soon
As to my breast of true belief one sparkle shall betide.
Tush, you which are in prosperous state and my pains have not tried [experienced],
Do think it but an easy thing, a sinner to repent
Him of his sins, and by true faith damnation to prevent.
  The healthful need not physic's art, and ye which are all hale
Can give good counsel to the sick, their sickness to eschew,
But here, alas, confusion and hell doth me assail   50
And that all grace from me is reft, I find it to be true.
My heart is steel, so that no faith can from the same ensue;
I can conceive no hope at all of pardon or of grace,

But out, alas, Confusion is alway before my face.
 And certainly, even at this time I do most plainly see
 The devils to be about me round, which make great
  preparation,
 And keep a stir here in this place which only is for me.
 Neither do I conceive these things by vain imagination,
 But even as truly as mine eyes behold your shape and fashion.
 Wherefore, desired death dispatch, my body bring to rest,   60
 Though that my soul in furious flames of fire be suppressed.
THEOLOGUS: Your mind corrupted doth present to you this false
  illusion,
 But turn awhile unto the spirit of truth in your distress,
 And it shall cast out from your eyes all horror and confusion,
 And of this your affliction it will you soon redress.
EUSEBIUS: We have good hope, Philologus, of your salvation
  doubtless.
PHILOLOGUS: What your hope is concerning me, I utterly contemn
  [scorn];
 My conscience, which for thousands stands, as guilty me
  condemns. . . .

(lines 2120–2197)

[There follows a disputation on the subject of justification by faith.]
THEOLOGUS: Alas, my friend, take in good part the chastment
  [chastisement] of the Lord,
 Who doth correct you in this world that in the life to come   70
 He might you save, for of the like the Scripture bears record.
PHILOLOGUS: That is not God's intent with me, though it be so with
  some
 Who after bodies' punishment have into favour come.
 But I, alas, in spirit and in soul these grievous torments bear.
 God hath condemn'd my conscience to perpetual grief and
  fear.
 I would most gladly choose to live a thousand thousand year,
 So that at length I might have ease, it would me greatly cheer.
 But I, alas, shall in this life in torments still remain,
 While God's just anger upon me shall be revealed plain,
 And I example made to all, of God's just indignation.   80
 O that my body were at rest, and soul in condemnation!
EUSEBIUS: I pray you, answer me herein: where you by deep despair
 Say you are worse here in this life than if you were in hell
 And for because to have death come you alway make your
  prayer,
 As though your soul and body both in torments great did dwell;
 If that a man should give to you a sword, I pray you tell,

Would you destroy yourself therewith, as do the desperate,
Which hang, or kill, or into floods themselves precipitate?
PHILOLOGUS: Give me a sword – then shall you know what is in mine
    intent.
EUSEBIUS: Not so, my friend, I only ask what herein were your will.   90
PHILOLOGUS: I cannot, neither will I tell whereto I would be bent.
THEOLOGUS: These words do nothing edify, but rather fancies fill,
    Which we would gladly, if we could, endeavour for to kill.
    Wherefore I once again request, together let us pray,
    And so we will leave you to God, and send you hence away.
PHILOLOGUS: I cannot pray. My spirit is dead, no faith in me remains.
THEOLOGUS: Do as you can, no more than might we can ask at your
    hand.
PHILOLOGUS: My prayer turned is to sin, for God doth it disdain.
EUSEBIUS: It is the falsehood of the spirit, which do your health
    withstand,   100
    That teach you this. Wherefore, in time reject his filthy band.
THEOLOGUS: Come kneel by me, and let us pray the Lord of
    heaven unto.
PHILOLOGUS: With as good will as did the devil out of the deaf man
    go.
    O God, which dwellest in the heavens –
    Tush sirs, you do your labours lose. See, where Beelzebub doth
    come,
    And doth invite me to a feast. You therefore speak in vain,
    Yea, if you ask aught more of me, in answer I will be dumb,
    I will not waste my tongue for naught. As soon shall one small
    grain
    Of mustardseed fill all the world, as I true faith attain.
THEOLOGUS: We will no longer stay you now, but let you hence
    depart.   110
EUSEBIUS: Yet will we pray continually that God would you convert.
THEOLOGUS: Gisbertus and Paphinitius, conduct him to his place,
    But see he have good company; let him not be alone.
AMBO [BOTH]: We shall so do, God us assist with His most holy grace.
GISBERTUS: Come, father. Do you not think good that we from
    hence be gone?
PHILOLOGUS: Let go my hands at liberty! Assistance I crave none.
    O that I had a sword a while! I should soon eased be.
AMBO: Alas, dear father, what do you?
EUSEBIUS: His will we may now see.
Exeunt PHILOLOGUS, GISBERTUS, and PAPHINITIUS.

                            (lines 2314–2382)

NOTES

Introduction

p. 183 *the dagger*: Dr J.H. Jones has kindly pointed out to us these parallels in Widman.

1 *The History of the Damnable Life and Deserved Death of Doctor John Faustus* (pp. 186–238)

Chapter 1 (pp. 186–7)

10   *Eli*: 1 Sam. 2: 12.
14–15   *Cain, Reuben, Absalom*: Gen. 4: 1–16; 49: 4; 2 Sam. 15–18.
47   *many stripes*: Luke 12: 47.
48   *two masters*: Matt. 6: 24.
48   *Lord thy God*: Matt. 4: 7.

Chapter 2 (pp. 187–9)

47   *under heaven*: Ephesians 2: 2.
49   *long tarrying*: cf. '*Quid tu moraris?*' (Cf. 'Why do you delay?') (I. 3. 20).

Chapter 3 (pp. 189–90)

40   *St Valentine's farewell*: *S Veltins Griß* (a disease): 'a plague on you!'

Chapter 5 (pp. 191–2)

4   *St Antony*: the patron saint of swineherds, whose emblems are a pig and a bell.
15   *war with the gods*: the giants are Otus and Ephialtes, who tried to pile Ossa on Olympus, and Pelion on Ossa, in order to climb to heaven, and were destroyed by Zeus.
31   *O homo fuge*: 'Fly, O man!' (1 Tim. 6: 11).

Chapter 8 (pp. 194–5

32   *a thief and a murderer*: John 10: 10.

Chapter 10 (p. 197)

22   *as Raphael*: according to the *Historia*, Lucifer was originally called Raphael.

Chapter 14 (pp. 200–1)

21   *Saul*: 1 Sam. 16: 14.

22	*Tobias*: the reference is to the apocryphal book of Tobit. The seven husbands were all killed on their wedding night by the jealous devil, Asmodeus.
24	*ark of God was stolen*: 1 Sam. 4: 10–11.
25	*60,000*: 2 Sam. 24: 1–15.
26	*gods of the heathen*: 1 Kings 11: 1–8.

Chapter 15 (pp. 201–4)

32	*as nothing for thee to reckon upon*: an allusion to Christ's Harrowing of Hell.
37	*the first mobile*: in the Ptolemaic system of astronomy, the *primum mobile* is the tenth sphere, which carries with it all the others as it revolves from east to west.
61	*Pernicies and Exitium*: death and destruction.
110	*Dives*: Luke 16: 19–31.
118	*can be forgiven*: Gen. 4: 13, where Cain's words are 'My punishment is greater than I can bear.'

Chapter 18 (pp. 206–8)

22	*learn of me*: mostly P.F.'s addition from here to the end of the chapter.
23	The symbols are those of the seven primary planets: Saturn, Jupiter, Mars, the sun, Venus, Mercury, and the moon.
61–3	*the snow. . . in Manifesto*: the sign is that of Pisces, and '*Occulto*' is 'in eclipse'; the passage as a whole is obscure.
67	*jacinth*: hyacinth, formerly a blue-coloured stone, now a reddish-orange variety of zircon.

Chapter 19 (pp. 208–11)

22	*the image of God*: P.F. here omits the heretical creation myth of the German text, in which it is asserted that neither the world nor the human race had a beginning.

Chapter 21 (pp. 212–15)

87	*the sun abideth perpetually in his place*: P.F.'s interpolation from the beginning of this sentence to the end of the next paragraph.

Chapter 22 (pp. 215–18)

20	*Trier*: the 1608 reading is 'Trent'. The corresponding lines in the play (III. 1. 2–5) are more applicable to Trent than to Trier, suggesting that Marlowe used an edition of *EFB*, now lost, containing the mis-reading preserved in 1608 and not the revised edition of 1592 (see Jones, 1991: 469–70).
30	*kingdom of Naples*: a confusing translation of *und kam in Campanien, in die Statt Neapolis*, 'and came in Campania to the city of Naples'.
32	*the streets fair and large*: most of the details in these notices of Naples, Venice, Padua, and Rome are P.F.'s additions.

58   *the pyramid*: the obelisk brought from Egypt by Caligula in AD 37 and re-erected in its present site in the middle of St Peter's Square by order of Pope Sixtus V in 1586. In medieval times, when the obelisk stood beside St Peter's, it was believed that Julius Caesar's ashes rested on the top, enclosed in a sphere.

89   *smote the Pope on the face*: a mistranslation of *blieβ D. Faustus ihm in das Angesicht* 'Dr. Faustus blew in his face'.

111   *bell, book, and candle*: not in the German. Cf. III. 1. 91–2.

Chapter 29 (pp. 218–20)

57   *basilisk*: a fabulous reptile, whose look was believed to be fatal.

73   *the woman that raised the prophet Samuel*: the witch of Endor (1 Sam. 28: 7–20).

Chapter 48 (pp. 225–27)

24   *Acts of the Apostles*: Acts 8: 9–13.

32   *I will refresh you*: Matt. 11: 28.

34   *convert and live*: Ezek. 33: 11.

Chapter 63 (pp. 235–8)

129   *another book*: G.R. Widman claims to draw on Wagner's book in his *Wahrhafftige Historia* ('True History') (1599).

2 *The Ecclesiastical History* . . . (pp. 239–41)

58   *the lion and the dragon*: Psalm 91: 13.

3 *The Conflict of Conscience* . . . (pp. 242–5)

6   *O God, which dwellest*: a paraphrase of the Lord's Prayer.

32   *God hath it said*: cf. 1 John 1: 8–9.

49   good counsel to the sick: cf. Terence, *Andros*, 309: *Facile omnes quom valemus recta consilia aegrotis damus.*

103   *the deaf man*: probably a conflation of Mark 7: 32–7 and Mark 9: 25–9.

108   *one small grain*: see Matt. 13: 31–2.

THE MASSACRE
AT PARIS

INTRODUCTION

The Massacre at Paris is concerned with events in France from the infamous massacre of St Bartholomew in 1572 to the assassination of Henry III in 1589, a turbulent period of successive wars of religion on which Marlowe imposes a certain coherence and unity by emphasizing the rise to power and dramatic fall of the ambitious Duke of Guise. Like Marlowe's other plays, it is difficult to date. The only early edition of it is undated, but probably belongs to 1602; its earliest recorded performance was given by Lord Strange's Men at the Rose Theatre in January 1593. The date of composition must of course be later than Henry's death on 2 August 1589; the reference to 'Sixtus' bones' in Act V may imply (but not necessarily) that it is also later than the death of Pope Sixtus V on 27 August 1590. A consideration of Marlowe's sources for the play suggests that it may have preceded *The Jew of Malta*. Marlowe certainly made use of an account of the St Bartholomew massacre by the Huguenot lawyer, François Hotman, writing under the pseudonym Ernestus Varamundus, which first appeared in Latin in 1573 and, in the same year, in an English translation entitled *A True and Plain Report of the Furious Outrages of France*. In 1574 it was reprinted, without acknowledgement, as Book X of Jean de Serres's more extensive history, *The Three Parts of Commentaries*, and this was followed in 1576 by a fourth part containing Books XI and XII. All four parts are bound up together in the British Library copy. If Marlowe used de Serres, and if he consulted Book XI, he would have found an account of entering a besieged town through a water channel (see below, *The Jew of Malta*, Text 8, pp. 333–4). It may be that he recalled this incident when he makes Barabas adopt a similar stratagem, but it must be stressed that this is conjecture, not hard evidence.

Critical appraisal of *The Massacre at Paris* is rendered difficult by the unsatisfactory state of the text. The often garbled and perfunctory version which has survived is generally agreed to have been put together from actors' recollections of their parts; the existence of a manuscript leaf (the Collier leaf, now in the Folger Library) offers a tantalizing

251

glimpse of a lost fuller version, which allows the Duke of Guise a soliloquy in which to savour his shortlived triumph over the body of the murdered Mugeroun in place of the three-line speech in the printed text. Even allowing for this, the play has often been dismissed as nothing more than a crude, bloodthirsty, and historically inaccurate potboiler. More recently, however, critics have begun to take the view that, even with a very imperfect text, the play can be seen as a typical exercise in Marlovian irony, and it has been acknowledged that Marlowe's use of his sources for the play is more intelligent and responsible than had been supposed.

It is unfortunate that Paul H. Kocher's painstaking and indispensable work on the sources of the play (1941, 1947) did so little to rehabilitate it, but rather the reverse, leading him to the conclusion that Marlowe uncritically adopts the violently prejudiced views of the Protestant pamphlets so abundantly available in the aftermath of the St Bartholomew's Day massacre. John Bakeless (1937) had already pointed out Marlowe's dependence in this play on what he calls 'newsbooks'; in 1942, he suggested that some of the material may well have come, not from printed sources at all, but from hearsay. In the second half of the play at least, this is very likely to have been the case. The massacre itself, with which the first half of the play is concerned, was an event of Marlowe's childhood, and although the arrival of Huguenot refugees in Canterbury may have made an impression on him, it must have been a distant memory. The rest of the play covers the period from 1572 to the death of Henry III in 1589. In 1587 Marlowe was himself in France as a government agent, and recent evidence uncovered by R.B. Wernham (1976) and interpreted by Constance Kuriyama (1988) suggests that his career in the secret service may have continued until at least 1592. He must have been well acquainted with the political and religious turmoil in France in this period. He was, in short, well qualified to write a play dealing with events so contemporary that, within two months of his death, its ending was to be overtaken by the final irony of Henry of Navarre's conversion to Catholicism in order to claim the throne of France.

Unlike Bakeless, Kocher does not acknowledge the possibility that Marlowe may not have needed to depend entirely on printed material. Julia Briggs, however, in an article which takes a fresh look at Marlowe's use of sources in the play, restates the importance of oral information; she points out, for example, that Henry III's dismissal of his councillors in Scene 20, an incident which Kocher concludes must be invented because he could find no published account of it, is in fact authenticated by contemporary documents (Briggs 1983: 261–2). She also challenges the view that the play is no more than an exploitation of Protestant prejudices, arguing that in his treatment of the Duke of Guise's murder,

Marlowe not only takes details from Catholic League sources, but adopts their point of view as well.

Any discussion of the sources of the second half of the play must necessarily be tentative and conjectural. There is a great deal of pamphlet material and it is difficult to establish how much of it Marlowe knew; the texts printed here are included, for the most part, as illustrations of the range of material available to him. It is a different matter, however, with the massacre scenes, which, as Kocher (1941) has convincingly demonstrated, rely extensively on *The Furious Outrages of France*. There are some details, however, which are not accounted for by Hotman. Kocher has suggested that Guise's trampling of the dead Admiral, and the mention of the gallows at Montfaucon, where the latter's corpse is displayed, may have come from Hotman's *The Life of . . . Jasper Coligny* (Kocher 1941: 358–9); Kocher and Bakeless both think that the death of Ramus, which is mentioned only in passing in *The Furious Outrages*, may be based on *Le tocsin contre les massacreurs* (1579). But Jacques Ramel's discovery (1979) of another possible source for the play, the *Mémoires de l'état de France sous Charles neuvième* (1576), a compilation edited by Simon Goulart, shows that it may not have been necessary for Marlowe to pick up odd details from individual pamphlets. There are equivalents in the *Mémoires* for all these passages and for a number of Marlowe's other divergences from Hotman (see Text 2, pp. 274–7).

Goulart's account is dominated by the conviction that the massacre had been planned in advance, a view not supported by modern historians, who see it rather as a panic reaction to the botched assassination of Coligny, leading to an uncontrollable explosion of mob violence. Hotman does not expound the conspiracy theory, although he hints at it with an occasional parenthetical 'as it seemed'. He does adopt the Protestant view that Joan of Navarre was murdered, without naming a culprit; there is no proof, however, that her death was unnatural. For Goulart the deaths of Joan and of Coligny are all part of Catherine de Medici's elaborate plan to establish her own dominance, again a view no longer accepted, although there is no doubt that the assassination of the Admiral was planned or of the involvement of Catherine and the Duke of Guise. In Goulart the king also knows of the plot, but that is unlikely.

Only one pre-massacre council is reported in Hotman and this is also the only one dramatized by Marlowe, where it occurs before the visit of the royal party to the Admiral's sickbed and not afterwards, as in both Hotman and Goulart. H.J. Oliver comments in his edition of the play that the effect of this relocation is to 'add hypocrisy to the king's sins' (1968: 108). There is ample justification, however, for Charles's hypocrisy in Goulart and other Protestant sources; whether he actually deserves their excoriation is another matter. In any case, Marlowe's portrayal is of an irresolute and susceptible character rather than a villain. This is close to the historical reality, and there are suggestions for it in Goulart, in the last-minute midnight meeting in the king's chamber at which the queen mother fears that he will be daunted by the thought of horrors to come.

Marlowe's version of events departs markedly from both Hotman and Goulart in the prominence which it gives to the Duke of Guise. Imagination takes precedence over fact most strikingly in the long soliloquy in Scene 2 which transforms Guise into a villain–hero of titanic proportions; events follow in accordance with it. In the play it is Guise who orders the murder of the Queen of Navarre, not Catherine de Medici, and it is he alone who orders the shooting of the Admiral. He is present at the council in Scene 4, which was not the case (although he was present at the midnight meeting mentioned above), and he is shown committing murders of which history does not accuse him: those of Ramus, of Leranne, of Navarre's schoolmasters, and of the Protestants praying in a wood. The last of these crimes, reminiscent of his father's slaughter of Protestants at a sermon at Vassy in 1561, has no equivalent in accounts of the St Bartholomew's Day Massacre. These additional murders can be explained largely in terms of dramatic economy, as can those attributed to Anjou and Gonzague.

Marlowe's interpretation of relations between the Duke of Guise and Catherine de Medici also differs from the accounts of Hotman and Goulart, and more especially the latter, where the duke appears to be little more than a tool manipulated by the Machiavellian queen. The partiality she shows for him in the play is not accounted for in Marlowe's written sources, unless there is a hint in Hotman's statement that 'the queen had given all the offices and places of honour that his father had borne before [to the Duke of Guise], being unfit thereto by age, and against the ancient laws and customs' (fol. 3 verso). Later historians, however, for example Martha Freer (1858: III. 83), confirm that she did indeed have a soft spot for Guise. Like the Protestant pamphleteers, Marlowe shows Catherine as desiring power at any cost; her relationship with Guise could be seen as exploitative on her part, and does not necessarily conflict with her overriding motive. After Guise's murder, however, Marlowe brings out the pathos of her situation, out-manoeuvred by Henry, isolated, and close to her own death. Her outburst in Scene 22 is authenticated in several contemporary reports, including the League pamphlet, *Le martyre des deux frères* (see Text 6, pp. 284–5), but there her concern is rather for the consequences to Henry of his rash deed than for Guise or for the church.

The massacre itself is dramatized as a series of short scenes, each enacting a murder, a procedure which a number of critics have designated a 'snapshot' technique and which, as Ramel has pointed out, may be derived from the narrative method adopted by Goulart (Ramel 1979: 10). Goulart does, however, treat the death of the Admiral at great length, and, like Hotman, he strongly emphasizes Coligny's courage, fortitude, and piety. In the play, the Admiral's part is brief and unimpressive, but Marlowe is not, unlike Hotman or Goulart, writing Protestant hagiography; rather, he gives greater prominence to the scholar, Ramus, than to the Admiral. In Hotman, Ramus is no more than an item in a list. In the *Mémoires* and *Le tocsin contre les massacreurs* there is only a very brief account of how Ramus tried to buy his life from the assassins; the courageous and dignified Ramus of the play does not have gold to give. The discussion of Ramist logic in this comparatively long scene probably derives from Marlowe's own interest in the subject, which he would have studied at Cambridge when the Ramist controversy was at its height. There is no historical warrant either for the presence of Ramus's Catholic friend, Talaeus, who had been dead ten years, but, as John Glenn points out (Glenn 1973: 371), he earns his place in the scene with the line 'I am as Ramus is, a Christian' (Scene 9, line 14). The implication, which is supported by Marlowe's ironic treatment of religious hypocrisy in his other plays, strengthens the argument that he is not simply voicing Protestant propaganda.

Religious observance is not the focus of the Ramus scene, but it is prominent in all the other scenes of the massacre. In the case of the Admiral, it is introduced by altering his last words from 'Young man, consider my age and the weak case I am now in', as reported by Hotman, to 'O, let me pray before I die' (Scene 6, line 29). The element of sardonic humour in the reply, 'Then pray unto our Lady; kiss this cross', is a striking and characteristic contribution to this and to the other massacre scenes. Kocher comments that 'most of the deviations from Hotman seem aimed at. . . the heaping up of the horrible, and the stirring of vengeful passions in the audience' (Kocher 1941: 366), but Julia Briggs argues that in this grim parody of ritual Marlowe shows an acute insight into what a social historian of the period, Natalie Zemon Davis, has called 'the rites of violence' (Briggs 1983: 275–8). Professor Davis explains that such rites are 'intended to purify the religious community and humiliate the enemy and thus make him less harmful. . . . The crucial fact that the killers must forget is that their victims are human beings' (Davis 1975: 178, 181). Scene 11, in which Murderers One and Two debate what to do with the Admiral's corpse, is a particularly good example of this dehumanizing and the need of the massacre's perpetrators to rid themselves of what they see as defilement; it is also one of several passages in the play where, unusually for Marlowe, the common man is allowed to express his reaction to the events in which he is caught up.

255

Nearly the whole of the first half of the play is devoted to a space of a few months in 1572 (and much of it to the day of the massacre), but in Scene 10 Marlowe begins the process by which he telescopes the events of seventeen years into the second half of the play. This scene shows Anjou accepting the elective crown of Poland from the Polish ambassadors, on condition that, should his brother die, he be allowed to return to France. The visit of the ambassadors in fact occurred much later, in 1573, and there is no evidence that Anjou made any such proviso; on the contrary, some writers (for example, Jean Boucher in *La vie de Henri de Valois*, 1589) assert that he broke faith with the Poles and absconded when he heard of the death of his brother. No doubt Kocher is right to say that the scene is inserted here so that Anjou's return to France will not follow too swiftly on his departure (Kocher 1941: 365), but negotiations with the Poles were in progress during the time of the massacre and are fully reported in the *Mémoires*, though not mentioned by Hotman. Ramel points out that a reference to them occurs just before the visit to Montfaucon, just as it does in Marlowe, increasing the possibility that Marlowe did know this work (Ramel 1979: 9–10).

Kocher argues that Scene 10 also begins the process by which Marlowe starts to transform Anjou from one of the architects of the massacre into the 'sympathetic' ally of Navarre and of England that he becomes in the latter part of the play, thereby rendering the character 'wellnigh unintelligible' (Kocher 1941: 368). But if Anjou is regarded as a cunning politician throughout, who here ensures that accepting the Polish crown will not prevent him from grasping a larger prize, then the characterization is not inconsistent. As for Navarre, according to Kocher, he is 'the merest patchwork of Protestant commonplaces' (1947: 316), but many critics now take the view that his sanctimoniousness coexists with a hardheaded grasp of political realities. Marlowe shows Navarre to be, as in fact he was, a supreme opportunist.

The coverage of the political background in the second half of the play is understandably sketchy, though not badly informed. The latter part of Henry III's reign is a confused and confusing period of shifting alliances, in which the Guises re-formed the Holy League, dedicated to extirpating heresy, and in which their growing power culminated in the Day of the Barricades (1588), when the Parisians rebelled against the king. The latter resorted to the expedient of assassinating the Duke of Guise and his brother the Cardinal, and with Navarre's help set about regaining Paris; his own assassination by the League merely delivered the kingdom into Navarre's hands. To complain, as Kocher does, that the incident of the Barricades is 'a sad example of missed opportunities' (Kocher 1947: 173), is to wish for a different, and not necessarily better, play. Scene 20, which follows this event, uses a technique perfected in similar scenes of confrontation in *Edward II*; without in this case relying on any particular source, Marlowe uses the points at issue between the Duke of Guise and Henry III in an imaginative reconstruction which builds towards Henry's decision to murder his rival. Elsewhere important political events are subordinated to the personal lives of the characters, as when the battle of Coutras (1587) forms little more than a background to the story of Guise's cuckolding (which in fact took place nine years earlier).

Further parallels with *Edward II* begin to be apparent in Scene 14 (that of Henry's coronation). It is clear from Catherine's critical comments on her son that Marlowe's interpretation of Henry's character is influenced by what he knew about Henry's homosexuality, which is much emphasized in League pamphlets. Boucher (see Text 3, p. 279) describes the incident when the crown nearly falls from Henry's head as he looks round at his *mignons*. Marlowe does not use this, but he does introduce the unhistorical incident of the cutpurse, which bears a striking likeness to an anecdote recorded by Sir Nicholas L'Estrange (1603–55) in his manuscript jestbook (see Text 4, p. 281). It is of course possible that the anecdote may derive from the play, but not very likely. L'Estrange's collection is a fascinating record of oral tradition and this jest is entirely typical of it; the differences in detail from the play (L'Estrange's gentleman, for example, loses a purse and sets a trap for the thief) suggest that the two versions may be independent variants of the same story. In the play it serves the purpose of focusing attention on one of the *mignons*, Mugeroun, and it adds an element of irony to the scene in which summary justice is executed on Mugeroun in his turn for a more serious crime than stealing gold buttons.

If Marlowe's treatment of Henry is less inconsistent than has been supposed, it can be argued that there is a change of emphasis in his presentation of the Duke of Guise. Like his fellow Machiavellian, Barabas, in *The Jew of Malta*, Guise begins to appear vulnerable. Betrayed first by his wife and then by the king, he is seen as a victim both of his own sexual jealousy and inflexible pride, and of an enemy who is a more successful Machiavellian than he is. Guise's only triumph in this part of the play is not, as in reality, on the battlefield or at the Day of the Barricades, but over the adulterer, Mugeroun. No contemporary source for the Mugeroun episode available to Marlowe has yet been found, although there is an account of it by Jacques-Auguste de Thou first published in 1609 (see Text 5, pp. 282–3). De Thou, as a councillor of state, was a contemporary observer at the court of Henry III, although his *Historia sui temporis* (1604–9) did not begin to appear in print until long afterwards. A scholarly edition of this work, based on a comparison of the extant manuscripts, was published in 1733 and translated into French in 1734; the latter has been used in Text 5. Evidently Marlowe confused Mugeroun with St-Mégrin; if he relied on hearsay evidence (and this must have been a subject for gossip) the mistake is understandable. Boucher tells in detail how the former met his end in a three-sided duel; he describes St-Mégrin as a successor to Mugeroun and as 'une personne de pareille vie' (p. 43) – another reason, perhaps, why Marlowe confused or conflated them. De Thou confirms the essentials of Marlowe's story: the king's mockery of the cuckold, the misplaced confidence of the lover, the king's unavailing warning. Marlowe reduces the assassins lying in wait to one, whose coarse comments make the episode yet more degrading. In de Thou, however, it is stressed that Guise himself is not provoked to revenge, and that it is his brother, the Duc de Mayenne (Dumaine) who has Mugeroun killed. Marlowe's scene in which the furious husband confronts his wife makes a more dramatic subject and may have some basis in fact; Kocher cites the historian, Martha Freer, who refers to an intercepted correspondence between Madame de Guise and St-Mégrin and to a meeting in which Guise 'terrified his wife into better behaviour' (Freer 1858: II. 204–6). Dumaine does appear as a revenger in the play, but only at the end, when, Henry's plan to assassinate him having failed, he in turn plots to murder Henry.

In Scene 22, that of Guise's assassination, Marlowe depends very largely on League pamphlets, and if he does not, as they do, present Guise as blameless and devout, he does emphasize his courage on the one hand and Henry's perfidy on the other. In *La vie de Henri de Valois* there is a scene in which the latter lulls Guise's suspicions with feigned friendliness (see Text 3, p. 279); in the equivalent scene in the play, Henry uses similar expressions of affection (for example 'my loving cousin') but he does so moments before the actual killing, not days before as in Boucher's account. In the play the only warning Guise receives – again at the last moment – comes from one of the murderers; they show no such compunction in the sources, but in another of the Catholic pamphlets, *Le martyre des deux frères* (see Text 6, p. 285), the murderers of Guise refuse to carry out the order to kill his brother, the Cardinal, as well. *Le martyre* shows Guise disregarding several warnings and insisting that he would rather die a hundred times than prejudice the meeting of the Estates General at Blois. Marlowe's Guise is equally emphatic, though his response is prompted by egotism and pride, not devotion to duty. His line 'Yet Caesar shall go forth' (line 67) also occurs in *Julius Caesar*, and looks at first like an example of Shakespeare borrowing from Marlowe, since the latter play was probably written and performed in 1599. It is possible, though, that the compilers of Marlowe's text may have recalled Shakespeare's line and the borrowing is the other way round. The comparison of Guise with Caesar was well established in League writings, as Bakeless notes (1942: II. 85–6); Marlowe's own interest in Caesar's career is evident from his translation of the first book of Lucan's epic poem of civil war, the *Pharsalia*. Here the parallel is particularly apt, and among other resonances, it lays yet further emphasis on the king's act of betrayal.

Henry's emergence from his 'cabinet' to gloat over the body of his dead enemy parallels Guise's earlier triumph over the body of the Admiral. Marlowe again follows a League pamphlet, *Les cruautés sanguinaires* (see Text 7, p. 286), when Henry sends for Guise's son 'to behold his death' (line 93). If Marlowe were indeed merely voicing Protestant propaganda there would certainly have been no reason to include this incident, which increases sympathy for Guise and his son and intensifies Henry's guilt. Nor is it the case that Marlowe simply adopts the League viewpoint instead; what he seizes on is the dramatic potential of this incident, poignantly realized in the son's line 'Art thou king, and hast done this bloody deed?' (line 122). In *Le martyre*, as in Boucher, Henry's companion in this scene is Loignac, not Epernoun. The latter *mignon* is the subject of particularly violent attacks in the Catholic pamphlets, but Protestant writers such as Antony Colynet approve of him as a staunch opponent of the Leaguers. Kocher argues that Marlowe takes a Protestant line on Epernoun (Kocher 1947: 317) but his involvement in the murder of Guise (there is some evidence that he suggested it, as in the play, but not that he was present at it) hardly shows him in a favourable light.

The next scene shows the murder of the Duke of Guise's brother, the Cardinal of Guise, whom Marlowe conflates with their uncle, the Cardinal of Lorraine (died 1574), more probably as a way of telescoping time than out of ignorance. The sardonic humour of the prose dialogue, which recalls that of the earlier massacre scenes, was perhaps suggested by *Le martyre*, where the murderers are said to mock their victim, and the woodcut illustration, at least, shows them laughing. In the pamphlet the original murderers refuse to shed a churchman's blood; in the play it is the Cardinal who vainly pleads clerical exemption. The strangling, which gives Marlowe's joke its punchline, is also mentioned in *Le martyre*, although not in every account. Interpreted simply from a Protestant standpoint, the murder may be seen as a just revenge; from a League point of view, however, it is a sacrilege and as deserving of the term 'massacre' as the crimes of St Bartholomew's Day. Marlowe does not necessarily endorse either view, but his structuring of the play to bring out the parallels between the St Bartholomew massacre and the deaths of the Guise brothers, as Julia Briggs observes, emphasizes 'the combination of royal treachery and sacrilegious violence against men of the church' which is common to both (Briggs 1983: 200).

The final scene, the assassination of Henry III, cannot be shown to depend on any one source, though a number of its details can also be found in Colynet's account (see Text 8, pp. 287–91). Colynet mentions the poisoned knife and Henry's partiality for friars, for example, and the friar's claim to bring letters from the President of Paris. He does not say that Henry attacked the friar with the same knife, although other writers, Boucher among them, do; only in Marlowe, though, does Henry actually kill the friar. In Colynet, as in the play, the dying Henry gives Navarre charge of the realm, a point of importance to the Protestant cause, and one not mentioned by League writers; but he also dies in exemplary fashion, confessing his sins to a priest, and although he at first asks Navarre to take a just revenge, he eventually forgives his enemies. In contrast, Marlowe's king certainly does not die as a penitent Catholic, but vowing vengeance on the Catholic church in terms as violent as those he had used earlier at the massacre of St Bartholomew. The unhistorical presence of 'the English agent' and the appeal to 'my sister' Elizabeth are undeniably directed at an English Protestant audience, but it need not be assumed that Marlowe simply offers Henry's tirade for their approval. It could also be said that the scene amply justifies the League view of Henry as the 'hypocrite et apostat ennemi de la religion Catholique', to quote the title page of *La vie de Henri de Valois*. In the context of the play as a whole, the scene may well be interpreted as a dispassionate ironic comment on the cruel fanaticism of both sides.

TEXT 1

A True and Plain Report of the Furious Outrages of France . . .

François Hotman [Ernestus Varamundus]
(1574)

[The text is taken from the British Library copy (shelfmark 286. c. 29)
of Jean de Serres, *The Three Parts of Commentaries*, in which
The Furious Outrages, first published 1573, is reprinted as Book X.]

And so was the third civil war ended [1570], and the peace
concluded with the same conditions that were before, that every
man should have free liberty to use and profess the religion
[Protestantism]. . . .

(fol. 4 recto)

[Charles IX promises to observe the edict of pacification and to give
military aid to the Prince of Orange against Spain in the Netherlands.]

And for that there was old enmity between the Guisians and the
Admiral, whereby it was to be doubted that perilous dissensions
would arise in the realm of France, the king willed it to be signified
to them both in his name, that they should for his sake and the
commonweal's give over those displeasures [quarrels], and he
prescribed them a certain form of reconciliation and agreement, 10
the same whereof the foundations had been laid almost six years
before in the town of Moulins, where the king calling to him the
greatest estates of his realm, after consultation and deliberation
had upon the matter, pronounced the Admiral not guilty of the
death of the Duke of Guise, wherewith he was charged by the young
Duke of Guise and his kinsmen; and so the king by the advice of his
council had ended that controversy. . . .

But there was none greater and more assured token of public
peace and quietness than this, that the king purposed to give his
sister Margaret in marriage to the Prince Henry, the son of the 20
Queen of Navarre, which prince had in the last war defended the
cause of the religion and been sovereign of their army. Which
marriage the king declared that it should be the most strait [close]

261

bond of civil concord, and the most assured testimony of his goodwill to those of the religion.

Yea, and also because it was alleged that the said Prince Henry was restrained in conscience, so as he might not marry the Lady Margaret, being of a contrary religion, a Catholic, and given to the rites of the Romish church, the king for answer said that he would discharge her of the Pope's laws, and notwithstanding the crying out of all his courtiers to the contrary, he permitted him that without all ceremonies, in the porch of the great church of Paris, the marriage should be celebrate in such a form as the ministers of the reformed church misliked not.

Which thing being by report and letters spread through the world, it cannot be expressed how much it made the hearts of those of the religion assured and out of care, and how it cast out all fear and jealousies out of their minds, what a confidence it brought them of the king's good will toward them; finally, how much it rejoiced foreign princes and states that favoured the same religion. . . . The marriage was appointed to be holden in the town of Paris. For which cause the Queen of Navarre during those few days repaired thither to provide things for the solemnity of the wedding. . . .

(fos. 6 verso–7 recto)

[The Admiral is persuaded to come to Paris for the wedding; the French suffer a defeat in the Netherlands.]

Not long before this, Joan, Queen of Navarre above-mentioned, died in the court at Paris, of a sudden sickness, being about the age of forty and three years, whereas the suspicion was great that she died of poison, and her body being for that cause opened by the physicians, there were no tokens of poison espied. But shortly after, by the detection of one A.P., it hath been found that she was poisoned with a venomed smell of a pair of perfumed gloves, dressed by one Renat [René], the king's apothecary, an Italian, that hath a shop at Paris upon St Michael's bridge, near unto the palace; which could not be espied by the physicians, which did not open the head nor looked into the brain. . . .

By her death, the kingdom came to the Prince Henry, her son, to whom as is abovesaid, the king's sister was promised and contracted.

Things being, as it seemed, throughout all France in most peaceable estate, and the concord of all degrees well stablished, the day was appointed for the marriage of the King of Navarre, which day all they that fancied the religion esteemed so much the more joyful to them, because they saw the king wonderfully bent there-

262

unto, and all good men judged the same a most assured pledge and establishment of civil concord, whereas on the contrary part, the Guisians and other enemies of common quietness greatly abhorred the same marriage.

When the day came, the marriage was with royal pomp solemnized before the great church of Paris, and a certain form of words so framed, as disagreed with the religion of neither side, was by the king's commandment pronounced by the Cardinal of Bourbon, the King of Navarre's uncle; and so the matrimony celebrate with great joy of the king and all good men, the bride was with great train and pomp led into the church to hear Mass, and in the meantime, the bridegroom, who misliked these ceremonies, together with Henry, Prince of Condé, son of Louis, and the Admiral, and other noblemen of the same religion, walked without the church door, waiting for the bride's return. . . .

After the marriage ended at Paris, which was the time that the Admiral had appointed to return to his own house, he moved the king concerning his departure. . . . But when they that were sent from the reformed churches to complain of injuries commonly done to those of the religion understood of the Admiral's purpose to depart, they did with all speed deliver to him their books and petitions, and besought him not to depart from the court till he had dealt in the cause of the churches, and delivered their petitions to the king and his council. . . .

(fos. 9 recto–10 recto)

Concerning all these affairs, the Admiral (as he determined before) having access and opportunity for that purpose, moved the king's privy council the 22 of August [1572], which was the fifth day after the King of Navarre's marriage, and spent much time in that treaty. About noon, when he was in returning home from the council, with a great company of noblemen and gentlemen, behold, a harquebusier [from *harquebus*, a hand-gun] out of a window of a house near adjoining shot the Admiral with two bullets of lead through both the arms. When the Admiral felt himself wounded, nothing at all amazed, but with the same countenance that he was accustomed, he said, 'Through yonder window it was done; go see who are in the house. What manner of treachery is this?' Then he sent a certain gentleman of his company to the king to declare it unto him. The king at that time was playing at tennis with the Duke of Guise. As soon as he heard of the Admiral's hurt, he was marvellously moved, as it seemed, and threw away his racket that he played with on the ground, and taking with him his brother-in-law, the King of Navarre, he retired into his castle.

The gentlemen that were with the Admiral brake into the house from whence he received his hurt; there they found only one woman, the keeper of the house; and shortly after also a boy, his lackey that had done the deed, and therewithal they found the harquebus lying upon the table in that chamber from whence the noise was heard. Him that shot they found not, for he in great haste was run away out at the back gate, and getting on horseback, which he had waiting for him ready stabled at the door, he rode a great pace to St Antony's gate. . . . 110

At the suit of the King of Navarre and the Prince of Condé and other, the king by and by gave commission for enquiry to be made of the matter. . . . First, it was found that the same house belonged to a priest, a canon of St Germain, whose name is Villemur, which had been the Duke of Guise's schoolmaster in his youth, and still continued a retainer toward him. Then the woman which we said was found in the house, being taken and brought before them, confessed that a few days before, there came to her one Chailly, sometime a *maître d'hôtel* of the Duke of Guise's house, and now of the king's court, and commanded her to make much of the man that had done this deed, and to lodge him in the same bed and chamber where Villemur was wont to lie, for that he was his friend and very familiar acquaintance, and that Villemur would be very glad of it. . . . 120

While these things were doing, and the Admiral's wound in dressing, Téligny went by his commandment to the king, and most humbly besought him in the name of his father-in-law that His Majesty would vouchsafe to come unto him, for that his life seemed to be in peril, and that he had certain things to say, greatly importing to the king's safety, which he well knew that none in his realm durst declare to His Majesty. The king courteously answered that he would willingly go to him, and within a little while after he set forward. The queen mother went with him, and the Duke of Anjou, the Duke of Montpensier, a most affectionate subject to the church of Rome, the Count de Retz, the queen mother's great familiar, Chavigny and Entragny, which afterwards were chief ringleaders in the butchery of Paris. 130 140

When the king had lovingly saluted the Admiral as he was wont to do, and had gently asked him some questions concerning his hurt and the state of his health, and the Admiral had answered with such a mild and quiet countenance, that all they that were present wondered at his temperance and patience, the king being much moved (as it seemed) said, 'The hurt, my Admiral, is done to thee, but the dishonour to me; but by the death of God,' saith he, 'I swear I will so severely revenge both the hurt and the dishonour, that it shall never be forgotten.' 150

He asked him also how he liked of the judges that he had chosen, to whom he had given commission for examining the matter. The Admiral answered that he could not but very well like of those that His Majesty had allowed of, yet he besought him if he thought it good, that Cavaignes might be called to council with them, albeit that it was no hard matter to find out, for it was no doubt, said he, that this good turn was done him by the Duke of Guise, the revenge whereof he referred to God. This only he most heartily and humbly besought of his royal majesty, that the fact [crime] might be duly enquired upon. The king answered that he would take earnest care of it, and revenge that injury with no less severity than if it had been done to himself. Then the king's brethren and their mother withdrawing themselves awhile, the Admiral, as it was afterward known by his own report, began to advise the king to have in memory those things that he had oft told him of the dangerous intentions of certain persons; and he told him that though he himself had received a great wound, yet there was no less hanging over the king's head, and that long ago there was treason in practising against his life, which if he would do wisely he should avoid betimes. Further he said, that though so soon as God should take him to Himself out of this life, he doubted not but that his fame should be brought into sundry slanders by envious persons and such as ought [bore] him evil will by reason of the late wars; nevertheless he had oftentimes disclosed unto the king the authors of the dissensions, and opened the causes thereof, and that God was his witness of his most faithful heart to the king and the common weal, and that he had never holden anything dearer than his country and the public safety.

The king after such answer made hereunto as he thought best, spake aloud, and heartily entreated the Admiral to suffer himself to be removed into his castle of Louvre, for that he thought some peril, lest there should arise some sedition among the commons already in disorder, or any stir in that mad and troublesome city. Whereto this speech of the king tended could not then be understood. For though the commonalty of Paris hath ever been accounted the most foolish and mad of all other, yet is it ever most easily appeased, not only with the coming and presence of the king, but also with the very sound of his name. The Admiral most humbly and largely thanked the king, and made his excuse upon the counsel of the physicians, which feared that shaking would increase his pain, and therefore had taken order that he should not be stirred out of his place.

Then the Count de Retz, turning to certain gentlemen of the Admiral's friends, said, 'I would the Admiral would follow the

265

king's counsel, for it is to be feared that some such stir may arise in the town as the king shall not easily be able to appease.'

Which speech being uttered, although no man did yet suspect whereto that advice tended, yet the Admiral and his friends thought it good to request of the king to assign unto him certain of the soldiers of the guard for his safety. The king answered that he very well liked of that device, and that he was fully determined to provide as well for the Admiral's safety as for his own, and that he would preserve the Admiral as the ball of his eye, and that he had in admiration the constancy and fortitude of the man, and that he never before that time believed that there could be so great valiantness of courage in any mortal person.

Therewith the Duke of Anjou, the king's brother, commanded Cossin [Cosseins], captain of the king's guard, to place a certain band of soldiers to ward the Admiral's gate. There could hardly a man be found more hateful against the Admiral's part, nor more affected to the Guisians, than this Cossin, which the success [outcome] plainly proved, as hereafter shall appear. The Duke of Anjou further added that he thought it should be good for the Admiral if mo [more] of his friends and familiars that lodged in the faubourgs [suburbs] did draw nearer about him, and forthwith he commanded the king's harbingers [purveyors of lodgings] to warn those to whom they had before assigned lodgings in that street to remove from thence and to place the Admiral's friends in their rooms. Which counsel was such as none could possibly be devised more fit for those things that followed. For those which might have by flight escaped out of the suburbs were now holden fast enough, being enclosed not only within the walls of the town, but also within the compass of one narrow street. The next day after, the undermasters of the streets, commonly called quartermen, surveyed all the victualling houses and inns from house to house, and all the names of those of the religion, together with the place of every of their lodgings, they put in books, and with speed delivered over the same books to those of whom they had received that commandment.

After noon the queen mother led out the king, the Duke of Anjou, Gonzague, Tavannes, the Count de Retz called Gondi, into her garden called Tegliers [Tuileries]. This place, because it was somewhat far from resort, she thought most fit for this their last consultation. There she showed them how those whom they had long been in wait for were now sure in hold, and the Admiral lay in his bed maimed of both his arms and could not stir, the King of Navarre and Prince of Condé were fast lodged in the castle, the gates were kept shut all night, and watches placed, so as they were so snared that they could no way escape, and the captains thus taken, it was not to be feared that any of the religion would from thenceforth stir anymore. Now was a notable opportunity, said she, offered to dispatch the matter. For all the chief captains were fast closed up in Paris, and the rest in other towns were all unarmed and unprepared, and that there were scarcely to be found ten enemies to a thousand Catholics; that the Parisians were in armour, and were able to make threescore thousand chosen fighting men, and that within the space of one hour all the enemies may be slain, and the whole name and race of those wicked men be utterly rooted out. 'On the other side,' saith she, 'if the king do not take the advantage of the fitness of this time, it is no doubt but that if the Admiral recover his health, all France will shortly be on fire with the fourth civil war.'

The queen's opinion was allowed. Howbeit, it was thought best, partly for his age, and partly for the affinity's sake, that the King of Navarre's life should be saved. As for the Prince of Condé, it was doubted whether it were best to spare him for his age, or to put him to death for hatred of his father's name. But herein the opinion of Gonzague took place, that he should with fear of death and torment be drawn from the religion. So that council brake up, with appointment that the matter should be put in execution the next night early afore day, and that the ordering and doing of all should be committed to the Duke of Guise.

The Admiral, being informed of stir and noise of armour and threatenings heard everywhere throughout the town, and preparation of many things pertaining to tumult, sent word thereof to the king, who answered that there was no cause for the Admiral to fear, for all was done by his commandment, and not everywhere, but in certain places, and that there were certain appointed by him to be in armour, lest the people should rise and make any stir in the town.

When the Duke of Guise thought all things ready enough, he called to him the abovesaid Marcel [the provost of the merchants], and charged him that he should a little after midnight assemble together the masters of the streets, whom they call dizeners [tithingmen], into the townhouse, for he had certain strange and special matters in charge from the king, which his pleasure was to have declared unto them. They all assembled by time. Carron [Le Charron], the new provost of merchants, guarded with certain Guisians. . . made the declaration. He said that the king's meaning [intention] was to destroy all the rebels which had in these late years borne arms against His Majesty, and to root out the race of those wicked men. It was now very fitly happened that the chieftains and ringleaders of them were fast enclosed within the walls of the town, as in a prison, and that the same night they should first begin

267

with them, and afterward for the rest as soon as possibly might be, throughout all parts of the realm the king would take order; and the token to set upon them should be given, not with a trumpet, but with tocsin or ringing of the great bell of the palace, which they knew to be accustomed only in great cases; and the mark for them to be known from other should be a white linen cloth hanged about their left arm, and a white cross pinned upon their caps. In the meantime, the Duke of Guise made privy thereunto the captains of the king's guard, both Gascons, Frenchmen, and Switzers, and bade them be ready to go to it with good courage. Shortly after, the Duke of Guise and the bastard son of King Henry, commonly called the Chevalier, with a great band of armed men following them, went to the Admiral's house, which Cossin kept besieged with harquebusiers placed in order on both sides of the street.

The Admiral advertised of the stir and the noise of the armour, although he had scarcely ten persons in his house able to bear harness [arms], and in his chamber only two surgeons, one preacher, and one or two servitors, yet could not be made afraid, trusting (as he oft rehearsed) upon the king's goodwill toward him, approved by so many and so great means of assurance, having also confidence that the commonalty of Paris, if they once understood the king to mislike of their mad fury, how much soever they were in outrage, yet so soon as they saw Cossin warding the gate, they would be appeased. He repeated also the oath for keeping of the peace, so oft openly sworn by the king and his brethren and their mother, and entered in public records. . . the marriage of the king's sister solemnized but six days before, which it was not like that he would suffer to be defiled with blood; finally, the judgement of foreign nations and of posterity, shame, and the honour and constancy of a prince, public faith, and the sacred respect of the law of nations, all which it seemed monstrous and incredible that the king could assent to be stained with so outrageous a cruel deed.

Cossin, when he saw the noblemen draw near, knocked at the gate, which as is abovesaid, he was commanded by the Duke of Anjou to keep. Whereupon many applied the old proverb, 'A goodly guard to make the wolf keeper of the sheep'. When he was entered without in manner any difficulty, he carried in with him a great company of armed men, and after those followed the great lords. Such as Cossin found at the entry of and within the porch of the house, he slew with a partisan [spear] that he had in his hand. Which when the Admiral understood, he caused those that were about him to lift him out of his bed, and casting on a nightgown upon him, he rose upright on his feet. He bade his friends and servants to flee and make shift for themselves, and to take no more care for him, for he said that he was ready with most willing heart to render into the hands of God, now calling for it again, the spirit that He had lent him to use for a time; and said that this violent 330 cruelty was prepared not so much for his destruction, as for the dishonoring of Christ and the tormenting of so many churches, the defence of which churches he had at the petition of all godly men with his many dangers and calamities sustained.

In the meantime there came up the stairs into the higher part of the house one Benvese [Besme], a German, brought up in the house of the Duke of Guise, and to whom it is said that the Cardinal of Lorraine had given one of his bastard daughters in marriage; and with him came Cossin the Gascon, Attin, a Picard, a retainer and familiar of the Duke d'Aumale [uncle of the Duke of Guise], 340 one that a few years before sought to murder d'Andelot [the Admiral's elder brother] by treason, and also one Hamfort, an Avernois [Anversois? i.e. from Antwerp], all weaponed with swords and targets and armed with shirts of mail.

When they were broken into the Admiral's chamber, Benvese came to him, and bending his drawn sword upon him, said, 'Art not thou the Admiral?'

He, with a quiet and constant countenance (as we have since understood by themselves) answered, 'I am so called.' And then, seeing the sword drawn upon him, he said, 'Young man, consider 350 my age and the weak case that I am now in.'

But the fellow, after blaspheming God, first thrust his sword into the Admiral's breast, and then also struck him upon the head, and Attin shot him through the breast with a pistol. When the Admiral was with this wound not yet thoroughly dead, Benvese gave him the third wound upon the thigh, and so he fell down for dead.

When the Duke of Guise, which stayed in the court with the other noblemen, heard this, he cried out aloud, 'Hast thou done, Benvese?'

He answered, 'I have done.' 360

Then said the Duke of Guise, 'Our Chevalier,' (meaning King Henry's bastard abovesaid), 'unless he see it with his eyes will not believe it; throw him down at the window.'

Then Benvese with the help of his fellows took up the Admiral's body and threw it down through the window. When by reason of the wound in his head and his face covered with blood they could not well discern him, the Duke of Guise kneeled down on the ground and wiped him with a napkin, and said, 'Now I know him; it is he.'

And therewithal going out at the gate with the rest of the lords, he cried out to the multitude in armour, saying, 'My companions, 370 we have had a good lucky beginning; now let us go forward to the

269

rest, for it is the king's commandment,' which words he did oft repeat aloud, saying, 'Thus the king commandeth; this is the king's will; this is his pleasure.'

And then he commanded the token to be given by ringing tocsin with the great bell of the palace, and alarm to be raised, and he caused it to be published that the conspirators were in armour and about to kill the king. Then a certain Italian of Gonzague's band cut off the Admiral's head, and sent it preserved with spices to Rome to the Pope and the Cardinal of Lorraine. Other cut off his 380 hands and other his secret parts. Then the common labourers and rascals three days together dragged the dead body, thus mangled and berayed [defiled] with blood and filth, through the streets, and afterward drew it out of the town to the common gallows, and hanged it up with a rope by the feet.

In the mean time, those of the noblemen's bands brake into all the chambers of the Admiral's house, and such as they found either in their beds, or hidden, they mangled them with many wounds, and so slaughtered them. . . . Then the noblemen's bands and Cossin's soldiers went ransacking from house to house, and the 390 Admiral's house and all the other houses were all sacked and spoiled, even in like manner as is used to be done by soldiers greedy of prey in a town taken by assault, and many by this robbery were of beggars suddenly become rich men. For the Duke of Guise, the Duke of Montpensier, the Chevalier, King Henry's bastard, Gonzague, Tavannes, and the other great lords, did with the reward of the spoil and booty encourage the multitude to the slaughter, and cried out aloud that this was the king's will. So all the rest of the day, from morning to evening, the rascal multitude, encouraged by spoil and robbery, ran with their bloody swords raging throughout 400 all the town; they spared not the aged, nor women, nor the very babes. In joy and triumph they threw the slain bodies out at the windows, so as there was not in manner any one street or lane that seemed not strewed with murdered carcases.

While these things were thus a-doing in the town, the King of Navarre and the Prince of Condé, whom the king had lodged in his own castle of the Louvre, were by the king's commandment sent for and conveyed unto him. But their company, their servitors of their chambers, their friends retaining to them, their schoolmasters, and those that had the bringing up of them, crying out aloud to the 410 king's fidelity for succour, were thrust out of the chambers, and by the king's guard of Switzers hewed in pieces and slaughtered in the king's own sight. . . . Leranne [Léran], being thrust through with a sword, escaped and ran into the Queen of Navarre's chamber, and was by her kept and preserved from the violence of those that pursued him. Shortly after, she obtained his pardon of her brother, and committing him to her own physicians, who restored him both to life and health. . . .

The next day following, where any that had hidden themselves in corners at Paris could be found out, the slaughter was renewed; also common labourers and porters, and other of the most rascals of the people, and desperate villains, to have the spoil of their clothes, stripped the dead bodies stark naked and threw them into the river of Seine. . . .

420

(fos. 10 recto–16 recto)

This butcherly slaughter of Paris thus performed. . . immediately messengers were sent in post into all the parts of the realm, with oft shifting their horses for haste, to command all other cities in the king's name to follow the example of Paris, and to cause to be killed as many as they had among them of the reformed religion.

These commandments it is wonderful to tell how readily and cheerfully the greatest part of the cities of France did obey and execute. But the king, fearing (as it was likely) the dishonour of false treachery and perjury, sent letters to the governors of his provinces, and also speedy messengers into England, Germany, and Switzerland, to declare in his name that there was a great commotion and seditious stir happened at Paris, which he was very sorry for; that the Duke of Guise had raised the people, and with armed men made assault upon the band that was assigned to the Admiral for his guard, and had broken into the house and slain the Admiral and all his company and household servants, and that the king had hardly kept safe from those dangers his own castle of the Louvre, where he kept himself close with his mother and his brethren. . . . But the same most mighty, and by the consent of all nations commonly called the most Christian king, within two days after came into the Parliament, accompanied with a great train of his brethren and other princes. The council being assembled, he sitting in his throne, began to speak unto them. He declared that he was certified that the Admiral with certain of his accomplices had conspired his death, and had intended the like purpose against his brethren, the queen his mother, and the King of Navarre, and that for this cause he had commanded his friends to slay the said Admiral and all his confederates, and so to prevent the treason of his enemies. . . .

After the king's oration ended, Christopher Thuane [de Thou], President of that Parliament, a man very notable for his light [frivolous] brain and his cruel heart, did with very large words congratulate unto the king, that he had now with guile and subtlety

430

440

450

271

overcome these his enemies, whom he could never vanquish by arms and battle, saying that therein the king had most fully verified the old saying of Louis XI his progenitor, king of France, which was wont to say that he knew never a Latin sentence but this one, *Qui nescit dissimulare nescit regnare* ('He that cannot skill to dissemble, cannot skill to be a king'). But Pibrac, the advocate of the finances, made a short oration, the sum whereof was to this effect, that although the king had just and great cause to be displeased, yet he thought it more agreeable with His Majesty's clemency and goodness to make an end of the slaughters and common spoil. . . . An arrest [*arrêt*, decree] of Parliament with the king's royal assent being made to that effect, there were immediately heralds and trumpeters sent round about all the town, and an edict proclaimed in the king's name, that from thenceforth the slaughters and common butcherly murderings should cease, and that all persons should abstain from pillage and robbery.

This being known, there were divers speeches used of this matter throughout the town, and specially of learned men. The most part said that they had read many histories, but in all memory of all ages they never heard of any such thing as this. They compared this case with the horrible doings of King Mithridates. . . . Some compared it with the doing of Peter of Aragon. . . . But yet this difference appeared between those cases and this: that those kings had exercised their cruelty upon foreigners and strangers, but this king had done his outrage upon his own subjects. . . . Those kings used no guileful means, unworthy for the majesty of a king, to deceive; this king for a bait and an allurement abused the marriage of his own sister, and in a manner besprinkled her wedding robe with blood. . . .

(fos. 16 verso–17 verso)

[Further examples are adduced in condemnation of Charles's perfidy.]

Now as touching the Admiral's supposed conspiracy, who can think it likely that he should enterprise any such thing within the walls of Paris?. . . But be it that the Admiral and a few other of his confederates and followers had conspired, why yet proceeded the outrageous cruelty upon the rest that were innocent? Why upon ancient matrons, why upon noble ladies and young gentlewomen and virgins that came thither for the honour of the wedding? Why were so many women great with child, against the laws of all nations and of nature, before their delivery thrown into the river? Why were so many aged persons, many that lay sick in their beds, many gownmen, many councillors, advocates, proctors, physicians, many singularly learned professors and teachers of good arts, and among the rest Petrus Ramus, that renowned man throughout the world, many young students, executed without hearing, without pleading their cause, without sentence of condemnation?. . . 500

But now to return to our purpose. At such time as the king's prohibition abovesaid was proclaimed at Paris, not only in other towns, as at Orléans, Angers, Viaron, Troyes, and Auxerre, the like butcheries and slaughters were used, but also in the town of Paris itself, in the very gaols that are ordained for the keeping of prisoners, if any had escaped the cruelty of the day before, they were now tumultuously slain by the raging and outraging multitude. . . . And because we have made mention of Angers, we think it good not to to omit the case of Masson de Rivers [La Rivière]. This man was a pastor of the church, and esteemed a singular man 510 both in virtuousness of life, and in excellence of wit and learning, and was the first that had laid the foundation of the church at Paris. As soon as the slaughter was begun at Paris, Monsorel [Monsoreau], a most cruel enemy of the religion, was sent to Angers in post to prevent all other that might carry tidings of the murdering. As soon as he came into the town, he caused himself to be brought to Masson's house. There he met Masson's wife in the entry, and gently saluted her, and after the manner of France, specially of the court, he kissed her, and asked her where her husband was. She answered that he was walking in the garden; and by and by 520 [straightaway] she brought Monsorel to her husband, who gently embraced Masson and said unto him, 'Canst thou tell why I am come hither? It is to kill thee by the king's commandment at this very instant time, for so hath the king commanded, as thou mayst perceive by these letters.'

And herewith he showed him his dag [pistol] ready charged. Masson answered that he was not guilty of any crime; howbeit this one thing only he besought him, to give him space to call to the mercy of God, and to commend his spirit into God's hand. Which prayer as soon as he had ended in few words, he meekly received 530 the death offered by the other, and was shot through with a pellet, and died.

Now to return to Paris. The Admiral's body being hanged up by the heels upon the common gallows of Paris, as is aforesaid, the Parisians went thither by heaps to see it. And the queen mother, to feed her eyes with that spectacle, had a mind also to go thither, and she carried with her the king and both her other sons. But the next night following, the body was conveyed away and (as it is thought) buried. . . .

(fos. 18 verso–20 recto)

TEXT 2

Mémoires de l'état de France sous Charles neuvième . . .

edited by Simon Goulart
(1576–7)

[The text is translated from the copy in the Bodleian Library
(shelfmark 8° M 4 ART).]

Before continuing further with the war [in the Netherlands], we
ought to consider what happened to the Queen of Navarre. At the
beginning of May [1572], the king asked her to go to Paris to make
arrangements for the wedding. This she did, and setting off on
about the sixth, arrived in Paris on the fifteenth of the month. . . .
The queen mother did not want to lose this opportunity. She hated
the Queen of Navarre violently and knew her character of old. If
she allowed her to live, after having had the others massacred, she
feared that she would find herself in fresh difficulties. If she killed
her during the massacre she was preparing, on the pretext of the   10
quarrel between the factions headed by Guise and by Châtillon [i.e.
Coligny], she could not find an adequate excuse to lay the blame
on the former, who had no dealings with the Queen of Navarre.
Moreover, she despaired of bringing the Prince of Navarre, her
son-in-law, under her control while his mother lived; the latter,
being an intelligent woman, might find out about the ambush and
ruin everything. However, she made use of master René, her hired
poisoner, who. . . in selling his potions and perfumed collars to the
Queen of Navarre, found a way to poison her. And as a result, on
Wednesday, the fourth day of June, she fell ill in bed with a   20
persistent fever. . . of which she died five days afterwards, to the
great regret of those of the [Protestant] religion, and the joy of the
secret council. The illness was lodged in the brain, which was
affected by the poison, but which was not inspected [at the
autopsy]; the queen mother certainly had a hand in this, though
making a show of grief for the affliction suffered by her friend. . . .

(I. 298–9)

274

[Goulart's account of the wedding of Henry of Navarre and Marguerite de Valois is much more detailed than Hotman's, and includes descriptions of the masques presented at court and the text of the letter written by Admiral Coligny to his wife describing the occasion. Goulart goes on to report the secret meetings at which it is claimed that the death of the Admiral and the subsequent massacre were planned.]

The king's council, or secret council [consisting of the king, his mother, Anjou, Birague, and de Retz], put about the idea that the king would never see his realm at peace, unless the perpetrators of the troubles were exterminated. Now, they said, there were three leagues in the kingdom, i.e, the Montmorencies, the Châtillons, and the Lorraines or Guises, who for the sake of their private quarrels had so shuffled the cards that there would never be peace in the kingdom while these factions lasted. To achieve this end, it would be necessary to begin with the Admiral, who was the head of the Châtillons. . . and the occasion being so opportune, it would be necessary to consider what would benefit the kingdom, namely, the extermination of the Huguenots, who would be completely demoralized by the death of their leader. . . . To this end they resolved. . . to procure someone to kill the Admiral with a shot from a harquebus [hand-gun], immediately after the wedding. Other benefits for the king would ensue from this coup, in particular that the Huguenots, who were present in sufficiently large numbers in Paris, could not endure such an outrage without rebelling in some way, and this would give the king, who had forces a hundred times larger than theirs in the city, a very good pretext to wipe them out. . . . As for the princes who were with the Admiral [i.e. Navarre and Condé], when their support was removed, it would be easy to make them mend their ways by giving them servants sympathetic to the king and the queen mother who would spy on their actions and make sure they stayed loyal.

But the queen mother's council [Catherine, Birague, de Retz] went much further. For she and the Comte de Retz had long foreseen and more or less decided, that to consolidate their authority and manipulate the whole kingdom as they pleased and without check, there must first be not a single nobleman in France who was not the queen's creature. . . . She also greatly feared the king's disposition, which she had nurtured in dissimulation, and thought that if he lent an ear to the Admiral for long, he would realize that her secret council sought the ruin of the kingdom and in consequence might outwit his mother, in seeking the means to restore everything. . . . In short, she resolved that her government could not exist or survive while these great ones [i.e. the houses of

Montmorency, Châtillon, and Guise] were so powerful. First then, she, the Comte de Retz, and Birague conclude that the Admiral should head the list, but in such a way that the others do not escape. This is the plan which they consider the most appropriate in the world: someone must be hired who will kill the Admiral with a shot from a harquebus, the harquebusier placed in a house belonging to one of the servants of the house of Guise, and the deed must be done in broad daylight. As soon as the Admiral is dead, the Huguenots, knowing the house, will not fail to turn upon the Guisians, nor the Parisians to attack the Huguenots. . . so that each faction will wipe out the other. The king meanwhile will lock himself up at the Louvre, and have a troop ready to attack the victorious party promptly, in order to dispatch the principals without delay. That done, no one will remain unprepared to condemn those who had been killed, pity the king, and praise the queen mother and the officers who will have held themselves in readiness to protect the royal majesty. 70

80

The third council, or that of de Guise [Anjou, Catherine, Birague, de Retz, and others] included a decision in their resolutions not to allow the Admiral or the principal members of his suite to escape. The plan to kill him was also approved. The Duc de Guise sometimes used to say that the justice he was demanding of the king against the Admiral was to fight him in single combat. But that for many reasons would never have been allowed, above all because of the uncertainty of the outcome. However, the Guisians, foreseeing clearly what the queen intended, assembled sufficient forces in Paris to ensure that the Huguenots could have damaged them only with difficulty and the king himself with his forces could not have harmed them. 90

There was not long to wait before this plan was put into execution. Maurevert, the hired assassin of the king, of the queen, and of the Guisians, and in the pay of the city of Paris, was summoned to be present in Paris at the time of the wedding. . . .

(I. 357–61)

[Goulart's account of the massacre of St Bartholomew is very much fuller than Hotman's. The following passages contain details which are not found in Hotman, but which can be paralleled in Marlowe.]

Towards midnight, the queen mother was seen to enter the king's chamber. . . . The Duc de Guise. . . having arrived at the Louvre, found the council assembled, which included the king, the queen mother, the Duc d'Anjou, the Duc de Nevers, Tavannes, and the Comte de Retz. . . . This secret council lasted more than an hour, and although the appointed time was not far off, nevertheless, the 100 queen mother, impatient, and fearing that the king, thinking of the horror of so many crimes, might prevent the execution of part of the plans, urged with all her might that it should begin. . . .

(I. 387–8)

Now since the blow he [Admiral Coligny] had received on the head and the blood which covered his face prevented him from being recognized, the Duc de Guise, bending down, and wiping his face with a handkerchief, says, 'I know him; it is he'; then kicking the face of the poor corpse, that all the murderers of France had so   110 feared while he lived, goes out of the gate of the house. . . .

[The wording of *The Life of Coligny* (1576) is closer to that of the play: 'The Admiral's body, being thrown down out of a window, was trampled underfoot by the young Duke of Guise' (H2 verso). Cf. 'The Duke of Guise stamps on thy lifeless bulk!' (Scene 6, line 42).]

The mob having arrived there below, cut off the hands and the privy parts from the corpse, which, thus mutilated and bleeding, was dragged by this rabble for three days round the whole city, and finally taken to the gibbet of Montfaucon, where it was hung up by the heels. . . .

(I. 391–2)

The overseers, captains, wardmen and tithingmen of Paris went with their men from house to house where they believed they would find the Huguenots, breaking down the doors, and then massacring cruelly, without regard to sex or age, those whom they met, being   120 induced and urged to these deeds by the dukes of Aumale, Guise, and Nevers [Gonzague], who went through the streets crying 'Kill, kill them all; the king commands it.'

(I. 399–400)

Peter Ramus, professor of rhetoric, a man well known among the ranks of the learned, was not forgotten. He had many enemies, among others one named Jacques Charpentier, who sent the assassins to the college of Presles, where Ramus was in hiding. But when he was discovered, he paid a large sum to save his life. Notwithstanding, he was murdered, and thrown down out of an upstairs window so that his entrails spilled out over the stones; then   130 the entrails were dragged through the streets, and the body whipped by some students urged on by their masters, to the great disgrace of the very learning which Ramus had made his profession.

(I. 411)

TEXT 3

La vie et faits notables de Henri de Valois . . .

Jean Boucher
(1589)

[The text is translated from the copy in the British Library
(shelfmark 610. c. 21).]

[In this virulent League attack on Henry III he is shown to be reluctant
to accept the Polish crown, but he does not, as in the play, insist on a let-
out clause. It is also hinted that Catherine de Medici is responsible for
the poisoning of Charles IX (an accusation framed more explicitly in
the play).]

. . . when Henry de Valois was ready to leave, recalling to mind the
sweetness of the country of France, and visualizing the country of
Poland as it had been described to him; considering also the
somewhat uncouth and boorish manner of the Poles, even of those
who came to France, although in such affairs it is the most polished
who are employed; or perhaps for some other secret reason which
he kept to himself (to succeed his brother, as likely as not), he
made up his mind to defer his journey. . . .

[Charles insists that Henry should honour his promise to the Poles.]

. . . he [Henry] gave him [Charles] a ring as a token of remembrance, which the unfortunate king did not long wear thereafter;   10
for soon afterwards he began to feel ill and could do no more than
languish until he died at the Bois de Vincennes. Some thought
that he was poisoned by a pike sauce. Others hold that the queen
mother said on taking leave of Henry, 'Go boldly, my son, you will
not be away long' – which, it must be said, he believed, for once he
was in Poland, he waited every day only to hear news of the king's
death. However that may be, King Charles was poisoned. . . .

(pp. 11–13)

[Boucher's account of Henry's coronation, like Marlowe's, emphasizes
the presence of his favourites.]

278

... when the most noble Cardinal de Guise (uncle of the one who was massacred at Blois) had anointed him and placed the crown of Charlemagne on his head, he cried quite loudly that it hurt him; and as the ceremonies of anointing and crowning were being celebrated, and as he looked at his minions here and there, making some inappropriate and petulant gestures that demonstrated his vanity, the crown twice slipped off his head and would have fallen to the ground, if an official nearby had not prevented it. ...

20

(p. 27)

[Boucher's account of Guise's death includes Henry's hypocritical assurances of good faith, as does the play.]

But his [Henry's] conspiracy was not so secret that Monsieur de Guise did not have some warning of it; . . . which caused him to say to the king the next day that he had heard that the king wished him no good. . . . Henry de Valois then answered him, 'My cousin, do you believe that I have a soul so wicked as to wish you ill? On the contrary, I assure you, there is no one in my kingdom I love more than you, or to whom I am more bound, as I shall prove by good deeds, before long.'

30

. . . Henry de Valois, traitor and perjurer, on Friday morning, 23 December [1588]. . . sent for Monsieur de Guise, giving him to understand that he had something of importance to communicate to him. Monsieur de Guise, arriving first (since he was lodged in the castle), left all the lords and ordinary gentlemen of his suite in the antechamber in order to visit the king in his cabinet in the usual manner. And when he was in the porch, between the antechamber and the cabinet, he found (contrary to custom) four of the forty-five hired henchmen of the king in the porch, whom he began to scrutinize; however, not suspecting any treason, he went forward to enter the cabinet. One of the forty-five lifted the curtain, where-upon the duke encountered three others of the forty-five opposite him, at the door of the cabinet. And then they all together fell upon him, one seizing his sword, the others stabbing him several times with a dagger . . . causing the lord of Guise to fall down im-mediately. . . . And as he fell, he cried out, 'O God, is it for my sins?' And at once the king, who was in his cabinet with Loignac, each with drawn sword, came out, and then the king kicked the Duke of Guise to see if he was completely dead, and said, 'Now I shall rule the French as I please.'. . .

40

50

This cruel executioner, enemy of the Catholic Church, thought to do likewise to the dukes of Mayenne and Aumale, in the places where they were located, and by this means to achieve the aim of his iniquitous conspiracies with the King of Navarre; but as God has prevented that detestable enterprise, he did not have the said princes put to death. . . .

(pp. 93–8)

TEXT 4

Merry Passages and Jests

Sir Nicholas L'Estrange
(*c.* 1650)

[The text is taken from the edition by H.F. Lippincott (Salzburg, 1974).]

A gentleman at a play sat by a fellow that he strongly suspected for a cutpurse, and for the probation of him, took occasion to draw out his purse, and put it up so carelessly as it dangled down (but his eye watched it strictly with a glance) and he bent his discourse another way; which his suspected neighbour observing, upon his first fair opportunity, exercised his craft, and having got his booty began to remove away, which the gentleman noting, instantly draws his knife and whips off one of his ears, and vowed he would have something for his money. The cutpurse began to swear and stamp and threaten. 'Nay go to, sirrah', says the other, 'be quiet, I'll offer you fair; give me my purse again, here's your ear, take it, and be gone.'

(No. 143, p. 52)

TEXT 5

Histoire Universelle

Jacques-Auguste de Thou
(1609)

[The text is based on the 1734 translation by A.F. Prévost d'Exiles *et al.*
of the original Latin (British Library shelfmark 210. e. 8).]

At that time Paul Stuart de Caussade, Comte de St-Mégrin, was
numbered among the king's minions. He was a handsome young
man of Saintonge, and as noble as he was gracious. The king did
not merely love him because he took part in all his debaucheries:
he had managed to please this Prince by the relationship he had
formed, as rumour had it, with a lady of the highest quality, who
had married a lord of the court [the Duc de Guise] to whom Henry
wished no good. This lord was very powerful; and the monarch
believed himself well avenged for the humiliations he had received
from him, by the revenge which St-Mégrin took in dishonoring   10
him, and by the jokes he himself made about this affair, when he
was with his favourites.

The person who naturally should have appeared the most
affected by this affront was too occupied by important projects to
bother to give the matter the slightest attention. In fact Charles de
Lorraine, Duc de Mayenne [his brother], who had a very close
relationship with him, was the individual who believed it his duty to
avenge him. With this intention he stationed some assassins to kill
St-Mégrin at the first available opportunity. It was not long before
this gentleman learned of the Duc de Mayenne's plan: the king   20
himself was informed of it, and one night when St-Mégrin wished to
leave very late, this Prince urged him in every way possible to stay
the night at the Louvre. But the monarch's entreaties, instead of
weakening the young lord's naturally high mettle, which was made
yet prouder by the king's favour, served only to provoke him
further to despise the danger and to run to his doom. He replied
with an air of scorn that if these eunuchs, which is what he called
the Lorraines, only dared to attack him, he would know how to
make them realize he was a man. With these words he left the

Louvre, and he had hardly gone a few paces, when he was assaulted 30
by the assassins who had been stationed to seize him. A page who
carried a torch before him was first ambushed. As for St-Mégrin, he
was pierced with several deadly thrusts and left for dead on the
spot. From there he was taken to his town house where he died after
some hours. His body was afterwards taken to St Paul's and buried
near Quélus and Maugiron, who had been killed three years earlier
[in a duel, in April, 1578].

(VIII. 716–18)

TEXT 6

Le martyre des deux frères . . .
(1589)

[The text is translated from the copy in the New York Public
Library (shelfmark ZZ-31893).]

. . . many warnings from many and various sources, even from those
who had been present when the resolution to commit the murder
was taken, were given to the lord of Guise, to the most reverend
lord Cardinal his brother, and to lord d'Elboeuf [his cousin]
among others, of the treachery which this traitor [Henry III] with
his accustomed hypocrisy was brewing for them; and so certain
were these warnings that a council on this disagreement was held in
the house of the said lord, to decide whether he should withdraw or
not. Four were of the opinion that he should retire, but the lord
Primate of Lyon, a man of great learning to whose counsel the Duc   10
de Guise submitted most of his inclinations, pointed out the harm
he would do; that in retiring he would acquire the reputation of a
disturber of the public peace and would disrupt the whole assembly
[the Estates General at Blois], which had only met there as it were
under his wing. . . .

This good prince, interrupting the lord Primate, said to him, 'It
has always been my resolution, rather to die a hundred times than
to incur any bad opinion or to be the cause of breaking up such an
assembly, and if I had a hundred lives, I would freely give them
to be the means of bringing some relief to the poor afflicted   20
people.'. . .

(p. 23)

[For an account of Guise's death which is closer to Marlowe than that in
Le Martyre, see Text 3. *Le Martyre*, however, does have a scene in which
Henry confronts his mother after the duke's death, as there is in the
play (Scene 22).]

After this cowardly execution, an act truly worthy of this barbarous
madman, he goes to find the queen his mother, telling her that he
was king now, and that he had killed her companion. She (according to report), found this news scarcely agreeable, but after having

284

berated him a thousand times and prophesied all the disasters
which were ready to fall on his head for this murder, she asked if he
had ordered his affairs well, all the more so since Monsieur de
Guise had many friends; and when this fool, bereft of all sense, said
yes, she became so ill that she took to her bed, from which she has   30
not risen since. . . .

(pp. 35–6)

[*Le Martyre* goes on to tell how the murderers of the Duke of Guise
refuse to kill his brother, the Cardinal, out of reverence for his office.]

And therefore this monster, leaving his cabinet, that suburb of hell,
between nine and ten o'clock, commanded his cruel henchmen to
go and kill the prince (prince of the blood as the saying is),
cardinal, archbishop, and priest, holy and sacred. This command
appeared so outrageous, so alien, even to these executioners,
cutthroats who were already bloody and stained with the blood of
milord the Duc de Guise, that, deterred by either the reverence they
bore towards the purple robe of Jesus Christ, or the terror of such
an unheard-of act, or the remorse which tormented their con-   40
science for such an execrable deed committed earlier, they flatly
refused to obey that command, so that this Nero was forced to
employ other soldiers of the guard. . . .

(pp. 38–9)

. . . and then these accursed murderers, godless and without soul,
more cruel than tigers or enraged lions, and less feeling than the
hardest rocks, with rough words mockingly told him, 'Cardinal, you
must die,' and seized him, putting a cord round his neck; and
dragging him out, led him to the place of that dire massacre. With
great reluctance they allowed this prince to say a single prayer as he
knelt against a wall, and that finished, he covered his face with his   50
hands, commending his soul to God. These murdering scoundrels
at that moment drawing tight the cord which they had already
placed round his neck, stabbed his sacred body several times with
dagger and halberd, and so massacred him and put him to death.

(p. 40)

TEXT 7

Les cruautés sanguinaires . . .
(1589)

[The text is translated from the copy in the New York Public Library (shelfmark ZZ-31893).]

[This League pamphlet contains the only extant account of the incident, dramatized by Marlowe in Scene 22, in which the Duke of Guise's son is brought to view his father's body. In the pamphlet, Henry, having imprisoned other members of Guise's party, proposes to kill his son, but is persuaded otherwise; in the play, the son is sent to prison.]

That done, the young Prince de Joinville was brought, and in the same way the king showed him the dead body of the lord of Guise stretched out on the ground, a sight which so afflicted the heart of the young prince that he would have swooned over the body of his father, if the king had not held him. And at once the young prince, not being able to kiss his father to bid him a last farewell, began to pour out an endless flow of abuse against his father's murderers, which caused the king to command him to be put to death. And this would have been done, had not Charles Monsieur [Charles d'Angoulême, natural son of Charles IX], who was present, and who naturally loved the said Prince de Joinville, thrown himself on his knees before the king, begging him to allow him to guard the prince on condition of producing him when he should be required to do so. . . .

(p. 8)

TEXT 8

The True History of the Civil Wars of France . . .

Antony Colynet
(1591)

[The text is taken from the British Library copy
(shelfmark 286. d. 37).]

BOOK VI

[Colynet's account of the death of Henry III begins with a report of a council at which the Duc de Mayenne (Dumaine in the play) is present.]

Now therefore they must search out some way to bring such a bold and dangerous enterprise to possibility. He that shall happily undertake that feat ought to be willing, bold, sturdy, and quick-handed, and a man so qualified that without any suspicion may have a speedy and sure access to the king's person. Many offered themselves to be the executioners of that villainous act. But it was considered that they could not pass through so many guards and doors without suspicion, which if they should be taken, by torments they would be made confess the matter, and that would be a caveat to him to look more diligently to himself, which would bring the   10
matter to impossibility.

Many are solicited thereunto by great and fair promises, and lacked no good will, but only courage. But advising themselves of the king's more than superstitious heart, [they] concluded to make choice of some saucy desperate wretch, who, covered with the cloak of hypocrisy, might pierce through all the guards of the king's house without any suspicion or examination.

To spy out such a one as would undertake to achieve such a desperate parricide, was committed specially to one Pichnard, an incestuous and most villainous person. This Pichnard, therefore, to   20
give some good grace to this tragedy, brought in a friar to play the devil's part, and such a one as might at all times assure himself of free access. And forasmuch as among all other sects of idolatrous

friars, the Dominicans were most welcome to the king, he made his choice of one of that order for the determined execution, as shall hereafter be declared.

(pp. 400–1)

[There follows a vituperative attack on the Franciscan and Dominican orders of friars.]

Whereupon, he [Pichnard] solicited one James Clément, another St Dominic in all respects, in ignorance exceeding, so that he knew no more than his Portiforia [breviaries], such a one as for his lewdness, and for being taken often times in stews and whorehouses, had been by the order of their discipline diversely punished. . . .

Friar James is called in. There were the Dukes de Mayenne, Aumale, Nemours . . . . and to fill the mess there was Pagarola, Friar Sixtus his chaplain. . . . They had (poor silly friar) James Clément under *benedicite*; there they showed to this accursed parricide what a good deed he might do to deliver Holy Church from the tyranny of Henry the third, who was become an heretic, and that with one blow he might procure peace to the whole realm, and a blessed quietness to the holy church. . . .

(pp. 402–3)

Friar Clément desireth to know how he may do it surely and safely. The Leaguers therefore enter into deliberation about three things, to wit, the access to the king's person, the stroke, and secrecy. As for the first point to convey him to the king's person, they considered his coat, which for the reverence and love which the king did bear to it, would prepare him the way.

Secondly, whereas the rebels in seizing upon Paris after the death of the Duke of Guise, had taken the Senate prisoner, and did as yet hold a great many prisoners, and among other the first President of the Senate named the President Harlay. They had also in like sort many of the chiefest citizens for bearing goodwill to the king, or because they were rich, . . . whom they detained in like manner prisoners. The said Lord President and some of the said citizens procured to write letters unto the king, which should be delivered to Friar James Clément. They taught him also a lesson containing matters of importance, with commandment that they should not be disclosed unto any man but unto the king only, and that in secret.

As for the stroke, it must needs be deadly too, or else it would but increase their misery, and such a blow could not be given but by a secret weapon that might be hidden easily about him; for otherwise if it could be perceived, it would make the king more wary hereafter and careful of himself. But what could be more fit than a knife, which might be easily conveyed in the friar's sleeve, and whose noise might not detect the treachery. But yet there was another mischance to be prevented; for the wound of a knife might light upon such a place as could not be deadly, they find the means to work surely, that if he cannot kill him out of hand, yet that at length it may be his death. . . .

Now the friar hath on his hypocritical coat, his letters in his hand, his lesson in his head, his poisoned knife in his sleeve, order is taken that no intelligences may be given, the way is made plain before this devilish murderer, even as far as to the king's gate; the doors are made open to him by these means, the execution is to be performed speedily, lest delay should disappoint his enterprise. This murderer. . . the 21 of July, which by the new heaven of the Pope's making is the first of August, out of Paris taking his way to St Cloud, which is a town upon Seine beneath Paris two small leagues, and coming to the camp, he told them whom he met first, that he had letters from the first President and certain other Parisians well affected to the king, which contained matters of great importance, and beside that, he had great and weighty things to disclose to the king.

The king being scarce ready, and advertised of this accursed friar's coming, commanded that he should attend, and that speedily he should be admitted to his speech; the friar did attend with his letter in his hand, which he said was from the first President detained prisoner. . . .

The friar came before the king with a bold countenance. The king looking merrily upon him, said these words, '*Amice, ad quid venisti?*' ['Friend, for what reason have you come?']

The friar making a low and humble reverence, even to the ground, gave the king the letter, which he said came from the first President of Paris; which letters when the king had read, asked the friar what news he brought from Paris. The friar answered that he had matters of great importance to declare unto him. Whereupon the king commanded two gentlemen, who waited and served him at his uprising, to go forth out of the chamber, and sat down in a chair, to hear what the friar would say.

The friar drew nigh to the king, and falling upon his knees, began to tell a tale; the king stooping somewhat low, to hear what the friar was about to say, gave more attendance to his words than to his fingers. The friar drawing softly his knife out of his sleeve, stabbed the king therewith in the lower part of the belly, and made haste to get away.

The king, amazed at the sudden and unexpected stroke, cried out, and laying hand upon a dagger that lay near him, struck the friar, who, partly for the blow, and partly for fear, fell presently down. Upon this noise, the lords came running into the king's chamber, and after many wounds slew that cursed friar.

Some do report that the king commanded that he should not be slain, but taken up and examined, which declared who set him on, and the authors' names of so vile treachery. The wound was presently dressed, and, as the report went, seven stitches made in it. At length the wound being dressed, he was laid on his bed, and slept a little upon his pain and grief. 110

After his sleep he made his prayers unto God, and with a loud voice made a confession of his faith, and of the feeling which he had of his redemption.

The king, having made an end of his prayers, sendeth for his brother, the King of Navarre, and for the chiefest lords of his court, governors, and captains, but specially for the heads of the strangers, to the intent that if it were God's will that he should die, they might know his last will. 120

First, speaking to the King of Navarre, commended unto him the charge of his realm, the government of his subjects, the laws of France. . . .

The second day toward the evening, there appeared in the king accidents, prognosticating an assured danger, not so much through the nature of the wound, as through the poisoned contagiousness of the weapon wherewith the wound was made; so that all remedies being used by the physicians and surgeons to prevent the danger, and nothing prevailing, the king called again to him the King of Navarre, and other princes and lords, before whom he greatly bewailed the accursed civil wars which had been the undoing of his house, his nobility and realm, and the breeders of so many treacheries and treasons, whereof he feeleth the smart, imputing the causes thereof unto himself, in that he had always preferred the bad and violent counsel of his secret enemies before the good, wise, and moderate admonitions and warnings of the princes of his blood, and many other princes, strangers, and faithful friends: [and] willeth him [Navarre] to make a just revenge, for example sake, upon the authors of such a vile act. 130 140

The King of Navarre, with the rest of the princes and nobility departing very sorrowful and dismayed, the king called for his confessor, to whose ear he confessed his sins, and having craved pardon for his offences, said that he had a sensible feeling that they were forgiven him through Christ. The mediator desired to communicate of His sacred body, and that all might hear that he had received freely of God the forgiveness of sins, in like case he not only forgave the conspirators, but also the very murderer and procurers

of the murder. So the poison prevailing and scattering itself through,   150
did infect the noble parts, whereby the night following, the 22 of
July [i.e. 2 August], he yielded his soul unto God.

(pp. 404–8)

NOTES

1 *A True and Plain Report of the Furious Outrages of France* . . .
(pp. 261–73)

15   *death of the Duke of Guise*: François, Duke of Guise, was assassinated in 1563
       and Coligny was suspected of complicity in the murder.

478   *Mithridates*: King of Pontus (*c.* 131–63 BC), enemy of Rome, said to have
       caused 80,000 Italians to be put to death in Asia.

479   *Peter of Aragon*: Peter III (1239–85), King of Aragon from 1276 and of
       Sicily from 1282, responsible for the massacre of the French in Sicily
       known as the Sicilian Vespers (1282).

509   *case of Masson de Rivers*: Marlowe transfers this incident to Paris (Scene
       8); in the next scene Mountsorrell is despatched to Rouen. Hotman
       mentions further killings at Rouen, Dieppe, and Toulouse (fol. 22
       verso).

2 *Mémoires de l'état de France sous Charles neuvième* . . .
(pp. 274–7)

1   *the war*: Charles IX planned to join forces with Coligny in an expedition
       in the Netherlands in support of the rebellion against Spain, but the
       campaign ended in defeat.

3 *La vie et faits notables de Henri de Valois* . . . (pp. 278–80)

55   *places where they were*: in the case of du Mayenne, this was Lyons. The play
       has Orleans (Scene 24), probably as a result of a mishearing rather than
       a misreading.

5 *Histoire universelle* (pp. 282–3)

36   *three years earlier*: other authorities say that the interval was three months.

6 *Le martyre des deux frères* . . . (pp. 284–5)

31   *has not risen since*: Catherine de Medici died 5 January 1589, the Duke of
       Guise 23 December 1588.

8 *The True History of the Civil Wars of France* . . . (pp. 287–91)

33   *Friar Sixtus*: Pope Sixtus V (1585–90) was a Franciscan.

75   *first of August*: Pope Gregory XIII dropped ten surplus days from the calendar in 1582.

THE JEW OF MALTA

INTRODUCTION

The place of *The Jew of Malta* in the Marlovian canon is complicated by
the fact that the earliest extant edition to survive dates from as late as
1633. Yet, the appearance of an entry in the Stationers' Register for 17
May 1594 suggests that an edition was published within a short period of
that date, and the piece was undoubtedly popular when staged, being
presented at least thirty-six times between the earliest recorded performance on 26 February 1592 and 21 June 1596. However, not until 20
November 1632 does it reappear in the Stationers' Register, the ensuing
quarto being published with the addition of material relating to a
revival of the piece both at court and at the Cockpit playhouse in Drury
Lane by the prolific popular playwright Thomas Heywood. Heywood's
hand in the text of the play itself has often been suspected, but in the
main modern scholars believe that the 1633 version is substantially that
presented in Marlowe's lifetime.

It has never proved possible to pinpoint sources for *The Jew of Malta*
with the confident precision permissible in the case of virtually all
Marlowe's other plays. The genesis of Barabas the Jew of Malta, and the
antecedents of that strange amalgam of distorted facts and derivative
fiction through which he makes his grotesque progress, have never
been susceptible to firm identification or elucidation. However, although lacking historical validation, *The Jew of Malta*, along with *The
Massacre at Paris*, reflects the strongly topical dimension in Marlowe's
art. The shameful persecution of Jews resident in Western Europe,
chiefly but not exclusively encouraged by instruments of the Christian
Church (an injustice which persisted well into the playwright's lifetime), is too well documented to necessitate extensive illustration, yet
Marlowe was one of the first English writers to exploit for theatrical
purposes racial and sectarian tensions and animosities, and to savour
the ironies of religious bigotry and intolerance practised in the name
of a reputedly merciful and loving God. In his portrait of Barabas,
the strong element of suspicion and distaste manifested by many of
Marlowe's contemporaries is counterbalanced by an awareness of the

unscrupulous treatment all too commonly meted out in preceding decades to members of the Jewish faith by believers in the divinity of Christ.

A further vital strand in the drama derives from another historical factor. The rise of the Empire of the Ottoman Turks in the fourteenth century and its expansion into Eastern Europe and North Africa in the fifteenth, seemed destined to be succeeded in the sixteenth by Moslem dominance of all those countries bordering the Mediterranean. Stirring feats of Christian resistance constituted no more than brief setbacks along a path apparently leading inexorably towards a Moslem world-order. With the fall of Constantinople to Mohammed II on 29 May 1453, the Byzantine Empire was overthrown; by the time Mohammed's grandson, Selim I, died in 1520, not only had Egypt, Syria and Arabia passed into the hands of Islam, but the whole of the Greek mainland and most of the Balkan peninsula had been overrun. Moreover, with the attainment of a toehold on Italian soil, 'the Turk was astride the Adriatic'.

To aid or impede this seemingly irresistible advance, the most important of the islands in the Eastern Mediterranean – Malta, Rhodes, and Cyprus particularly – assumed great significance for the rival powers, offering as they did strategic control of several vital sea-routes. Crete or Candia, subject at this period to the Venetians, appears to have avoided attracting the unwelcome attentions of the Moslem power until the following century, but Malta, Rhodes, and Cyprus, all strongly garrisoned by Christian warriors of ancient renown and proven calibre, suffered intermittent Turkish attacks throughout the crisis. Early in the reign of Suleiman the Magnificent (1494–1566), that energetic Sultan under whom the Ottoman Empire spread its influence 'from the Atlantic to the Indian Ocean, . . . from Austria to the Persian Gulf', the Knight Hospitallers of the Order of St John of Jerusalem were forced to surrender Rhodes, their headquarters since 1309, and in 1522, despite having inflicted heavy casualties on their opponents, they evacuated the island, setting up a new base in Malta eight years later.

Here, so that they could 'perform in peace the duties of their Religion for the benefit of the Christian community and employ their forces and arms against the perfidious enemies of the Holy Faith', the Holy Roman Emperor Charles V granted them a home, coupling with his gift Gozo and the North African port of Tripoli. On the island the Knights prepared new fortifications, but the Turks were not prepared to allow this strategic asset to remain in alien hands indefinitely. After first failing to dislodge the Christians from their stronghold in 1551, they resumed the assault fourteen years later in one of the century's most celebrated sieges. From May to September 1565 Suleiman's army, outnumbering the defenders by at least four to one, made strenuous efforts to overcome the garrison, but after both sides had sustained heavy losses, the Knights, under their Grand Master La Valette, had the satisfaction of compelling the foe to withdraw, so stemming the remorseless onward surge of the infidel. Five years later the Turks fell on Cyprus, and so provoked the celebrated Battle of Lepanto of 1571 which in large measure terminated Turkish marine supremacy in the Eastern Mediterranean. Yet, as if to prove that they were far from a spent force, in 1573 the Ottoman power enjoyed the consolation of seeing the Venetians pressurized into yielding up the island, and in this way obtained a large measure of control over naval access to the Levant.

While it is obvious that *The Jew of Malta* makes no pretence to historical veracity, it is against this background of Great Power rivalry for the Mediterranean and of recent Jewish repression and dispossession within Christian Europe that Marlowe's account of the rise and fall of Barabas must be viewed. Just as Shakespeare in *Othello* was to set his tragedy of love and military ambition against a background of recent East–West tension, so did Marlowe conceive of a pertinent milieu for his central characters. Necessarily the dramatist adapted the facts to fit his fiction: in neither 1551 nor 1565 did Malta succumb to Turkish arms; at no time did its inhabitants pay tribute-money to the Turks or boast a governor called Ferneze, the name in fact deriving from that of a Governor of Tripoli. Moreover, it is beyond doubt that Barabas himself is not directly taken from any actual historical figure. Yet from among the personalities and episodes associated with the struggle for mastery of the Mediterranean seaways, and with the battle for recognition and respite from hostility among Jewish communities within Europe, Marlowe assimilated impressions which went to create *The Jew of Malta*. At the time in question, national and religious antagonisms dominated the European political scene; corruption and extortion, double-dealing, treachery and espionage were inescapable facts of existence; the ruthless conduct and characters of men capable of inspiring the dramatic constructs which are Ferneze and Barabas were common knowledge. Here was richly suggestive material for any aspiring playwright possessed of Marlowe's lively powers of imagination and invention.

The earliest attempts to supply a real-life prototype for the figure of Barabas (Kellner 1887) focused on the slightly suspect career of one Joseph Mendez-Nassi or João Micques (died 1579), a rich and influential Portuguese Jew of Marrano stock, none of whose activities ever bore directly on the fate of Malta. The epithet 'Marranos' or 'the Damned' was applied to those continental Jews forced or prepared to embrace the outward forms of Christian belief, but who still maintained in secret the observation of Judaic rites and practices, such customs rendering them liable to periodic spells of penalization, repression, and, too often, extermination. From such a stock sprang Micques, who, after quitting Portugal, spent some years in a number of prominent

European commercial centres including Antwerp, and Venice where he found the yoke of the Republic bore heavily on his shoulders, while outward conformity to the demands of Roman Catholicism proved equally repugnant.

In 1547 Micques led an exodus consisting of some 500 Jews from Venice to the Turkish capital of Constantinople, where he established himself and his family at the head of a powerful and flourishing community. Here a much more sympathetic and tolerant attitude towards Judaism prevailed, and sweetened relationships between Micques, now Nassi, and the Turkish rulers, so much so that the Jewish grandee rose to a position of considerable power and influence with the Sultanate. Appointed adviser to Selim, son of Sultan Suleiman II, and made a member of the Crown Council, he negotiated with foreign diplomats and dignitaries; on Selim's accession in 1566, Nassi was created Duke of Naxos, an island in the Cyclades which the Turks had recently captured from the Venetians. In this respect at least his career parallels one of the roles adopted by his dramatic counterpart: here is a rich Jewish financier placed in command of a Mediterranean island captured from Christians by Turks.

Nassi's star was now at its zenith: he undertook financial and diplomatic transactions on behalf of the Ottoman Empire, and his own commercial enterprise was legendary. Only with Selim's death in 1574 did his influence decline, and in 1579 in honourable if enforced retirement Nassi died. Perhaps his greatest triumph came in 1570 when he allegedly persuaded Selim II to undertake the removal of Cyprus from the grip of the Venetians, and it is this aspect of his activities, most briefly presented in two extracts from François de Belleforest's expanded version of Sebastian Münster's *Cosmographia*, known as *La Cosmographie Universelle de Tout le Monde* (Text 1 p. 306), which made the greatest impact on Western chroniclers. Belleforest, in common with the longer accounts to be discovered in Lonicerus's *Chronicorum Turcicorum*, and Pietro Bizari's history of the armed struggle for Cyprus (which Belleforest himself translated into French in 1573) maintains the standard West European, hostile and anti-Semitic view of him, emphasizing the popular belief that it was at Nassi's instigation that the sluggish Selim set out to deprive Venice of its sway in Cyprus. However, apart from his vast wealth, his race and contemporary reputation for unscrupulous dealings, the historical Nassi was in all other respects as unlike Marlowe's protagonist as it is possible to imagine.

It is scarcely surprising that diligent researches culminated in the 1920s with the advocacy of an ostensibly more promising candidate for the role of a 'real-life Barabas'. In David Passi, double-agent, master-manipulator, and wily intriguer whose devious machinations eventually backfired on himself, C.F. Tucker Brooke (1922) claimed to have

298

discovered the true prototype of Marlowe's protagonist; the case can never be strong, given the lack of information concerning Passi's overall history. However, this Jewish resident of Constantinople emerges from the many official papers transmitted between 1585 and 1591 by Venetian diplomatic representatives in the Porte to their masters in the Serenissima (Text 2, p. 309) as an intriguing instance of a prominent double- or treble-agent, of whose activities Marlowe could have known, if only from gossip and rumour. If an actual original for Marlowe's animated creation needs to be identified, then David Passi's career-pattern – cunning self-advancement, over-ambitiousness, ignominious downfall – accords very well with the curve described by his stage counterpart. But as with Nassi, while the Jew's connections with the Ottoman Empire are firmly attested, the links with Malta appear to be non-existent. Though his activities provide an intriguing parallel to those of Barabas, there is no firm evidence to suggest that the career of David Passi played an indisputable part in inspiring Marlowe's drama.

Nor should this be a matter for surprise. *The Jew of Malta* makes no pretence to be history, even history in the popularized form it was apt to assume on the Elizabethan stage. In establishing Barabas's ancestry, theatrical traditions may be every bit as important as potential proto-types from the murkier corners of sixteenth-century politics. Several 'stage-Jews' call for comment. In the so-called *Croxton Play of the Sacrament* (*c.* 1465), Jonathas, the Semite at the centre of an action which dramatizes the traditional *canard* in which a group of Jews desecrate the Holy Sacrament, delivers an opening soliloquy which Arthur Freeman (1962) claims is more than casually related to Barabas's introductory speech in *The Jew* (Text 3, p. 313). In the same way, a connection has been perceived between the remarks which open Marlowe's first scene and those with which Avarice introduces himself at the start of the Tudor political morality *Respublica* (*c.* 1553), usually attributed to Nicholas Udall (Text 4, p. 315). Udall's personification is never identified as being Jewish, and his affinities are primarily with the morality Vice of convention, but Avarice's spirited self-projection certainly anticipates the manic *faux bonhomie* of his Marlovian successor, and his address to his money-bags later in the action, should it have come to the Elizabethan playwright's notice, may possibly have suggested Barabas's frenzied greeting to his gold in Act II Scene 1 of *The Jew.* At the dénouement of *Respublica* when his bluff is called and he is exposed, Avarice is char-acteristically evasive, and his fate – to be pressed like a sponge – is the harshest punishment meted out to those who have wronged the state. In both particulars this may be felt to have foreshadowed more than coincidentally the ultimate downfall of Barabas.

But greater interest attaches to two later plays, one a late morality entitled *The Three Ladies of London* (*c.* 1584) by Robert Wilson, the other a less didactic work which, although English in origin, exists only in a garbled German translation. *The Three Ladies* is of relevance primarily for the unexpectedly generous manner in which its noble-hearted Jew deals with a Christian debtor in the context of the kind of scenario in which Barabas attempts to star at the opening of Marlowe's play. The unprincipled merchant with his broken English is effectively contrasted with the Turkish Jew Gerontus, who belies his Western racial stereotype in all he says and does, and ends by being outwitted by the devious capitalist Mercadore (see Dessen 1974). But the Judge's observation that conventional moral expectations have been overturned – 'Jews seek to excel in Christianity and Christians in Jewishness' – comes curiously close to similar reversals of received prejudice to be discovered in *The Jew of Malta* (Text 5, p. 317).

While it is entirely possible that *Der Jud von Venedig*, a German version of an English comedy featuring a mercenary Jew, derives from Marlowe's play rather than influencing its creation, it is at least worth considering as the possible *fons et origo* of both *The Jew of Malta* and *The Merchant of Venice*. In *The School of Abuse* published in 1579 Stephen Gosson alludes to a stageplay entitled *The Jew* in which 'the greediness of worldly choosers, and bloody minds of usurers' evidently featured, and a manuscript text preserved in Vienna (Codex 13791) (reprinted in Meissner, 1884) suggests that this piece or something like it formed part of the repertoire of those English theatre companies who toured Germany between the closing years of the sixteenth century and the late 1600s. Certainly a play variously titled but with 'the Jew of Venice' as its chief element can be traced to Passau (1607), Graz (1608), Halle (1611), Dresden (1626), Prague (1651), and in 1674 to Dresden once more. How many of these performances were based on the playtext which survives in Vienna is unclear, but the Vienna manuscript of *Das Wohlgesprochene Uhrteil* or *Der Jud von Venedig* is our only route, however tenuous, to a potential precursor of Marlowe's piece. Significant elements include the oppression of the Jews by their superiors, the suggestion that the Jews should be fleeced of their wealth under threat of expulsion, and the resistance of the Jew Barabas. The donning of disguise to which the protagonist resorts in *The Jew* appears in Act 1 Scene 4 of the German piece, when Barabas arranges to follow the Prince to Venice; the vengeance wreaked by Marlowe's protagonist on Ferneze's son Lodowick has its counterpart in the determination with which Barabas in *Der Jud von Venedig* proposes to get even with the young Prince. While most scholars would be wary of asserting the primacy of the original of *Der Jud* over Marlowe's tragedy, brief translated extracts have been included in the selection which appears here (Text 6, p. 324), to give readers an opportunity for exercising personal judgement in the matter.

For some of the background and 'local colour' which informs his portrait of Malta under siege, Marlowe may well have been indebted to a contemporary account of a visit paid to the island in the course of a journey to Constantinople, undertaken in 1551 by the Lord of Aramont, French Ambassador to the Porte. Among those lords and knights accompanying him was the young French nobleman Nicolas de Nicolay, geographer to King Charles IX; in 1568 Nicolay published at Lyon a narrative of his journey in four books, which appeared in Thomas Washington's translation of 1585 as *The Navigations, Peregrinations and Voyages, Made Into Turkey*. . . . Passages in *Tamburlaine* suggest that Marlowe knew this work, and while composing *The Jew* he might well have recalled from Nicolay (Text 7, p. 329) the exotic delights of Malta (which included a plethora of courtesans), the abortive Turkish assault on the island in 1551, and the subsequent siege of Tripoli at which Nicolay was present (an event which involved a stratagem to infiltrate the citadel by effecting an undergound entry, a device to which Barabas has recourse in Act V Scene 1). However, some commentators regard the notion of underground entrance as a commonplace, and point to other instances, most notably an account given by Jean de Serres in his *Fourth Part of Commentaries of the Civil Wars in France*, which relates to the successful capture of Villeneuve-de-Berg by the employment of tactics similar to those of Barabas (Text 8, p. 333). In the course of reading for *The Massacre at Paris* Marlowe might have come across the account and utilized it in *The Jew of Malta*, though it would be rash to assume that de Serres was citing this as a unique instance of such a manoeuvre.

Historical material deployed in similar fashion may lie behind Barabas's stratagem towards the end of the play to lure the army of the victorious Turks into a monastery outside the town, and then blow them all up. In John Foxe's *Acts and Monuments* (1583), N.W. Bawcutt (1968) discovered a passage describing an incident associated with the besieging of a town in Hungary by Turkish forces, which may possibly have provided Marlowe with a brief account of the dramatic situation he required:

At the first beginning of the siege, there stood a little without [outside] the munitions [defences] in the front of the city, a certain church or monastery, which the citizens, pretending to maintain and keep against the Turks, had privily conveyed light matter easily to take flame, with powder, in secret places thereof, and had hid also fire withal. Which done, they (as against their wills being driven back) withdrew themselves within the munitions, waiting the occasion when this fire would take. Thus the Turks having the possession of the church, suddenly the fire coming to the powder, raised up the church, and made a great scatter and slaughter among the barbarous Turks.

(I. 754)

In the same way the researches of Paul H. Kocher (1963) have thrown up another event of contemporary if more parochial interest, which in theory could well lie at the back of one of Barabas's more sensational acts of villainy. In late 1529 or early 1530 in the Kentish city of Rochester, a Richard Rose or Rouse committed a sensational crime whereby, in the words of Sir Francis Bacon, speaking in 1615,

poison was put into a little vessel of barm [yeast] that stood in the kitchen of the Bishop of Rochester's house; of which barm porridge or gruel was made, wherewith seventeen of the Bishop's family were poisoned. Nay, divers of the poor that came to the Bishop's gate, and had the poison in alms, were likewise poisoned.

So horrified was the nation, shortly to be engulfed in the controversies of the incipient Reformation – the Bishop of Rochester in question was St John Fisher – that the offence of wilful poisoning of which Rose was accused was made high treason, and the appropriate punishment adjudged to be boiling to death. Rose was tried and sentenced by Parliament itself, and the statute and the penalty remained in force until 1547 when they were mitigated as being too severe. Evidently the case became so notorious that Marlowe may well have heard it spoken of during his years in Canterbury, some twenty-six miles from Rochester, or in some other part of Kent. The conjunction of poisoned porridge and boiling to death in *The Jew of Malta*, and a flagrant crime executed in Marlowe's home county, seems at least significant.

Of similar relevance may be the alleged machinations of that Richard Baines or Baynes whose role in Marlowe's downfall in 1593 still remains shadowy, but whose ostensibly damning testimony submitted to the Privy Council contributed to the case which stood against the play-wright at the time of his death, re-examined by Nicholl (1992). Baines first appears as a government spy planted in the important English Roman Catholic seminary at Rheims, formerly at Douai, where many English Catholics trained for the priesthood and as propagandists for the faith, and with which Marlowe himself had links in the 1580s. Here Baines's subterfuge was exposed by a confidant to whom he had revealed not only his attempt to ensnare the Rector William Allen, but also admitted that he thought it feasible to remove all the inmates of the seminary by introducing poison into the well or the bath which provided the establishment at Rheims with its supply of water (Boas 1949). Perhaps knowledge of this detail inspired Marlowe to include it in Barabas's confession to Ithamore: 'Sometimes I go about and poison wells' (II. 3. 178), though such an accusation was frequently levelled at the Jewish people down the centuries as part of the Christian campaign to vilify their race. In this context it is worth recording (Purcell 1966) that Whetstone's *English Mirror,* possibly employed for *Tamburlaine,* contains much vilification of Jews, atheists, Machiavels, and their associates, and may have contributed to Marlowe's portrait of Barabas:

> you monsters of humanity, that are drunken with the strength of your own wits and are bewitched with the success of your own policies, esteem it for sound counsel that I give you to understand that the eternal God, whom you neither fear, love, nor do acknowledge, seeth all your wicked policies in his vengeance and frustrateth them with his mercy; he searcheth the reins [seat of the affections] and hearts, and will give to every man according to his works. If you dig a pit to bury the innocent, look to fall into it yourselves; if you raise a gallows to hang them, be you sure that you shall suffer thereupon; if you edge your sword to pierce their hearts, trust to it, your own entrails will be the sheath thereof. What you do, or would do, unto them, shall be done unto you. . . .
>
> (Book III, Chapter 8, pp. 241–2)

By contrast, the dramatist also makes use of anti-Catholic propaganda in the course of *The Jew of Malta,* not least in his portrayal of the 'two religious caterpillars', the friars Jacomo and Barnadine who are instrumental in gaining Abigail admission to the nunnery, and who ultimately vie to convert Barabas to Christianity. The satirical portrayal of these worldly priests is of long standing, but the culminating stroke in Barabas's scheme by which Jacomo is persuaded that he has murdered the already strangled Barnadine during Act IV Scene 1 derives from a popular tale of widely-attested provenance, which may well have been familiar to the playwright from his earliest years. The device by which a relative innocent is led to believe that he has 'killed' a corpse is traditional; some of the most frequently cited analogues include 'The Tale of the Hunchback' from the *Arabian Nights*; a story (that of the Emperor Plebeius) from the medieval collection of fictitious Latin narratives known as the *Gesta Romanorum*; as well as a number of *fabliaux.* However, the closest parallels to Marlowe's version, in that they feature two clerics, are represented by 'A Merry Jest of Dan Hugh Monk of Leicester', a poem preserved in the Bodleian Library, which tells of a sequence of farcical happenings arising from the murder of a lecherous young friar; the same plot is utilized in the first narrative of a collection of fifty stories composed in a vein strongly hostile to 'false ministers of religion' by the Italian author Masuccio di Salerno, and published in Naples as *Il Novellino* in 1476. The anti-clerical strain is more pronounced in the sophisticated Italian *novella* than it is in the homely coarseness of the English, but there is no need to identify the contempt for religious hypocrisy which appears in Marlowe as directly resulting from Masuccio's influence.

Interest also attaches to this narrative as a result of its appearance in 1624 in works by Thomas Heywood, both as the sub-plot for his play *The Captives; or, The Lost Recovered*, and in his compilation, Τυναικέιον or, Nine Bookes of Various History Concerning Women, where it is entitled 'The Faire Ladie of Norwich'. Said to be based on an incident involving two Norwich friars in the reign of Henry V, Heywood's version almost certainly derives from Masuccio, according to A.C. Judson in his edition of 1921. However, the possibility that Heywood played some part in revising *The Jew of Malta* for performance and publication in 1633 has raised the suggestion that the incident was imported into *The Jew* by Heywood rather than by Marlowe, and formed no part of the original text. There has always been some dissatisfaction with the text as it stands, but, as we have already said, on the whole scholars take the view that the 1633 version of the play is still substantially Marlowe's, and furthermore that it is unlikely that Heywood as a professional man of letters would have made such repetitious use of a single plot situation on three separate occasions.

Attention must finally focus on the part played by the Italian political commentator and thinker Machiavelli in the genesis of Marlowe's play, and particularly in the creation of the portrait of the man popularly identified as the arch-enemy of Elizabethan society which appears at the opening of *The Jew of Malta*, serving as prologue to the whole ensuing action. However, the degree to which Barabas's conduct may be deemed truly 'Machiavellian' has been extensively discussed, especially by critics (for example, Catherine Minshull 1982) who perceived that it is the Christian Governor Ferneze rather than the Jewish 'villain' who is most notably successful in deploying those techniques of manipulation and control commended by the Italian.

It has been sometimes claimed that the notion of permitting the stage figure of 'Machevill' to indulge in an address of blatant self-confession was inspired by a twenty-six line Latin monologue, *Machiavelli ipse loquitur*, created by Gabriel Harvey and inserted as one of the additions to his *Gratulationes Valdinenses* as part of his campaign against the Catholic Duc d'Alençon and his supporters active at the royal court during the summer of 1578. Thomas Jameson (1941) has shown that Harvey as an adherent of the Earl of Leicester's Protestant party had reason to resent the apparent success of the Englishman's rival for the royal hand, and that the satire against Machiavelli as Alençon's assumed role-model can be traced to hostility towards the foreigner who might displace Leicester in Elizabeth's esteem. By using the sentiments of popular anti-Machiavellianism Harvey articulated a warning against alien influences, and it is just possible that Marlowe knew the poem, and used it as a basis for the opening speech of *The Jew*. Common to both is the notion that while Machiavelli might be dead, his influence still remained an active force in European politics; yet it is true that the resemblance between the two passages has been challenged in recent years as being of too broad a nature. Readers may formulate their own conclusions by a comparison between Marlowe's Prologue and Harvey's original which appears in English translation below with the Latin text appended for interest's sake (Text 9, p. 335).

The larger question of the relationship between the political philosophy of the Italian as understood by the Elizabethans and Marlowe's personal opinions on matters of ethical government or public morality has been amply explored and is regrettably too complex to be extended in detail here. All one may agree is that it is perilous to wax over-dogmatic on the question of the playwright's interest in, and detailed knowledge of, Machiavelli's writings, however tempting it may be to speculate on the possibility that Marlowe was an avid student of the Machiavellian position, and the numerous contemporary reactions it inspired. Though the plays are often associated in the public mind with *Realpolitik* and the frank presentation of ruthless political and moral opportunism, it would be rash to believe that Marlowe's perception of these manifestations of the *Zeitgeist* was based on a facile adherence to the tenets of a single and perhaps imperfectly understood authority, whatever additional spurious glamour either playwright or politician may derive from the association.

TEXT 1

La cosmographie Universelle de tout le monde ... beaucoup plus augmentée, ornée, et enrichie, par François de Belleforest

(1575)

[The text is translated from the British Library copy
(shelfmark 568.h.5).]

Suleiman's successor [in 1566] was Selim, the most slothful and
least courageous of all his offspring, to whom nevertheless his
presence was most dear, being the sole survivor among the numerous sons that his predecessor begot on various women; for Bajazet
lay dead in Persia. Now Mohammed Pasha, seeing Suleiman dead
in his camp before Seghet [Szigetvar], concealed his death so that
no unrest should break out among the army and so prevent the
capture of the town which was already half-conquered. This was in
order that Selim could meanwhile seize the city of Constantinople
in his own person, and be saluted and proclaimed as monarch   10
there, an end he actually achieved, while Mohammed led the
troops back out of Hungary into Greece to forestall mutinies and to
calm those distubances which were breaking out in Asia on all sides.
For although Bajazet was dead, it was a fact that the Arabs
who live among the lonely wastes of Arabia Deserta, tent-dwellers
tending their flocks, already emancipated by the previous civil war
from subjection to the Turks, incited the neighbouring provinces
to revolt, and this provided the occasion which compelled Selim to
make a truce with Emperor Maximilian in order to keep matters
peaceful on the border with Hungary. The Arabs made themselves   20
the lords of Mecca, a town they held in honour as having been the
birthplace of their false prophet Mohammed, and the Turk had to
dispatch armed forces to that place in order to punish them and
restore them to a state of servitude. In the end they reached an
agreement – not that the Turk ever defeated the Arab, since the
latter has never offered the former tribute, but rather the Turk has

306

allowed the Arab the freedom to enjoy his beloved Mecca in peace for a long spell, fearing lest he should ally himself with the Persian or the Portuguese; the Arab, holding the fort of Aden in Arabia Felix, and several other fortresses, having the goodwill of these thieves and vagabonds, has been able to make himself supreme master of the entire Arabian coastline of the Red Sea, seeing that almost all the rest on the border with Egypt is subject to the monarch of Ethiopia.

This storm having blown over, Selim, a man addicted to his pleasures, a lecher, a drunkard (although his Law forbade the use of wine) and a true likeness of Sardanapalus, would have remained docile, if a dissolute Jew named Micques, a shrewd, crafty and villainous man, had not suggested to him how well it would pay him if he were to hurl himself on the Christians, seeing that religious disagreements stood in the way of all the mightiest Latin [western Christian] monarchs becoming reconciled and settling their differences. And he advised him to attack the Venetians and take from them the isle of Cyprus. . . . To which advice Selim lent an ear, and made such good provision that by capturing the island's two principal cities, Nicosia and Famagusta, he made himself their possessor by peaceful means, as we shall set out more fully when we reach the description of Cyprus.

(II. cols 579–80)

It is a fact that Sultan Suleiman, having become scrupulous during his declining years, never wished to confront the Venetians, with whom he had sworn a truce, however much the Corsair pirates, Barbarossa and Dragut, might set about the task of stirring up his feelings against the Venetian Signoria. But his son Selim was not so zealous to keep faith that he felt himself obliged to be bound by promises made by his father. For having succeeded to the crown, and after having calmed the disturbances in Arabia and other neighbouring provinces which had rebelled following the death of Suleiman, it was needful that in keeping with the ancient custom of the Ottoman family, he should on his advancement to the throne wage war on one of the Christian powers. He had himself made peace with Maximilian Emperor of the West, and if he were to take up arms against the Spaniard, the length and the difficulties of the voyage would be formidable. Thus he saw no better means [of accomplishing his aim] than to attack the Venetians.

Towards this end he was impelled by a wicked Marrano [overt convert to Christianity] called Jean Micques, a Jew and a Spaniard, or else a descendant of the Jews whom Ferdinand formerly [in 1492] harried from Spain, an astute and cunning man, and one

who had departed from no Christian province where he had not   70
been arrested; for he had lived for a long time at Lyon as a
merchant trading in France, then in Marseilles; from thence he
removed to Rome, visited Sicily, and betook himself to Venice
where he was strongly urged to convert to Christianity. But since he
was crafty and villainous, stung to feelings of hatred against the
Signoria, he departed at the moment when it was least expected,
and retained these charitable thoughts in his heart until that time
when, retiring among the Turks in Constantinople, he obtained
the friendship of Selim.

The Sultan's father being dead, Micques fomented his ill-will
towards the Venetian Signoria. This born-again wretch set before   80
the circumcised Turk how important for him the isle of Cyprus was,
and how greatly it dishonoured his name that the Venetians should
retain such a handsome possession right in the heart of his empire.
This incited the tyrant to demand it back, and to declare war on the
citizens of St Mark if they refused to abandon the island.

(II. col. 785)

TEXT 2

Calendar of State Papers
(Venetian)
(1585–91)

[The extracts below are taken from Volume VIII, which covers
the years 1581–91.]

Lorenzo Bernardo, Venetian Ambassador in Constantinople, to the
Doge and Senate, Vigne di Pera, 30 October 1585:

The French agent who came to call on me said that in an audience
with the Magnificent Pasha [the Grand Vizir] a long report on the
political situation, the work of David Passi, had been read to him. . . .

(p. 123)

Lorenzo Bernardo, Venetian Ambassador in Constantinople, to the
Doge and Senate, Vigne di Pera, 25 November 1585:

Last week two Englishmen arrived here from Ragusa [Dubrovnik],
and, after stopping here a few days, set out on their return journey
by way of Poland. There was some suspicion that they came here on   10
a secret mission, especially as one of them is very clever, and has a
wide knowledge of the world. I could not find out their object,
although I asked them to dinner on purpose. But now another
Englishman has reached this [place] by way of Poland. He is lodged
with the English Ambassador, who for many days has been very
busy, and in constant conferences with David Passi. . . .

(pp.125–6)

Lorenzo Bernardo, Venetian Ambassador in Constantinople, to the
Doge and Senate, Vigne di Pera, 26 December 1585:

A few days ago two Englishmen left here in company with a Jew
belonging, as I understand, to the household of David Passi. Many   20
conjectures as to their mission are made, but I have no definite
information to give your Serenity.

(p. 128)

Tomaso Contarini, Venetian Ambassador in Spain, to the Doge and
Senate, Madrid, 11 November 1589:

I am informed from a trustworthy source that the Spanish are in relations with David Passi in Constantinople, the same [man] as was in relation with Secretary Salazar [the Spanish Secretary in Venice]. The Viceroy of Naples has written advising his Majesty [Philip II] to confer a regular salary on the Jew.

(p. 474)

Hieronimo Lippomano, Venetian Ambassador in Constantinople, to the Doge and Senate, Vigne di Pera, 5 January 1590/1:

Every time during my residence here that I am advised of the preparation of a great fleet, I do my best to find out the purpose for which it is being constructed. . . .

The Queen of England is exerting herself, by making large promises, to persuade the Sultan to attack the King of Spain, in order to prevent that Sovereign from acquiring still greater power. . . . She hopes to counterbalance the power of Spain by support from the Turk. . . . The result is that the Grand Vizir [Sinan Pasha] has issued orders to the Capudan Pasha [the Turkish High Admiral] and to the Aga of the Janizaries to prepare an armament with all speed. . . .

Great is the excitement and genuine the preparations as yet at the beginning. Consultations between the Grand Vizir, the Capudan, the Aga, the Sultan's secretary, the English Ambassador and David Passi take place almost daily.

. . . I have been forced to admit David Passi, the Jew, to my confidence, for I found that the Sultan himself has ordered the Grand Vizir to consult with Passi, to listen to him, to favour him. The Grand Vizir refused, whereupon the Sultan said that slaves like the Vizir he had in abundance, but never a one like David, probably alluding to all the information about Christendom with which Passi furnishes the Sultan. Passi is a man of natural ability, and sufficient knowledge. I carefully weigh and balance all he says, but I have frequently had occasion to find him correct; and so I think it well to attach him [win him over] as much as may be, for he is able to do great harm and great good.

(pp. 512–14)

Hieronimo Lippomano, Venetian Ambassador in Constantinople, to the Doge and Senate, Vigne di Pera, 19 January 1590/1:

The Grand Vizir is in frequent and secret conference with a Chavass [a Turkish official], who was for a long time the slave of Don Juan de Cardona, and is therefore well acquainted with the possessions of King Philip. He declares that one hundred thousand men will rise in Granada on the appearance of the Turkish fleet in those waters; and that for long these men have had their weapons hidden underground in expectation of such an event. David Passi, the Jew, is present at all these conferences. . . . David Passi is also in continual relations with the Capudan Pasha, and communicates to the Capudan all his information about Christendom before furnishing it to the Sultan in writing. 70

(p. 519)

Hieronimo Lippomano, Venetian Ambassador in Constantinople, to the Doge and Senate, Vigne di Pera, 2 February 1590/1:

The Capudan and the Aga of Janizaries are in frequent consultation at the house of the Grand Vizir Sinan, and David Passi, the Jew, is always present. They discuss the preparations for the fleet, the question of the fortresses, the expenditure of the Sultan, the King of Spain, and the King of France, the political situation in Christendom, the destination of the proposed expedition, upon which point I am unable to discover the Sultan's real intention. All the Ministers in complete accord declare that the destination is 80 Spain. And at this very moment David Passi is on the point of despatching Guglielmo di Savoy, [another spy] with all secrecy, to King Philip to give him warning,and to persuade him to attempt to divert the expedition by means of money. If the attack on Spain is abandoned, Malta or Fez will be selected for attack.

(p. 521)

Hieronimo Lippomano, Venetian Ambassador in Constantinople, to the Doge and Senate, Vigne di Pera, 16 February 1590/1:

David Passi is very closely allied with the Aga and the Capudan, and [all three] recently agreed in urging the Grand Vizir to send a Chavass to Venice with letters demanding the island of Crete; for 90 now that Spain is occupied in attending to her own defences, and cannot assist Venice, the Sultan will either get that island or half a million of gold to spare it. This David, for one truth tells a hundred lies; he would betray us if he could; he is agent for Don Antonio of Portugal and in the confidence of the King of Spain; he is the warm supporter of Venice, and the trusty spy of the Sultan. . . .

(p. 525)

Hieronimo Lippomano, Venetian Ambassador in Constantinople, to the Doge and Senate, Vigne di Pera, 16 March 1591:

David Passi has fallen into disgrace with the Grand Vizir, for he wrote to the Grand Chancellor of Poland, saying that Sinan Pasha 100 had written the letter of accord and reconciliation on his own authority only, without binding the Sultan, and this with a view to deceiving them, and drawing money from them. Sinan, on learning this, flew into a violent rage, and having obtained leave from the Sultan to avenge himself except on the life of Passi, he could not wait to catch David quietly, but must send for him at midnight, at a time when he happened not to be at home. The result of this haste is that David has taken refuge in the house of the new Beglierbey [provincial governor]. Sinan, they say, hoped to be able to secure the drowning of David. The lapse of time and the intervention of friends, however, will, it is thought, cause the Sultan to spare his life, and perhaps to reinstate him. Sinan considers that he has been accused of treachery, and nurses his anger, though he dissimulates for the present. The Sultan's Secretary said to me that the Republic ought to consider Passi's removal as worth a million in gold. But seeing that he is supported by people of the highest authority, who assure the Sultan that he is the only truthful and well-informed spy against Christian powers, I will watch the issue of events, and see that your Serenity's interests are not affected. . . .

(p. 533)

Lorenzo Bernardo, Venetian Ambassador in Constantinople, to the Doge and Senate, Vigne di Pera, 15 July 1591:

The Grand Vizir has caused the Jew, David Passi, to be publicly placed in irons with a chain round his neck, in his own house. Shortly afterwards Passi was sent on board a galley, and rumour goes that he is to be deported to Tunis; but it is thought that as soon as the galley is out of harbour, he will be thrown into the sea. He was a man who was filled to the full with vanity. This will be a lesson to others not to meddle in affairs of State. The cause of his fall was the discovery of certain letters which he had written to the Grand Chancellor of Poland.

(p. 550)

Lorenzo Bernardo, Venetian Ambassador in Constantinople to the Doge and Senate, Vigne di Pera, 21 September 1591:

David Passi has come back from Rhodes. His face shows the terror he has gone through. I imagine, if he has any brains at all, he will leave affairs of State alone for the future. . . .

(p. 556)

TEXT 3

The Play of the Sacrament

(*c.* 1460)

[The extract is taken from *Non-Cycle Plays and Fragments*,
published by the Early English Text Society in 1970.]

*Now shall the merchant's man withdraw him and the Jew Jonathas shall make
his boast.*

JONATHAS: Now, almighty Mahomet, mark in thy majesty,
Whose laws tenderly I have to fulfil [observe],
After my death bring me to thy high see [seat],
My soul for to save, if it be thy will;
For my intent is for to fulfil,
As my glorious God thee to honour;
To do again[st] thy intent it should grue me ill
   [make me fearful],
Or again thine law for to report [speak].

For I thank thee haily [greatly] that hast me sent   10
Gold, silver, and precious stones,
And abundance of spices thou hast me lent
   [granted],
As I shall rehearse before you once:
I have amethysts, rich for the nonce,
And beryls that be bright of blee [in colour];
And sapphire seemly I may show you at once,
And crystals clear for to see;

I have diamonds, dearworthy to dress [precious to
   place in a setting],
And emeralds – rich I trow they be –
Onyx and agates both more and less,   20
Topazines, smaragdes of great degree,
Pearls precious, great plenty;
Of rubies rich I have great renown;
Crapauds and chalcedonies seemly to see,
And curious carbuncles here ye find moun [may];

313

Spices I have, both great and small
In my ships, the sooth for to say;
Ginger, liquorice, and galingale,
And figs fat to please you to pay [satisfy you];
Pepper and saffron and spices small,   30
And dates well dulcet [sweet] for to dress,
Almonds and rice, full every male [sack],
And raisins both more and less:

Cloves, grains [of paradise], and ginger green,
Mace, mastic [gum] that mighty is;
Cinnamon, sugar, as you may seen;
Long pepper and Indas [Indian] liquorice;
Oranges and apples of great apprize [excellence],
Pomegranates and many other spices –
To tell you all I have now, i-wis,   40
And much other merchandise of sundry spices
    [species?].

Jew Jonathas is my name –
Jazon and Jazdon, they waiten on my will;
Masfat and Malchus, they do the same,
As ye may know, it is both right and skill.
I tell you all, by dale and by hill,
In Eraclea is none so much of might:
Wherefore ye owe [ought] tenderly to tend me
    till [pay me attention],
For I am chief merchant of Jews, I tell you,
    by right.

                                    (lines 149–96)

TEXT 4

Respublica

Nicholas Udall (?)
(1553)

[The text is taken from the Early English Text Society edition
published in 1952.]

[Enter AVARICE.]

AVARICE: Now godigood [greetings] everyone, both great
    and small;
  From highest to lowest, Godigood to you all!
  Godigood – what should I say? – even or morrow?
  – If I mark how the day goeth, God give me sorrow!
  But Godigood each one, twenty and twenty score
  Of that ye most long for – for what would ye have more?
  Ye must pardon my wits, for I tell you plain,
  I have a hive of humble-bees swarming in my brain,
  And he that hath the compass [scope] to fetch that I
    must fetch,
  I may say in counsel, had need his wits to stretch!   10
  But now what my name is and what is my purpose,
  Taking you all for friends, I fear not to disclose.
  My very true unchristian name is Avarice,
  Which I may not have openly known in no wise;
  For though to most men I am found commodious,
  Yet to those that use me my name is odious:
  For who is so foolish that the evil he hath wrought
  For his own behoof [advantage], he would to light
    should be brought?
  Or who had not rather his ill-doings to hide
  Than to have the same bruited [advertised] on every
    side?   20
  Therefore to work my feat I will my name disguise,
  And call my name Policy instead of Covetise.
  The name of Policy is praised of each one,

315

But to rake gromwell seed [accumulate a cash return?],
   Avarice is alone.
The name of Policy is of none suspected;
Policy is ne'er of any crime detected,
So that under the name and cloak of Policy,
Avarice may work facts [commit crimes] and 'scape all
   jealousy [suspicion].
For now is the time come that, except I be a beast,
E'en to make up [fill] my mouth and feather my nest –   30
A time that I have waited for a great long space –
And now may I speed my purpose, if I have grace . . .
                        (I. 1. 1–32)

[AVARICE *enters, dragging his bags of gold behind him.*]

AVARICE: Come on, sweet bags of gold, come on with a good will,
         I on you so tender and ye so froward [obstinate] still?
         Come forward, I pray you, sweet bags. Ah, will ye so?
         Come, or I must draw you, whether ye will or no.
         I know your desire; ye would fain be in my chest;
         When the belly is full, the bones would be at rest.
         Be content awhile; I will couch you all up soon
         Where ye shall not be spied, neither of sun nor moon.   40
         What now, brother Honesty? What, pry ye this way?
         Is there anything here that is yours, can ye say?
         Look off from my bags! it is a pretty matter;
         Ye can see no green cheese, but your teeth will water!
                           (III. 4. 1–12)

TEXT 5

A right excellent and famous Comedy called the Three Ladies of London . . .

Robert Wilson
(1584)

[The extracts are taken from the Tudor Facsimile Text
reprint published in 1911.]

[Love and Conscience being out of fashion, Lady Lucre is the only one
among the three ladies of London to hold sway there. An Italian
merchant, Mercatore or Mercadorus, is one of those supplicating for
her favours; he agrees to export produce from England to Turkey, and
in return to supply the people of London with trashy imported goods of
little value. In this way Lucre will be the beneficiary, and the merchant
will grow rich.

Mercatore, having been despatched to Turkey to purchase luxuries
with which to beguile the English consumer, meets with Gerontus, a
Jewish businessman, who demands the settlement of a past debt.]

Enter MERCADORUS *the Merchant and* GERONTUS *a Jew.*

GERON: But Signor Mercadorus, tell me, did ye serve me well
　　　　or no,
　　　　That having gotten my money, would seem the country to
　　　　　forgo?
　　　　You know I lent you two thousand ducats for three
　　　　　months' space,
　　　　And ere the time came you got another thousand by
　　　　　flattery and your smooth face.
　　　　So when the time came that I should have received my
　　　　　money,
　　　　You were not to be found but was fled out of the country;
　　　　Surely if we that be Jews should deal so with one another,
　　　　We should not be trusted again of our own brother.
　　　　But many of your Christians make no conscience to falsify
　　　　　your faith and break your day [of repayment]:

317

I should have been paid at the month's end, and now it is
two year you have been away. 10
Well, I am glad you be come again to Turkey; now I trust
I shall receive the interest of you so well as the
principal.

MERCA: Ah good-a Master Geronto, pray heartily bear-a me a little
while,
Me have-a much business for buy pretty knacks to send to
England;
Good-a sir, bear-a me four or five days, me'll despatch your
money out of hand.

GERON: Signor Mercadore, I know no reason why, because you
have dealt with me so ill;
Sure you did it not for need, but of set purpose and will.
And I tell ye, to bear with ye four or five days goes sore
against my mind,
Lest you should steal away, and forget to leave my money
behind.

MERCA: Pray heartily do tink-a no such ting, my good friend-a me;
By my trot' and fait', me'll pay you all every penny! 20

GERON: Well, I'll take your faith and troth once more; I'll trust to
your honesty,
In hope that for my long tarrying, you will deal well with me.
Tell me, what ware you would buy for England – such
necessaries as they lack?

MERCA: Oh, no lack! Some pretty fine toy or some fantastic new
knack!
For da gentlewomans in England buy much tings for
fantasy [whim];
You pleasure-a me, sir, what me mean-a dareby?

GERON: I understand you, sir, but keep touch [faith] with me,
and I'll bring you to great store,
Such as I perceive you came to this country for:
As musk, amber, sweet powders, fine odours, pleasant
perfumes, and many such toys [trifles],
Wherein I perceive consisteth that country
gentlewoman's joys. 30
Besides, I have diamonds, rubies, emeralds, sapphires,
smaragdines, opals, onyxes, jacinths, agates, turquoise,

and almost of all kind of precious stones;
And many moe [more] fit things to suck away money from
such green-headed wantons.

MERCA: Fatta, my good friend, me tank you most heartily alway;
Me shall-a content your debt within dis two or tree day.

GERON: Well, look you do keep your promise, and another time
you shall command me:
Come, go we home where our commodities you may at
pleasure see.

[*They exit.*]

[Later in the play the merchant and the Jew reappear.]

Enter MERCADORUS *reading a letter to himself, and let* GERONTUS *the Jew*
follow him, and speak as followeth:

GERON: Signor Mercadore, why do you not pay me? Think you I
will be mocked in this sort?
This is three times you have flouted me; it seems you make
thereat a sport.
Truly, pay me my money, and that even now presently
[immediately],
Or by mighty Mahomet I swear, I will forthwith arrest ye.   40

MERCA: Ha, pray-a bear wit' me tree or four days, me have much
business in hand;
Me be troubled with letters you see here, dat comes from
England.

GERON: Tush, this is not my matter; I have nothing therewith to do;
Pay me my money or I'll make you, before to your lodging
you go!
I have officers stand watching for you, so that you cannot
pass by;
Therefore you were best to pay me, or else in prison you
shall lie.

MERCA: Arrest me, dou scall'd [scabby] knave? Marry, do and if
thou dare;
Me will not pay dee one penny; arrest me, do; me do not
care.

319

      Me will be a Turk; me came hither for dat cause;

      Darefore me care not for dee so much as two straws!   50

GERON: This is but your words, because you would defeat me;

      I cannot think you will forsake your faith so lightly;

      But seeing you drive me to doubt, I'll try your honesty:

      Therefore be sure of this, I'll go about it presently.   *Exit.*

MERCA: Marry, farewell, and be hanged; shitten scall'd drunken

        Jew!

      I warrant ye, me shall be able very well to pay you.

      My Lady Lucre have sent me here dis letter,

      Praying me to cozen [cheat] de Jews for love-a her.

      Darefore me'll go to get-a some Turks' apparel,

      Dat me may cozen da Jew, and end dis quarrel.   *Exit.*   60

[Gerontus now arraigns the merchant before a judge.]

    Enter the JUDGE *of Turkey, with* GERONTUS *and* MERCADORUS.

JUDGE: Sir Gerontus, because you are the plaintiff, you first your

        mind shall say;

      Declare the cause you did arrest this merchant yesterday.

GERON: Then, learned judge, attend. This Mercadorus whom you

        see in place,

      Did borrow two thousand ducats of me, but for a five

        weeks' space.

      Then, sir, before the day came, by his flattery he obtained

        one thousand more,

      And promised me at two months' end, I should receive

        my store.

      But before the time expired, he was closely [secretly] fled

        away,

      So that I never heard of him at least this two years' day:

      Till at the last I met with him, and my money did demand,

      Who sware to me at five days' end, he would pay me out

        of hand.   70

      The five days came, and three days more, then one day he

        requested;

      I, perceiving that he flouted me, have got him thus

        arrested.

      And now he comes in Turkish weeds to defeat me of my

        money,

      But I trow he will not forsake his faith; I deem he hath

        more honesty.

JUDGE: Sir Gerontus, you know, if any man forsake his faith, king,
country, and become a Mahomet,
All debts are paid – 'tis the law of our realm – and you
may not gainsay it.

GERON: Most true, reverend judge, we may not, nor I will not
against our laws grudge.

JUDGE: Signor Mercadorus, is this true that Gerontus doth tell?

MERCA: My Lord Judge, de matter and de circumstance be true,
me know well;
But me will be a Turk, and for dat cause me came here.   80

JUDGE: Then it is but a folly to make many words. Signor
Mercadorus, draw near:
Lay your hand upon this book, and say after me –

MERCA: With a good will, my Lord Judge, me be all ready.

GERON: Not for any devotion, but for Lucre's sake of my money.

JUDGE: Say: 'I, Mercadorus, do utterly renounce before all the
world, my duty to my Prince, my honour to my parents,
and my goodwill to my country. Furthermore, I protest
and swear to be true to this country during life, and
thereupon I forsake my Christian faith.'

GERON: Stay there, most puissant judge! Signor Mercadorus,
consider what you do;   90
Pay me the principal – as for the interest I forgive it you;
And yet the interest is allowed amongst you Christians, as
well as in Turkey;
Therefore respect your faith, and do not seem to deceive
me.

MERCA: No point da interest; no point da principal.

GERON: Then pay me the one half, if you will not pay me all.

MERCA: No point da half, no point denier [tiny sum]; me will be a
Turk, I say;

321

Me be weary of my Christ's religion, and for dat me come
away.

GERON: Well, seeing it is so, I would be loth to hear the people say
it was 'long of me,
Thou forsakest thy faith, wherefore I forgive thee frank
and free;
Protesting before the judge and all the world, never to
demand penny nor halfpenny.   100

MERCA: O Sir Gerontus, me take-a your proffer, and tank you
most heartily!

JUDGE: But, Signor Mercadorus, I trow ye will be a Turk for all
this?

MERCA: Signor, no, not for all da good in da world me forsake-a
my Christ.

JUDGE: Why, then, it is as Sir Gerontus said, you did more for the
greediness of the money,
Than for any zeal or goodwill you bear to Turkey?

MERCA: Oh, sir, you make a great offence;
You must not judge-a my conscience!

JUDGE: One may judge and speak truth, as appears by this;
Jews seek to excel in Christianity, and Christians in
Jewishness.

Exit.

MERCA: Well, well, but me tank you, Sir Gerontus, with all my very
heart.   110

GERON: Much good may it do you, sir; I repent it not for my part.
But yet I would not have this bolden you to serve another so;
Seek to pay, and keep day with men, so a good name on
you will go.

Exit.

MERCA: You say well, sir ! It does me good dat me have cozened de
Jew;
Faith, I would my Lady Lucre de whole matter now knew !

What is dat me will not do for her sweet sake?
But now me will provide, my journey toward England to
   take:
Me be a Turk? No! It will make my Lady Lucre to smile,
When she knows how me did da scalled Jew beguile.

                                            Exit

TEXT 6

Das Wohlgesprochene Uhrteil,
or
Der Jud von Venedig

[The extracts are translated from J. Meissner, *Die Englischen Comoedianten zur Zeit Shakespeares in Oesterreich*, Wien, 1884.]

I.1

The play begins with a meeting between the King of Cyprus, two of his councillors, and his son the Prince of Cyprus. The King asks his son why he requires his judgement on this occasion, when normally he governs and make decisions without consulting him. The Prince replies that he wishes to consult him on a serious and worrying matter which concerns the security of the whole kingdom. He explains to his father that at first 'the despised nation of the Jews' had been obedient and humble, conscientiously paying their taxes, but that now he receives daily complaints about them, despite everything done to limit their sphere of activity. Through usury   10
both nobles and commoners have lost their goods, and the Jews have even been involved in areas of activity which were strictly the royal domain. This state of affairs could no longer be tolerated, and therefore he wished to obtain his father's advice.

The King agrees that the situation has got out of hand, adding that the number of Jews has also increased, and he calls on his councillors for their opinions. The first says that since they have carried out illegal trade the Jews should be got rid of completely by being sent out of the land 'naked and bare' and their goods confiscated by the King, either to return to those who can prove   20
they have lost money to the Jews or else for the King himself to retain. The second councillor agrees with the first, and the Prince then says:

> I too am of this opinion, for if we allow them to live in this land any longer, we shall have something worse to fear from their usury and financial dealings. We all know what they recently planned in Malta. One of these days they could indeed betray this whole kingdom to the Turks.

The King praises his son's assessment of the situation and empowers
him to do what he feels necessary to put things to rights.   30

I.2

Pickelhäring, the Prince's servant, who also plays the role of fool,
reads out a number of somewhat comic supplications to the King
and Prince. The last of these concerns the Jews, who say they will
gladly leave the country once they have managed to acquire the
goods of the Prince and the King, as well as those of their subjects.
The King commands the most important Jew to be brought before
them and informed of the judgement. The councillors go to give
orders for the Jews' houses and shops to be appropriated and for
the Jews themselves to be driven out of the land. Pickelhäring tells
Barrabas the leader of the Jews to come in, informing him that the   40
King is inviting him to a dinner of sausages and sauerkraut. Their
conversation continues:

I.3

JEW: No, Pickelhäring; that's not what I eat.

PICK: But a pretzel that the ropemaker had baked – that would
         be just right for your neck.

JEW (*to the* PRINCE *and* KING): Did your majesties send for me?

PRINCE: Yes, we did send for you, but after this we shall not send
         for you again. You know, Jew, how bare and poor your
         nation came into this country. Now you have enriched
         yourselves so much, not only attracting to yourselves our   50
         subjects' money and goods, but you have also made
         complete estates with all their goods you own.
         Therefore, my father and the whole kingdom have
         unanimously decided to punish you and no longer
         permit your trafficking and trade.

JEW: What, O gracious lord! Who has given your lordship
         such a report of us? We penniless Jews, we came here
         poor, are still poor and will indeed remain poor. We
         need to do something in order to be able to feed our
         wives and children. We practise no usury other than to   60
         lend Christians money on occasion in return for
         something they pawn. When they return and restore the
         money to us, they receive back the item they have
         pawned after paying a small amount of interest for it.
         We do the country more good than harm.

325

PICK: Jew, I know you are lying. Once my father pawned a blind horse for half a thaler, but when he brought you back the money the horse had already died.

JEW: Why didn't he collect his horse on time?

PICK: Why didn't you feed him, you gallows bird? 70

PRINCE: Be quite, Pickelhäring! Listen, Jew, we know well enough your usury and greed; also how your houses are filled with goods and your chests with money. Since you brought nothing to us when you came into this land, and people know when something belongs to them and when it does not, therefore your goods and chattels including your house and land are confiscated and given over to us. As you value your life you should all be gone from the land tomorrow along with your wives and children. 80

JEW (*kneeling*): But your majesty, how have we deserved this? I implore you, most merciful Prince, show us some mercy! Shall we Hebrews turn our backs on everything? If we have earned anything and got it for ourselves, we have done so through hard work. Oh, Pickelhäring, do me a favour and I will give you a good ducat.

PICK: You don't have any ducats any longer: they all belong to the King. However, I will ask a favour for you. (*kneeling*) Oh, my lord King and Monsieur Prince, let not the poor villainous thieving Jews be chased out of the land; let 90 them all be brought to the gallows instead.

KING: What the Prince our son has spoken must stand. Throw out the villain immediately; we do not wish to see him before our eyes any longer.

PICK: Get out, rogue; you stink!

JEW: Just wait, Pickelhäring; I shall remember you.

PICK: Wait, you rogue, are you threatening me? (*Hits him on the neck*).

JEW: I beg you for mercy in the name of the God of Abraham, Isaac and Jacob.

PICK: Go and plead with the hangman and the torturer's 100 knaves. (*The Jew leaves*)

The Prince now answers the petitions presented to him earlier: to the one concerning the Jews he orders that the Jews must either leave the land or be executed. To the King the Prince says that their action against the Jews of Cyprus will provide a good example for other countries to follow and relieve Cyprus of a great burden. Moreover, the new situation will enable him to carry out a long-cherished plan to visit Venice. Reluctantly the King agrees to let him go, and only on condition that he first goes in disguise with only one servant and stays for a maximum of one year. Pickelhäring wishes to accompany the Prince and persuades the King to release him from the court.

I.4

Barrabas appears disguised as a soldier with a plaster over one eye, and knocks at the Prince's door. He informs the Prince that he is a poor soldier who has served in the war against the King of Crete. Because he had lost his eye in the war, he asks for a favour. Telling the Prince that he is a native of Venice and having heard that the Prince intends to go there, he wonders if he could be taken along. The Prince agrees. In a soliloquy which ends the scene the Jew announces that Pickelhäring and his master will in due course find out what sort of a fellow he really is. He explains how on being told to flee Cyprus he had returned home, dressed himself in different clothes and taken with him as much gold and and as many jewels as he could hide on his person. He says that he will now go to Venice with the Prince (his wife and children following), and that he has enough money with him to buy the services of bandits to kill the Prince. He states that the Prince will not succeed in getting rid of the Jews, and that he himself will recover all the goods he has lost.

II.3

The scene has now shifted to Venice, where Barrabas in soliloquy informs us that thanks to his brothers and his own hard work he is now richer than he had been before. While the Prince is a foreigner in Venice, he himself is at home there, and while the Prince is in disguise, he himself is free to proclaim himself a Jew. He mocks the Christians for thinking that they can eradicate the Jews so easily. The Jews, he says, are extremely resilient and manage to flourish even more when they are oppressed. He says:

On the journey [from Cyprus] I had only one eye, now I have two to enable me to look out precisely for what will benefit me. Then I had to make do with a ragged coat, now I have clothes not just as bare necessities but for splendour and magnificence. Before I was called Barrabas; now I have taken on the name of Joseph. Just look out, my Prince, for Joseph is seeking your downfall. I am not in fact Joseph of Arimathea, but if I catch you in my claws, I shall certainly be the Joseph who will help you to your grave.

[The only other scenes with a possible bearing on *The Jew of Malta* are III. 4 and III. 5, in which the Prince, seeking to woo the lovely Anciletta, seeks to disguise himself as a French doctor, and orders Pickelhäring to borrow suitable clothing and a false beard for him from one of the Venetian Jews. By chance it is Barrabas who is visited, and he, recognizing the Prince's servant, decides that this is a chance for him to revenge himself. Barrabas decides to spread deadly poison on the clothes so that whoever wears them will die, and with this in mind asks Pickelhäring to return in two hours to collect the clothing. However, Pickelhäring says that he will go elsewhere rather than wait, and the Jew gives him the clothes untreated, reasoning that it is worth developing this contact with the Prince, so that he can be revenged at some later date.]

TEXT 7

The Navigations, Peregrinations and Voyages made into Turkey . . .

Nicolas de Nicolay

translated out of the French by
T. Washington the Younger
(1585)

[The texts are taken from *The English Experience*
facsimile edition published in 1968.]

BOOK I CHAPTER 16

Description of the Isle of Malta.

Malta, which by the ancients was called Melita, is an isle in the Sea
Mediterranean between Sicily and Tripoli in Barbary which from
the west to the east containeth in length two and twenty miles, in
breadth eleven, and in circuit threescore. It is an island low and
stony, and hath five fair and large ports, all issuing at one mouth: at
the entry of which isle is the castle (where the Grand Master
keepeth), by art and nature almost inexpugnable [invincible],
being furnished with good quantity of ordnance, and situated
upon a high rock of three parts environed with the sea; and on the
side towards Cande [Crete], separated with a large channel from   10
the bourg [town] which lieth underneath it, very great, and well-
inhabited, full of fair houses and palaces, well-builded, every one
with a cistern [water-tank]; for they have neither there nor in the
castle neither wells nor fountains. There be also many fair churches,
both Greek and Latin, and in the midst of the great place a great
pillar erected, where the malefactors are punished. True it is that
this bourg is not defensible against any great siege, because it is
environed with great hills, unto which of all sides it is subject. She
is inhabited and peopled with a great number of commanders,
knights and merchants of all nations; and above all, there is great   20
abundance of courtesans, both Greek, Italian, Spaniards, Moors

and Maltese. The common sort wear none other clothing, because of the extremity of the heat, than a long linen white smock, girded under their breasts, and over the same a fine white woollen mantle, by the Moors called [a] barnuche [burnous]. . .

The city is distant six miles from the castle, situated upon the top of a mountain, environed on the three parts with great valleys full of gravel and large stones very painful to go [walk] upon. On the south side about two miles from the city is a great fountain, bringing forth such a marvellous number of eels, that it is a matter hard to be believed; which have so sharp teeth that there cannot be a string so good, but they will bite it asunder, so as such as will take them are forced to strengthen their lines about the hook with a silk or cotton thread, and as soon as they feel them taken, be very ready to pull them up. And out of this fountain our galleys took their fresh water.

There are in this island sixty castles or villages, all well inhabited and very abundant of barley, cunego (which is a grain which they mingle amongst their corn to make bread), cotton, citrons, oranges, melons and other fruits of exceeding goodness, but for wheat and wine they do furnish themselves out of Sicily; there are bred very good mulets and horses of the race of Spain. . .

(fos. 17 recto–17 verso)

[The French Ambassador and his retinue depart from Malta for Tripoli in an attempt to persuade the Turkish Captain-General Sinan Pasha to lift the siege, but find themselves the unwilling witnesses of his efforts to dislodge the Knights Hospitallers of St John from the fortress.]

The Ambassador, accompanied of his gentlemen, went to declare unto him [the Pasha] the cause of his coming, praying him in the name and behalf of the king to refrain from such an enterprise, which the Pasha would not agree unto, but to the contrary, made him answer that the great Turk was much aggrieved that the Knights at the giving-over of the Rhodes [in 1522] having sworn at no time after to wear arms against the Turkish nation, had not only contrary to their oath aided and succoured all the enterprises of the Emperor [i.e. Charles V]: namely [especially] at the taking of the city of Africa against Dragut, but also of themselves did daily make war unto His Highness [i.e. the Sultan], and did thereunto all the worst they could. And that he therefore was moved to dress [draw up] this army to chastise their temerity, and if it were possible, to drive them out of Africa, and in all that lay in him to endamage them. . . .

(fol. 19 verso)

BOOK I CHAPTER 19

Of Bazaar where were sold the Christians taken in the isle[s] of Sicily, Malta and Gozo; and of the manner of trenches, gabions [containers for excavated earth] and batteries of the Turk.

Having well considered the placing of the camp, the town and castle, we returned to the Pasha, with whom the Ambassador talked a while, and in the meanwhile I went to see the market of the Turks (which they call Bazaar), being hard by where the poor Christians of Sicily, Malta and Gozo were sold unto those that most offered for them and last enhancers [raisers of the price], being permitted unto those that bought them (as the ancient custom of the oriental barbarians is) to strip them stark naked and to make them go [move], to the intent to see if they have any natural impediment in their bodies, visiting afterwards their teeth and eyes, as though they   10
had been horses. And standing there, I saw creeping upon the ground a scorpion of yellow colour, being of length more than a long finger. . . .

(fol. 21 verso)

[Despite the spirited resistance of the Knights, the fortress is finally betrayed to the enemy.]

Notwithstanding, the end was such that an unhappy [wretched] soldier of Provence, born in Cavaillon, being the Pope's country, which by the long frequentation he had had in those countries, had learned the language and served as a spy unto the enemy, seeing the occasion to be come to that pass, which his knavery and dissimuled treason had wished for, and being corrupted with money, found the means to flee unto the camp, where he declared   20
unto the Turks the weakest places of the castle, by the which it might be battered and soon taken. And it was against the Governor's lodging, which standing towards the ditch and having underneath it the cellars to retire [store] the munition, could not be repaired nor fortified. Which the Pasha having understanded, caused the battery there to be planted, laying the pieces so low that easily they did beat the vaults and cellars in such sort as in small time they did pierce the walls. Whereupon followed that the height, being charged with ramparts, through the continual battery began greatly to sink, which amazed the soldiers for that they knew no means to   30
repair the same, that setting all honour aside, quitting themselves of their weapons, concluded together to take some party [decision], giving their captain to understand that having unto that

instant quitted themselves as good men and valiant soldiers, seeing their matters to be in despair of succour, and not able to hold out any longer, he would not think evil of them, if they thought to practise some way for their surety.

(fos. 22 recto–23 verso)

[Despite the remonstrations of their senior officers, the defending force insists on Vallier the Governor surrendering the castle under a flag of truce. Sinan on his part deceives the Governor and the inhabitants into surrendering their stronghold, and the city falls to the Turks.]

TEXT 8

The Fourth Part of Commentaries of the Civil Wars in France . . .

Jean de Serres

translated by Thomas Tymme
(1576)

[The text is taken from the British Library copy
(shelfmark 286.c.29).]

THE ELEVENTH BOOK OF COMMENTARIES

About this time there befell a new occasion to further the affairs of
the [Protestant] religion in Languedoc. . . . Concerning Villeneuve
[-de-Berg] which was intercepted [cut off] by Monsieur Leugère,
we have spoken before. The banished citizens of Villeneuve used
these means to recover their city: we said before that a little town
called Mirebelle was taken by Monsieurs Baron and Pradelle,   10
whither the most earnest favourers of the religion of Villeneuve
fled. They therefore, being in Mirebelle which was situate upon the
higher ground, from whence they might see far off, had always
Villeneuve before their eyes, insomuch that the present occasion
[necessity] was always in the minds of the poor banished citizens to
recover their country [district]. Amidst the straits [privations] of
the siege of Sommiron, those extremities of Mirebelle [were]
repeated, being beseiged round about with enemies.

There came to M. Pradelle a certain soldier, a coppersmith,
which was newly come from Villeneuve, who affirmed that he had
devised a way to take the city, in show [ostensibly] ridiculous and
fond [foolish], but yet such he said as was not to be rejected, being
much more easy than that which was practised in taking of Nîmes in
the time of the former war.   20

There was at the walls of Villeneuve a hole, out of the which the
water of the town, only in the time of rain, runneth to purge the
ways and channels, and the same had an iron grate before it. That
hole this soldier had viewed, and reported the same to be such, that

333

the bars of iron might easily be broken up, through the which, he affirmed, they might easily pass into the town.

The matter being told to M. Baron, a captain, was jested at. Notwithstanding, at the instance of M. Pradelle, it was agreed that this device should be put into practice. . . .

They of the religion came unto the city when all things were at rest, through the compassing valleys shadowed with hills, with the which Villeneuve was compassed on that side. And when the iron bars were pulled up, they entered in at the foresaid hole. And they that entered first came unto the chief watch and slew certain soldiers whom they found asleep, and some between sleeping and waking. And thus they ran through the city, crying 'The town is taken!' Thus the greater part, being entered in at the hole, not one shot being discharged from the walls against them, opened one gate. Whomsoever they met, they slew. M. Leugère [the Catholic commander], being waked with the noise of this tumult, went out of his house, but being constrained by force to retire again, he kept himself close in the same, being lately well fortified. The Catholics also betook them to the tower of the greater gate, and to another also of great height beside the temple. But such as were found armed in any place of the city were slain by them of the religion, insomuch that the streets were filled with dead bodies.

Many popish prelates also were slain, which were come thither from divers cities thereabouts, to hold a synod. And after they had assailed the two towers and the house of M. Leugère, to the hurt and detriment of both parts, the said three places were yielded the third day, and M. Leugère departed, being in great peril of the Catholics, insomuch that he could scarcely be in safety in his house, being accused of treason. (Thus faith being violated, he is also accused of treason by false surmise.) So great fear came upon all this country [region], that no doubt they of the religion might easily have taken the next [neighbouring] city, but that the soldiers, being busied about the prey, would not go elsewhere. A great booty was carried out of this little town, and much money for ransoms was received, which by the negligence of the captains was put to private uses.

(pp. 55–7)

TEXT 9

Gratulationum Valdinensium libri quattuor

Gabriel Harvey
(1578)

[The text is translated from the British Library copy (shelfmark C. 60. h. 17 (2)). The Latin is given below.]

Epigrams on the image of Machiavelli: Machiavelli speaks in person

You ask me who might I be? The King of all Kings is my answer:
On the tip of my finger I balance command of this wide world.
Unfit for rule is the man who lacks knowledge of Machiavelli;
Set no store by his wisdom unless he is steeped in my dogmas.
All other matters are shadows and smoky, playthings and follies;
Ruling is all I can speak of, sovereign sway and dominion.
Infants and dotards crave peace, miserable old men and women;
Military camps are my sole theme; I can speak only of warfare.
Love of the people is nothing; still less is penurious Virtue: 10
Abandoning mere words to others, I carry out marvellous actions.
Look in my eyes: Anger resides there; in one hand I brandish a
     flintstone;
The other makes free with a sword; my mouth conceals poisons.
A thousand venomous liquids stream from each one of my features:
Iron is my brow, my heart is well worthy the dark god of Hades.
My motto remains as it has been: 'There is pleasure in high
     aspiration;
Be Caesar or nothing' – and he was a pupil of our school.
Moderation in all things is hateful; I nurture sublime designs only;
Milk is a foodstuff for children, blood is the thing that sustains me.
Let a thousand deaths ravage the rabble, provided I seize on the
     sceptre;   20
I am indifferent to bloodshed, slaughter weighs little in my book.
Let wretched souls perish in Hell; let them be carted to Hades!
I am the only wise mortal; I live in my own deeds to triumph.
Who does not know what comes next? Deceit is my ultimate virtue:

335

Close to it Brute Force stands; I recognize no gods but these two.
Leaf through my *Prince,* that monument reared to my brilliance:
Then you will not need to ask: 'Who was this Machiavelli?'

Epigramma in effigiem Machiavelli: Machiavelli ipse loquitur

Quaeris, ego qui sim? Rex Regum: totius orbis
    Imperium digito nititur omne meo.   30
Nemo regat, qui non Machiavellica dogmata callet:
    Ne sapuisse putes qui minus ista sapit.
Caetera sunt umbrae, fumi, ludibria, risus,
    Regna ego sola loquor, sceptra ego sola loquor,
Pacem optent pueri, vetulaeque, senesque, miselli,
    Castra ego sola loquor, bella ego sola loquor.
Plebis amor nihil est; nihilo minus, Indiga Virtus:
    Verba ego linquo aliis; facta ego mira patro.
Ecce oculos: Furor iis habitat: manus altera saxum;
    Altra ensem torquet: toxica in ore latent.   40
Spiritus hinc, atque hinc perfusus mille venenis:
    Ferrea frons, Orci pectora digna Deo.
Emblema est, semperque fuit; *Iuvat ire per altum*:
    Aut nihil, aut Caesar; noster Alumnus erat.
Nil mediocre placet: sublimia sola voluto:
    Lac pueris cibus est: sanguine vescor ego.
Mille neces obeat vulgus, modo sceptra capessam;
    Non flocci cruor est, non laniena mihi.   50
Dispereant abjectae animae: trudantur ad Orcum:
    Solus ego sapio, vivo, triumpho mihi.
Caetera quis nescit? *Fraus* est mea maxima Virtus:
    Proxima, *Vis*: alios non ego nosco Deos.
Ingenii monumenta mei Regalia volue:
    Nec post hac quaeres: Quid Machiavellus erat?

NOTES

1 *La cosmographie Universelle de tout le monde* . . . (pp. 306–8)

1   *Suleiman*: Suleiman the Magnificent (1494–1566) died in early August 1566, besieging Szigetvar in Hungary, to be succeeded as Ottoman Sultan by Selim II (1524–74).
15   *Arabia Deserta*: the predominantly desert area of the Arabian peninsula.
29   *Arabia Felix*: the fertile south-western corner of the peninsula.
65   *Marrano*: a Jew overtly converted to Christianity who continued to observe Jewish customs and traditions.

2 *Calendar of State Papers (Venetian)* (pp. 309–12)

15   *English Ambassador*: the English Ambassador to the Porte from 1583 to 1588 was William Harborne; he was succeeded in August 1588 by Edward Barton, then aged 26.

36   *the Sultan*: Murad III who ruled the Ottoman Empire from 1574 to 1595.

3 *The Play of the Sacrament* (pp. 313–14)

21   *smaragdes*: precious emerald-green stones.

24   *crapauds*: gemstones toad-like in shape or colour, or supposedly derived from the toad, which popular legend alleged wore one in its head.

47   *Eraclea*: Heraclea, 'the city of Hercules', allegedly in Spain, the ostensible setting for *The Play of the Sacrament*.

6 *Das Wohlgesprochene Uhrteil* (pp. 324–8)

Title: *Das Wohlgesprochene Uhrteil*: 'The Happy (lit. 'well-delivered') Verdict'.

7 *The Navigations, Peregrinations and Voyages made into Turkey . . .* (pp. 329–32)

Title: *Nicolas de Nicolay*: Seigneur d'Arfeuille, Nicolay (1517–83) was geographer to Charles IX.

Book 1 Chapter 16

2   *Barbary*: Saracen territories on the North African coast between Morocco and Libya, famous as a base for pirates.

10   *Cande*: western Crete (in Latin *Candia*).

52   *Dragut*: a notable Corsair pirate.

EDWARD II

INTRODUCTION

Marlowe's principal source for *Edward II* is Raphael Holinshed's *Chronicles*, but scholars have long agreed that he also made use of the chronicles of Robert Fabyan and John Stow. From Fabyan he took the ballad with which the Scots mocked the defeated English after Bannockburn; his most obvious debt to Stow is for the story of Edward's journey towards his death at Berkeley castle, but his dependence on this chronicle is much greater than has been generally recognized. There is also a strong possibility that he consulted the brief but informative account of the reign in the 1570 edition of John Foxe's *Acts and Monuments*, and John Bakeless conjectures that he may have come across Jean Boucher's *Histoire tragique et mémorable de Pierre de Gaverston* (1588) when he was working on *The Massacre at Paris* (Bakeless 1942: II.88). Boucher's pamphlet, which is based on the late fourteenth- to early fifteenth-century chronicles of Thomas Walsingham, is an attack on Henry III's favourite, Epernon, intended as a warning to the French king to beware the fate of Edward II. Whether or not Marlowe knew this work, he certainly may have been prompted to write *Edward II*, as Julia Briggs has suggested, by the striking parallels between the two reigns (Briggs 1983: 264). Some details of Marlowe's play, as Briggs points out, seem more appropriate to Henry III's court than to Edward's; the former's liking for extravagant and sometimes transvestite entertainments may underlie Gaveston's proposals for a masque in the opening scene.

Whether Marlowe consulted any of the medieval chronicles, most of them in Latin, from which his immediate sources in turn derived their information is a matter of doubt. There seems to be no convincing evidence that he went directly to any of these earlier writers. Many of them remained in manuscript in his time, except for those few published by Caxton, and between 1567–74 under the auspices of Archbishop Matthew Parker. Bakeless further suggests that as a student at Cambridge Marlowe would have had access to copies of some of Walsingham's chronicles and of Geoffrey le Baker's *Vita et Mors Edwardi*

Secundi which had been bequeathed to the library of Corpus Christi college by the archbishop (Bakeless 1942: II. 23). R.I. Page (1977) has recently shown, however, that the college did not receive the Parker legacy until 1593, well after Marlowe's time there and much later than Bakeless had supposed. The *Vita et Mors* is an abbreviated extract from Baker's *Chronicon*, a work which provides Stow with much of his material, but the Corpus Christi manuscript does not contain the episode in which Edward is shaved with puddle water, something which Marlowe certainly does include.

There is one episode in the play which could have come from Walsingham's *Historia Anglicana*. When in Act II Scene 4 Edward 'posts away' with Gaveston, his unkindness to Isabella derives ultimately from Walsingham, who is the originator of the story that she begged the king to stay with her (in the play she asks only for a farewell). Fabyan, Holinshed, and Stow do not include this detail, but Boucher and Foxe both follow Walsingham's account. Foxe's version is as follows:

> And hearing there that Newcastle was taken, [Edward] taketh shipping and saileth from thence (notwithstanding the queen there, being great with child, with weeping tears and all instance desireth him to tarry with her, as safely he might) but he, nothing relenting to her, took Peter his compeer with him, and coasted over to the castle of Scarborough.
>
> (1570: I. 461)

Holinshed gives an account of Isabella's later grievances against the Spencers, but is curiously silent about Edward's neglect of her for Gaveston. Her former plight, which is a prominent feature of Marlowe's play, is described by most early chroniclers and is mentioned by Foxe and Stow.

Although Holinshed's chronicle did not provide Marlowe with all his material, it is still the most detailed single source of information available to him. Holinshed himself is not the only author of the huge work commonly referred to by his name, to which he contributed the histories of England and Scotland in the first edition of 1577; after his death in 1580, it was revised and extended by various contributors for a second edition in 1587. There are no substantial differences between the two editions as far as the reign of Edward II is concerned (although 1587 adds to Holinshed's moralizing comments, often attaching Latin tags to them) and no conclusive evidence to show which edition Marlowe used, but there are some indications that, as in Shakespeare's case, it may have been the later of the two. It has been noted by Josie S. Shumake (in an unpublished dissertation which is to date the most detailed study of Marlowe's sources for *Edward II*) that Marlowe uses the forms 'Penbroke' and 'Killingworth', as does the 1587 edition of

Holinshed, but that the 1577 edition has 'Pembroke' and 'Kenilworth' (Shumake 1984: clviii).

A similar question arises with regard to the two relevant editions of Stow. A second edition of his *Chronicles* of 1580 appeared in 1592 with a new title, *The Annals of England*, and Dr Shumake again suggests that Marlowe used the later edition, a point which has important conse-quences for the dating of the play (Shumake 1984: clxii–clxxvi). She bases her argument on two passages which were added in 1592. In the first, the barons are said to fear to raise war, 'yet the peril being weighed, they found that so long as Piers lived, there could be no peace in the kingdom, nor the king to abound in treasure, nor the queen to enjoy the king's true love' (see Text 2, p. 374). Certainly Marlowe's handling of the baronial revolt over Gaveston shows similarities to this succinct account but he could have found a very similar passage in Foxe (1570: I.461); both writers follow Walsingham closely here. The second passage carries more weight. In this, Stow spells out both meanings of the ambiguous letter sent to Edward's jailers, as well as the reason for the ambiguity, which is to escape blame. Marlowe's version is closer in both respects to the 1592 edition of Stow than to Holinshed, who gives only one of the possible meanings of the letter and does not explain the writer's motive. Again, the evidence cannot be regarded as conclusive, but if Marlowe did use the second edition – and it seems likely – then the play must have been completed after May 1592 (the date of Stow's epistle dedicatory). A late date for the play (which may well be Marlowe's last) is in any case indicated by the statement on the title page of the 1594 edition that 'it was publicly acted' by the Earl of Pembroke's Men, since no London productions by this company are recorded before the winter of 1592–3.

There are a number of other significant details for which Marlowe is indebted to Stow. For example, Stow says that Edward called Gaveston 'brother', as he does in the play: 'What call you this but private libelling / Against the earl of Cornwall and my brother?' (II. 2. 34–5). Marlowe also follows Stow (and Foxe) in placing Gaveston's marriage to one of the sisters of the Earl of Gloucester after his return from Ireland rather than before Edward's coronation, as in Holinshed. At this point in the play (II. 2) the younger Spencer and Baldock make their first appear-ance. Holinshed does not mention either of the Spencers (or Baldock) until after Gaveston's death, but Marlowe could have read in Stow about the participation of the elder Spencer at least in the Gaveston episode. Finally, Stow's dramatic account of Mortimer's arrest, which like that of Edward's last journey is based on eye-witness reports transmitted by Geoffrey le Baker, provides Marlowe with Isabella's line 'For my sake, sweet son, pity Mortimer' (V. 6. 55). (For all these passages in Stow, see Text 2, pp. 373–8.)

Marlowe's principal task in writing *Edward II* was to impose unity and coherence on a vast and formless mass of chronicle material covering the twenty years of Edward II's reign and the first three years of Edward III's, a process which involved some very severe pruning. Holinshed and Stow, by contrast, like their medieval predecessors, observe no principle of organization other than the chronological, and although they include character sketches of kings, again following medieval tradition, it cannot be said that they display much interest in character and motive. Faced with the problems of adapting chronicle history to the 'abstract and brief chronicles' of the stage, Marlowe, like Shakespeare, adopts methods which closely resemble those of humanist historians such as Sir Thomas More and Polydore Vergil, who do impose a coherent structure on their material and who are concerned with the analysis of motives.

Marlowe may well have profited by Shakespeare's pioneering example in the three plays of *Henry VI* (staged 1591-2); if *Edward II* was not completed until late in 1592, he would certainly have had the opportunity to do so. There are a number of similarities between the two reigns; Shakespeare too had to deal with a long, turbulent, and confused period of history, a weak king, a fierce queen, powerful and quarrelsome barons, and civil war, but with three plays at his disposal, the problem of organization was less acute. Some of his methods anticipate Marlowe's, for example, the disregard of chronology in the interests of speeding up the action or of bringing a character into prominence, as when the future Richard III is made to take part in the first battle of St Albans when in historical fact he was a child of three. Shakespeare's achievement in *3 Henry VI* is described by Bullough as 'an astonishing *tour de force* in its handling of sprawling, recalcitrant material' (Bullough 1960: III. 167): the same might well be said of *Edward II.*

Marlowe's solution is to focus the play on the personality of Edward and on his relationships with his favourites, his barons, and his wife. It is a highly selective approach, producing a series of dramatic confrontations, but which brings the past alive at the expense of strict chronology. Edward II's reign (1307-27) divides into three distinct phases. Briefly, the first is dominated by the struggle over Gaveston, ending with the latter's death (1312), the second by the ascendancy of the Earl of Lancaster, ending with a second baronial revolt and the king's victory at Boroughbridge (1322), and the third by the tyranny of the king's new favourites, the Despensers (the Spencers in the play), culminating in Isabella's and Mortimer's invasion (1326). In Marlowe's version, the baronial opposition to the Spencers is eclipsed by the more inherently dramatic Gaveston episode; the first two acts are devoted to it and the Spencers are drawn into it. The second phase of the reign, which with its series of military defeats and natural disasters, the episode of a pretender to the throne, and complicated shifts of allegiance among the barons, is not good dramatic material, virtually disappears. The historian William Stubbs's summing-up helps to explain why: 'The reign of Edward II possesses, in its more prominent events, an extraordinary amount of tragic interest; but outside of the dramatic crisises [sic] it may be described as exceedingly dreary. . . . This absence of inspiring topics renders certain parts of the reign simply unreadable' (Stubbs 1882–3: II. lxxv). Marlowe deals with the problem by eliminating the time-gap between the death of Gaveston and the battle of Boroughbridge, so that the latter seems like an immediate response to the former. Most sources, including Holinshed (see Text 1, p. 360), agree that the beheading of Lancaster was indeed an act of revenge for the beheading of Gaveston, but it was a long-delayed revenge, brought about by events that had nothing to do with Gaveston and much to do with the Spencers. Marlowe's account of the reign is admittedly in many ways unhistorical, but it may also be seen as an illustration of Sir Philip Sidney's argument in the *Apology for Poetry* that a poet may be better able than a historian to tell the esential truth about the past. Certainly at least one historian, Natalie Fryde, thinks so: 'Marlowe's play. . . has captured the essential atmosphere of the regime perhaps better than any historian has since been able to do' (Fryde 1979: 7).

The crucial change is the prominence given to Mortimer. There is not much information about him in the chronicles before the period of his virtual reign after the accession of Edward III, when his pride and misgovernment are condemned; Marlowe's characterization of him as in every way Edward's antithesis and as a man corrupted by power is almost entirely his own creation. From the beginning of the play Mortimer is portrayed as a leader of the baronial opposition to Edward, claiming in his very first speech that, together with his uncle and the Earl of Lancaster, he had sworn an oath to the dying Edward I never to allow Gaveston to return to the realm. In fact this oath was sworn by the earls of Warwick, Lincoln, and Pembroke; moreover, the Earl of Lancaster was a far more important figure than Mortimer during most of Edward's reign. In Holinshed Mortimer is not even mentioned until 1315, when he is heard of fighting against the invader Edward Bruce, brother of Robert Bruce, in Ireland. His uncle, the elder Mortimer, who also plays an unhistorically large part in the early scenes of the play, is said to have been captured in Scotland, but did not in fact take part in the Scottish wars. In Holinshed the younger Mortimer does not appear again until 1321, when he and his uncle are among the Marcher lords outraged by the Spencers' acquisition of the lands of Sir William de Braose (an event mentioned in passing in the play at III. 2. 53–5). The Mortimers did not fight at Boroughbridge, having prudently submitted earlier to the king (as Marlowe would have learned from Stow, not

Holinshed). In Marlowe's version of events it may perhaps seem anomalous that Mortimer should not be summarily executed with the other rebels after Boroughbridge, but it can also be argued that the inconsistency is only too typical of Edward's lack of political acumen.

Isabella is linked with Mortimer from her first entrance, when it is his perception of her distress that prompts her emotional outburst against Gaveston. In the chronicles, her liaison with Mortimer is not apparent before 1325. Foxe, following Walsingham, mentions rumours of her over-familiarity with Mortimer during her stay in France (Foxe 1570: I. 464), but Holinshed makes no explicit comment until Mortimer's arrest in 1330. Fabyan perhaps provides Marlowe with a precedent for the sequence of events in the play when he says that Mortimer on his escape went to join Isabella in France (Fabyan 1559: 180); in Holinshed and Stow Mortimer's escape precedes Isabella's embassy. There is a good deal of scope here for reading between the lines of history; Marlowe's version is a not implausible fiction.

The major problem Marlowe faced with Isabella is her transformation from the wronged and long-suffering wife to the pitiless and hypocritical 'she-wolf of France' who orders Edward's death. Marlowe's imaginative reconstruction of Edward's cruel treatment of her is a partial explanation, but the change is made more credible by the way in which he interprets her role as peacemaker. The invented sequence (I. 4. 225–73) in which she pleads for the repeal of Gaveston's banishment hints both at her collusion with Mortimer and that it is she who initiates the plan to kill Gaveston. Marlowe places her final break with Edward at Tynemouth (II. 4). In the account given by Foxe, quoted above, she is at her most pathetic here; only in Marlowe does she go on to betray Gaveston's whereabouts to the barons, resolve to return to France, and consider committing herself to Mortimer.

By such means Marlowe makes his fictional Isabella more consistent in her inconsistency than the Isabella of the chronicles. In Holinshed it is she and Adam de Orleton, Bishop of Hereford, who send the ambiguous letter ordering Edward's death. Marlowe makes Mortimer the sender of the letter, as does Foxe (1570: 469); the 'friend of ours' who is the actual author of it may be an allusion to Orleton, but the latter does not appear in the play. It is Isabella, though, who first proposes Edward's death, 'so it were not by my means' (V. 2. 45). At the end of the play Isabella is sent to the Tower by her own son to await trial on suspicion of complicity in Edward's death; in actual fact she got off much more lightly (see Text 1, p. 372). The alteration of history here illustrates Sidney's point that a poet, unlike a historian, may mete out the justice which real life often fails to deliver and so make men fear to be tyrants.

Marlowe's handling of the relationship between Isabella and Mortimer involves a good deal of invention; that between Edward and

Gaveston is more closely based on historical evidence. The play focuses on Gaveston in its opening lines, with the soliloquy in which he reads Edward's letter inviting him back to England and which at once makes clear the intense and homoerotic nature of the relationship. In this Marlowe builds on the implications of the chronicles, implications which have not always been admitted by later commentators, although Gaveston's latest biographer, J.S. Hamilton, says that 'there is no question that the King and his favorite were lovers' (Hamilton 1988: 16). Marlowe handles the matter with a mixture of sympathy and criticism not unlike that of the *Vita Edwardi Secundi*, whose anonymous author, a contemporary observer, compares Edward and Gaveston with David and Jonathan, with the proviso that David's love was not, like Edward's, excessive (Denholm-Young 1957: 15). Implicit in this comparison is the idea of mutual love, although no chronicler actually considers Gaveston's feelings; he is always portrayed as a venal opportunist. Marlowe, on the other hand, omits or plays down the usual references to Gaveston's thefts of the king's treasures, and in his version Gaveston does reciprocate Edward's love.

Marlowe's concentration on the relationships between Edward, Gaveston, Isabella, and Mortimer means that the Spencers play a less important part than they did in reality. The greed and ambition for which they were so bitterly resented and which led to the second baronial revolt and to Isabella's invasion are not emphasized, although the younger Spencer is presented at first as an unscrupulous upstart. This, though a vivid piece of satire, is not historically accurate; neither he nor Baldock was ever a dependant of the Gloucester household and the Spencers were members of the baronial order, albeit not of the first rank. The emotional expressions of affection for the king which all three make on the occasion of his capture at Neath show them in a very different light from that in which they usually appear in the chronicles. The younger Spencer and Baldock are universally condemned, but Holinshed's report of the former's refusal to eat and the latter's 'extreme grief of mind' after their capture at Neath could support Marlowe's interpretation. Geoffrey le Baker, followed by Stow, gives an unusually favourable picture of the elder Spencer as a worthy knight destroyed by his excessive love for his son and Marlowe may have remembered Stow's phrase 'in arms valiant' when in Act III Scene 2 he makes the elder Spencer enter armed with a truncheon, bringing soldiers to Edward's aid.

Marlowe has sometimes been accused of unduly narrowing the focus of his play by concentrating on the personal aspects of Edward's reign to the exclusion of larger political issues. It would be more accurate to say that the play is concerned with the intersection of the personal and the political, an approach which seems justified in view of J.S. Hamilton's comment that 'perhaps the one unifying theme of this disjointed reign is the important role of personalities in shaping events' (1988: 12). Holinshed ends his account with condemnation both of the king's bad judgement and of the barons' disloyalty. Marlowe's view is similar, but he focuses much more closely than does Holinshed on whether it can ever be right to depose a king.

The foreshortening of time in the play has the effect of accumulating the various failures and disasters of the reign, so that towards the end of Act II Scene 2, which brings to a head the barons' resentment against Gaveston, they can claim not only that the king's treasury has been drawn dry, but also that he suffers military reverses in France, Scotland, and Ireland, and in England at the hand of the Scots. Edward did make one unsuccessful expedition against the Scots, accompanied by Gaveston, but Bannockburn, which is in question here, and which occurred in 1314, was the more spectacular and humiliating defeat. It was not until after Bannockburn that the Scots invaded Ireland or raided almost as far south as York; the French did not seriously threaten Gascony until 1322. The effect of piling up these accusations is a massive indictment of Edward's folly and irresponsibility and appears to give the barons an overwhelming case.

Marlowe concentrates the central dilemma of the play in a character, that of the king's brother (in reality, step-brother), Edmund, Earl of Kent. In the chronicles too Kent changes sides and back again, but his shifts of allegiance are unexplained. The little we learn about him in Holinshed and Stow is not very creditable (see Text 1, p. 371); Marlowe's characterization, building perhaps on Foxe's description of him as one 'who loved the king and the realm' (Foxe 1570: I. 470), is far more sympathetic. As with Mortimer, the restructuring of the time scheme requires Kent to be an active participant in the Gaveston episode when in fact he appears much later in the story (in 1307 he was only six years old). He did not join Mortimer, as in the play, on the latter's escape from the Tower, nor was he ever exiled; his defection did not occur until some time after his diplomatic mission to France in 1324 to negotiate about the territories in dispute between the French and English kings. The chronicles tell us only that he accompanied Mortimer and Isabella in their invasion of 1326. In the play the important issues raised by Edward's reign are concentrated in the Gaveston episode, and it is at this stage that Kent's inner conflict begins to encapsulate them. His loyalty to his brother and his king underlines the temerity of the barons, but he sees that 'your love to Gaveston / Will be the ruin of the realm and you' (II. 2. 207–8). Marlowe's version of events requires his reluctant conversion to the barons' cause and subsequent banishment; in fact, he fought on his brother's side at Boroughbridge. The chroniclers also say nothing of

Kent's reasons for his second change of front; reading between the lines of history, Marlowe recreates Kent's anguished remorse at his betrayal of his brother and in doing so presents the idea of the sanctity of kingship in vividly personal terms.

It is in the scenes of Edward's capture, deposition and imprisonment that Marlowe most movingly puts the case for him. In contrast to the earlier part of the play, he slows down Holinshed's narrative here, building a detailed picture of Edward's suffering, but never losing sight of the folly that had caused it. At this point he takes a substantial passage from Stow describing Edward's last journey. Stow in turn had it from a writer of royalist sympathies, Geoffrey le Baker, who had heard it 'from William Bishop, who was in charge of Edward's guards, which he confessed and repented, hoping for divine mercy' (Baker 1889: 31). Stow leaves out the allusions in le Baker which, following the cult of the murdered king, present Edward as a Christlike martyr; Marlowe goes further, omitting the mock-crowning with hay, but the effect is still to increase sympathy for Edward. Conversely, Mortimer's hiring of the assassin, Lightborn, to kill Edward increases his guilt; Lightborn's very name, which as W.D. Briggs (1914: 193) and Harry Levin (1952: 101) have noted, may be taken from that of a devil in one of the Chester mystery plays, brings a suggestion of hell. No such character appears in any historical source; the local tradition (referred to by Laurie Lee in *Cider with Rosie*) that the leader of Edward's murderers was called Lightly possibly originates from the play.

Marlowe makes a significant alteration to his sources when he omits all reference to Edward's repentance (reported in detail by Fabyan, who includes the penitential verses Edward is supposed to have written in prison). In the deposition scene in Holinshed Edward is meek indeed, begging pardon for his offences and grateful for his son's election. The Edward of the play is by no means so tractable. He is not repentant, here or later; he does not know how he has erred. He still thinks of revenge, and he at first refuses to give up the crown. He is also allowed to make some pertinent objections; when the Bishop of Winchester claims that 'it is for England's good, / And princely Edward's right we crave the crown', Edward replies, rightly, 'No,'tis for Mortimer, not Edward's head' (V. 1. 38–40). The deposition as reported in Holinshed has at least an appearance of legality, conferred in part by Edward's voluntary resignation. Marlowe's handling of the scene undermines the rebels' case.

If Edward's last days are treated in harrowing detail, the three years between his death and that of Mortimer are virtually eliminated; there is certainly no time to mention the inglorious Scottish campaign for which Mortimer and Isabella were blamed. The effect of this foreshortening is to leave the impact of Edward's death undiminished and to make Edward III seem more decisive than he actually was at this stage of his reign. By the end of the play he is – in marked contrast to his father – an embodiment of justice and of filial piety, who exercises his power wisely and with the loyal support of his barons.

TEXT 1

The third volume of Chronicles . . .

Raphael Holinshed
(Second edition 1587)

[The text is taken from the copy in the British Library,
(shelfmark 629. n. 3). Passages marked * are additions first
appearing in the 1587 edition.]

Edward, the second of that name, the son of Edward the first, born
at Caernarfon in Wales, began his reign over England the seventh
day of July, in the year of our Lord 1307. . . . His father's corpse was
conveyed from Burgh upon Sands unto the abbey of Waltham,
there to remain, till things were ready for the burial, which was
appointed at Westminster.

Within three days after, when the Lord Treasurer, Walter de
Langton, Bishop of Coventry and Lichfield (through whose complaint Piers de Gaveston had been banished the land) was going
towards Westminster, to make preparation for the same burial,   10
he was upon commandment from the new king arrested, committed to prison, and after delivered to the hands of the said
Piers, being then returned again into the realm, who sent him
from castle to castle as a prisoner. His lands and tenements
[holdings] were seized to the king's use, but his moveables were
given to the foresaid Piers. . . .

But now concerning the demeanour of this new king, whose
disordered manners brought himself and many others unto destruction: we find that in the beginning of his government, though
he was of nature given to lightness, yet being restrained with the   20
prudent advertisements of certain of his counsellors, to the end he
might show some likelihood of good proof, he counterfeited a kind
of gravity, virtue, and modesty; but yet he could not throughly be so
bridled, but that forthwith he began to play divers wanton and light
parts, at the first indeed not outrageously, but by little and little,
and that covertly. For having revoked again into England his old
mate the said Piers de Gaveston, he received him into most high
favour, creating him Earl of Cornwall, and Lord of Man, his

351

principal secretary, and Lord Chamberlain of the realm, through whose company and society he was suddenly so corrupted that he burst out into most heinous vices; for then using the said Piers as a procurer of his disordered doings, he began to have his nobles in no regard, to set nothing by their instructions, and to take small heed unto the good government of the commonwealth, so that within a while, he gave himself to wantonness, passing his time in voluptuous pleasure, and riotous excess; and to help them forward in that kind of life, the foresaid Piers, who (as it may be thought, he had sworn to make the king to forget himself, and the state to the which he was called) furnished his court with companies of jesters, ruffians, flattering parasites, musicians, and other vile and naughty ribalds, that the king might spend both days and nights in jesting, playing, banqueting, and in such other filthy and dishonorable exercises, and moreover, desirous to advance those that were like to himself, he procured for them honorable offices. . . .

[At the parliament of 13 October, 1307] a marriage was concluded betwixt the Earl of Cornwall, Piers de Gaveston, and the daughter of Gilbert de Clare, Earl of Gloucester, which he had by his wife, the Countess Joan de Acre, the king's sister, which marriage was solemnized on All-hallows' Day next ensuing.

About the two and twentieth of January [1308], the king sailed over into France, and at Boulogne in Picardy on the four and twentieth day of January, he did homage to the French king [Philip IV] for his lands of Gascony and Ponthieu, and on the morrow after, married Isabel, the French king's daughter, and on the seventh of February he returned with her into England, and coming to London, was joyfully received of the citizens, and on the five and twentieth day of February . . . they were solemnly crowned by the Bishop of Winchester. . . .

(pp. 318–19)

The malice which the lords had conceived against the Earl of Cornwall still increased, the more indeed through the high bearing of him, being now advanced to honour. For being a goodly gentleman and a stout [brave], as would not once yield an inch to any of them, which worthily procured him great envy amongst the chiefest peers of all the realm, as Sir Heny Lacey, Earl of Lincoln, Sir Guy, Earl of Warwick, and Sir Aymer de Valence, Earl of Pembroke, the earls of Gloucester, Hereford, Arundel, and others, which upon such wrath and displeasure as they had conceived against him, thought it not convenient to suffer the same any longer, in hope that the king's mind might happily be altered into a better purpose, being not altogether converted into a venomous disposition, but so that it might be cured, if the corrupter thereof were once banished from him.

Hereupon they assembled together in the parliament time, at the New Temple, on Saturday next before the feast of St Dunstan [1308], and there ordained that the said Piers should abjure the realm, and depart the same on the morrow after the Nativity of St John Baptist at the furthest, and not to return into the same again at any time then after to come. To this ordinance the king (although against his will), because he saw himself and the realm in danger, gave his consent, and made his letters patents to the said earls and lords, to witness the same. . . . The Archbishop of Canterbury . . . did pronounce the said Piers accursed, if he tarried within the realm longer than the appointed time, and likewise all those that should aid, help, or maintain him, as also if he should at any time hereafter return again into the land. To conclude, this matter was so followed, that at length he was constrained to withdraw himself to Bristol, and so by sea as a banished man to sail into Ireland.

The king being sore offended herewith, as he that favoured the earl more than that he could be without his company, threatened the lords to be revenged for this displeasure, and ceased not to send into Ireland unto Piers, comforting him both with friendly messages and rich presents, and as it were to show that he meant to retain him still in his favour, he made him ruler of Ireland as his deputy there. A wonderful matter that the king should be so enchanted with the said earl, and so addict himself, or rather fix his heart upon a man of such a corrupt humour, against whom the heads of the noblest houses in the land were bent to devise his overthrow. . . .

The lords, perceiving the king's affection, and that the treasure was spent as lavishly as before, thought with themselves that it might be that the king would both amend his past trade of life, and that Piers being restored home, would rather advise him thereto, than follow his old manners, considering that it might be well perceived, that if he continued in the encouraging of the king to lewdness, as in times past he had done, he could not think but that the lords would be ready to correct him, as by proof he had now tried their meanings to be no less. Hereupon, to retain amity, as was thought on both sides, Piers by consent of the lords was restored home again [1309], the king meeting him at Chester, to his great comfort and rejoicing for the time, although the malice of the lords was such, that such joy lasted not long. . . .

The king indeed was lewdly led, for after that the Earl of Cornwall was returned into England, he showed himself no changeling (as writers do affirm), but through support of the king's favour, bare himself so high in his doings, which were without all good order, that he seemed to disdain all the peers and barons of the realm. And after the old sort he provoked the king to all naughty [evil] rule and riotous demeanour, and having the custody of the king's jewels and treasure, he took out of the king's jewel-house a table and a pair of trestles of gold. . . .

(pp. 319–20)

[Gaveston accompanies the king on an unsuccessful expedition against the Scots.]

In this fifth year of the king's reign [1311]. . . Henry Lacy, Earl 120 of Lincoln . . . departed this life. . . . Lying on his death-bed, he requested (as was reported) Thomas, Earl of Lancaster, who had married his daughter, that in any wise he should stand with the other lords in defence of the commonwealth, and to maintain his quarrel against the Earl of Cornwall, which request Earl Thomas faithfully accomplished; for by the pursuit of him, and of the Earl of Warwick chiefly, the said Earl of Cornwall was at length taken and beheaded (as after shall appear). Some write that King Edward the first upon his death-bed charged the earls of Lincoln, Warwick, and Pembroke, to foresee that the foresaid Piers returned not again 130 into England, lest by his evil example he might induce his son the prince to lewdness, as before he had already done. . . .

The lords perceiving the mischief that daily followed and in-creased by that naughty [wicked] man, as they took it, the Earl of Cornwall, assembled at Lincoln, and there took counsel together, and concluded eftsoons [again] to banish him out of the realm, and so thereupon shortly after. . . he was exiled into Flanders, sore against the king's will and pleasure, who made such account of him, that (as appeared) he could not be quiet in mind without his company, and therefore about Candlemas [2 February, 1312] he 140 eftsoons revoked him home.

But he being nothing at all amended of those his evil manners, rather demeaned himself worse than before he had done, namely [especially] towards the lords, against whom using reproachful speech, he called the Earl of Gloucester, 'bastard', the Earl of Lincoln lately deceased, 'bursten belly', the Earl of Warwick, 'the black hound of Arden', and the Earl of Lancaster, 'churl'. Such lords and other more that were thus abused at this Earl of Cornwall's hands, determined to be revenged upon him, and to dispatch the realm of such a wicked person; and thereupon assembling their 150 powers together, came towards Newcastle, whither the king from York was removed, and now hearing of their approach, he got him to Tynemouth, where the queen lay, and understanding there that Newcastle was taken by the lords, he leaving the queen behind him, took shipping, and sailed from thence with his dearly beloved familiar, the Earl of Cornwall, unto Scarborough, where he left him in the castle, and rode himself towards Warwick. The lords hearing where the Earl of Cornwall was, made thither with all speed, and besieging the castle, at length constrained their enemy to yield himself into their hands, requiring no other condition, but that he might come to the king's presence to talk with him. 160

The king, hearing that his best beloved familiar was thus apprehended, sent to the lords, requiring them to spare his life, and that he might be brought to his presence, promising withal that he would see them fully satisfied in all their requests against him. Whereupon, the Earl of Pembroke persuaded with the barons to grant to the king's desire, undertaking upon forfeiture of all that he had to bring him to the king and back again to them, in such state and condition as he received him. When the barons had consented to his motion, he took the Earl of Cornwall with him to 170 bring him where the king lay, and coming to Deddingon [near Oxford], left him there in safe keeping with his servants, whilst he for one night went to visit his wife, lying not far from thence.

The same night it chanced that Guy, Earl of Warwick, came to the very place where the Earl of Cornwall was left, and taking him from his keepers, brought him unto Warwick, where incontinently [immediately] it was thought best to put him to death, but that some, doubting the king's displeasure, advised the residue to stay; and so they did, till at length an ancient grave man amongst them exhorted them to use the occasion now offered, and not to let slip 180 the mean to deliver the realm of such a dangerous person, that had wrought so much mischief, and might turn them all to such peril, as afterwards they should not be able to avoid, nor find shift how to remedy it. And thus persuaded by his words, they caused him straightways to be brought forth to a place called Blacklow, otherwise named by most writers Gaversley Heath, where he had his head smitten from his shoulders, the twentieth day of June, being Tuesday. *A just reward for so scornful and contemptuous a merchant [fellow], as in respect of himself (because he was in the prince's favour) esteemed the nobles of the land as men of such 190 inferiority, as that in comparison of him they deserved no little jot or mite of honour. . . . *

When the king had knowledge hereof, he was wonderfully displeased with those lords that had thus put the said earl unto death, making his vow that he would see his death revenged, so that the rancour which before was kindled betwixt the king and those lords began now to blaze abroad, and spread so far, that the king ever sought occasion how to work them displeasure. This year, the thirteenth of November, the king's eldest son named Edward (which succeeded his father in the kingdom by the name of Edward the third) was born at Windsor. King Edward now after that the foresaid Piers Gaveston, the Earl of Cornwall, was dead, nothing reformed his manners, but as one that detested the counsel and admonition of his nobles, chose such to be about him, and to be of his privy council, which were known to be men of corrupt and most wicked living (as the writers of that age report); amongst these were two of the Spencers, Hugh the father, and Hugh the son, which were notable instruments to bring him unto the liking of all kind of naughty [wicked] and evil rule.

By the counsel therefore of these Spencers he was wholly led and governed, wherewith many were much offended, but namely Robert, the Archbishop of Canterbury, who foresaw what mischief was like to ensue, and therefore to provide some remedy in time, he procured that a parliament was called at London, in the which many good ordinances and statutes were devised and established, to oppress the riots, misgovernance and other mischiefs which as then were used; and to keep those ordinances, the king first, and after his lords, received a solemn oath, that in no wise neither he nor they should break them. By this means was the state of the realm newly restored and new counsellors placed about the king. But he, neither regarding what he had sworn, neither weighing the force of an oath, observed afterwards none of those things, which by his oath he had bound himself to observe. And no marvel, for surely (as it should seem by report of Thomas de la More), the lords wrested [coerced] him too much, and beyond the bounds of reason, causing him to receive to be about him whom it pleased them to appoint. For the younger Spencer, who in place of the Earl of Cornwall was ordained to be his chamberlain, it was known to them well enough that the king bare no good will at all to him at the first, though afterwards through the prudent policy and diligent industry of the man, he quickly crept into his favour, and that further than those that preferred him could have wished. . . .

(pp. 320–1)

In this mean time, Robert Bruce recovered the most part of all Scotland, winning out of the Englishmens' hands such castles as they held within Scotland, chasing all the soldiers which lay there in garrison out of the country, and subduing such of the Scots as held on the English part.

[1314] King Edward to be revenged hereof, with a mighty army bravely furnished, and gorgeously apparelled, more seemly for a triumph than meet to encounter with the cruel enemy in the field,

entered Scotland, in purpose specially to rescue the castle of
Stirling, as then besieged by the Scottishmen. But at his approaching near to the same, Robert Bruce was ready with his power to give
him battle. In the which King Edward, nothing doubtful of loss, had
so unwisely ordered his people, and confounded their ranks, that
even at the first joining, they were not only beaten down and
overthrown by those that coped with them at hand, but also were
wounded with shot afar off by those their enemies which stood
behind to succour their fellows when need required, so that in the   250
end the Englishmen fled to save their lives, and were chased and
slain by the Scots in great number.

The king escaped with a few about him, in great danger to have
been either taken or slain. Many were drowned in a little river
called Bannocksburn, near to the which the battle was foughten.
There were slain of noblemen. . . to the number of forty-two, and of
knights and baronets to the number of sixty-seven. There were slain
of all sorts upon the English part that day about ten thousand men,
over and beside the prisoners that were taken. . . .

(p.322)

[An account follows of a long and dreary period in which the Scots
make frequent incursions into England, 'doing much mischief with
fire and sword'; an attempt by the English in 1319 to counter these
attacks is easily overcome at Myton-on-Swale, near York. All this is
summed up in two lines in the play, 'Unto the walls of York the Scots
made road, / And unresisted drave away rich spoils' (II. 2. 164–5). The
Scots also invade Ireland, led by Robert Bruce's brother, Edward; the
first mention of Roger Mortimer occurs in this connection, when in
1315 he is defeated by Edward Bruce at Kenlis (i.e. Kells) in Co. Meath.
These years (1315–19) are also marked by bad harvests, cattle disease
and high prices; the poor are forced to eat the flesh of dogs and
horses, and many die. In 1318 John Poidras or Ponderham claims to be
Edward I's true heir.]

Thus all the king's exploits by one means or other quailed, and   260
came but to evil success, so that the English nation began to grow in
contempt by the unfortunate government of the prince, the which
as one out of the right way, rashly and with no good advisement
ordered his doings, which thing so grieved the noblemen of the
realm, that they studied day and night by what means they might
procure him to look better to his office and duty, which they judged
might well be brought to pass, his nature being not altogether evil,
if they might find shift to remove from him the two Spencers, Hugh
the father, and Hugh the son, who were gotten into such favour
with him, that they only did all things, and without them nothing   270

was done, so that they were now had in as great hatred and indignation. . . both of the lords and commons, as ever in times past was Piers de Gaveston, the late Earl of Cornwall. But the lords minded not so much the destruction of these Spencers, but that the king meant as much their advancement, so that Hugh the son was made High Chamberlain of England, contrary to the mind of all the noblemen, by reason whereof he bare himself so haughty and proud, that no lord within the land might gainsay that which in his conceit seemed good. . . .

About this season [1321], the lord William de Bruce [Braose], 280 that in the marches of Wales enjoyed divers fair possessions to him descended from his ancestors, but through want of good government was run behindhand, offered to sell a certain portion of his lands called Gower's land, lying in the marches there, unto divers noblemen that had their lands adjoining to the same, as to the Earl of Hereford, and to the two lords Mortimers, the uncle and nephew. . . . But at length (as unhap would) Hugh Spencer the younger, Lord Chamberlain, coveting that land because it lay near on each side to other lands that he had in those parts, found such means through the king's furtherance and help, that he went away 290 with the purchase, to the great displeasure of the other lords that had been in hand to buy it.

Hereby such heartburning rose against the Spencers, that upon complaint made by the Earl of Hereford unto the Earl of Lancaster of their presumptuous dealing, by ruling all things about the king as seemed best to their likings, it was thought expedient by the said earls that some remedy in time (if it were possible) should be provided. Whereupon the said earls. . . [with other lords, including the two Mortimers] assembling together at Sherburn in Elmdon [Elmet], swore each of them to stand by other, till they had 300 amended the state of the realm. But yet, notwithstanding this their oath, the most part of them afterwards forsaking the enterprise, submitted themselves to the king. . . .

(p. 325)

[The disaffected barons attack a number of castles and manors belonging to the Spencers.]

Finally, after they had satisfied their desires in such riotous sort, they raised the people, and constrained them to swear to be of their accord, and so came forward with the like force towards the parliament that was summoned to be holden at London three weeks after midsummer. At their coming to St Albans, they sent the bishops of London, Salisbury, Ely, Hereford, and Chichester to the king with their humble suit in outward appearance, though in 310 effect and very deed more presumptuous than was requisite. Their chief request was that it might please his highness to put from him the Spencers, whose counsel they knew to be greatly against his honour, and hereof not to fail if he tendered [valued] the quiet of his realm. . . .

(p. 326)

[The king is forced to submit to this demand, but the Spencers are not in exile for long; in the play the king is petitioned to 'remove' the Spencers (III. 2. 156–71), but they are not exiled at all. Spurred by the episode in which the queen, 'who had ever sought to procure peace, love, and concord betwixt the king and his lords', is denied entry to Leeds castle in Kent, Edward, with the support of his brothers and the barons who had remained loyal to him, raises 'a mighty army' to besiege the castle and to pursue the rebels.]

. . . about the first Sunday in Lent [1322], he [Edward] set forward towards his enemies, having with him to the number of sixteen hundred men of arms on horseback, and footmen innumerable. . . . At his coming to a little village called Caldwell, he sent afore him certain bands to Burton-upon-Trent, where he meant to have 320 lodged; but the earls of Lancaster and Hereford . . . and many other, being gotten thither before, kept the bridge. . . .

The earls of Richmond and Pembroke were appointed to pass by a ford which they had got knowledge of, with three hundred horsemen in complete armour, and the king with his brother the Earl of Kent should follow them, with the residue of the army. . . . But after that the earls of Lancaster and Hereford with their complices heard that the king was passed with his army, they came forth with their people into the fields, and put them in order of battle; but perceiving the great puissance which the king had there 330 ready to encounter them, without more ado they fled, setting fire on the town. . . .

. . . the earls of Lancaster and Hereford, with the other barons, being come unto Pomfret [Pontefract], fell to council in the Friars there, and finally, after much debating of the matter. . . it was concluded that they should go to the castle of Dunstan- burgh, and there remain till they might purchase the king's pardon, sith [since] their enterprise thus quailed under their hands; and herewith setting forward that way forth, they came to Boroughbridge, where Sir Andrew de Harcla with the power of 340 the Countess of Cumberland and Westmoreland had forelaid the passage [lay in wait], and there on a Tuesday, being the 16 of March, he setting upon the barons, in the end discomfited them, and chased their people.

[In this fight, the Earl of Hereford is killed and the Earl of Lancaster is taken prisoner.]

Upon the one and twentieth of March, came Sir Andrew de Harcla unto Pomfret, bringing with him the Earl of Lancaster and other prisoners. . . . On the morrow after, being Monday, the two and twentieth of March, he [Lancaster]. . . was arraigned of high treason, for that he had raised war against the king and . . . was thereupon adjudged to die, according to the law in such cases provided, that is,   350
to be drawn, hanged, and headed. But because he was the queen's uncle, and son to the king's uncle, he was pardoned of all save heading, and so accordingly thereunto suffered at Pomfret the two and twentieth of March.

Thus the king seemed to be revenged of the displeasure done to him by the Earl of Lancaster, for the beheading of Piers de Gaveston, Earl of Cornwall, whom he so dearly loved, and because the Earl of Lancaster was the chief occasioner of his death, the king never loved him entirely after. *So that here is verified the censure of the Scripture expressed by the wisdom of Solomon, that the anger   360
and displeasure of the king is as the roaring of a lion, and his revenge inevitable. . . .*

(pp. 329–31)

At this time also, master Robert Baldock, a man evil beloved in the realm, was made Lord Chancellor of England. This Robert Baldock, and one Simon Reading, were great favourers of the Spencers, and so likewise was the Earl of Arundel, whereby it may be thought, that the Spencers did help to advance them into the king's favour, so that they bare no small rule in the realm, during the time that the same Spencers continued in prosperity, which for the term of five years after that the foresaid barons . . . were brought to confusion,   370
did wonderfully increase, and the queen for that she gave good and faithful counsel, was nothing regarded, but by the Spencers' means clearly worn out of the king's favour. . . .

Here is to be noted, that during the time whilst the civil war was in hand betwixt King Edward and his barons, the Scots and Frenchmen were not idle, for the Scots wasted and destroyed the country of the bishopric of Durham . . . and the Frenchmen made roads [inroads] and incursions into the borders of Guyenne, alleging that they did it upon good and sufficient occasion, for that King Edward had not done his homage unto the King of France, as   380
he ought to have done, for the duchy of Aquitaine, and the county of Ponthieu. . . .

(p. 332)

[In 1323, after more raids and humiliating defeats inflicted on the English, a thirteen-year truce is negotiated with the Scots.]

About the same time, the lord Roger Mortimer of Wigmore, giving his keepers a drink that brought them into a sound and heavy sleep, escaped out of the Tower of London where he was prisoner. This escape of the lord Mortimer greatly troubled the king, so that immediately upon the first news, he wrote to all the sheriffs of the realm that if he chanced to come within their rooms [domains], they should cause hue and cry to be raised, so as he might be stayed and arrested; but he made such shift, that he got over into France, 390 where he was received by a lord of Picardy. . . .

(p. 334)

[The new French king, Charles IV, on Edward's continued refusal to do homage for his lands in France, 'seized into his hands divers towns and castles in Aquitaine'. (Cf. III. 2. 60–4, where Marlowe substitutes Normandy for Aquitaine.) Edmund, Earl of Kent, is sent to France as ambassador, but having failed to 'light upon any good conclusion', leads the resistance to the incursion of the French king's uncle, Charles of Valois. More ambassadors are sent and a peace treaty concluded.]

[1325] Finally, it was thought good that the queen should go over to her brother, the French king, to confirm that treaty of peace upon some reasonable conditions . . . and . . . she being the mediatrix, it was finally accorded that the King of England should give to his eldest son the duchy of Aquitaine and the county of Ponthieu, and that the French king receiving homage of him for the same, he should restore into his hands the said county, and the lands in Guyenne, for the which they were at variance. . . .

Upon the covenants the French king wrote his letters patents 400 into England, and other letters also of safe conduct, as well for the son as for the king himself, if it should please him to come over himself in person. Upon which choice great deliberation was had . . . but the Earl of Winchester [i.e. the elder Spencer] and his son, the Lord Chamberlain, that neither durst go over themselves with the king, nor abide at home in his absence . . . at length prevailed so, that it was fully determined that the king's eldest son, Edward, should go over, which turned to their destruction, as it appeared afterward. . . .

(p. 336)

In the beginning of the next spring, King Edward sent into France 410 unto his wife and son, commanding them, now that they had made an end of their business, to return home with all convenient speed. The queen receiving the message from her husband, whether it was

361

so that she was stayed by her brother, unto whom belike she had complained after what manner she was used at her husband's hands, being had in no regard with him, or for that she had no mind to return home, because she was loth to see all things ordered out of frame by the counsel of the Spencers, whereof to hear she was weary, or whether (as the manner of women is) she was long about to prepare herself forward, she slacked all the summer, and sent letters ever to excuse her tarriance. But yet because she would not run in any suspicion with her husband, she sent divers of her folks before her into England by soft [leisurely] journeys. *A lamentable case, that such division should be between a king and his queen, being lawfully married, and having issue of their bodies . . . but (alas) what will not a woman be drawn and allured unto, if by evil counsel she be once assaulted? And what will she leave undone, though never so inconvenient to those that should be most dear unto her, so her own fancy and will be satisfied? And how hardly is she revoked from proceeding in an evil action, if she have once taken a taste of the same?. . .*

But to the purpose. King Edward, not a little offended with King Charles, by whose means he knew that the woman thus lingered abroad, he procured Pope John to write his letters unto the French king, admonishing him to send home his sister and her son unto her husband. But when this nothing availed, a proclamation was made in the month of December [1325]. . . that if the queen and her son entered not the land by the octave of the Epiphany next ensuing in peaceable wise, they should be taken for enemies to the realm and crown of England. Here authors vary, for some write that upon knowledge had of this proclamation, the queen determined to return into England forthwith, that she might be reconciled to her husband.

Others write, and that more truly, how she being highly displeased, both with the Spencers and the king her husband, that suffered himself to be misled by their counsels, did appoint indeed to return into England, not to be reconciled, but to stir the people to some rebellion, whereby she might revenge her manifold injuries, which (as the proof of the thing showed) seemeth to be most true, for she being a wise woman, and considering that sith [since] the Spencers had excluded, put out, and removed all good men, from and besides [away from] the king's counsel, and placed in their rooms such of their clients, servants and friends as pleased them, she might well think that there was small hope to be had in her husband, who heard no man but the said Spencers, which she knew hated her deadly. Whereupon, after that the term prefixed in the proclamation was expired, the king caused to be seized into his

420

430

440

450

hands all such lands as belonged either to his son, or to his wife. . . .

(pp. 336–7)

But in the meantime, Walter Stapledon, Bishop of Exeter, which 460 hitherto had remained with the queen in France, stole now from her, and got over into England, opening to the king all the counsel and whole mind of the queen. . . .

The king of England stood not only in doubt of the Frenchmen, but more of his own people that remained in France, lest they through help of the French should invade the land, and therefore he commanded the havens and ports to be surely watched, lest some sudden invasion might happily [perhaps] be attempted, for it was well understood, that the queen meant not to return, till she might bring with her the lord Mortimer, and the other banished 470 men, who in no wise could obtain any favour at the king's hands, so long as the Spencers bare rule. . . .

King Edward, understanding all the queen's drift, at length sought the French king's favour, and did so much by letters and promise of bribes with him and his council, that Queen Isabel was destitute in manner of all help there, so that she was glad to withdraw into Hainault, by the comfort of John, the lord Beaumont, the Earl of Hainault his brother. . . .

The Spencers (some write) procured her banishment out of France. . . . Also I find that the Spencers delivered five barrels of 480 silver, the sum amounting unto five thousand marks, unto one Arnold of Spain, a broker, appointing him to convey it over into France, to bestow it upon such friends as they had there of the French king's counsel, by whose means the king of France did banish his sister out of his realm. But this money was met with upon the sea by certain Zealanders [Dutchmen] and taken, together with the said Arnold, and presented to the Earl of Hainault. . . .

Sir John de Hainault, lord Beaumont, was appointed with certain bands of men of arms, to the number of four hundred or five hundred, to pass over with the said queen and her son into 490 England, and so thereupon began to make his purveyance for that journey, which thing when it came to the knowledge of King Edward and the Spencers, they caused musters to be taken through the realm, and ordained beacons to be set up, kept and watched . . . that the same upon occasion of the enemy's arrival might be set on fire, to warn the countries adjoining to assemble and resist them.

But Queen Isabel and her son, with such others as were with her in Hainault, stayed not their journey for doubt of all their adversaries' provision, but immediately after that they had once

made their purveyances, and were ready to depart, they took the 500
sea, namely the queen, her son, Edmund of Woodstock, Earl of
Kent, Sir John de Hainault aforesaid, and the lord Roger Mortimer
of Wigmore, a man of good experience in the wars, and divers
others, having with them a small company of Englishmen, with a
crew of Hainaulters and Almains [Germans], to the number of
2,757 armed men, the which sailing forth towards England, landed
at length in Suffolk, at an haven called Orwell besides Harwich, the
twenty fifth day of September [1326]. Immediately after that the
queen and her son were come to land, it was wonder to see how
fast the people resorted unto them. . . . 510

(p. 337)

[The king, having failed to gain the support of the citizens of London,
'departed towards the marches of Wales, there to raise an army against
the queen', and issues a proclamation in which he sets a thousand
marks on Mortimer's head. The queen also issues a proclamation
willing all men to hope for peace, the Spencers and Baldock only
excepted, and setting a price of two thousand pounds on Hugh Spencer
the younger's head.]

Then, shortly after, the queen with her son making towards
London, wrote a letter to the mayor and the citizens, requiring to
have assistance for the putting down of the Spencers, not only
known enemies of theirs, but also common enemies to all the realm
of England. To this letter no answer at the first was made, wherefore another was sent . . . containing in effect, that the cause of their
landing and entering into the realm at that time, was only for the
honour of the king and wealth of the realm, meaning hurt to no
manner of person, but to the Spencers. . . .

[The king retreats to Bristol, which he entrusts to the elder Spencer.]

And with the earls of Gloucester [the younger Spencer] and 520
Arundel, and the Lord Chancellor, Sir Robert Baldock, he sailed
over into Wales, there to raise a power of Welshmen, in defence of
himself against the queen and her adherents, which he had good
hope to find amongst the Welshmen, because he had ever used
them gently, and showed no rigour towards them for their riotous
misgovernance.

[The queen follows Edward towards Wales and comes to Oxford.]

Here Adam de Orleton, the Bishop of Hereford, which lately
before had been sore fined by the king, for that he was accused to
stir the people to rebellion, and to aid the barons . . . made a pithy
oration to the army, declaring that the queen and her son were 530

returned only into England to the intent to persecute the Spencers, and reform the state of the realm. . . .

(pp. 338–9)

[The queen reaches Bristol, where the elder Spencer is taken and hanged.]

The king with the Earl of Gloucester and the Lord Chancellor taking the sea, meant to have gone either into the Isle of Lundy, or else into Ireland, but being tossed with contrary winds for the space of a week together, at length he landed in Glamorganshire, and got him to the abbey and castle of Neath, there secretly remaining upon trust of the Welshmens' promises. . . .

But now touching the king, whilst he was thus abroad, and no man wist where he was become, proclamations were made in the queen's army daily, in the which he was summoned to return, and to take the rule of the realm into his hands, if he would be conformable to the minds of his true liegemen; but when he appeared not, the lords of the land assembled in council at Hereford, whither the queen was come from Bristol, and there was the lord Edward, Prince of Wales and Duke of Aquitaine, made Warden of England by common decree, unto whom all men, as to the Lord Warden of the realm, made fealty, in receiving an oath of allegiance to be faithful and loyal to him. . . .

The queen remained about a month's space at Hereford, and in the meanwhile sent the lord Henry, Earl of Leicester, and the lord William la Zouch, and one Rice [Rhys] ap Howell . . . into Wales, to see if they might find means to apprehend the king by help of their acquaintance in those parts. . . . They used such diligence in that charge, that finally with large gifts bestowed on the Welshmen, they came to understand where the king was, and so on the day of St Edmund the Archbishop, being the sixteenth of November, they took him in the monastery of Neath . . . together with Hugh Spencer the son, called Earl of Gloucester, the Lord Chancellor, Robert de Baldock, and Simon de Reading, the king's marshal. . . .

The king was delivered to the Earl of Leicester, who conveyed him by Monmouth and Ledbury to Killingworth [Kenilworth] castle, where he remained the whole winter. The Earl of Gloucester, the Lord Chancellor, and Simon de Reading were brought to Hereford, and there presented to the queen, where on the four and twentieth of November, the said earl was drawn and hanged on a pair of gallows of fifty foot in height. . . .

On the same day was Simon de Reading drawn and hanged on the same gallows. . . . The common fame went, that after this Hugh Spencer the son was taken, he would receive no sustenance,

540

550

560

570

wherefore he was the sooner put to death. . . . John, Earl of Arundel was taken on St Hugh's Day, in the parts about Shrewsbury, and the same day sevennight before the execution of the Earl of Gloucester, Hugh Spencer the younger . . . the said earl . . . [with two others] were put to death at Hereford, by procurement of the lord Mortimer of Wigmore, that hated them extremely, by reason whereof they were not like to speed much better, for what he willed the same was done, and without him the queen in all these matters did nothing. . . .

(pp. 339–40)

[Baldock is taken to Newgate 'where shortly after through inward sorrow and extreme grief of mind he ended his life'.]

After Christmas, the queen with her son and such lords as 580 were then with them, removed to London, where at their coming thither, which was before the feast of the Epiphany [1327], they were received with great joy, triumph, and large gifts, and so brought to Westminster, where the morrow after the same feast, the parliament which beforehand had been summoned began, in which it was concluded and fully agreed by all the states (for none durst speak to the contrary) that for divers articles which were put up against the king, he was not worthy longer to reign, and therefore should be deposed, and withal they willed to have his son Edward, Duke of Aquitaine, to reign in his place. This ordinance was openly 590 pronounced in the great hall at Westminster by one of the lords . . . to the which all the people consented. The Archbishop of Canterbury, taking his theme *Vox populi, vox Dei*, made a sermon exhorting the people to pray to God to bestow of His grace upon the new king. . . . But the Duke of Aquitaine, when he perceived that his mother took the matter heavily in appearance, for that her husband should be thus deprived of the crown, he protested that he would never take it on him without his father's consent, and so thereupon it was concluded that certain solemn messengers should go to Killingworth to move the king to make resignation of his 600 crown and title of the kingdom unto his son. . . .

The bishops of Winchester and Lincoln went before, and coming to Killingworth, associated with them the Earl of Leicester . . . that had the king in keeping. And having secret conference with the king, they sought to frame his mind, so as he might be contented to resign the crown to his son, bearing him in hand [pretending], that if he refused so to do, the people in respect of the evil will which they had conceived against him, would not fail but proceed to the election of some other that should happily not touch him in lineage. And sith [since] this was the only mean to bring the land in 610 quiet, they willed him to consider how much he was bound in conscience to take that way that should be so beneficial to the whole realm.

The king, being sore troubled to hear such displeasant news, was brought into a marvellous agony; but in the end, for the quiet of the realm, and doubt of further danger to himself, he determined to follow their advice, and so when the other commissioners were come, and that the Bishop of Hereford had declared the cause wherefore they were sent, the king in presence of them all, notwithstanding his outward countenance discovered how much it inwardly grieved him, yet after he was come to himself, he answered that he knew that he was fallen into this misery through his own offences, and therefore he was contented patiently to suffer it, but yet it could not, he said, but grieve him, that he had in such wise run into the hatred of all his people; notwithstanding, he gave the lords most hearty thanks that they had so forgotten their received injuries, and ceased not to bear so much good will towards his son Edward, as to wish that he might reign over them. Therefore to satisfy them, sith [since] otherwise it might not be, he utterly renounced his right to the kingdom, and to the whole administration thereof. And lastly he besought the lords now in his misery to forgive him such offences as he had committed against them.
* Ah, lamentable ruin from royalty to miserable calamity, procured by them chiefly that should have been the pillars of the king's estate, and not the hooked engines to pull him down from his throne! So that here we see it verified by trial that

> . . . *miser atque infelix est etiam rex,*
> *Nec quenquam (mihi crede) facit diadema beatum.*

['Wretched and unfortunate indeed is a king, / For the crown (believe me) makes no one happy.']*

The ambassadors with this answer returning to London, declared the same unto all the states, in order as they had received it, whereupon great joy was made of all men, to consider that they might now by course of law proceed to the choosing of a new king. And so thereupon the nine and twentieth day of January in session of parliament then at Westminster assembled, was the third King Edward, son to King Edward the second, chosen and elected king of England, by the authority of the same parliament. . . . On the same day Sir William Trussell, procurator for the whole parliament, did renounce the old king in name of the whole parliament, with all homages and fealties due to him. . . .

(pp. 340–1)

367

But now to make an end of the life, as well as of the reign of King Edward the second, I find that after he was deposed of his kingly honour and title, he remained for a time at Killingworth, in custody of the Earl of Leicester. But within a while the queen was informed by the Bishop of Hereford (whose hatred towards him had no end) that the Earl of Leicester favoured her husband too much, and more than stood [accorded] with the surety of her son's state, whereupon he was appointed to the keeping of two other lords, Thomas Berkeley and John Maltravers, who receiving him of the 660 Earl of Leicester, the third of April, conveyed him from Killingworth unto the castle of Berkeley. . . .

But forsomuch as the lord Berkeley used him more courteously than his adversaries wished him to do, he was discharged of that office, and Sir Thomas Gurney appointed in his stead, who together with the lord Maltravers conveyed him secretly (for fear lest he should be taken from them by force) from one strong place to another, as to the castle of Corfe, and such like, still removing with him in the night season, till at length they thought it should not be known whither they had conveyed him. And so at length they 670 brought him back again in secret manner unto the castle of Berkeley, where whilst he remained (as some write) the queen would send unto him courteous and loving letters with apparel and other such things, but she would not once come near to visit him, bearing him in hand [pretending] that she durst not, for fear of the people's displeasure, who hated him so extremely. *Howbeit, she with the rest of her confederates had no doubt laid the plot of their device for his dispatch, though by painted words she pretended a kind of remorse to him in this his distress, and would seem to be faultless in the sight of the world. . . . * 680

But as he thus continued in prison, closely kept, so that none of his friends might have access unto him, as in such cases it often happeneth, when men be in misery, some will ever pity their state, there were divers of the nobility (of whom the Earl of Kent was chief) began to devise means by secret conference had together, how they might restore him to liberty, discommending greatly both Queen Isabel and such other as were appointed governors to the young king, for his father's strict imprisonment. The queen and other the governors understanding this conspiracy of the Earl of Kent, and of his brother, durst not yet in that new and green world 690 go about to punish it, but rather thought good to take away from them the occasion of accomplishing their purpose. And hereupon the queen and the Bishop of Hereford wrote sharp letters unto his keepers, blaming them greatly, for that they dealt so gently with him . . . and withal the Bishop of Hereford under a sophistical form of words signified to them by his letters that they should dispatch him out of the way, the tenor whereof wrapped in obscurity ran thus:

Edwardum occidere nolite timere bonum est:
To kill Edward will not to fear it is good.   700

Which riddle or doubtful kind of speech, as it might be taken in two contrary senses, only by placing the point in orthography called comma, they construed in the worse sense, putting the comma after '*timere*', and so presuming of this commandment as they took it from the bishop, they lodged the miserable prisoner in a chamber over a foul filthy dungeon, full of dead carrion, trusting so to make an end of him, with the abominable stench thereof, but he bearing it out strongly, as a man of a tough nature, continued still in life, so as it seemed he was very like to escape that danger, as he had by purging either up or down avoided the force of such poison as had been   710 ministered to him sundry times before, of purpose so to rid him.

Whereupon when they saw that such practices would not serve their turn, they came suddenly one night into the chamber where he lay in bed fast asleep, and with heavy featherbeds or a table (as some write) being cast upon him, they kept him down and withal put into his fundament an horn, and through the same they thrust up into his body an hot spit, or (as other have) through the pipe of a trumpet, a plumber's instrument of iron made very hot, the which passing up into his entrails, and being rolled to and fro, burnt the same, but so as no appearance of any wound or hurt outwardly   720 might be once perceived. His cry did move many within the castle and town of Berkeley to compassion, plainly hearing him utter a wailful noise, as the tormentors were about to murder him, so that divers being awakened therewith (as they themselves confessed) prayed heartily to God to receive his soul, when they understood by his cry what the matter meant.

The queen, the bishop, and others, that their tyranny might be hid, outlawed and banished the lord Maltravers and Thomas Gurney, who fleeing unto Marseilles, three years after being known, taken, and brought toward England, was beheaded on the sea, lest   730 he should accuse the chief doers, as the bishop and other. John Maltravers, repenting himself, lay long hidden in Germany, and in the end died penitently. Thus was King Edward murdered, in the year 1327, on the 22 of September. . . .

All these mischiefs and many more happened not only to him, but also to the whole state of the realm, in that he wanted judgement and prudent discretion to make choice of sage and discreet counsellors, receiving those into his favour that abused the same to their private gain and advantage, not respecting the

advancement of the commonwealth, so they themselves might attain 740
to riches and honour, for which they only sought, insomuch that by
their covetous rapine, spoil, and immoderate ambition, the hearts
of the common people and nobility were quite estranged from the
dutiful love and obedience which they ought to have showed to their
sovereign, going about by force to wrest him to follow their wills,
and to seek the destruction of them whom he commonly favoured,
wherein surely they were worthy of blame, and to taste (as many of
them did) the deserved punishment for their disobedient and
disloyal demeanours. For it was not the way which they took to help
the disfigured state of the commonwealth, but rather the ready 750
mean to overthrow all, as if God's goodness had not been the
greater it must needs have come to pass, as to those that shall well
consider the pitiful tragedy of this king's time it may well appear.

(pp. 341–2)

Edward the third of that name . . . began his reign as king of
England, his father yet living, the twenty-fifth day of January . . . in
the year of our Lord 1327. . . . And because he was but fourteen
years of age, so that to govern of himself he was not sufficient, it was
decreed that twelve of the greatest lords within the realm should
have the rule and government till he came to more perfect years.
[The twelve lords, who include the Earl of Kent, are listed.] But this 760
ordinance continued not long, for the queen, and the lord Roger
Mortimer took the whole rule so into their hands, that both the
king and his said counsellors were governed only by them in all
matters both high and low. . . .

(p. 343)

And first you shall understand that in the beginning of this king's
reign the land truly seemed to be blessed of God; for the earth
became fruitful, the air temperate, and the sea calm and quiet.
This king, though he was as yet under the government of other,
nevertheless he began within a short time to show tokens of great
towardness, framing his mind unto grave devices, and first he 770
prepared to make a journey against the Scottishmen, the which in
his father's time had done so many displeasures to the Englishmen,
and now upon confidence of his minority, ceased not to invade the
borders of his realm. . . .

(p. 346)

[In spite of these good auguries, the expedition is a failure and the
Scots elude the English army at Stanhope Park. Isabella and Mortimer
persuade the king to accept the treaty of Northampton (1328), which
conceded to the Scots everything they had fought for.]

After the quindene [fifteenth day] of St Michael [1328], King Edward held a parliament at Salisbury, in which the lord Roger Mortimer was created Earl of March. . . . But the Earl of March took the most part of the rule of all things pertaining either to the king or realm into his own hands, so that the whole government rested in a manner betwixt the queen mother and him. The other of the council that were first appointed were in manner displaced, for they bare no rule to speak of at all, which caused no small grudge to arise against the queen and the said Earl of March, who maintained such ports [style of living], and kept among them such retinue of servants, that their provision was wonderful. . . .

The king about the beginning, or (as other say) about the middle of Lent [1330], held a parliament at Winchester, during the which, Edmund of Woodstock, Earl of Kent, the king's uncle, was arrested the morrow after St Gregory's Day, and being arraigned upon certain confessions and letters found about him, he was found guilty of treason. . . . the earl upon his open confession before sundry lords of the realm, declared that not only by commandment from the Pope, but also by the setting on of divers nobles of this land (whom he named), he was persuaded to endeavour himself by all ways and means possible how to deliver his brother King Edward the second out of prison, and to restore him to the crown, whom one Thomas Dunhead, a friar of the order of preachers in London, affirmed for certain to be alive. . . .

The Bishop of London and certain other great personages whom he had accused were permitted to go at liberty. . . . The earl himself was had out of the castle gate at Winchester, and there lost his head the nineteenth day of March, chiefly (as was thought) through the malice of the queen mother and of the Earl of March, whose pride and high presumption the said Earl of Kent might not well abide. His death was the less lamented, because of the presumptuous government of his servants and retinue which he kept about him, for that they riding abroad, would take up things at their pleasure, not paying nor agreeing with the party to whom such things belonged. . . .

Also in a parliament holden at Nottingham about St Luke's tide [1330], Sir Roger Mortimer, the Earl of March, was apprehended the seventeenth day of October within the castle of Nottingham, where the king with the two queens, his mother and his wife, and divers other were as then lodged. . . . From Nottingham he was sent up to London . . . [and] committed to prison in the Tower. Shortly after was a parliament called at Westminster, chiefly (as was thought) for reformation of things disordered through the misgovernance of the Earl of March. But whosoever was glad or sorry for the trouble of

780

790

800

810

371

the said earl, surely the queen mother took it most heavily above all other, as she that loved him more (as the fame went) than stood well with her honour: For, as some write, she was found to be with child by him. They kept as it were house together, for the earl to have his provision the better cheap, laid his penny with hers, so that her takers served him as well as they did her, both of victuals and carriages. *Of which misusage (all regard to honour and estimation neglected) every subject spake shame. For their manner of dealing, tending to such evil purposes as they continually thought upon, could not be secret from the eyes of the people. . . . * But now in this parliament holden at Westminster he was attainted of high treason, expressed in five articles, as in effect followeth. 830

1 First, he was charged that he had procured Edward of Caernarfon, the king's father, to be murdered in most heinous and tyrannous manner within the castle of Berkeley.
2 Secondly, that the Scots at Stanhope Park through his means escaped.
3 Thirdly, that he received at the hands of the lord James Douglas, at that time general of the Scots, great sums of money to execute that treason, and further to conclude the peace upon such dishonorable covenants as was accorded with the Scots at the parliament of Northampton. 840
4 Fourthly, that he had got into his hands a great part of the king's treasure, and wasted and consumed it.
5 Fifthly, that he had impropried [impropriated] unto him divers wards that belonged unto the king, and had been more privy with Queen Isabel, the king's mother, than stood either with God's law, or the king's pleasure.

These articles with other being proved against him, he was adjudged by authority of the parliament to suffer death, and according thereunto, upon St Andrew's Even next ensuing, he was at London drawn and hanged at the common place of execution, 850 called in those days The Elms, and now Tyburn. . . .

In this parliament holden at Westminster, the king took into his hand, by advice of the states there assembled, all the possessions, lands, and revenues that belonged to the queen his mother, she having assigned to her a thousand pounds by year, for the maintenance of her estate, being appointed to remain in a certain place, and not to go elsewhere abroad, yet the king to comfort her would lightly [customarily] every year once come to visit her.

(pp. 347–9)

TEXT 2

The Annals of England . . .

John Stow
(Second edition 1592)

[The text is taken from the Huntington Library copy
(shelfmark 69560).]

Edward the second, son to the first Edward, born at Caernarfon,
began his reign the seventh day of July, in the year of Christ 1307.
He was fair of body, but unsteadfast of manners, and disposed to
lightness, haunting the company of vile persons, and given wholly to
the pleasure of the body, not regarding to govern his commonweal
by discretion and justice, which caused great variance between him
and his lords. . . . He ordained Walter Reynolds to be his chancellor,
and caused Walter Langton, Bishop of Chester, Lord Treasurer of
England, to bring the king his father's body from Carlisle to
Waltham Cross, and then to be arrested by Sir John Felton, Con- 10
stable of the Tower, and sent to Wallingford, there to be shut up in
prison, and his goods confiscate, because in his father's lifetime he
had reproved him of his insolent life, etc. He also called out of exile
Piers of Gaveston, a stranger born, which lately in his father's days
had for certain causes been banished this land. He gave to the said
Piers the earldom of Cornwall, the Isle of Man, and the lordship of
Wallingford, otherwise assigned to Queen Isabel. . . .

The king gave unto Piers of Gaveston all such gifts and jewels as
had been given to him, with the crowns of his father, his ancestors'
treasure, and many other things, affirming that if he could, he 20
should succeed him in the kingdom, calling him brother, not
granting anything without his consent. The lords therefore envying
him, told the king that the father of this Piers was a traitor to the
king of France, and was for the same executed, and that his mother
was burned for a witch, and that the said Piers was banished for
consenting to his mother's witchcraft, and that he had now bewitched the king himself. . . .

(pp. 320–1)

Then the king taking counsel of Piers, Hugh Spencer the treasurer,

the chancellor and others, he appointed to answer the barons at
the parliament on Hock Day [second Tuesday after Easter]. The   30
barons being departed out of London, the city gates were shut up
and chained, great watch kept, and Hugh Spencer made Constable
of London. The king with Peter of Gaveston went toward Wallingford castle with a great company of soldiers, as well strangers as
English, and Hugh Spencer [the elder] tarried still at London. . . .

[Parliament decrees Gaveston's banishment to Ireland.]

The king intended to give Gascony to the French king, Scotland to
Robert Bruce, Ireland and Wales to others, hoping thereby to have
aid against his barons. . . .
    The king sent for Piers of Gaveston out of Ireland. He landed at
Caernarfon, on the even of St John Baptist; the king met him at the   40
castle of Flint with great joy, and gave to him the Earl of Gloucester's
sister in marriage. . . .

(p. 322)

The abbot of St Denis in France, being sent legate from the Pope
to demand the legacy that King Edward's father gave to the Holy
Land, did earnestly request King Edward to remove from him
Peter Gaveston, with whose conversation all the world was as it
were infected.

(p. 323)

[Gaveston is again banished, this time to Flanders.]

Piers of Gaveston, conceiving an affiance [confidence] in the
favour of King Edward, and of the young Earl of Gloucester, whose
sister he had married, taking with him many strangers, returned   50
into England, and a little before Christmas came to the king's
presence, whom the king, forgetting all oaths and promised pacts,
received as a heavenly gift.
    King Edward kept his Christmas at York, where Piers of Gaveston
was present with his outlandish [foreign] men, the king rejoicing
and being in a great jollity because he had received Piers of
Gaveston in safety, all the court and queen being sorrowful, because they saw the king not very sound. The mighty men of the land
therefore sought how they might set an end to the trouble at hand,
for they feared to raise war, and durst not disquiet the king, yet the   60
peril being weighed, they found that so long as Piers lived, there
could be no peace in the kingdom, nor the king to abound in
treasure, nor the queen to enjoy the king's true love. Thus after
they had long considered the perils past, present, and to come, they
determined rather to try all extremities, than to be despised and

374

set at naught by a stranger. They chose a captain then for their business to come, Thomas of Lancaster, noble in lineage, valiant in arms, excellent in fame for his manners and justice. . . .

(p. 324)

[Gaveston's capture and execution are briefly described; there is no mention, for example, of Edward's request to see Gaveston.]

This year [1313] therefore by consent of the prelates and certain nobles, Hugh Spencer the son was appointed the king's chamber-   70
lain in place of Peter of Gaveston, whom they the rather preferred, because they knew the king hated him; nevertheless, not long after, by his great diligence, he brought himself into the king's favour. The father of this Hugh being old, was yet living, a knight of great virtue, in counsel wise, in arms valiant, whose confusion and shameful end he won unto himself by natural love though dis-ordinate towards his son, who was in body very comely, in spirit proud, and in action most wicked, whose covetousness and am-bition, by the disheriting of widows and strangers, wrought the death of the nobles, the fall of the king, with the utter destruction   80
of himself and his father. . . .

(pp. 325–6)

[Stow's account of events leading up to the battle of Boroughbridge and to Isabella's invasion includes two important details about the Mortimers, given below, which Holinshed omits.]

King Edward held his Christmas at Cirencester [1321], and after Christmas leaving Gloucester and Worcester, he with his army went to Shrewsbury and Bridgnorth. Both the Mortimers meeting the king, reverently and peaceably submitted themselves unto him; but the king sent them both to the Tower of London. . . .

(p. 333)

The second day of August [1322] the two Mortimers were adjudged to be drawn and hanged at Westminster, for divers robberies and murders which the king laid against them, but no execution of that judgement was done, by reason of a writ that the king sent to Sir   90
Richard de Swardstone, then Constable of the Tower, to stay the judgement, and the king granted them their lives, to be in perpetual prison. . . .

(p. 335)

[Stow's description of the treatment inflicted on Edward by order of the 'fierce and cruel' Isabella and the Bishop of Hereford, Adam de Orleton, is more detailed than Holinshed's and includes Edward's journey to Berkeley castle, the source for Act V Scene 3.]

These tormentors of Edward [i.e. Thomas Gurney and John Maltravers] exercised towards him many cruelties, unto whom it was not permitted to ride, unless it were by night, neither to see any man, or to be seen of any. When he rode, they forced him to be bareheaded; when he would sleep, they would not suffer him, neither when he was hungry would they give him such meats as he desired, but such as he loathed; every word that he spake was contraried by them, who gave it out most slanderously that he was mad. And, shortly to speak, in all matters they were quite contrary to his will, that either by cold, watching, or unwholesome meats, for melancholy [or] by some infirmity he might languish and die. But this man being by nature strong to suffer pains, and patient through God's grace to abide all griefs, he endured all the devices of his enemies; for as touching poisons, which they gave him often to drink, by the benefit of nature he dispatched away.

These champions bring Edward towards Berkeley, being guarded with a rabble of hell-hounds, along by the grange belonging to the castle of Bristol, where that wicked man Gurney, making a crown of hay, put it on his head, and the soldiers that were present, scoffed, and mocked him beyond all measure, saying 'Tprut, avaunt sir king', making a kind of noise with their mouths, as though they had farted. They feared to be met of any that should know Edward; they bent their journey therefore towards the left hand, riding along over the marish [marshy] grounds lying by the river of Severn. Moreover, devising to disfigure him that he might not be known, they determined for to shave as well the hair of his head, as also of his beard; wherefore, as in their journey they travelled by a little water which ran in a ditch, they commanded him to light from his horse to be shaven, to whom, being set on a mole-hill, a barber came unto him with a basin of cold water taken out of the ditch, to shave him withal, saying unto the king, that that water should serve for that time. To whom Edward answered, that would they, nould they, he would have warm water for his beard, and, to the end that he might keep his promise, he began to weep, and to shed tears plentifully.

At length they came to Berkeley castle, where Edward was shut up close like an anchor [hermit]. Isabel his wife, taking it grievously that her husband's life (which she deadly hated) was prolonged, made her complaint to her schoolmaster Adam de Orleton, feigning that she had certain dreams, the interpretation whereof she misliked, which if they were true, she feared lest, that if her husband be at any time restored to his old dignity, that he would burn her for a traitor, or condemn her to perpetual bondage. In like sort the bishop being guilty in his own conscience stood in like

fear. The like fear also struck the hearts of other for the same
offence; wherefore it seemed good to many of great dignity and
blood, as well spiritual as temporal, both men and women, that all 140
such fear should be taken away, desiring his death. Whereupon
there were letters colourably [deceitfully] written to the keepers
of Edward, greatly blaming them, for looking so slenderly [slackly]
to the king, suffering him to have such liberty and nourishing him
too delicately.

Moreover, there was a privy motion made unto them, but yet in
such sort, as it might seem half done, that the death of Edward
would not be misliking unto them, whether it were natural or
violent. And in this point, the great deceit of sophisters stood in
force, set down by the bishop, who wrote thus: 150

Edwardum occidere nolite timere bonum est.
Kill Edward do not fear, it is a good thing:
Or thus:
To seek to shed King Edward's blood
Refuse to fear I count it good.

Which sophistical saying is to be resolved into two propositions,
whereof the first consisting of three words, to wit, *Edwardum occidere
nolite,* 'do not kill Edward', and the second of other three, that is,
timere bonum est, 'fear is a good thing', do seem to persuade subtly
from murdering of the king; but the receivers of these letters, not 160
ignorant of the writing, changed the meaning thereof to this sense,
Edwardum occidere nolite timere, 'to kill Edward do not fear', and
afterwards these words, *bonum est,* 'it is good', so that they being
guilty, turned a good saying into evil.

The bishop being thus determinately purposed touching the
death of Edward, and warily providing for himself, if by any chance
he should be accused thereof, craftily worketh that the authority
which he gave by writing might seem to be taken expressly contrary to his meaning, by reason of accenting and pointing of
the same. . . . 170

(pp. 343–4)

[The play follows Stow's account of Mortimer's arrest in some respects;
Holinshed omits this incident 'because of the diversity in report
thereof by sundry writers'.]

There was a parliament holden at Nottingham, where Roger
Mortimer was in such glory and honour, that it was without all
comparison. No man durst name him any other than Earl of March;
a greater rout of men waited at his heels than on the king's person;
he would suffer the king to rise to him, and would walk with the

377

king equally, step by step, and cheek by cheek, never preferring the
king, but would go foremost himself with his officers. . . . By which
means a contention rose among the noblemen, and great murmur-
ing among the common people, who said that Roger Mortimer, the
queen's paragon [companion] and the king's master, sought all the
means he could to destroy the king's blood, and to usurp the regal
majesty, which report troubled much the king's friends, to wit,
William Montacute [Montagu] and other, who for the safeguard of
the king swore themselves to be true to his person, and drew unto
them Robert de Holland, who had of long time been chief keeper
of the castle, unto whom all secret corners of the same were known.
Then upon a certain night, the king lying without the castle, both
he and his friends were brought by torchlight through a secret way
underground, beginning far off from the said castle, till they came
even to the queen's chamber, which they by chance found open.
They therefore being armed with naked swords in their hands, went
forwards, leaving the king also armed without the door of the
chamber, lest that his mother should espy him. . . . From thence
they went toward the queen mother, whom they found with the
Earl of March, ready to have gone to bed, and having taken the said
earl, they led him out into the hall, after whom the queen followed,
crying, '*Bel fils, bel fils, ayez pitié de gentil Mortimer*' ('Good son, good
son, take pity upon gentle Mortimer'), for she suspected that her
son was there, though she saw him not. . . .

The next day, in the morning very early, they bring Roger
Mortimer and other his friends taken with him, with an horrible
shout and crying . . . towards London, where he was committed to
the Tower, and afterward condemned at Westminster in presence
of the whole parliament on St Andrew's Even next following, and
then drawn to the Elms [i.e. Tyburn], and there hanged on the
common gallows. . . .

(pp. 349–50)

TEXT 3

The Chronicle of Fabyan . . .

Robert Fabyan
(Fourth edition 1559)

[The text is taken from the British Library copy
(shelfmark G. 6018).]

It was not long after that word was brought unto the king how
Robert le Bruce was turned [returned] into Scotland, and had
caused the Scots to rebel of new. Ye have before heard, in the thirty
third year of Edward the first, how the said Edward chased the
forenamed Robert le Bruce out of Scotland into Normandy. But
when he had heard of the misguidings of the realm of England, and
specially of the division between the king and his lords, he anon
with a small aid of the Normans or Norways [Norwegians] returned
into Scotland.

Where he demeaned him in such wise to the lords of Scotland   10
that he in short process was again made king of that realm, and
warred strongly upon the king's friends, and won from them castles
and strongholds, and wrought unto Englishmen much sorrow and
teen [damage]. . . .

In the seventh year, for to oppress the malice of the Scots, the
king assembled a great power, and by water entered the realm of
Scotland, and destroyed such villages and towns as lay or stood in
his way. Whereof hearing, Robert le Bruce with the power of
Scotland coasted toward the Englishmen, and upon the day of the
Nativity of St John the Baptist, met with King Edward and his host   20
at a place called Estryvelin [Stirling], near unto a fresh river that
then was called Bannocksburn, where between the English and the
Scots that day was foughten a cruel battle. But in the end the
Englishmen were constrained to forsake the field.

Then the Scots chased so eagerly the Englishmen that many of
them were drowned in the forenamed river, and many a nobleman
of England that day was slain in that battle. . . . And the king
himself from that battle scaped with great danger, and so with a few
of his host that with him escaped came unto Berwick, and there

379

rested him a season. Then the Scots inflamed with pride, in   30
derision of the Englishmen, made this rhyme as followeth:

Maidens of England, sore may ye mourn
For your lemans [sweethearts] ye have lost at Bannocksburn,
With heave a low.
What weeneth the king of England
So soon to have won Scotland?
With rumbelow.

This song was after many days sung, in dances, in the carols of the
maidens and minstrels of Scotland, to the reproof and disdain of
Englishmen, with divers other, which I overpass. And when King   40
Edward had a season tarried in Berwick, and set that town in surety,
as he then might, he returned with small honour into England, and
came secretly to Westminster. . . .

(II. 168–9)

NOTES

1 *The third volume of Chronicles* . . . (pp. 351–72)

9   *banished the land*: According to Holinshed (p. 313), two years earlier
Edward I had imprisoned his son for trespassing into a park belonging to
Langton at Gaveston's instigation and had sent Gaveston into exile (but
in fact this first exile did not take place until 1307).

47   *Earl of Gloucester*: Gilbert de Clare, 6th Earl of Gloucester, died 1295.

74   *New Temple*: Holinshed is the only authority to name the New Temple as
the location for this meeting, which is also specified in the play (I. 2. 75).

137   *exiled into Flanders*: Marlowe conflates Gaveston's exile in Flanders with
the earlier exile to Ireland.

225   *Sir Thomas de la More*: a reference to the *Chronicon* of Geoffrey le Baker,
written for his patron, Sir Thomas de la More, who provided him with an
eye-witness account of Edward's abdication, and has often been wrongly
credited with the authorship of this work.

345   *one and twentieth of March*: many other barons were executed. Marlowe
includes Warwick, who had in fact died in 1315, among them, an
alteration of history which underlines the element of revenge for
Gaveston's death in Edward's victory at Boroughbridge.

361   *the roaring of a lion*: Proverbs 19: 12.

463   *mind of the queen*: cf. the role of Levune, an invented character, in the play.

533   *Earl of Gloucester*: the younger Spencer, who married one of the sisters
and co-heiresses of the 7th Earl of Gloucester (killed at Bannockburn),
is often referred to as Earl of Gloucester, though in fact he was never
given that title. Nor was he ever Earl of Wiltshire (the title conferred on
him in the play at III. 2. 49); his father, however, was created Earl of
Winchester in 1322 and in Marlowe's time at least the son of the
Marquess of Winchester was known as Earl of Wiltshire.

649   *Sir William Trussell*: It is clear from Stow's account that Trussell made his formal renunciation at Kenilworth. .

2 *The Annals of England* (pp. 373–8)

27   *bewitched the king himself*: cf. I. 2. 55: 'Is it not strange that he is thus bewitched?'

43   *legate from the Pope*: Marlowe transfers the title of legate to the Pope (I. 4. 51) from the Abbot of St Denis to the Archbishop of Canterbury.

SELECT BIBLIOGRAPHY

[This listing asterisks those primary materials from which texts in the main body of the book have been drawn; where modern editions of early printed texts exist, they have been cited. General materials have been cited only where they have particular relevance to a study of Marlowe's sources.

Where a work has been reprinted in facsimile in the *English Experience* series, the following publication details apply below, where only the volume number and year are cited: *The English Experience, its Record in Early Printed Books Published in Facsimile*: Amsterdam: Theatrum Orbis Terrarum; New York: Da Capo Press.]

PRIMARY TEXTS

DIDO QUEEN OF CARTHAGE

Caxton, William, *The Recuyell of the Histories of Troy . . . translated . . . out of French . . . by W. Caxton*, Bruges, 1473–4; ed. H.O. Sommer, 2 vols, London: David Nutt, 1894.

* Dolce, Lodovico, *Didone*, Vinegia [Venice]: Aldus, 1547.

Douglas, Gavin, *The XIII books of 'Aeneidos' of the famous poet Virgil translated out of Latin verses into Scottish metre*, London: W. Copland, 1553; ed. D.F.C. Coldwell, 4 vols, Edinburgh and London: Blackwood, (Scottish Text Society), 1957–64.

Gager, William, *Dido, tragedia*, in A.R. Roberts-Baytop, *Dido, Queen of Infinite Literary Variety*, Salzburg: Institut für Englishe Sprache und Literatur, 1974, pp. 37–94.

Giraldi-Cinthio, Giambattista, *Didone*, in *Le Tragedie di G.G.C.*, ed. G. Giraldi, Venetia: Cagnacini, 1583.

Howard, Henry, Earl of Surrey, *The fourth book of Virgil. . . translated into English*, London: J. Day, 1554; *Certain books of Virgil's 'Aeneis' turned into English metre*, London: R. Tottel, 1557; in *Poems*, ed. E.L. Jones, Oxford: Clarendon Press, 1964.

Jodelle, Etienne, *Didon se sacrifiant*, in *Les Oeuvres . . . d'Etienne Jodelle*, ed. C. de la Mothe, Paris, 1574; ed. E. Balmas, 2 vols, Paris: Gallimard, 1965–8 (vol. II).

* Lydgate, John, *The History, Siege and Destruction of Troy (Troy Book)*, 1412–20, London: R. Pynson, 1513; T. Marshe, 1555; ed. Henry Bergen, 4 vols, London: Oxford University Press (Early English Text Society), 1906–35.

Nashe, Thomas, *Works*, ed. R.B. McKerrow, revised F.P. Wilson, 5 vols, Oxford: Blackwell, 1958.

* (Ovid) Publius Ovidius Naso, *The Heroical Epistles of the Learned Poet P. Ovidius Naso in English verse, set out and translated by George Turbervile, Gent,* London: Henry Denman, 1567. Modern translation in *Heroides and Amores,* ed. E.H. Warmington, London: Heinemann; Cambridge, Mass.: Harvard University Press, 1971.

*—— *The XV Books of P. Ovidius Naso, entitled Metamorphoses, translated out of Latin into English metre, by Arthur Golding, Gentleman,* London: William Seres, 1567. (*The English Experience* 881 [1977].) Ed. J.F. Nims, New York: Macmillan, 1965.

Pazzi, Alessandro, *Dido in Carthagine,* in *Le Tragedie Metriche di A. Pazzi de' Medici,* ed. A. Solerti, Bologna, 1887 (reprinted 1969).

Stanyhurst, Richard, *The first four books of Virgil his 'Aeneis' translated into English heroical verse,* Leyden: J. Pates, 1582; London: H Bynneman; ed. Dirk Van der Haar, Amsterdam: H.J. Paris, 1933.

* (Virgil) Publius Virgilius Maro, *The seven first books of the 'Aeneidos' of Virgil, converted in English metre by Thomas Phaer, Esquire,* London: J. Kyngston for R. Jugge, 1558. Subsequent editions, 1562, 1573, 1584. Modern translation in *The Aeneid,* ed. H. Rushton Fairclough, 2 vols, London: Heinemann; Cambridge, Mass.: Harvard University Press, 1947.

TAMBURLAINE THE GREAT

Aeneas Silvius Piccolomini [Pope Pius II], *Pii II Pon. Max. Asiae Europaeque elegantissima descriptio. . .,* Venetiis [Venice], 1477; Paris: Claudius Chevallonius, 1534.

Ashton, Peter, *A short treatise upon the Turks' Chronicles, compiled by Paulus Jovius Bishop of Nucerne. Drawn out of the Italian tongue into Latin, by F. Niger Bassianates, and translated out of Latin into English by P. Ashton,* London: Edward Whitchurch, 1546.

* Belleforest, François de, *La cosmographie Universelle de tout le monde,* 2 vols, Paris, 1575.

* Bishop, John, *Beautiful Blossoms, gathered by John Bishop, from the best trees of all kinds, divine, philosophical, astronomical, cosmographical, historical, etc.,* London: Henry Cockyn, 1577.

Bodin, Jean, *The Six Books of a Commonweal. . . out of the French and Latin copies, done into English, by Richard Knolles,* London: Adam Islip, 1606; facsimile edition, ed. Kenneth Douglas McRae, Cambridge, Mass.: Harvard University Press, 1962.

* Bonfinius, Antonius, *Antonii Bonfinii Rerum Ungaricarum Decades Quattuor cum dimidia. . .,* 1543, Basileae [Basle]: ex officinia Oporiniana, 1568; Frankfurt: apud A. Wechelum, 1581. (See Knolles below.)

* Cambinus, Andreas, *Libro. . . della origine de Turchi et imperio delli Ottomanni,* Firenze, 1529. (See Shute below.)

* Chalcocondylas, Laonicus, *L[aonici] Chalcocondylae Atheniensis, de origine et rebus gestis Turcorum libri decem nuper e Graeco in Latinum conversi: Conrado Clausero,* Basle, 1556.

* Fortescue, Thomas, *The Forest or Collection of Histories no less profitable than pleasant and necessary, done out of French into English by Thomas Fortescue,* London: J. Kingston for W. Jones, 1571.

* Foxe, John, *The first volume of the Ecclesiastical History, containing the Acts and Monuments of things passed in every king's time in this realm, especially in the Church of England. . . Newly recognized and enlarged by the author,* 2 vols, London: John Day, second edition, 1570. First edition, 1563; subsequent editions, 1576,

1583, etc. Modern edition G. Townsend (ed.) 8 vols, London, 1843–9; repr. New York: AMS Press, 1965.

* Fulgosius, Baptista, *De Dictis Factisque memorabilis collectanea* . . ., Mediolani [Milan], 1509; Parrhisius [Paris], 1518.

* Gascoigne, George and Francis Kinwelmershe, *Jocasta A Tragedy written in Greek by Euripides, translated and digested into Act [sic] by G. Gascoigne and F. Kinwelmershe of Gray's Inn, and there by them presented,* in *The Posies of George Gascoigne Esquire,* 1566; London: Richard Smith, 1575. Reprinted in John W.Cunliffe (ed.), *The Complete Works of George Gascoigne,* 2 vols, Cambridge: Cambridge University Press, 1907–10 (Vol. I).

Gruget, Claude, *Les Diverses Leçons de Pierre Messie gentilhomme de Sevile. Contenants variables et memorables histoires: mises en Français par Claude Gruget Parisien,* Paris: pour Jan Longis, 1552; Lyon, 1563.

* Harington, Sir John, *Orlando Furioso in English Heroical Verse,* London: Richard Field, 1591. Ed. and introduced G. Hough, London: Centaur Press, 1962.

* Ive, Paul, *The Practice of Fortification: Wherein is showed the manner of fortifying in all sorts of situations. . . Compiled in a most easy and compendious method, by Paul Ive. Gent.,* London: Thomas Orwin, 1589. (*The English Experience* 29 [1968].)

* Jovius, Paulus [Giovio, Paolo], *Elogia virorum bellica virtute illustrium, veris imaginibus supposita,* Florentiae, 1551; Basileae [Basle], 1571.

Knolles, Richard, *The General History of the Turks . . . Together with the Lives and Conquests of the Othoman Kings and Emperors,* London: A. Islip, 1603. Subsequent editions 1610, 1621, 1631, etc.

La Primaudaye, Pierre de, *The French Academy. . .newly translated into English by T.B.,* London, 1586.

* Lonicerus, Philippus, *Chronicorum Turcicorum in quibus Turcorum origo, principes, . . . bella &c exponuntur. . .,* 3 vols, Frankfurt am Main, 1578.

Mexía, Pedro, *Silva de Varia Lección,* Seville, 1542; ed. Justo Garcia Soriano, 2 vols, Madrid: Sociedad de Bibliofilos Espanoles, 1933.

The Mulfuzāt Tīmūry or Autobiographical Memoirs of the Moghul Emperor Timur. . ., trans. Major Charles Stewart, London: John Murray *et al.,* 1830.

Newton, Thomas, *A Notable History of the Saracens. Briefly and faithfully describing the original beginning, continuance and success as well of the Saracens, as also of Turks, Soldans, Mamelukes, Assassins, Tartarians and Sophians . . . Drawn out of Augustine Curio and sundry other good Authors by Thomas Newton,* London: William How for Abraham Vele, 1575.

Nicolay, Nicolas de, *The Navigations, Peregrinations and Voyages made into Turkey by Nicholas Nicholay Dauphinois, Lord of Arfeuile, Chamberlain and Geographer Ordinary to the King of France. . . Translated out of the French by T. Washington the Younger,* London: Thomas Dawson, 1585. (*The English Experience* 48 [1968].)

* Perondinus, Petrus, *Magni Tamerlanis Scytharum Imperatoris Vita Petro Perondino Pratense conscripta,* Florentiae, 1553.

Platina, Bartholomeus Sacchi de, . . . *in vitas sumorum pontificum ad Sixtum iiij,* Venezia, 1479.

* Shute, John, *Two Very Notable Commentaries the one of the original of the Turks and Empire of the house of Ottomanno written by Andrew Cambine. . .faithfully translated out of Italian into English by John Shute,* London: Rowland Hall for Humphrey Toye, 1562. (*The Engl ish Experience* 235 [1970].)

Spenser, Edmund, *The Faerie Queene. Disposed into twelve books, fashioning xii moral virtues. . .,* 2 vols, London: W. Ponsonby, 1590–6.

* Whetstone, George, *The English Mirror. A Regard Wherein all Estates may behold the Conquests of Envy. . .,* London: J. Windet, 1586. (*The English Experience* 632 [1973].)

DOCTOR FAUSTUS

Aglionby, E. (trans.), *A notable and marvellous Epistle of the famous Doctor, Matthew Gribald, Professor of the Law in the University of Padua. . . .*, 1550; London: H. Denham for W. Norton, 1570.

Becon, Thomas, *The Dialogue between the Christian Knight and Satan: wherein Satan moveth unto desperation, the Knight comforteth himself with the sweet promise of the Holy Scripture* in *Works*, 3 vols, London: J. Day, 1560–4. Modern edition by J. Ayre in *The Catechism of Thomas Becon*, Cambridge: Cambridge University Press (Parker Society), 1844.

* Foxe, John (see under *Tamburlaine* above).

Greene, Robert, *The Honourable History of Friar Bacon and Friar Bungay, as it was played by Her Majesty's Servants*, London: Edward White, 1594. Various modern editions, incl. W.W. Greg (ed.), Malone Society Reprints, 1926; J.A. Lavin (ed.), New Mermaids, 1969.

Historia von D. Johann Fausten, dem weitbeschreiten Zauberer und Schwarzkünstler. . ., Frankfurt am Main: Johann Spies, 1587. Reprinted in H.W. Geissler (ed.), *Gestaltungen des Faust*, 3 vols, München: Parcus Verlag, 1928 (vol. I).

The Most Famous History of the Learned Friar Bacon. . ., London: Thomas Norris, c. 1715.

* P. F., *The History of the Damnable Life and Deserved Death of Doctor John Faustus, newly imprinted and in convenient places imperfect matter amended, according to the true copy printed at Frankfurt, and translated into English by P.F., Gent.*, London: Thomas Orwin, 1592. (*The English Experience* 173 [1969].)

Pulci, Luigi, *Il Morgante Maggiore*, Firenze: Francesco di Dino, 1482; ed.F. Ageno, *La Letteratura Italiana, Storià e Testi 17*, Milano e Napoli, 1955.

Rhegius, Urbanus, *An Homily or sermon of good and evil angels. . .*, trans. Richard Robinson, London: J. Charlewode, 1583; subsequent editions, 1590, 1593.

Scot, Reginald, *The Discovery of Witchcraft*, London: W. Brome, 1584. (*The English Experience* 299 [1971].)

Widman, Georg Rudolff, *Wahrhafftige Historia. . .*, Hamburg, 1599.

* Woodes, Nathaniel, *An excellent new comedy entitled The Conflict of Conscience, containing the most lamentable history of the desperation of Francis Spira, who forsook the truth of God's gospel for fear of the loss of life and worldly goods*, London: Richard Bradocke, 1581; ed. H. Davis and F.P. Wilson, Oxford: Oxford University Press (Malone Society Reprints), 1952.

THE MASSACRE AT PARIS

* Boucher, Jean, *La vie et faits notables de Henri de Valois. . .où sont contenues les trahisons, perfidies, sacrilèges, exactions, cruautés, et hontes de cet hypocrite et apostat ennemi de la religion Catholique. . .*, Paris: Didier Millot, 1589.

* Colynet, Antony, *The True History of the Civil Wars of France, between the French King Henry the fourth and the Leaguers. . .*, London: Thomas Woodcock, 1591.

* *Les cruautés sanguinaires excercées envers feu Monseigneur le Cardinal de Guise. . .*, Paris, 1589.

* Goulart, Simon (ed.), *Mémoires de l'état de France sous Charles neuvième contenant les choses les plus notables, faites, et publiées. . .depuis le troisième édit de pacification fait au mois d'âout 1570 jusques au regne de Henri troisième*, 3 vols, Meidelbourg [Geneva]: Heinrich Wolf [Vignon], 1576–7. Subsequent editons, 1578; 1578–9.

* Hotman, François [Ernest Varamundus], *De furoribus Gallicis. . .*, Basle and

London, 1573. Translated as *A True and Plain Report of the Furious Outrages of France. . .*, London: H. Bynneman, 1573; reprinted in Jean de Serres, *The Three Parts of Commentaries, containing the whole and perfect discourse of the civil wars of France, translated out of Latin by Thomas Tymme*, London: Henry Middleton, 1574.

—— *The life of the most godly, valiant, and noble captain and maintainer of the true Christian religion in France, Jasper Coligny Châtillon, sometime great Admiral of France. Translated out of Latin by Arthur Golding*, London: Thomas Vautrollier, 1576.

* L'Estrange, Nicholas, *Merry Passages and Jests, c.* 1650 (MS Jestbook, ed. W.J. Thoms, *Anecdotes and Traditions*, London: Camden Society, 1839; ed. H.F. Lippincott, Salzburg: Institut für Englische Sprache und Literatur, Universität Salzburg, 1974.

* *Le martyre des deux frères contenant au vrai toutes les particularités les plus notables des massacres et assassinats commis ès personnes de . . . Messeigneurs le Reverendissime Cardinal de Guise . . . et de Monseigneur le Duc de Guise . . .*, Paris, 1589.

* Thou, Jacques-Auguste de, *Jac. Aug. Thuani Historiarum sui temporis*, Paris, 1604–9; ed. Thomas Carte, London, 1733; translated by A.F. Prévost d'Exiles *et al.* as *Histoire universelle de Jacques-Auguste de Thou depuis 1543 jusqu'en 1607*, 16 vols, London, 1734.

Le tocsin contre les massacreurs et auteurs des confusions en France, Rheims, 1579.

THE JEW OF MALTA

* Belleforest, François de (see under *Tamburlaine* above).

Bizarus, Petrus, *Persicarum rerum historia in xii libros descripta. . .*, Antwerp, 1583.

* Brown, Horatio F. *et al.* (eds), *Calendar of State Papers and Manuscripts, relating to English Affairs, existing in the Archives and Collections of Venice. . . .*, 38 vols, London: HMSO, 1864–1947 (vol. VIII, 1581–1591).

* Davis, Norman (ed.), *The Play of the Sacrament* (*c.* 1460) in *Non-Cycle Plays and Fragments*, London: Oxford University Press, pp. 58–89. (Early English Text Society [Supplementary Series 1 (1970)].)

* Harvey, Gabriel, *Gabrielis Harveii gratulationum Valdinensium libri quattuor*, London: H. Bynneman, 1578.

Hazlitt, W.C. (ed.), *A Merry Jest of Dan Hugh Monk of Leicester*, in *Remains of the Early Popular Poetry of England*, III, London: J.R. Smith, 1866, pp. 130–46.

Lonicerus, Philippus (see under *Tamburlaine* above).

Masuccio di Salerno, *The Novellino of Masuccio*, trans. W.G. Waters, 2 vols, London: Lawrence & Bullen, 1895, I, 13–28.

* Nicolay, Nicolas de (see under *Tamburlaine* above).

* Serres, Jean de, *The Fourth Part of Commentaries of the Civil Wars in France translated out of Latin by Thomas Tymme*, London, 1576 (see under *The Massacre at Paris* (Hotman) above).

* (?) Udall, Nicholas, *A merry interlude entitled Respublica, made in the year of our Lord 1553, and the first year of the most prosperous Reign of our most gracious Sovereign Queen Mary the first.* Included in the Macro manuscript (Library of Carl H. Pforzheimer, MS 40 A). Modern edition by W.W. Greg, London: Oxford University Press. (Early English Text Society [Original Series 226 (1952)].)

* Wilson, Robert, *A right excellent and famous Comedy called the Three Ladies of London. . . Written by R.W.*, London: Robert Warde, 1584; ed. J.S. Farmer, Tudor Facsimile Texts, 1911.

* *Das Wohlgesprochene Uhrteil* or *Der Jud von Venedig* in Johann Meissner, *Die Englischen Comoedianten zur Zeit Shakespeares in Oesterreich*, Wien, 1884.

EDWARD II

Boucher, Jean, *Histoire tragique et mémorable de Pierre de Gaverston, gentilhomme Gascon, jadis le mignon d' Edouard II, Roi d' Angleterre, tirée des Chroniques de Thomas Walsingham. . .*, Paris, 1588.

Denholm-Young, N. (ed. and transl.), *Vita Edwardi Secundi: The Life of Edward II*, London: Nelson, 1957.

* Fabyan, Robert, *The Chronicle of Fabyan, which he nameth the concordance of histories, newly perused. . .*, 2 vols, London: John Kyngston, fourth edition, 1559. Previous editions R. Pynson, 1516; W. Bonham, 1542; William Rastell, 1553. Modern edition by H. Ellis, London: F.C. and J. Rivington, 1811.

Foxe, John (see under *Tamburlaine* above).

* Holinshed, Raphael, *The first and second volumes of Chronicles, beginning at Duke William the Norman, commonly called the Conqueror, and descending by degrees of years to all the kings and queens of England in their orderly successions. . . . Now newly recognized, augmented and continued. . .*, 2 vols, London: John Harrison, George Bishop, Ralph Newbery, Henry Denham, and Thomas Woodcock. Second edition, 1587. First edition 1577. Modern edition by H. Ellis, 6 vols, London: J. Johnson, 1807–8.

Le Baker, Geoffrey, *Le Chronicon Galfridi le Baker de Swynebroke*, ed. E. Maunde Thompson, Oxford: Clarendon Press, 1889.

* Stow, John, *The Annals of England, faithfully collected out of the most authentical authors, records, and other monuments of antiquity, from the first inhabitation until this present year 1592*, London: Ralph Newbery, second edition, 1592. (First edition 1580, under the title *The Chronicles of England, from Brute unto this present year of Christ 1580*.)

Stubbs, W. (ed.), *Vita Edwardi II* and *Vita et Mors Edwardi II* in *Chronicles of the reigns of Edward I and Edward II*, 2 vols, London: Longman (Rolls series), 1882–3 (vol. II).

Walsingham, Thomas, *Historia Anglicana*, London: Henry Bynneman, 1574 (under the title *Historia Brevis*) ; ed. H.T. Riley, 2 vols, London: Longman (Rolls series), 1863–4.

SECONDARY MATERIALS

DIDO QUEEN OF CARTHAGE

Boas, F.S. (1914) *University Drama in the Tudor Age*, Oxford: Clarendon Press.

Brooke, C.F. Tucker (ed.) (1930) *The Life of Marlowe and The Tragedy of Dido Queen of Carthage*, London: Methuen.

Gill, Roma (1977) 'Marlowe's Virgil: *Dido Queene of Carthage*', *Review of English Studies* 28, 141–55.

Koskenniemi, I. (1972) 'Did Marlowe use any dramatic sources for *Dido Queen of Carthage*?' *Neuphilogische Mitteilungen* 73, 143–52.

Oliver, H.J. (ed.) (1968) *Dido Queen of Carthage and The Massacre at Paris*, London: Methuen.

Pearce, T.M. (1930) 'Marlowe's *Tragedie of Dido* in relation to its Latin source', unpublished Ph.D. thesis, University of Pittsburgh, Pennsylvania.

Smith, Mary E. (1976) ' Marlowe and Italian Dido Drama', *Italica* 53, 223–35.
—— (1977) *'Love kindling Fire: A Study of Christopher Marlowe's "The Tragedy of Dido Queen of Carthage"'*, Salzburg: Institüt für Englische Sprache und Literatur.

TAMBURLAINE THE GREAT

Battenhouse, Roy W.(1941) *Marlowe's Tamburlaine: A Study in Renaissance Moral Philosophy*, Nashville, Tennessee: Vanderbilt University Press.
—— (1973) 'Protestant apologetics and the subplot of *2 Tamburlaine*', *English Literary Renaissance* 3, 30–43.
Brown, William J. (1971) 'Marlowe's Debasement of Bajazeth: Foxe's *Actes and Monuments* and *Tamburlaine, Part 1*', *Renaissance Quarterly* 24, 38–48.
Cole, Douglas (1962) *Suffering and Evil in the Plays of Christopher Marlowe*, Princeton: Princeton University Press.
Cunningham, J.S. (ed.) (1981) *Tamburlaine the Great*, Manchester: Manchester University Press; Baltimore, Maryland: Johns Hopkins Press.
Cutts, John P.(1958) 'The ultimate source of Tamburlaine's white, red, black and death?' *Notes and Queries* 203, 146–7.
Danchin, F.C. (1912) 'En marge de la seconde partie de Tamburlaine', *Revue Germanique* 8, 23–33.
Dick, Hugh G. (1949) *'Tamburlaine*'s sources once more', *Studies in Philology* 46, 154–66.
Ellis-Fermor, Una (ed.) (1930) *Tamburlaine the Great*, London: Methuen; second revised edition, 1951.
Fisher, H.A.L. (1938) *A History of Europe*, revised edition, 3 vols, London: Eyre & Spottiswoode.
Gardner, Helen (1942) 'The Second Part of *Tamburlaine the Great*', *Modern Language Review* 37, 18–24.
Herford, C.H. and Wagner, A. (1883) 'The sources of Marlowe's *Tamburlaine*', *Academy* 24, 265–6.
Hookham, Hilda (1962) *Tamburlaine the Conqueror*, London: Hodder & Stoughton.
Izard, Thomas C. (1943) 'The principal source for Marlowe's *Tamburlaine*', *Modern Language Notes* 58, 411–17.
O'Connor, John J. (1955) 'Another human footstool', *Notes and Queries* 200, 332.
Ribner, Irving (1953) 'The idea of history in Marlowe's *Tamburlaine*', *English Literary History* 20, 251–66.
Seaton, Ethel (1921) 'Marlowe and his authorities', *Times Literary Supplement*, 16 June, 388.
—— (1924) 'Marlowe's Map', *Essays and Studies* 10, 13–35.
Spence, Leslie (1926–7) 'The influence of Marlowe's sources on *Tamburlaine I*', *Modern Philology* 24, 181–207.
—— (1927) 'Tamburlaine and Marlowe', *PMLA* 42, 604–22.
Summers, Claude J. (1974) 'Tamburlaine's opponents and Machiavelli's *Prince*', *English Literary History* 11, 256–8.
Taylor, Robert T. (1957) 'Maximinus and Tamburlaine', *Notes and Queries* 202, 417–18.

DOCTOR FAUSTUS

Bevington, D. and Rasmussen, E. (eds) (1993) *Doctor Faustus A- and B- Texts*, Manchester and New York: Manchester University Press (The Revels Plays).

Birringer, J.H. (1984) *Marlowe's 'Dr. Faustus' and 'Tamburlaine': Theological and Theatrical Perspectives*, Frankfurt am Main, Bern and New York: Peter Lang.

Boas, F.S. (ed.) (1932) *The Tragical History of Doctor Faustus*, London: Methuen.

Brennan, M.G. (1991) 'Christopher Marlowe's *Dr Faustus* and Urbanus Rhegius's *An Homelye. . . of good and evil angels*', *Notes and Queries* 38, 466–9.

Brown, B.D. (1939) 'Marlowe, Faustus, and Simon Magus', *PMLA* 54, 82–121.

Butler, E.M. (1952) *The Fortunes of Faust*, Cambridge: Cambridge University Press.

Campbell, Lily B. (1952) '*Doctor Faustus*: a case of conscience', *PMLA* 67, 219–39.

Deats, Sara Munson (1976) '*Doctor Faustus*: from chapbook to tragedy', *Essays in Literature* (Western Illinois University) 3, 3–16.

—— (1981) 'Ironic Biblical allusion in Marlowe's *Doctor Faustus*', *Medievalia et Humanistica* 10, 203–16.

Dreher, D.E. (1983) '"*Si pecasse negamus*": Marlowe's *Faustus* and *the Book of Common Prayer*', *Notes and Queries* 30, 143–4.

Eriksen, R.T. (1985) 'Giordano Bruno and Marlowe's *Faustus* (B)', *Notes and Queries* 32, 463–5.

Gardner, Helen (1948) 'Milton's "Satan" and the theme of damnation in Elizabethan tragedy', *English Studies* n.s. 1, 46–66.

Greg, W.W. (ed.) (1950) *Marlowe's 'Doctor Faustus' 1604–1616: Parallel Texts*, Oxford: Clarendon Press.

Jackson, MacDonald P. (1971) 'Three old ballads and the date of *Doctor Faustus*', *AUMLA* 36, 187–200.

Johnson, F.R. (1946) 'Marlowe's astronomy and Renaissance skepticism', *English Literary History* 13, 241–54.

Jones, John Henry (1991) '"Invirond round with ayrie mountaine tops": Marlowe's source for *Doctor Faustus*', *Notes and Queries* 38, 469–70.

—— (1994) *The English Faust-book*, Cambridge: Cambridge University Press.

Kocher, Paul H. (1942) 'Nashe's authorship of the prose scenes in *Faustus*', *Modern Language Quarterly* 3, 17–40.

Oliver, L.M. (1945) 'Rowley, Foxe, and the *Faustus* additions', *Modern Language Notes* 60, 391–4.

Palmer, P.M. and More, R.P. (1936) *The Sources of the Faust Tradition*, New York: Oxford University Press.

Pettitt, Thomas (1980) 'The Folk-Play in Marlowe's *Doctor Faustus*', *Folklore* 9, 72–7.

—— (1988) 'Formulaic dramaturgy in *Doctor Faustus*' in Friedenreich *et al.*, pp. 167–91.

Searle, John (1936) 'Marlowe and Chrysostom', *Times Literary Supplement* 15 February, 139.

Thaler, Alwin (1923) 'Churchyard and Marlowe', *Modern Language Notes* 38, 89–92.

THE MASSACRE AT PARIS

Bakeless, John (1937) 'Christopher Marlowe and the Newsbooks', *Journalism Quarterly* 14, 18–22.

Bennett, H.S. (ed.) (1931) *The Jew of Malta and The Massacre at Paris*, London: Methuen.

Briggs, Julia (1983) 'Marlowe's *Massacre at Paris*: a reconsideration', *Review of English Studies* 34, 257–78.

Davis, Natalie Zemon (1975) *Society and Culture in Early Modern France*, London: Duckworth.
Freer, M.V. (1858) *Henry III, King of France and Poland: His Court and Times*, 3 vols, London: Hurst & Blackett.
Glenn, J.R. (1973) 'The martyrdom of Ramus in Marlowe's *The Massacre at Paris*', *Papers on Language and Literature* 9, 365–79.
Kocher, Paul H. (1941) 'François Hotman and Marlowe's *The Massacre at Paris*', *PMLA* 56, 349–68.
—— (1947) 'Contemporary pamphlet backgrounds for Marlowe's *The Massacre at Paris*', *Modern Language Quarterly* 8, 157–73, 309–18.
Oliver, H.J. (ed.) (1968) *Dido Queen of Carthage and The Massacre at Paris*, London: Methuen.
Ramel, J. (1979) '*Le Massacre de Paris* de Christopher Marlowe et *Les Mémoires de l'Etat de France Sous Charles Neuvième*', *Confluents* 5, 5–18.

THE JEW OF MALTA

Bawcutt, N.W. (1968) 'Marlowe's "Jew of Malta" and Foxe's "Acts and Monuments"', *Notes and Queries* 15, 250.
Bennett, H.S. (ed.) (1931) (see under *The Massacre at Paris* above).
Boas, F.S. (1949) 'Informer against Marlowe', *Times Literary Supplement*, 16 September, 608.
Brooke, C.F. Tucker (1922) 'The prototype of Marlowe's Jew of Malta', *Times Literary Supplement*, 8 June, 380.
Dessen, Alan C. (1974) 'The Elizabethan Stage Jew and Christian example: Gerontus, Barabas, and Shylock', *Modern Language Quarterly* 35, 231–45.
Freeman, Arthur (1962) 'A source of *The Jew of Malta*', *Notes and Queries* 207, 139–41.
Graetz, H. (1892) *The History of the Jews*, trans. Bella Löwy, 6 vols, London: David Nutt.
Jameson, Thomas H. (1941) 'The "Machiavellianism" of Gabriel Harvey', *PMLA* 56, 645–56.
Kellner, Leon (1887) 'Die Quelle von Marlowe's "Jew of Malta"' *Englische Studien* 10, 80–111.
Kocher, Paul (1963) 'English legal history in Marlowe's *Jew of Malta*', *Huntington Library Quarterly* 26, 155–63.
Minshull, Catherine (1982) 'Marlowe's "Sound Machevill"', *Renaissance Drama* 13, 35–53.
Purcell, H.D. (1966) 'Whetstone's "English Myrror" and Marlowe's "Jew of Malta"', *Notes and Queries* 13, 288–90.

EDWARD II

Briggs, Julia (1983) (see under *The Massacre at Paris* above).
Briggs, W.D. (ed.) (1914) *Edward II*, London: David Nutt.
Charlton, H.B. and Waller, R.D. (ed.) (1933), *Edward II*, London: Methuen; revised F.N. Lees, 1955.
Fryde, Natalie (1979) *The Tyranny and Fall of Edward II 1321–1326*, Cambridge: Cambridge University Press.
Hamilton, J.S. (1988) *Piers Gaveston, Earl of Cornwall 1307–1312: Politics and Patronage in the Reign of Edward II*, Detroit, Michigan: Wayne State University Press; London: Harvester Wheatsheaf.

Shumake, J.S. (1984) 'The sources of Marlowe's *Edward II*', unpublished Ph.D. thesis, University of South Carolina.

GENERAL

Bakeless, John (1942) *The Tragicall History of Christopher Marlowe*, 2 vols, Cambridge, Mass.: Harvard University Press.

Boas, F.S. (1940) *Christopher Marlowe: A Biographical and Critical Study*, Oxford: Clarendon Press.

Braden, Gordon (1978) *The Classics and English Renaissance Poetry: Three Case Studies*, New Haven and London: Yale University Press.

Bullough, Geoffrey (1957–75) *Narrative and Dramatic Sources of Shakespeare*, 8 vols, London: Routledge; New York: Columbia University Press.

Cornelius, R.M. (1984) *Christopher Marlowe's Use of the Bible*, New York: Peter Lang.

Dawson, Giles (ed.) (1965) *Records of Plays and Players in Kent 1450–1642*, *Collections* VIII, Oxford: Oxford University Press (Malone Society Reprints).

Doran, Madeleine (1954) *Endeavors of Art: A study of form in Elizabethan Drama*, Madison: University of Wisconsin Press.

Friedenreich, K., Gill, R., and Kuriyama, C. (eds.) (1988) *'A Poet and a filthy Playmaker': New Essays on Christopher Marlowe*, New York: AMS Press.

Gill, Roma (ed.) (1987–90) *The Complete Works of Christopher Marlowe*, vols I and II, Oxford: Clarendon Press.

Godshalk, W.L. (1974) *The Marlovian World Picture*, The Hague and Paris: Mouton.

Henslowe, Philip (1961) *Henslowe's Diary*, ed. R.A. Foakes and R.T. Rickert, Cambridge: Cambridge University Press.

Hyde, Mary Crapo (1949) *Playwriting for Elizabethans 1600–1605*, New York: Columbia University Press.

Kelsall, Malcolm (1981) *Christopher Marlowe*, Amsterdam: Brill.

Kocher, Paul (1946) *Christopher Marlowe: A Study of his Thought, Learning, and Character*, Chapel Hill: University of North Carolina Press.

Kuriyama, C.B. (1988) 'Marlowe's Nemesis: the identity of Richard Baines' in Friedenreich *et al.*, pp. 343–60.

Levin, Harry (1952) *The Overreacher: A Study of Christopher Marlowe*, Cambridge, Mass.: Harvard University Press.

Nelson, Alan H. (ed.) (1989) *Records of Early English Drama: Cambridge*, 2 vols, Toronto: University of Toronto Press.

Nicholl, Charles (1992) *The Reckoning*, London: Cape.

Page, R.I. (1977) 'Christopher Marlowe and the library of Matthew Parker', *Notes and Queries* 24, 510–14.

Sanders, Wilbur (1968) *The Dramatist and the Received Idea*, Cambridge: Cambridge University Press.

Seaton, Ethel (1929) 'Fresh Sources for Marlowe', *Review of English Studies* 5, 385–401.

—— (1959) 'Marlowe's light reading' in H. Davis and H. Gardner (eds), *Elizabethan and Jacobean Studies Presented to F.P. Wilson*, Oxford: Clarendon Press, pp. 17–35.

Urry, William (1988) *Christopher Marlowe and Canterbury*, London: Faber.

Voegelin, Eric (1951) 'Machiavelli's *Prince*: background and formation', *Review of Politics* 13, 142–68.

Wernham, R.B. (1976) 'Christopher Marlowe at Flushing in 1592', *English Historical Review* 91, 344–5.

HISTORICAL TABLE

1284	Birth of future Edward II at Caernarfon Castle
1301	Edward created Prince of Wales
1307	Edward succeeds to English throne (8 July); Piers de Gaveston created Earl of Cornwall (September)
1308	Edward crowned; appoints Gaveston guardian of England; marries Isabella of France
1311	English nobles issue Ordinances limiting royal power; Gaveston banished but returns
1312	Gaveston executed (19 June); birth of future Edward III at Windsor (13 November)
1314	Scots defeat English at Bannockburn (24 June)
1322	Edward rescinds Ordinances; Thomas Earl of Lancaster put to death
1323	Truce agreed with Scots (30 May)
1327	Edward forced to abdicate by Queen and Roger de Mortimer (20 January); king put to death at Berkeley Castle (September)
1330	Edward III executes Mortimer (29 November) and banishes Queen
1336	Birth of Timur or Tamerlane at Kesh or Karshi
1347	Bajazeth born
1378	The Great Schism in the Church: two popes in office
1389	Turks defeat Serbs at Kossovo (15 June); assassination of Murad I; Bajazeth succeeds as Turkish Sultan
1391– 1425	Reign of Manuel II Palaeologus as Emperor of the East (Byzantium)
1396	Bajazeth defeats Christians under Sigismund of Hungary at Nicopolis (28 September)
1398	Tamerlane conquers northern India; Battle of Panipat
1401	Tamerlane conquers Damascus and Baghdad
1402	Battle of Angora (Ankara) (20 July); Tamerlane defeats Turks
1403	Death of Bajazeth in captivity (8 March)
1405	Death of Tamerlane en route for China (19 January)

1415	Council of Constance; Sigismund betrays John Huss
1416	Huss executed (6 July)
1421–51	Murad II Sultan of the Turks
1444	Vladislaus III of Hungary defeated by Turks at Battle of Varna (10 November)
1451–81	Mohammed II Sultan of the Turks
1453	Turks capture Constantinople (29 May); Byzantine Empire dissolves
1492	Conquest of Granada (2 January); Jews expelled from Spain (31 March)
1494	Suleiman the Magnificent born
1520	Death of Sultan Selim I. Suleiman II ('the Magnificent') succeeds as ruler of Ottoman Empire
1522	Knights Hospitallers ejected from Rhodes (December)
1530	Charles V installed as Holy Roman Emperor (24 February); Knights Hospitallers settle on Malta as their new base
1558	Elizabeth I succeeds to English throne (17 November)
1564	BIRTH OF CHRISTOPHER MARLOWE at Canterbury (6 February?)
1565	The Great Siege of Malta (May – September)
1566	Joseph Mendez-Nassi (Micques) created Duke of Naxos; death of Suleiman II
1571	Turks defeated at the Battle of Lepanto (7 October)
1572	The Massacre of St Bartholomew's Day (23–24 August)
1574	Death of Charles IX of France; Henri III succeeds to throne; Selim II succeeded by Murad III as Turkish Sultan
1578	The Duc d'Alençon active at English court
1579	Death of Nassi in Constantinople
1584	The Catholic League formed in France (September–December)
1585	Protestantism proscribed in France (July); 'the War of the Three Henris' follows
1588	The Duc de Guise assumes control in Paris, supplanting Henri III (May); Spanish Armada defeated (July–August); Guise assassinated at Blois (23 December); League leaders suppressed
1589	Henri III assassinated (2 August)
1593	DEATH OF CHRISTOPHER MARLOWE in Deptford (30 May); Henri IV of France converts to Catholicism (July)

INDEX TO THE INTRODUCTIONS

Figures in bold type denote main entries

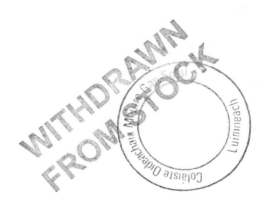